Innovation in Natural Resource Management

**Other Books Published in Cooperation with
the International Food Policy Research Institute**

*Intrahousehold Resource Allocation in Developing Countries:
Models, Methods, and Policy*
Edited by Lawrence Haddad, John Hoddinott, and Harold Alderman

*Sustainability, Growth, and Poverty Alleviation: A Policy and
Agroecological Perspective*
Edited by Stephen A. Vosti and Thomas Reardon

Famine in Africa: Causes, Responses, and Prevention
By Joachim von Braun, Tesfaye Teklu, and Patrick Webb

Paying for Agricultural Productivity
Edited by Julian M. Alston, Philip G. Pardey, and Vincent H. Smith

*Out of the Shadow of Famine: Evolving Food Markets and Food Policy
in Bangladesh*
Edited by Raisuddin Ahmed, Steven Haggblade,
and Tawfiq-e-Elahi Chowdhury

Agricultural Science Policy: Changing Global Agendas
Edited by Julian M. Alston, Philip G. Pardey, and Michael J. Taylor

*The Politics of Precaution: Genetically Modified Crops
in Developing Countries*
By Robert L. Paarlberg

*Land Tenure and Natural Resource Management: A Comparative Study
of Agrarian Communities in Asia and Africa*
Edited by Keijiro Otsuka and Frank Place

*Seeds of Contention: World Hunger and the Global Controversy over
GM Crops*
By Per Pinstrup-Andersen and Ebbe Schiøler

Reforming Agricultural Markets in Africa
By Mylène Kherallah, Christopher Delgado, Eleni Gabre-Madhin,
Nicholas Minot, and Michael Johnson

*The Triangle of Microfinance: Financial Sustainability, Outreach,
and Impact*
Edited by Manfred Zeller and Richard L. Meyer

Innovation in Natural Resource Management

The Role of Property Rights and Collective Action in Developing Countries

EDITED BY RUTH MEINZEN-DICK, ANNA KNOX,
FRANK PLACE, AND BRENT SWALLOW

Published for the International Food Policy Research Institute

The Johns Hopkins University Press
Baltimore and London

The Johns Hopkins University Press
2715 North Charles Street
Baltimore, Maryland 21218-4363
www.press.jhu.edu

International Food Policy Research Institute
2033 K Street, N.W.
Washington, D.C. 20006
(202) 862-5600
www.ifpri.org

LIBRARY OF CONGRESS CATALOGING-IN-PUBLICATION DATA
Innovation in natural resource management : the role of property rights
and collective action in developing countries / edited by Ruth
Meinzen-Dick . . . [et al.].
        p.   cm.—(International Food Policy Research Institute)
    Includes bibliographical references and index.
    ISBN 0-8018-7142-5 (hard : alk. paper)—ISBN 0-8018-7143-3 (pbk. :
    alk. paper)
    1. Natural resources—Developing countries—Management.   2. Right of
property—Developing countries—Case studies.   I. Meinzen-Dick, Ruth
Suseela.   II. International Food Policy Research Institute (Series)
HC59.7 .I5374   2002
333.7′09172′4—dc21   2002005782

A catalog record for this book is available from the British Library.

Contents

Figures

Tables

Foreword

The Rio and Johannesburg Earth Summits have highlighted the problems of environmental degradation, which have particularly severe impacts on poor, resource-dependent communities in developing countries. Much research and farmer innovation has gone into developing technologies and natural resource management practices to address these problems. But in many cases farmers do not adopt these innovations, indicating that we must look beyond technical solutions to environmental problems.

This volume demonstrates the critical role that institutions of property rights and collective action play in effective natural resource management. Whereas technologies for managing natural resources were once viewed as relevant primarily to individual farms, it is increasingly clear that such technologies have long-term relevance for the entire landscape. If they are to adopt new technologies that will not yield immediate benefits, farmers need to be assured of rights to particular resources, such as land, for sufficient lengths of time. In addition, if individual farmers must work together to benefit from technologies that apply to an entire area, they must have a mechanism for achieving collective action. Yet the links between property rights, collective action, and technology adoption for natural resource management are not always straightforward. Land titles do not guarantee that farmers will make long-term investments in their land, and farmers will not necessarily work together just because an extension agent tells them to.

This volume takes a closer look at the how property rights and collective action influence farmers' decisions about technologies for managing natural resources. It presents a conceptual framework for analyzing the links and follows with case studies that reflect a range of countries and technologies. The cases show that property rights and collective action are dynamic institutions that change according to a number of factors, such as population density, resource scarcity, and market access. Property rights and collective action can differ between socially differentiated groups, and other factors beyond property rights and collective action can also affect technology adoption.

Although many of the studies have been carried out by economists, others draw from a range of disciplines, including political science, geography, anthropology, sociology, and the natural sciences. Still other studies are interdisciplinary. Thus the volume will be of interest to those involved in research and policy in any of these fields. Ultimately, the volume points to the goals of increasing agricultural productivity, conserving natural resources, and, most important, improving the welfare of millions of resource-dependent households.

Per Pinstrup-Andersen
Director General
International Food Policy Research Institute

Preface

The institutions of property rights and collective action affect how people manage natural resources. Together, they shape people's incentives for undertaking sustainable and productive management strategies and influence who benefits from natural resources and how much. A better understanding of the linkages between property rights, collective action, and natural resource management is important because these linkages have implications for the adoption of innovative technologies and practices, economic growth, equity and poverty alleviation, and environmental sustainability.

Secure property rights (to give people long-term incentives) and collective action (to coordinate individuals' actions) have become particularly relevant for international agricultural research as it expands beyond agricultural technologies that can be employed on individual farms to natural resource management techniques that operate at the landscape level. Many centers in the Consultative Group on International Agricultural Research (CGIAR) have been grappling with these issues. Because there are few rigorous, cross-comparable case studies of these institutions, researchers have had difficulty developing locally relevant policy recommendations and internationally generalizable lessons that can help focus government activities and create an enabling environment for local-level efforts. In response to this need for better understanding, the CGIAR has begun a Systemwide Program on Collective Action and Property Rights (CAPRi) to promote comparative research on the role played by these institutions in shaping the efficiency, sustainability, and equity of natural resource systems.

One of the most important topics for the CAPRi program concerns how property rights and collective action affect farmers' adoption of innovation in agricultural technologies and natural resource management practices. Although many national and international agricultural research centers were investigating the extent to which property rights constrained the adoption of new technologies, there had been little effort to bring this work together, to develop a clear conceptual framework for understanding the linkages, or to critically examine the methodologies and findings of the various studies.

This volume originated in a workshop called "Property Rights, Collective Action, and Natural Resource Management" sponsored by the CAPRi program in November 1997 in Aleppo, Syria. The workshop, hosted by the International Center for Agricultural Research in the Dry Areas (ICARDA), provided an opportunity to examine ongoing studies and to identify critical gaps in understanding. The papers presented, the comments by discussants, and the group discussions helped to shape our collective understanding. We are grateful to ICARDA for the outstanding hospitality at the workshop and for an enlightening field trip, to all those at ICARDA who made the workshop possible, and to all the paper authors, discussants, and other participants for their contributions. Selected papers from the workshop have since been refined (and often rewritten) as chapters for this volume. New chapters have been added, particularly on the role of collective action in the adoption of natural resource management practices, which was a major gap in the existing studies.

We hope that this volume will not only provide information on the extent to which institutions of property rights and collective action facilitate or constrain the application of specific technologies in particular places, but also show the relevance of these social institutions for agricultural research and natural resource management and encourage further research in this area.

Innovation in Natural Resource Management

1 Introduction

RUTH MEINZEN-DICK, ANNA KNOX,
BRENT SWALLOW, AND FRANK PLACE

Are indigenous land tenure systems a constraint to the adoption of "modern" agricultural technologies? Is collective action a viable approach to achieving more sustainable management of natural resources? These have been recurring issues for policymakers, social science researchers, and technical specialists in agriculture, forestry, and fisheries management over at least the past century.[1] Much hangs in the balance: not only levels of agricultural productivity and the conservation of natural resources, but more important, the welfare of millions of resource-dependent households. Yet the evidence on these issues has been fragmentary, with incomplete understanding of the complex interrelationships between people's rights to land, water, and trees, the way that people organize and work together to achieve common objectives, and the adoption and use of agricultural and natural resource management practices. As a result there is a very real risk that policymakers and planners will develop and implement policy decisions that disrupt, rather than promote, equitable and sustainable agricultural growth. There is also a risk that millions of dollars will be spent on research and dissemination of technologies that fail to meet the needs of key target groups.

This volume seeks to contribute to a better understanding of the ways in which property rights and collective action may facilitate or constrain the adoption of agricultural technologies and natural resource practices. It does this by developing several complementary lines of evidence. First, it presents a conceptual framework for examining the direct and indirect relationships between property rights, collective action, and application of various technologies and a review of the evidence on these relationships from around the developing

---

1. For example, the question of whether African systems of property rights were insecure, and hence limited investment in agriculture, formed a major issue of policy debate in colonial Kenya (Swynnerton 1954), as well as for the World Bank in the 1980s (Feder and Noronha 1987; Bruce and Migot-Adholla 1994). Questions of how to achieve collective action for irrigation management received considerable attention at both the beginning and close of the 20th century in India (Great Britain 1904; INCID 1996; India 1997).

world. Second, it presents a number of new case studies of how property rights, collective action, or both shape the individual and collective behavior of farm families from developing countries in Africa, Asia, and Latin America. These case studies apply a range of quantitative and qualitative research techniques, including some new techniques for community-level and spatial analysis. Third, the volume also presents methodological approaches and "best practices" for further research needed on the roles of property rights and collective action institutions in shaping incentives to adopt technologies and manage natural resources.

Definitions and Approaches

Although both "property rights" and "collective action" are commonly used terms, a lack of clear and consistent understanding of these concepts has led to problems in both research and policy regarding natural resources. Therefore it is useful to begin with definitions and to clarify the broad approach taken to both concepts in this volume.

Property rights can be defined as *"the capacity to call upon the collective to stand behind one's claim to a benefit stream"* (Bromley 1991, 15, emphasis in original) or "social institutions that define or delimit the range of privileges granted to individuals to specific assets . . . [they] critically affect decision making regarding resource use and, hence, affect economic behaviour and performance" (Libecap 1989 in Ensminger 1992, 124). As such, they are recognized as an important factor shaping the use of different technologies.

Definitions provided by Place, Roth, and Hazell (1994) and Roth, Wiebe, and Lawry (1993) stress that the necessary components of secure property rights, or tenure security, include excludability, duration, robustness, and assurance. *Excludability* allows those with rights to exclude those without rights to a particular resource such as land. *Duration* refers to the temporal extent of one's rights. To have secure tenure, one must possess a sufficient time horizon to reap the benefits of one's investments. *Robustness* refers to the number and strength of the bundle of rights an individual possesses. The bundles of rights may include various types of rights to access, use, manage, control, or transfer a resource (Schlager and Ostrom 1992). Different individuals or institutions (including the state) may hold different bundles of rights over the same piece of land or other type of resource. Finally, *assurance* derives from an institutional framework capable of enforcing an individual's rights to land. It is important to note that property rights may be held by individuals, families, collectives, or other groups.

The institutional framework that enforces property rights may comprise multiple sources of authority, including the state. In examining property rights, it is useful to employ the perspective of legal pluralism, recognizing that there is not just one legal system that applies nor a simple division between de jure (statutory) and de facto (locally practiced) rules, but rather that there are over-lapping legal and normative frameworks related to property rights.[2] Not only statutory laws, but also customary and religious laws, and even unwritten local norms may all address the rights and responsibilities related to natural resources. Current users and potential future users can base their resource claims on one or another of these legal frameworks, and the overlap and even inconsistencies give scope for negotiation and evolution of property rights. This reality implies that it is not enough to look only at official statutes or at "customary law" in isola-tion and that changes in government laws alone do not necessarily change prop-erty rights at the local level. It further implies that to understand property rights in practice it is necessary to begin not with the formal laws as defined by any system—whether state, religious, or customary—but with individuals and to look at what property rights and other institutions affect them.

Some confusion in empirical findings stems from lack of clarity regarding the scale at which property rights are measured: whether at the plot, farm, or community level (see Chapter 3). To assess what incentives individuals have to adopt technologies or how adoption may vary from plot to plot, it is essen-tial to look at the property rights over individual plots and who controls them. This approach is especially important for assessing households that may have plots under different types of tenure and the effects of gender differences within households.

In much of Sub-Saharan Africa, households operate more than one plot of land, and women and men have separate plots and separate responsibilities for production (Lastarria-Cornhiel 1997). In other cases, the full set of property rights held by a household may indicate the types of livelihood strategies the members can employ. For example, households may be able to try out new tech-nologies on some types of holdings because they have other land to meet sub-sistence needs (for an example of analysis at different levels, see Quisumbing et al. 2001).

Concepts of tenure security have largely been confined to property con-trolled by individuals or households rather than common property, which is controlled by one or more groups of individuals or communities. To define tenure security for the users of a common property pool resource, three dimen-sions need to be considered. First, the group or community should have secure property rights over the collectively managed resource, in the same sense as al-ready defined for individually controlled resources. Second, secure member-ship in the group is required to ensure that an individual will have continued

---

2. This concept draws on the legal anthropological literature on legal pluralism (for exam-ple, Griffiths 1986; Merry 1988; Spiertz and Wiber 1996). Vandergeest (1997) presents similar ideas on the complexity of property rights, and the law and economics literature deals with the importance of norms (for example, Ellickson 1991).

use rights to the resource over time. Third, there must be an effective local institution to manage and regulate the use of the resource, to assure members that if they abide by the rules, others will also. Today many common properties are under increasing pressure and are degenerating toward open-access situations. One major reason is that population expansion is exerting increased competition for resources and producing a growing number of people with group membership claims. Breakdowns in common property management also occur when the ownership rights of the community are challenged by outsiders, including in some cases the state (such as nationalization of rangelands and forests), and when market forces, policy interventions, and other institutional and technological forces undermine the institutions that have managed the resource (Bromley and Cernea 1989; Jodha 1992; Richards 1997).

The Oxford Dictionary of Sociology (Marshall 1998, 85) defines collective action as: "action taken by a group (either directly or on its behalf through an organization) in pursuit of members' perceived shared interests." Organizations can facilitate collective action, but the two concepts are not the same. Many government decentralization and devolution programs, for instance, measure the number of formal organizations as a target for and indicator of local involvement, but collective action can occur without a coordinating organization, and many formal organizations never produce any action. Collective action is particularly visible in community-level efforts to build and maintain local infrastructure for natural resource management.

Just as the term "property rights" encompasses a number of aspects, so also collective action covers a range of activities. In addition to joint investment in purchase, construction, or maintenance of technologies, such actions as deciding on and implementing rules to exploit (or refrain from exploiting) a resource; representing the group to outsiders; and devising mechanisms for sharing information and other resources are especially relevant for agriculture and natural resource management techniques.

Themes of the Book

Despite the wide variation in countries and technologies presented in the case studies in this volume, there are some recurring themes and approaches:

- the complexities of property rights and the components of tenure security;
- the need to understand property rights and collective action as dynamic institutions that change in response to a number of factors, including population density, resource scarcity, and market access;
- the importance of differences in property rights and collective action between socially differentiated groups; and
- the recognition that property rights and collective action are not the only factors affecting technology adoption.

First, the analyses of property rights go beyond the conventional focus on "ownership," as defined by state law, to grapple with the complexities of rights as they manifest themselves in the experience of rural people who depend on natural resources. Although the cases cut across examples of private, common, and public property, the focus is not on classifying property rights regimes, but on the range of rights held by individuals and households and how these affect their incentives and ability to adopt a range of technologies and resource practices. Emphasis is therefore placed on the bundles of rights held by different parties—for example, rights to use, manage, or transfer the resource to others (Bromley 1991; Schlager and Ostrom 1992; Benda-Beckmann et al. 1997). Tenure security also emerges as a critical aspect of property rights—not only what rights people hold, but the time horizon of those rights and how confident they are that those rights will be respected (see Roth, Wiebe, and Lawry 1993; Place, Roth, and Hazell 1994).

Property rights do not derive from state law alone. While statutory law may be very important, cases in this book demonstrate that customary law and even local norms may be a more important source of property rights than state laws. Property rights are only as strong as the institutions that stand behind them. Where the state is weak, state law may not be an effective source of rights, but if local institutions are eroding, customary property rights may also be weakening. Indeed, Smucker, White, and Bannister's case from Haiti (Chapter 6) and the Syrian case by Rae et al. (Chapter 7) argue that state regulations and moves to formalize tenure have reduced tenure security by weakening the social institutions that underpinned customary property rights systems without replacing them with effective state institutions. At the same time, local law is also not rigid and unchanging: "customary" rights also change in response to a number of forces (as seen, for example, in the case studies by Place and Otsuka in Chapter 4, and Kimberly Swallow in Chapter 13).

Although property rights and collective action are conceptually distinct, the examples in Chapters 4 and 6 through 9 show that there is considerable overlap. Collective action is often at the heart of property rights enforcement. This situation is clearest in the case of common property systems, but it also applies to communal property systems where land is "owned" by a lineage with use rights allocated to individuals (Otsuka and Place 2001) and even to individual private property. Unruh's case from Mozambique (Chapter 8) demonstrates how major social disruptions such as war undermine the social foundation to support even private property, and the resulting tenure insecurity has important consequences for the adoption of technologies.

The case studies dealing with property rights show that these institutions are dynamic, responding to many changes (including to the introduction of technologies themselves). Collective action is even more dynamic. The term itself suggests movement, and the case studies dealing with these institutions highlight how various forms of collective action change in response to internal and external forces, including projects and the studies themselves (see, for example, Ravnborg et al., Chapter 12). All of the cases dealing with collective action analyze factors affecting the degree and type of collective action that emerges or takes place. Following the work of Boserup (1981) and Hayami and Ruttan (1985), the case studies by Place and Otsuka (Chapter 4), Birner and Gunaweera (Chapter 9), and Pender and Scherr (Chapter 10) analyze institutional change using induced innovation hypotheses, which focus particularly on the role of population density, resource security, and market conditions.

Rights and actions vary not only over time, but also between different social groups. Indeed, property rights are often used as a way of distinguishing socioeconomic classes, especially landlord and tenant. Rights also vary dramatically between ethnic groups, whether tribes (as in Rae et al.), castes (as in Birner and Gunaweera), or locals and migrants (as in Unruh). Even within the household there may be differences in property rights. Similarly the extent of collective action can vary considerably between, and even within, communities (as in Pender and Scherr and Brent Swallow et al.).

As important as property rights and collective action may be, they are not the only factors affecting adoption of agricultural technologies. The conceptual framework chapter reviews many of the other factors that are likely to be influential. Overemphasizing the effect of property rights and collective action can be as misleading as ignoring these institutions. The chapters in this volume recognize this risk and attempt to address other factors affecting use of technologies. Some do this by controlling for different variables in econometric analysis, others by employing different techniques of qualitative analysis. While the exact findings will certainly vary from one place and technology to another, the issues and approaches represented in this volume have broader applicability.

The conceptual framework and case studies draw from a range of disciplines. The majority of chapters are by economists, who apply both neoclassical and institutional economics approaches (such as Birner and Gunaweera). Others draw more from political science, geography, anthropology, sociology, and natural sciences. Many of the studies have been interdisciplinary, with innovative combinations of techniques, such as between econometric and spatial analysis in Chapter 11 by Brent Swallow et al. Each approach has something valuable to offer, and given the richness and complexity of property rights and collective action in natural resource management, no single discipline is likely to have all the answers. We hope that this volume shows how interdisciplinary research can provide better understanding.

Organization of the Volume

Following this introduction, the chapter by Knox, Meinzen-Dick, and Hazell presents a review of the literature and a conceptual framework for analyzing the linkages between property rights, collective action, and technologies for natural resource management. It lays out where and why we would expect these institutions to affect use of different technologies (and where we would not). The conceptual framework therefore provides an entry point into the complex study of these relationships. In particular, long time scales (temporal externalities) call for attention to tenure security, and large spatial scales (spatial externalities) call for attention to the degree of collective action.

The framework chapter is followed by a cluster of three chapters examining the links between property rights and agricultural technologies. The first of these chapters, by Place and Swallow, identifies best-practice methodologies for studying the relationships. The authors begin by looking at what types of questions a study might be trying to address, then address the implications for the level and type of data collection required, approaches to ensuring high-quality data on complex issues such as tenure, and analytic techniques to ensure that questions are addressed correctly.

The following chapter by Place and Otsuka applies many of these techniques to examining the relationship between different types of land tenure and tree cover on private and communal land in Malawi and Uganda. Because households use both on- and off-farm tree resources for economic and environmental benefits, data collection and analysis are done across all landscapes at the community, rather than household, level.

Going beyond a single technology, Gavian and Ehui compare the total factor productivity of relatively insecure, informal tenure (sharecropped, rented, and borrowed) with more formal tenure contracts in Ethiopia and find that, although plots with insecure tenure are less efficient, they actually receive more inputs rather than less.

The next four chapters deal more with the complexities of property rights and the interface between property rights and collective action. Based on a number of studies of land tenure in Haiti, Smucker, White, and Bannister find that land registers and other types of formalization often proposed to increase tenure security would in fact *not* improve adoption of agroforestry or other technologies for resource management. This is because formalization would not increase tenure security in a context where people rely primarily on social networks to defend their property rights and where most rural residents lack the education or connections required to register their claims or defend them in courts of law.

A case from Syria by Rae et al. shows the limitations of state authority in the interaction between state and tribal institutions and how state and tribal interactions shape property rights over rangelands. They argue that this institutional dynamic, as well as the dynamic nature of rangeland resources, influences the potential success of technical approaches such as fodder shrub plantations.

Unruh's study of land tenure and adoption of agroforestry following the war in Mozambique highlights not only the importance of social institutions to provide evidence of property rights and settle disputes, but also the effects of trees and other technologies on property rights. Contrary to assumptions that trees are likely to be cut when individuals have insecure tenure, Unruh reports that old trees were being maintained because they provided the most secure form of evidence of property rights. Ironically, productivity was therefore reduced because old cashew trees were not being replaced with younger, better-yielding trees.

Conflicts arise not only as a result of major disruptions, but also with intensification of resource use, as seen in Birner and Gunaweera's chapter from Sri Lanka. The Sri Lanka case shows triadic relationships between property rights, technology (in this case, irrigation), and collective action. The authors demonstrate how collective action at all levels is needed to address the conflicts arising over property rights, especially to mediate between irrigated and pastoral production systems as they compete for land and water rights.

The final four chapters deal most directly with collective action for natural resource management. Pender and Scherr look at the factors affecting the number of local organizations involved in natural resource management in Honduras and how organizations in turn affect individual and collective investment in resources. They find that local organizations do play a substantial role in increasing collective action for resource management, but they do not affect investment by individuals. External government organizations, on the other hand, appear to displace collective investment but have more positive effects on the adoption of conservation practices by individual farmers.

Because insects rarely respect farm boundaries, pest management represents a clear case of spatial externalities that, in Knox, Meinzen-Dick, and Hazell's conceptual framework, calls for collective action. Both Brent Swallow et al. and Helle Ravnborg et al. incorporate this spatial dimension in their analysis of the extent of collective action for pest management. Examining the adoption of pouron applications to control livestock pests and diseases in Ethiopia, Swallow et al. make innovative use of geographic information systems (GIS) to create "neighborhood" variables (for example, to characterize neighbors and distance to treatment center) for use in econometric analysis of the probability of adoption by households. The analysis revealed that spatial patterns interact with local organizations in influencing cooperation and were instrumental in adjusting the program to increase adoption throughout the area.

Ravnborg et al. examine the control of leaf-cutter ants, a component of a participatory watershed management program in Colombia. Spatial analysis in this detailed community case study consisted of mapping ant nests and their radius of activity along with farm boundaries to help farmers recognize the spatial externalities. Technologies were not developed on a research station and presented to the community; the case study shows how the farmers identified the problem themselves, helped to identify and test alternative techniques to control the ants, and engaged in innovative processes (such as local contests) to increase collective action in ant control.

Kimberly Swallow's case study deals with the process of change in collective action when intensified cattle feeding was introduced in a village in Kenya and how this change altered the definitions of property rights themselves. Her analysis at the community and individual levels shows how social networks can both facilitate and constrain the adoption of different feed options. The analysis shows how intensifying dairy production is more than just a technical or economic issue. It involves a shift from relying primarily on community transactions (in free grazing) to reciprocal transactions (in tethered grazing) to private sector transactions (for most stall feeding)—a process that involves many contested "gray areas" and illustrates again the strong links between collective action, property rights, and technology adoption.

In the final chapter of the volume (Chapter 14), we draw out the major conclusions and policy recommendations that emanate from the various chapters. Simplistic policy prescriptions that call for giving title as a way to stimulate investment can be misleading, because there is more to tenure security than just statutory title and more factors influencing investment than just tenure security. The need for collective action for adoption of many technologies and natural resource management practices is also gaining recognition in development projects and policies, but sustained local involvement requires more than just external programs. Thus successful policies toward natural resource management require an understanding of the interaction between local and external institutions, and this volume attempts to show how such an understanding can be developed.

Although these studies did not grow out of a common project or framework, they do illustrate the many-faceted relationships among property rights, collective action, and techniques for natural resource management. The conceptual framework and case study findings presented in this volume indicate where these institutions are most likely to facilitate or constrain the application of agricultural and resource management technologies, while the methodologies presented offer ways of investigating the linkages and pointing to what programs and policies can (and cannot) do. Our hope is that this will contribute to more effective ways for communities, researchers, and policymakers to work together for sustainable communities and sustainable resource management.

References

Benda-Beckmann, K. von, M. de Bruijn, H. van Dijk, G. Hesseling, B. van Koppen, and L. Res. 1997. *Rights of women to the natural resources land and water*. Women and Development Working Paper 2. The Hague: Netherlands Development Assistance (NEDA).

Boserup, E. 1981. *Population and technological change*. Chicago: University of Chicago Press.

Bromley, D. W. 1991. *Environment and economy: Property rights and public policy*. Oxford, U.K.: Basil Blackwell.

Bromley, D. W., and M. M. Cernea. 1989. *The management of common property natural resources: Some conceptual and operational fallacies.* World Bank Discussion Paper 57. Washington, D.C.: World Bank.

Bruce, J. W., and S. Migot-Adholla, eds. 1994. *Searching for land tenure security in Africa.* Washington, D.C.: World Bank.

Ellickson, R. C. 1991. *Order without law: How neighbors settle disputes.* Cambridge, Mass., U.S.A.: Harvard University Press.

Ensminger, J. 1992. *Making a market: The institutional transformation of an African society.* Cambridge: Cambridge University Press.

Feder, G., and R. Noronha. 1987. Land rights, systems, and agricultural development in Sub-Saharan Africa. *World Bank Research Observer* 2 (2): 143–169.

Great Britain. 1904. *Report of the Indian Irrigation Commission 1901–03.* Parliamentary Papers, Cd. 185.

Griffiths, J. 1986. What is legal pluralism? *Journal of Legal Pluralism* 24: 1–55.

Hayami, Y., and V. W. Ruttan. 1985. *Agricultural development: An international perspective.* Baltimore, Md., U.S.A.: Johns Hopkins University Press.

INCID (Indian National Committee on Irrigation and Drainage). 1996. *Water user's associations in India: A status report.* New Delhi.

India. 1997. *Draft report of the working group on major and medium irrigation program for the IX five-year plan (1997–2002).* New Delhi: Ministry of Water Resources, Central Water Commission.

Jodha, N. S. 1992. *Common property resources: A missing dimension of development strategies.* World Bank Discussion Paper 169. Washington, D.C.: World Bank.

Lastarria-Cornhiel, S. 1997. Impact of privatization on gender and property rights in Africa. *World Development* 25 (8): 1317–1334.

Marshall, G. 1998. *A dictionary of sociology.* New York: Oxford University Press.

Merry, S. E. 1988. Legal pluralism. *Law and Society Review* 22 (5): 809–896.

Otsuka, K., and F. Place. 2001. Issues and theoretical framework. In *Land tenure and natural resource management: A comparative study of agrarian communities in Asia and Africa,* ed. K. Otsuka and F. Place. Baltimore, Md., U.S.A.: Johns Hopkins University Press.

Place, F., M. Roth, and P. Hazell. 1994. Land tenure security and agricultural performance in Africa: Overview of research methodology. In *Searching for land tenure security in Africa,* ed. J. W. Bruce and S. Migot-Adholla. Washington, D.C.: World Bank.

Quisumbing, A. R., E. Payongayong, J. B. Aidoo, and K. Otsuka. 2001. Women's land rights in the transition to individualized ownership: Implications for tree-resource management in western Ghana. *Economic Development and Cultural Change* 50 (1): 157–181.

Richards, M. 1997. Common property resource institutions and forest management in Latin America. *Development and Change* 28 (1): 95–117.

Roth, M., K. Wiebe, and S. Lawry. 1993. Land tenure and agrarian structure: Implications for technology adoption. In *Proceedings of a workshop on social science research and the CRSPs: June 9–11, 1992, University of Kentucky, Lexington, KY.* Washington, D.C.: U.S. Agency for International Development.

Schlager, E., and E. Ostrom. 1992. Property rights regimes and natural resources: A conceptual analysis. *Land Economics* 68 (3): 249–262.

Spiertz, J., and M. G. Wiber, eds. 1996. *The role of law in natural resource management.* Gravenhage, The Netherlands: VUGA Uitgeverij B.V.
Swynnerton, R. J. M. 1954. *A plan to intensify the development of African agriculture in Kenya.* Nairobi: Government Printer.
Vandergeest, P. 1997. Rethinking property. *Common Property Resource Digest* 41: 4–6.

2 Property Rights, Collective Action, and Technologies for Natural Resource Management: A Conceptual Framework

ANNA KNOX, RUTH MEINZEN-DICK,
AND PETER HAZELL

The technologies people use play a fundamental role in determining how fast agricultural productivity grows and in shaping how that growth affects the poor and the condition of natural resources. As a result substantial investments have been made in research to improve agricultural technologies, from new crop varieties to natural resource management practices. Improved agricultural and natural resource technologies are of little value, however, unless farmers judge them to be appropriate and subsequently adopt them. Many factors constrain farmers' technology choices, but the lack of secure property rights is one common and important barrier to adoption, particularly for longer-term investments in things like tree crops and improvements to natural resources. For technologies and natural resource management practices that require farmers to make joint decisions and cooperate in implementing them, inadequate and ineffective institutions for managing collective activity can also be a constraint to adoption.

Property rights and collective action (PRCA) are important in determining *who* benefits from productivity increases, both directly by determining who can reap the benefits of improvements in productivity and indirectly through their effects on land markets, access to credit, and the like. PRCA also affects the way farmers manage their natural resources, hence the longer-term sustainability of their farming systems and the state of the environment.

The links between technology adoption and PRCA are best understood in a dynamic rather than static context. Besides the effects that PRCA introduces, technological change and the resulting changes in agricultural productivity, poverty, and the environment can redefine underlying economic and social

The authors wish to acknowledge the valuable contributions of Brent Swallow, particularly to the development of Figure 2.1, and the comments of Frank Place, Pablo Eyzaguirre, and Douglas Vermillion, as well as the input of all participants at the Workshop on Property Rights, Collective Action, and Technology Adoption, held in Aleppo, Syria, November 22–25, 1997. This chapter builds on the conceptual framework for the System-wide Program on Property Rights and Collective Action of the Consultative Group on International Agricultural Research (see Meinzen-Dick, Jackson, and White 1996).

FIGURE 2.1 Conceptual framework: Links between property rights and collective action and technological change

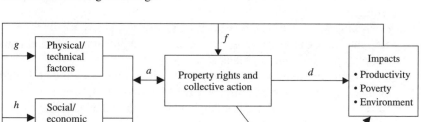

forces and induce changes in PRCA institutions themselves. This process of evolutionary change leads to a dynamic interplay between PRCA and technology adoption.

This chapter begins by developing the conceptual framework for understanding the links between PRCA, technology adoption, and its impacts. It then reviews the empirical literature on the direct and indirect roles of PRCA in affecting farmers' decisions to adopt. The indirect effects arise from interactions between PRCA and those factors that often impact directly on technology adoption. It discusses how PRCA conditions the impact of adopted technologies on productivity, poverty, and the environment and considers how technological change and its effects on productivity, poverty, and the environment feed back to change existing property rights and collective action relationships.

A Conceptual Framework

Figure 2.1 summarizes the conceptual framework used in this chapter. Three important relationships are portrayed in this figure: (1) how PRCA and other factors condition technology adoption; (2) how PRCA affects the impact of new technology on agricultural productivity, poverty, and the environment; and (3) how technological change and its impacts on productivity, poverty, and the environment modify existing PRCA relationships.

PRCA and Technology Adoption

The empirical literature has identified a number of variables as important constraints to technology adoption. These variables include:

- lack of or inadequate *infrastructure and information* to enable acquisition of technological inputs, marketing of output, and knowledge regarding the returns from adoption;
- *environmental and price risk*, whereby risk-averse and low-wealth farmers are reluctant to adopt because of their need to stabilize income and consumption streams and to protect scarce assets;
- *low wealth and lack of access to credit*, which limit people's ability to finance the acquisition and maintenance of technologies;
- *labor bottlenecks*, resulting from higher labor requirements that new technologies often introduce and seasonal peaks that may overlap with other agricultural activities;
- *price policies* that discriminate against agriculture and thereby lower incentives for adoption of capital- or cash-intensive technologies; and
- *other conditioning factors*, such as agroecological conditions, institutions, cultural norms, and power structures that render technologies unsuitable for particular environments.

Some studies also identify PRCA as an important variable, but they usually define it narrowly in terms of tenure security. Many studies, for example, evaluate whether share tenancy contracts lead to different farmer adoption behavior than fixed rental contracts, or compare investments by farmers on owner-operated parcels to those on rented or borrowed land. But as one moves from, for instance, Green Revolution technologies that yield quick returns to farmers to technologies with longer maturation periods (such as trees) or that involve cooperation between farmers (such as watershed development), then more complex measures of PRCA become relevant. The next section explains these relationships more in depth.

In Figure 2.1, PRCA *directly* affects technology adoption (arrow *c* going from the PRCA box to the technology choice box). But PRCA also has *indirect* impacts on technology adoption through its interactions with the other factors mentioned in conditioning technology adoption. Figure 2.1 groups these other factors into three categories: physical/technical factors such as agroclimatic conditions (including risk) and infrastructure; social and economic factors including human capital, information, economic risk, social networks, wealth, credit availability, labor patterns, and social norms; and policy and government factors such as pricing policies or legislation regarding resource use. Each of these factors is assumed to have a direct impact on technology adoption (arrow *b* extending directly from the factor boxes to the technology choice box). Each factor also has an indirect impact by interacting with the PRCA arrangements that exist. We hypothesize a two-way mapping (arrow *a* linking the factor boxes with the PRCA box). Going from left to right, the factors themselves influence the types of PRCA that exist. For example, population pressures may stimulate the emergence of more privatized forms of land tenure, which may in turn reorient technological choices toward smaller-scale technologies that can be better managed by families and individuals. In Chapter 10 Pender and Scherr test the effect of population growth and other socioeconomic variables on the development of local organizations and collective action in Honduras and relate these variables to intensification of coffee, horticulture, forestry, basic grains, or other enterprises. Going from right to left, PRCA helps shape the other constraints. For example, forcible sedentarization of pastoral populations may expose them to greater environmental and food security risks, causing them to take up crop technologies and reduce their stock numbers.

PRCA and Technology Impact

The right-hand side of Figure 2.1 shows that technology adoption has a direct impact on agricultural productivity, poverty, and environmental outcomes (arrow *e*). PRCA also conditions these impacts, either directly (arrow *d*) or indirectly (arrows *c* and *e*).

Technological Change and Induced Changes in PRCA

The dynamism of PRCA and technology linkages is underscored by the effect of technological change and productivity, poverty, and the environment outcomes on the economic and social conditions that in turn shape PRCA arrangements. The induced innovation model (Boserup 1965) predicts that institutions will evolve to meet the changing needs of communities. For example, productivity increases or commercial opportunities arising from technology adoption can change relative factor prices and scarcities leading to pressures to change existing PRCA relationships. In West Africa the introduction of cocoa crops and taxation by Europeans resulted in the evolution of tenancy arrangements as well as separation of rights to trees versus land to accommodate migrating cocoa farmers (Bruce 1988). In a more general context, North (1992) describes how institutions respond to increased technical specialization and impersonalization of markets. This kind of feedback is represented by arrow *f* in Figure 2.1. But technological change can also have feedback effects on other factors that condition PRCA and technology adoption, which amount to an indirect impact on PRCA (represented by arrows *g, h,* and *i* leading to *a*).

Direct Impacts of PRCA on Technology Adoption

When assessing the effect of property rights and collective action on technology adoption, it is useful to consider the spatial and temporal dimensions of a particular technology. Irrigation technology or integrated pest management (IPM) technology, for example, require substantial space to operate effectively, and collective action can help facilitate their adoption (see Chapters 11 and 12). In general, the broader the space occupied by the resource and the larger the number of individuals dependent on its benefits, the greater the potential for collective action strategies to promote adoption of improved technologies and natural resource management practices.[1] Once a threshold size is reached in terms of the transaction costs of sustaining collective action, a role for the state may be warranted.

The temporal dimensions of a technology carry implications for tenure security. In cases where technologies require long time horizons to generate returns on investment, if property rights, whether individualized or communal, do not offer the resource user sufficient duration to reap the benefits of investing in a particular technology, adoption will not be forthcoming. For example, Fortmann, Antinori, and Nabane's 1997 study of tenure security and gender differences in tree planting in Zimbabwe found that where women's tenure security is of shorter duration, they are less likely to plant trees.

Figure 2.2 places several technologies within a spectrum of their relative spatial versus temporal scale. The vertical axis ranges from the plot through the farm and village to the region, and the horizontal axis ranges from a single season to many years or even generations. These scales are then matched to corresponding institutions that facilitate adoption on the parallel axes. Technologies with a larger spatial scale (left-hand vertical axis) call for stronger collective action (right-hand vertical axis);[2] those with a longer temporal scale (lower horizontal axis) call for stronger tenure security (upper horizontal axis).

For example, high-yielding cereal varieties (HYVs)—the linchpin of the Green Revolution—are in the lower left-hand corner because the benefits could be captured within a single agricultural season and hence do not require secure property rights. Indeed, even sharecropping tenants with single season leases are able to adopt. Nor do they require collective action; individual farmers can adopt regardless of what their neighbors decide to do. These features make adoption decisions relatively simple and help explain why Green Revolution technologies spread so quickly and widely in diverse local socioeconomic conditions.

Lynam (1994) notes that moving from agricultural to natural resource management technologies generally expands both the temporal and spatial scale of research and adoption. Even technologies that are applied at the farm level require widespread adoption to become effective. Integrated pest management, for example, requires that all farmers in an area work together; the technology

---

1. This is not to say that the association, monitoring, and enforcement costs of collective action do not increase with space, but that the coordination costs and efficiency losses of managing large-scale resources privately will, after a certain level or size, often overwhelm other costs, making collective action an economically superior alternative, at least in terms of social costs and benefits.

2. Depending on average farm sizes within a given area and the variation and distribution of farms of different sizes, a technology serving 100 hectares could be internalized and adopted within a single farm in some areas, or require coordination of hundreds of farmers in other areas.

FIGURE 2.2 Property rights, collective action, and sustainable agriculture and natural resource management practices

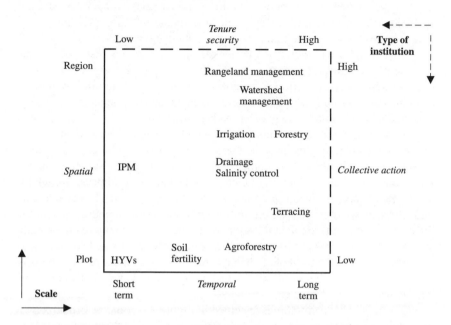

NOTE: Location of specific technologies is approximate, for illustrative purposes. IPM is integrated pest management. HYVs are high-yielding varieties.

does not work if some farmers continue to spray indiscriminately or if there is not adequate synchronization of planting dates.

The returns, however, are relatively quick, so secure property rights are less of an issue. For these reasons IPM appears partway up the vertical axis of Figure 2.2. In contrast, the planting of trees on farms (agroforestry) is a long-term investment that requires secure property rights. But since trees can be planted by individual farmers regardless of what their neighbors do, then farm trees appears partway along the horizontal axis.

Most natural resource management technologies and practices, such as salinity control, irrigation systems, rangeland management, or forestry, have both larger spatial scales and longer time horizons. They therefore appear in the upper right-hand quadrant, indicating that both property rights and collective action are important. Watershed development, for example, requires secure property rights because it involves long-term investments in check dams, land contouring, and tree planting in water catchment areas, and it is most successful if the entire community living within the relevant landscape is mobilized to support collective action. If these institutional conditions are not met, then the technology is not likely to be adopted and maintained, regardless of its profitability and scientific soundness. This explains why, as resource degradation issues have gained greater public attention and as research agendas have responded with an increased focus on the sustainable use of natural resources, PRCA issues have become much more prominent and complex.

Finally, river basin management takes place on such a vast spatial scale and incurs such large transaction costs that it extends beyond the realm of strictly local collective action as a feasible option. Here state (and sometimes even international) intervention or comanagement arrangements involving the state and local institutions may offer the best solution.

Viewing technologies in this framework allows more precise identification of whether property rights or collective action are likely to be constraining or enabling factors in technology choices. The framework can also help guide the development and dissemination of technologies that are appropriate for the institutional context. For example, technologies that operate on a landscape scale may be more appropriate where traditions of cooperation are strong, whereas those that require an extended duration to produce benefits may realize greater success where tenures are long term and reasonably secure, at least for those resources linked to the technology being applied. Conversely, areas where many farmers have insecure tenure call for technologies that have significant short-term returns.

Several of the technologies specified in Figure 2.2 could be broken down into subgroups to more accurately reflect their spatial and temporal characteristics. The "irrigation" category should distinguish between small tubewells serving a few hectares and a large canal system serving thousands of hectares. Within the agroforestry category, community nurseries tend to require extensive collective action to sustain them, but security-enhancing property rights are less important given the short time necessary to derive benefits from the technology. By contrast, agroforestry aimed at production of fuelwood or poles requires an extended duration for production, yet the practice is more individualized and requires much less, if any, coordination beyond the household level. Similarly, whereas comprehensive watershed management often has a large spatial scale and long time horizon, specific components such as contour plowing can be applied on smaller areas with shorter-term pay-offs.

Property Rights and Technology Adoption

As discussed in Chapter 1, the components of tenure security include excludability, duration, assurance, and robustness. The empirical literature linking property rights with technology adoption has demonstrated mixed conclusions concerning the importance of tenure security, often depending which of these or other dimensions is used to define tenure security (Barrows and Roth 1990; Bruce 1993; Roth, Cochrane, and Kisamba-Mugerwa 1993; Roth, Wiebe, and Lawry 1993). The Swynnerton Plan emerging out of colonial Kenya equated tenure security with ownership and title to land as practiced by Western countries (Swynnerton 1954). Indeed, many of the policy prescriptions for Africa and other developing countries that emerged in the next three decades followed suit in arguing for the need to replace community-based land tenure institutions with freehold tenure backed by formal titles (Dorner 1972; Feder and Onchan 1987; Harrison 1987; Feder et al. 1988).

Subsequent research has revealed that title and privatization of land-ownership are not always necessary to ensure tenure security and in fact may in some cases weaken it (Shipton 1988; Bruce 1993; Place and Hazell 1993; Roth, Unruh, and Barrows 1994; Ensminger 1997). This result stems from the strength and effectiveness of indigenous property rights institutions that still exist in much of Africa, particularly in the components of assurance, duration, and excludability. Their legitimacy often supersedes national land laws in the eyes of local people. Even in other regions, indigenous property rights institutions have often proven effective in recognizing and enforcing secure property rights for community members, and where these institutions persist, a title does little to strengthen the land rights of community members. In Chapter 6 Smucker, White, and Bannister report that in Haiti local tenure systems are a source of protection against the insecurity that comes from involvement with formal state tenure systems, which often bring a threat of urban elites taking land. Where indigenous local systems have broken down (because of either internal factors or external threats to the security of tenure, such as outsiders attempting to claim land), registration or land titling may be needed. It may also be needed where commercialization has advanced to the point of creating a need for efficient credit and land markets in which non–community members become important agents (Cohen 1980; Noronha 1985; Bruce 1993).

In other cases, tenure security depends on which resource is being considered. For example, Adesina, Chianu, and Mbila (1997) found that, after controlling for other factors such as fuel and fodder scarcity, secure land rights were not a significant factor in adoption of alley farming in Cameroon, though secure tree tenure was. How tenure security is defined has also played a significant role in shaping policy outcomes.

Apart from tenure security considerations, other components of property rights and technologies can shape the interaction between these two. Grabowski (1990) maintains that the high cost of negotiating tenancy and fixed-rent contracts will induce landlords to adopt mechanized agricultural processes in the face of technological change, whereas Bardhan (1979) finds that technology has different impacts on tenure arrangements depending on whether it is labor intensive or land augmenting. In other cases, it is not property rights arrangements themselves, but rather factors underlying the choice of property rights, that shape technology choice. Several studies examine the effects of landlord-tenant arrangements on incentives to adopt yield-enhancing technologies and find that the expected gains from adoption can be quite low when one figures in the increased risk borne by the tenant and the potential for weakening the lucrative patron-client relationship from the perspective of the landlord (Bahduri 1973; Scandizzo 1979). Other literature argues that poor terms of trade and information asymmetries, rather than landlord-tenant contracts, act as adoption constraints, because these contracts are by-products of the asymmetries (Ghose and Saith 1976; de Janvry 1979).

Collective Action and Technology Adoption

Collective action becomes particularly relevant for natural resource management techniques that operate at the landscape level. This is seen clearly in farmer-managed irrigation systems (Leach 1961; Mahendrarajah 1981; Coward 1986; Yoder 1994). Drijver, van Wetten, and de Groot (1995) present evidence from the floodplains regions of Lake Chad of village participation in digging canals and constructing protected fish spawning areas, which are owned by groups of villagers. Groups take annual turns refraining from fishing in spawning areas in order to augment the fish population, a sacrifice that is rewarded by a guaranteed percentage of the subsequent communal catch. Failure to consider and subsequently organize for collective action, however, can result in a number of viable natural resource management practices never being conceived or taking hold.

A growing body of research outlines conditions for creating and effectively sustaining collective action for managing common pool resources (for example, Runge 1986; Uphoff 1986; Wade 1988; Ostrom 1990, 1994; Oakerson 1992; Nugent 1993; Rasmussen and Meinzen-Dick 1995; White and Runge 1995; Baland and Platteau 1996). A resource that is to be managed or improved collectively should be small enough so that group members can effectively control and monitor the resource and exclude outsiders. Federations of groups can facilitate collective action for managing larger resources or resources that are linked over larger areas (such as watersheds), though very large areas (such as river basins and oceans) often require state involvement. Greater social cohesion within the group is facilitated by a smaller number of users and higher net benefits derived from group membership.

Evidence is varied on the effect of wealth heterogeneity on collective action. Examining the political structure of Fulani society, Vedeld (1997) concludes that heterogeneity in endowments can foster collective action and improve resource management. Yet Baland and Platteau (1998) argue that wealth inequality can induce less efficient collective regulation and more disparate effects on participants. Wealth and power differentials aside, there appears to be general agreement that shared values and objectives are likely to promote group cohesion (Baland and Platteau 1995; Schlager and Blomquist 1998).

Institutional design is also important. Ostrom (1994) has identified seven design principles for effective local organizations for common property management: (1) a clear definition of the members and the boundaries of the resource to be managed or improved; (2) a clear set of rules and obligations that are adapted to local conditions; (3) ability of members to collectively modify those rules with changing circumstances; (4) an adequate monitoring systems in place, with (5) enforceable sanctions, preferably graduated to match the seriousness and context of the offense; (6) effective mechanisms for conflict resolution; and (7) an organization that, if not empowered or recognized by government authorities, is at least not challenged or undermined by those authorities.

Davis and North (1971) base their principles for organizational capacity on transaction costs and how these influence the time between when people realize the potential benefits of collective action and when they organize for it. Collective action is enabled when participants are fewer and share sociocultural values, the net benefits of cooperation are large and relatively certain, participants are less risk averse, there is access to transportation and communications infrastructure, and there are existing organizational structures for pursuing new collective action. Birner and Gunaweera's study of *chena* farmers in Sri Lanka (Chapter 9) attributed their lack of organizational capacity to their large numbers, sociocultural heterogeneity, lack of access to infrastructure and communication facilities, and aversion to risk.

Motivation to cooperate depends not only on quantifiable economic costs and benefits, but also on factors such as time involved and social tensions or gratification from participation. Where there are sufficient incentives but governance mechanisms are lacking, local leaders or external community organizers can play an instrumental role in developing local mechanisms. This assistance can be seen as reducing the transaction costs of organizing. To be sustainable over time, however, these governance mechanisms must be institutionalized and not dependent on the actions of a single person.

Lack of boundedness of the resource is more complex. Clear boundaries are important in monitoring and enforcing and in ensuring that those who participate in collective action (either by contributing or refraining from taking too much) will be the ones who benefit from improvements. In some cases, however, somewhat fuzzy boundaries may be preferred, especially in highly variable contexts, where people recognize that they may need to tap others' resources under crisis conditions (such as drought) and are therefore willing to allow others to use their resources under similar conditions (Cleaver 1998; Ngaido and Kirk 2001; McCarthy 2002).

In many cases property rights and collective action are interrelated, especially in natural resource management. This situation is clearest in common property regimes, which require both clearly defined property rights for the group and a relatively high degree of collective action within the group. Conversely, shared property rights can reinforce collective action among a group, whereas privatization of a resource or government claims of "ownership" can erode local management institutions (Coward 1986; Wade 1988; Bromley and Cernea 1989). But even private property regimes require collective action to uphold private rights, and managing resources (with or without joint ownership rights) often requires coordination between individuals and households.

Indirect Effects of PRCA on Technology Adoption

Much of the empirical literature focuses on the direct links between PRCA and technology adoption, yet there is increasing evidence to show that PRCA also has important indirect impacts through its interactions with other socioeconomic factors that affect adoption. In this section, we review how PRCA interacts with each of the factors listed earlier.

Infrastructure and Information

Property rights are intrinsically linked to the distribution of technological inputs and information. At the community level, extension services have often favored those who control the greatest quantity of resources—that is, the wealthy. At the intrahousehold level, the norm in most patrilineal societies is for male heads of household to either own or have primary rights over land and other natural resources, even when they are not the primary users of the resource. Although this right does not necessarily imply that they can easily exercise the right to deprive other family or community members of use rights over the resources they control, it does tip the balance of technology and information access in their favor. One sees a recurring pattern where extension services have largely targeted male heads of household, mainly because they were seen as the ones who controlled the land, even if women were directly engaged in cultivation (Fortmann and Rocheleau 1985; Kilkelly 1986; Agarwal 1994; Lastarria-Cornheil 1997).

Collective action, in its capacity to build relationships and alliances between individuals, may act to strengthen the bargaining power of disadvantaged community interest groups (Agarwal 1994; Kurien 1995). This occurs through a process of knowledge sharing and building common objectives that identify the group and magnify the voice of individuals via the collective. If it succeeds in altering the distribution of local power and voice, collective action has the potential for realigning the distribution of technologies and resources (Chen 1983; Sarin and Khanna 1993; Agarwal 1994; Meinzen-Dick et al. 1997).

Likewise, formation of networks among community members can facilitate access to information by reducing the cost of acquiring it, thereby enabling coordination of technology adoption efforts, whether individual or collective. For example, a communally managed seed bank may be established to facilitate individual tree planting and also provide a forum for information sharing about the technology or other matters. In Chapter 11 Brent Swallow and his coauthors show how the spread of information through *kabeles* (cooperatives) and interaction among neighbors facilitate the adoption of tsetse control measures in Ethiopia.

Environmental and Price Risk

Prevailing property rights and collective action institutions can affect farmers' ability to manage risk efficiently. For example, plot scattering, which takes advantage of microclimate variations and reduces the possibilities that a farmer's full range of crops will be lost to pest or weather problems, requires either institutionalized systems of land inheritance or active land markets so that farmers can optimally diversify their holdings through land swaps, purchases, or leases. The performance of land markets, in turn, depends on the presence of secure property rights. Plot scattering also requires that the government does not prohibit fragmentation, as often occurs based on the belief that land consolidation is necessarily more efficient.

Rules for joint access to common pool resources frequently function as a buffer against risk. During drought periods, for example, agricultural households often resort more to village commons to meet their subsistence needs, particularly for fuelwood and food (Jodha 1992). Pastoral and agropastoral populations occupying arid and semi-arid regions rely on herd mobility on communal rangelands to mitigate their risk exposure, engaging in opportunistic grazing (Behnke 1994; Galaty 1994; Swallow 1994). Collective action among herders not only establishes the membership, rules, and enforcement of common property, it also enables risk sharing and diversification and inspires mechanisms for collective self-help (Thompson and Wilson 1994; Waller and Sobania 1994; Mearns 1996).

The bundle of property rights held by an individual bears significantly on their capacity to manage risk. In many parts of West Africa, "stranger" farmers originating from outside the community and women are restricted from planting and owning trees since doing so would confer greater land rights on them (Berry 1988; Fortmann 1988; Rocheleau and Edmunds 1997). Inevitably, this limits their adoption of agroforestry and reforestation practices as well as other tree technologies that could diminish their exposure to risk (Rocheleau 1988; Neef and Heidhues 1994).

Collective action can also play a critical role in smoothing consumption in the face of uncertain and variable production. Support networks and reciprocity norms are frequently present in low-wealth rural communities to cope with these hazards, particularly given insufficient or complete lack of insurance markets. Sharing of output or other resources, and even participation in collective action, can be seen as an investment in social capital, which can prove invaluable for the survival of the poor in the face of risk. White and Runge (1994, 1995) show that people in Haiti often contribute labor for watershed management programs out of a sense of solidarity and reciprocity even if they do not directly benefit economically from land improvements.

The spatial characteristics of risk are important for understanding the adoption or nonadoption of different technologies and for designing improved technologies that match the preferences of low-wealth individuals to mitigate risk. Idiosyncratic risks affect the individual or household. Family illness, death of an animal, or localized crop failure are some examples. Covariate risks, by contrast, are associated with environmental disasters like drought, flooding, or large-scale pest attack or economic crises like a major fall in output prices, which take their toll on large groups, communities, and even entire countries.

Different forms of collective action and social capital may be needed depending on whether risks are idiosyncratic or covariate. In the case of covariate risk, collective action networks may need to involve a larger number of participants and be more heterogeneous so that the impact of the risk on individuals is differentiated. Large groups and heterogeneity may, however, introduce coordination problems and conflict, diminishing the potential success of collective action (Olson 1971; Hansmann 1988, 1990; Lawry 1989; Tang 1992; Nugent 1993; Quiggan 1993; Baland and Platteau 1996; Mearns 1996). In contrast, collective action designed to confront idiosyncratic risk can be coordinated with an informal set of reciprocity rules or norms in a small community setting or even among a few neighbors and hence is more likely to be an effective strategy (Fafchamps and Minten 1998).

Wealth

In agrarian societies, natural resources are key assets; therefore wealth is intricately linked to property rights over natural resources. Asset control conditions the ability to generate income and has a strong effect on people's options with regard to technology. In Pakistan, for example, farmers owning more land are wealthier and are more likely to install tubewells; the control over groundwater that tubewells provide further increases their wealth (Meinzen-Dick 1996).

The bundle of one's property rights and the security of those rights combined with one's level of assets, income, and food security affect the degree to which one discounts possible future gains. Those who possess a higher quantity and quality of endowments will place a higher future value on the medium- and long-run benefits produced by investment in technologies. This is because they are less constrained by food insecurity and risks that undermine the ability to meet basic needs than are low-wealth actors. Furthermore, social structures and power distributions bias technologies and the flow of technical information in favor of the wealthy, shaping adoption outcomes accordingly (Grabowski 1990).

Collective action can be a means for the poor to garner control over assets, thereby alleviating food insecurity and other survival risks they bear disproportionately. With reduced risk, the poor would lower the degree to which they discount possible future gains and thus lower the constraints on technology adoption. By facilitating the adoption of more advanced technologies that require "lumpy" investments, collective action can realign the distribution of gains from a resource more in favor of the poor. For example, in Bangladesh and Pakistan, groups of small-scale farmers as well as landless people and women obtain rights to groundwater through collective purchases and management of wells and pumps, which provide for the water needs of members or other farmers in the community (Wood and Palmer-Jones 1990; van Koppen and Mahmud 1995; Meinzen-Dick 1996). Documenting the decollectivization of Mongolian pastoralism, Mearns (1996) notes that herders jointly purchase lumpy technologies that tend to be beyond the capacity of individual households to acquire. By investing and acting collectively, groups spread out the costs associated with a particular technology among their members, lowering individual risk exposure and thereby potentially facilitating adoption. When people apply collective action to enhance resource access, wealth is less of a constraint to obtaining rights to resources and adopting technologies.

Credit

One of the primary arguments made in favor of privatization of land tenure is that farmers need title to their land so that they can offer it as collateral for credit. For farmers who tend to have little or no collateral, it is hypothesized that privatization will give them access to financial markets and increase the supply of credit available to them (Feder and Noronha 1987; *Economist* 2001). As a result, agricultural investment and technology adoption is expected to follow. Feder et al. (1988) provide a good example of this linkage from Thailand.

Formal financial institutions, however, remain a rarity in many rural settings, particularly for the purposes of agricultural lending (Place and Hazell 1993; Roth, Cochrane, and Kisamba-Mugerwa 1993). In fact, it is questionable how important a constraint formal collateral actually is relative to the overwhelming transaction costs involved in rural lending. Even when means are found to reduce the transaction costs of lending, other forms of collateral may still prove more appropriate, or even more effective, for reducing the risks of lending to low-wealth borrowers. For example, many informal financial institutions undertake successful group lending schemes using joint liability mechanisms (Berger and Buvinic 1989; Chen 1989; Adams and Fitchett 1992; Bhole and Bhavani 1995; Zeller 1996). These programs substitute collective action (group formation and backing) and norms of social accountability for conventional property rights as a form of collateral. Implementing more progressive models of financial service provision may therefore accelerate investment in agricultural and natural resource management technologies.[3]

---

3. Because informal financial institutions are typically limited by the number of clients they can reach and vulnerable to covariate risk (especially in agriculture), widespread access to credit by the poor is likely to happen only if linkages are made with the formal financial system. For such linkages to be forged and sustainable, formal banks will need to be trained in more effective means of banking with the poor.

Some of the most noted forms of collective action in the literature center on the dynamics of credit and savings groups. In addition to establishing mutual accountability for repayment, they act to lower transaction costs of financial services (whether funds are internally raised or received from external lenders). Such groups provide a forum for building assets and self-reliance via savings programs as well as opportunities via credit for purchasing technologies and inputs to develop and maintain technologies. Group credit may also make larger-scale, expensive technologies more feasible to acquire and operate if members share the costs of acquisition and the subsequent use and maintenance of the technology (Agarwal 1994). Finally, credit groups may play a role in strengthening social capital formation and producing network externalities in a way that enhances opportunities for collective action in natural resource management and technology adoption (Anderson, Locker, and Nugent 2000). If groups have already formed around a common purpose and have established a history of coordination and trust, this experience reduces the information and coordination costs of their involvement in another activity (Wade 1988; North 1990; Nugent 1993; Baland and Platteau 1996; Mearns 1996). A study of watersheds in India by Kerr et al. (2000) found that when nongovernmental organizations (NGOs) initiated microcredit and other organizational activities with the poorest in the community before introducing watershed management activities, they achieved substantially more equitable distribution of benefits.

Labor

Within the households of most rural societies, property rights fail to correspond closely to labor responsibilities. One statistic on the status of African women states that they perform around two-thirds of all the hours spent on agriculture-related work and own only 1 percent of the property (FAO 1985).[4] In some cultures women may need to contribute labor to their husbands' plots in order to get access to plots for their own production (Berry 1988; Carney 1992; Meinzen-Dick et al. 1997; van Koppen 2000). The introduction of new technology (such as irrigation) can shift these labor demands and responsibilities.

Von Braun and Webb (1989) attribute declines in women's labor productivity in a Gambian setting to their lesser access to labor-saving and yield-enhancing technologies and shifting labor responsibilities away from agricultural production. Berry (1988) and Quisumbing et al. (2001) explore how the spread of cocoa as a commercial crop in western Ghana led men to demand a greater share of women's labor to farm cocoa crops owned by men. In some cases this development has led men to give women a stronger claim over land in compensation for the added labor burden (also see Okali 1983), which can be expected to have positive results for technology adoption by women.

---

4. Given the pervasiveness of community-based land tenure in Africa, one assumes that the term "own" refers to holding primary use rights to land.

Power and asset ownership are also frequently used to influence labor relations to preserve the interests of dominant groups (von Braun and Webb 1989; Grabowski 1990; Folbre 1997). In the initial stages of an irrigation project, officials and local male elites in Burkina Faso took land and water rights away from women who had been cultivating rice and reallocated them as "family" plots, controlled by men, resulting in declining productivity, as well as increased work burdens for women (van Koppen 2000). In central Mali the distribution of cattle ownership began shifting from Fulani pastoralists to Bambara farmers, who hired Fulani herders who had lost their animals as a result of drought (Toulmin 1992), illustrating how asset ownership influences the direction of labor relationships.

Collective action can be used to exert control over individuals' own labor. In her study of a contract farming irrigation scheme in The Gambia intended to target women, Carney (1988) describes how women's property rights to land for rice cultivation were undermined by village men. In several communities women jointly responded by withdrawing their labor from rice cultivation, thereby undermining the successful adoption of contract farming technology. Collective action and reciprocity arrangements may also be used to overcome labor shortages faced by individual households, particularly in cash-scarce economies, thereby facilitating the use of more labor-intensive technologies (Kirk 1988; White and Runge 1995).

Other Conditioning Factors

Besides property rights institutions, other statutory laws and formal and informal community rules, norms, or ideas can act to expand or constrain people's choices with regard to technology. Erenstein and Cadena Iniguez (1997) partially attribute the adoption of conservation tillage practices in Chiapas, Mexico, to state agricultural policies, including a law prohibiting the burning of crop residues. In South Asia taboos forbid women to use plows, restricting agricultural productivity and reinforcing women's dependence on men (Agarwal 1994). Nevertheless, property rights institutions are pervasive in their scope; they frequently shape and reinforce other rules, both legal and normative. Property rights vested in the state provide the means by which laws are enacted to forbid the cutting of trees, which can then discourage cultivation of crops (Freudenberger 1994).

Although on the surface cultural norms that hinder technology adoption may appear to have equity, productivity, or environmental drawbacks, it is important to understand their more profound implications and not to write them off as irrational. In many African rural societies, the capacity to perpetuate a cohesive community and lessen exposure to risk is rooted in kinship and marital practices, which have implications for the distribution of property rights (see Eyzaguirre 1988). In patrilineal societies, when men and women marry, women often move to their husbands' community and acquire secondary use rights to land without retaining rights to land in their birth community. Likewise, the practice of having multiple wives means that male household heads must periodically redistribute land to accommodate women as well as children. Altering the principles and property regimes that facilitate a cohesive community may increase exposure to environmental risk and diminish social security for women, at least in the short term. In sum, the failure to adopt technologies often arises from cases in which the costs of altering rules and norms—including transaction costs and livelihood risks—exceed the potential benefits of the technology.

PRCA and the Impact of Technology Adoption

Adoption of new technologies is not an end in itself for agricultural researchers, policymakers, or people who employ them in farming or managing natural resources. Rather, the outcome of technological change should be evaluated in terms of the contribution to broader goals of sustainable development. Agricultural productivity growth, poverty reduction, and environmental sustainability form a "critical triangle" for development (Vosti and Reardon 1997). Although there may be trade-offs between these three objectives, all are necessary and interlinked. The way these play out in practice is strongly influenced by the nature of property rights and the degree of collective action.

Agricultural Productivity

Because PRCA affects access to information and key inputs associated with yield-enhancing technologies, when farmers adopt new technologies, their yields are directly related to PRCA. PRCA can also affect decisions to invest in improving natural resources that in turn affect their productivity. Several studies have attempted to estimate the net impact of PRCA on productivity (usually measured by yield) using reduced-form econometric equations. Results are mixed, with weak and insignificant relationships in Africa (Carter, Wiebe, and Blarel 1991; Place and Hazell 1993; Gavian and Ehui in Chapter 5) and stronger ones in Asia (Feder et al. 1988). This difference may occur in part because credit markets are more developed in Asia and property rights affect one's ability to mortgage land.

Simplistic analyses of PRCA-productivity relations can lead to misleading results. For example, econometric analysis of the relation between agricultural productivity and titling in the Njoro District of Kenya reveals that the positive relationship between the two does not stem from improved tenure security or access to credit afforded by titles (Carter, Wiebe, and Blarel 1991). Rather, because larger-scale farmers have access to imperfect labor, capital, and insurance markets that smallholders do not, their productivity is often greater, an outcome that can be further improved by titling their land. Similarly, in Chapter 5 Gavian and Ehui found that in Ethiopia, land with less secure tenure had lower total factor productivity, but not because farmers were applying fewer inputs; rather, it was the low quality of inputs or low skill in applying them that limited productivity.

Results may also depend on how productivity is measured. Many customary tenure regimes permit different users to exploit different "niches." Examples include pastoralists and cultivators on the same land; irrigation, fishing, and domestic use of water; or timber, firewood, and minor forest products (Swallow et al. 1997). Technologies that increase the production of one of those components at the expense of other outputs do not necessarily improve overall productivity. For example, introducing new tree species or forest management practices may maximize production of logs but sacrifice kindling and minor forest products critical to the livelihoods of local residents (Meinzen-Dick et al. 1997).

Privatization of resources held under common property and of land under communal tenure tends to lead to loss of multiple user rights in favor of more concentrated resource holding by a less diverse set of interests (Jodha 1992; Rocheleau and Edmunds 1997; Swallow et al. 1997). The logic underpinning the privatization of tenure in Kenya during the 1950s rested on the belief that more entrepreneurial and supposedly more efficient farmers would acquire land from less efficient farmers (Swynnerton 1954). Subsequent research has linked conversion to freehold tenure to rising loss of access to land and other resources by customary landholders and large-scale land acquisitions by wealthy producers, government officials, and speculators, with dubious gains for total productivity and definite losses by the poor (Hitchcock 1980; Shipton 1988; Jodha 1992). Although evidence is mixed on the relation between land markets, patterns of landholding, and investments in land improvements, where the purchases are by large-scale producers and speculators who are interested in short-term profits and have little stake in the long-term productivity of the land, soil fertility and other natural resources may be depleted (Gupta 1987; Jodha 1988, 1992; Arnold and Stewart 1989; Chambers, Saxena, and Shah 1989; for counterevidence, see Migot-Adholla et al. 1994).

Although a large literature points to the inefficiencies of collective efforts like agricultural cooperatives, some technologies are more efficiently employed with collective adoption after material and transaction costs are assessed, whereas others are more amenable to individual adoption. In Katon, Pomeroy, and Salamanca's (1997) study of a fishers' organization in the Philippines and Kurien's (1995) case of artisanal fishermen in India, local groups constructed artificial reefs to lure more fish and increase their food supply. Alternatively, collective action may influence technological choices based not only on efficiency concerns, but also on equity and environmental sustainability. Quiggan (1993) points to joint ownership of harvesting equipment by small farmers as an example of efficiency gains from employing a technology held as common property rather than private property, which might otherwise impose spatial limitations on adoption, particularly for the poor, who could face access limitations under a private property renting mechanism.

Poverty

Access to natural resources is a key factor in determining the size and distribution of the gains from technological change in agriculture. Because the poor typically have access to the least amount of land and other natural resources, they typically gain the least from technologies that improve the productivity of those resources. Some offsetting gains may occur in the labor market, but even this is not assured. The literature on these linkages is large and evolving and continues to be debated. Critics of the Green Revolution argue that, because of their better access to irrigation water, fertilizers, seeds, and credit, large-scale farmers were the main adopters of the new technology, and smaller farmers were either left unaffected or were made worse off because the Green Revolution resulted in lower output prices, higher input prices, and efforts by larger farmers to increase rents or force tenants off the land. It has also been argued that the Green Revolution encouraged unnecessary mechanization, with a resulting reduction in rural wages and employment, the net result of which has been an increase in the inequality of income and land distribution, an increase in landlessness, and a worsening of absolute poverty in areas affected by the Green Revolution (see, for example, Griffin 1972, 1974; Frankel 1976; Farmer 1977, 1986; Pearse 1980; Freebairn 1995).

Meanwhile, a host of other studies have emerged with findings to the contrary (see, for example, Blyn 1983; Pinstrup-Andersen and Hazell 1985; Lipton and Longhurst 1989; Hazell and Ramasamy 1991). These studies show that while small farmers did lag behind large farmers in adopting Green Revolution technologies, most of them eventually adopted and benefited from increased production, as well as from greater employment opportunities and higher wages in the agricultural and nonfarm sectors. Other evidence demonstrates that distribution of land did not worsen in most cases (Rosegrant and Hazell 1999) and that other poor people also benefited from the Green Revolution through increased employment and business earnings in the farm and nonfarm sectors and from lower food prices (Pinstrup-Andersen and Hazell 1985). Studies from both sides of the debate have contributed to a better understanding of the conditions under which Green Revolution and other yield-enhancing technologies are likely to be equitable. These include (1) a scale-neutral technology package that can be profitably adopted on farms of all sizes; (2) an equitable distribution of land with secure ownership or tenancy rights; (3) efficient input, credit, and product markets so that farms of all sizes have access to needed modern farm inputs and receive similar prices for their products; (4) a mobile labor force that can migrate or diversify into the rural nonfarm economy; and (5) policies that do not discriminate against small farms (for example, no subsidies on mechanization or scale-biases in agricultural research and extension).

Common property resources may also contribute to the livelihoods of the poor and improve equity by accommodating multiple users beyond the household level. In this respect, common property may be better equipped than private property to spread benefits more evenly. Technologies geared to improving the performance of resources held as common property likewise may have more positive effects on the poor. Recent research, however, has cautioned against assuming that common property regimes and collective action embody impartial sharing rules and equal distribution of power (Agrawal and Gibson 1997). Although users have equal rights to the resource, their ability to exploit the resources is often conditioned by their access to private means of production. Also, because collective action implies the exclusion of nonparticipants, negative outcomes for some poor people are possible. In his research on communally owned land in Portugal, Brouwer (1992) maintains that mechanisms of social redistribution and security shape equity outcomes of resource exploitation, rather than property rights themselves.

Technological change that benefits poor households may not be enough if there are important gender differences in access to and control over technology and resources within households. Women may be accorded less voice in the decisionmaking process while still being accountable for labor contributions or being otherwise affected by the new management practices (Mayoux 1993; Athukorala and Zwarteveen 1994; Sarin 1995; Ahluwalia 1997). Although male dominance in many societies does not necessarily stem from men's monopoly on property rights, ownership or primary rights to resources enhance the status and bargaining power of individuals within both the household and community (Agarwal 1994, 1997; Folbre 1997; Meinzen-Dick et al. 1997). Greater control over resources tends to enhance men's influence over community power structures and wield political leverage with government officials and others responsible for technology distribution as well as infrastructure and market development. The same is true for the wealthier strata of society (Grabowski 1990; Kurien 1995). Technologies and their supporting infrastructure will therefore mainly reflect the interests of men who control substantial resources unless a sufficient degree of collective action emerges capable of reshaping political outcomes so that government and other suppliers of technology and infrastructure intervene with policies to override these biases.

Environment

PRCA affects incentives to conserve and improve natural resources. Secure property rights are necessary if farmers are to have the right long-term incentives to make such investments (Pender and Kerr 1998; Otsuka and Place 2001).

Yet even when rights are secure, degradation problems can arise because the effects of environmental damage are not experienced by those who impose the damage. With sufficient distance, those who cause the damage may not even be aware of the costs they impose on others or they may feel little social pressure to do anything about it. Stakeholders may also be separated in time; for example, future generations cannot make their voices heard to change the behavior of those whose actions are degrading resources today. There are also instances in which the affected party cannot be properly represented at the bargaining table; this is the case for many plant and animal species whose future depends on how successful environmentalist are in voicing their fate.

According to economic theory, if appropriate property rights systems could be defined over all natural resources with little or no transaction costs, then the different stakeholders might be able to negotiate market solutions to these environmental problems (Coase 1960). Unfortunately, defining appropriate property rights can be difficult when there are off-site effects from environmental damage (for example, the right to "clean" water, not just water), and the transaction costs of negotiating solutions can also be formidable. It is therefore not surprising that adequate solutions to these problems are rarely found through property rights approaches alone. Rather, collective action often plays a large role in improving environmental conditions and abating externalities by bringing stakeholders together and thereby enabling them to appreciate the impacts felt by others, negotiate solutions, choose mutually beneficial technologies, and forge a stronger sense of community responsibility (Ashby, Knapp, and Ravnborg 1998; Knox, Swallow, and Johnson 2001).

Trade-offs between the Components of the Critical Triangle

The objectives of increased productivity, poverty reduction, and environmental sustainability frequently involve trade-offs. Increasing productivity involves allocating production factors, whether it is managers, labor, capital, or land. Some factors will become less valuable relative to others, and this change leads to inequitable outcomes. Even within input categories, substitutions are made. For example, efficiency-enhancing technology improvements can increase the demand for skilled labor at the expense of unskilled labor.

Productivity and environmental goals are often at odds as well. Productivity measures tend to assess only the private financial costs of inputs and neglect social and environmental costs. Privatization of such resources as rangelands and fisheries has been advocated as a measure to control stocking rates and improve resource management so as to enhance profitability (Foss 1960; Demsetz 1967; Cheung 1970; Johnson 1972; Picardi 1974). In Africa, however, failure to account for environmental variability and fragility has resulted in overgrazing, soil erosion, and other forms of environmental degradation on many privatized ranches and areas appropriated by sedentarization schemes (Gilles and Jamtgaard 1981; Hogg 1987; Keya 1991). Technologies designed for large-scale agriculture may also carry environmental implications. For instance, use of pesticide technology by large farmers may generate negative externalities for small farmers if they do not have access to it, especially if the chemicals eliminate predators who would otherwise keep the pest in check. Likewise, inadequate access to resources and environmentally friendly technology by the poor can lead to overexploitation and degradation.

However, the trade-offs are perhaps overstated. In the case of natural resource management techniques such as agroforestry and soil conservation, environmental degradation can raise the perceived value of products and conservation of the resource base to the point where it becomes worthwhile to invest in such practices (Scherr and Hazell 1994; Hazell and Wood 2000). Also, when productivity measures include the value of nontraded goods and services that poor households (and especially women within those households) obtain for their livelihood and security, an equitable distribution of resources, or technologies that favor the disadvantaged, may be seen as highly productive. Appreciation of less tangible economic and social dynamics broadens the scope of technologies deemed to be productivity improving so that they are less biased toward concepts of efficiency that consider only physical inputs and a narrow range of outputs. Recognition and attention to the complexity of defining and measuring efficiency is necessary to prevent the poor from being left behind or hurt by technologies and to narrowing equity gaps.

Impact of Technological Change on PRCA

As shown in Figure 2.1, technological change and its impacts on productivity, poverty, and the environment have important feedback effects on the structure of property rights, collective action, and other socioeconomic constructs. For example, Kimberly Swallow's (Chapter 13) study shows how the adoption of new cattle-feeding technologies in Kenya changed the rules of access to a variety of feed sources, affecting both property rights and collective action. Quisumbing et al. (2001) demonstrate how changes in physical and economic conditions such as the introduction of cocoa production, population growth, and scarcity of natural forests in Ghana has led to changes in the types of property rights found within communities; the property rights found within communities in turn set the options available to households; meanwhile, household allocation of rights to particular plots affect the resources available to individuals. In effect, the framework displayed in Figure 2.1 is dynamic, driven by endogenous forces that operate at different levels. The choice of natural resource management technologies inevitably shapes the institutions underlying property rights and collective action. Technologies embodying substantial spatial externalities such as irrigation are likely to induce demand for common property regimes and collective action given the gains to be realized from coordinated efforts. If incentives for adoption are not built into PRCA institutions, however, information asymmetries are profound and transaction costs of coordination and enforcement are not reduced. Then technology adoption will not succeed and unsustainable outcomes may prevail. Using North's language (1992), the "adaptive efficiency" of a society or community is the critical variable in ascertaining the potential for technical and institutional change.

Technologies with temporal externalities whereby the benefits of the technology are reaped at some future point in time carry implications for enhancing tenure security. Planting trees may establish a claim on land and often contribute to greater tenure security. Unruh (Chapter 8) shows how cashew agroforestry technology in Mozambique has become a particularly important source of evidence for defending land claims in the aftermath of war when many other forms of evidence have been weakened. While tree planting may produce positive effects in terms of halting environmental degradation, promoting such practices without understanding the implications for tenure can lead to serious problems. In The Gambia, for example, elite men used a tree-planting program as a means of reclaiming land that had been given to women, who had been using the land for high-value horticultural produce (Schroeder 1993).

More generally, technologies that increase the value of a resource may induce privatization, enclosure, and the exclusion of some customary uses. Yet the gains to some households and individuals from such institutional change frequently result in losses to others, usually the more vulnerable. Empirical studies have revealed a negative correlation between household income and reliance on the commons for subsistence purposes (Jodha 1986, 1992; Hopkins, Scherr, and Gruhn 1994). Women especially depend on resources accessed through common property and "interstitial spaces" of private property (such as hedgerows and reed beds) to provide for their family's needs (Rocheleau 1988; Agarwal 1994; Maggs and Hoddinott 1997; Rocheleau and Edmunds 1997) or for their own tenure security where private property does not guarantee them access in the case of widowhood or divorce (Fortmann, Antinori, and Nabane 1997). Well-defined and secure property rights to common property and protection of secondary access and use rights on private lands are therefore highly important for the poor, and poor women in particular. Support for common property regimes and technologies that are compatible with them are likely to be effective poverty reduction strategies given their potential to enhance production over the long term and ensure fairer distribution of resources to more marginalized interest groups.

Conclusions

Going beyond the realm of crop technologies to understand the use of technologies and practices for appropriate natural resource management requires a deeper appreciation of the spatial and temporal externalities embodied in various technologies, as well as the role played by property rights and collective action in facilitating or impeding adoption. As yet, little empirical research has been carried out documenting factors influencing technology choices applied to common pool resources and how traditionally identified constraints interact with various property rights regimes to either weaken or assist in expanding the use of resource-enhancing technologies. Similarly, collective action, by internalizing the externalities produced by spatially dispersed resources and by lowering transaction costs of institutional change, may be instrumental in facilitating technological change in natural resource management.

Despite the important implications of property rights and collective action, it is important not to view these institutions as the single key for identifying constraints or enabling factors for adoption of natural resource management technologies. Other constraining factors abound. For instance, lack of market infrastructure and human capital constraints may hinder the use of mechanized wells for improved livestock management, given the inability to acquire spare parts and lack of indigenous knowledge to repair the wells. Property rights may constitute a separate issue constraining adoption in this context, being relatively independent of other constraints.

Because so many things tend to be related to property rights, it is easy to confound the effects of property rights with the effects of other related variables. By modifying the existing property rights structure or facilitating collective action responses, more fundamental barriers can be overlooked and more problems may be created than solved. Instead of focusing on property rights or collective action in isolation, the purpose in introducing the PRCA framework to evaluate technology choices is to stimulate greater appreciation for how these issues manifest themselves in people's decisions about which technologies to employ, and the process of technology change itself, as illustrated by the cases in this volume.

References

Adams, D. W., and D. A. Fitchett. 1992. *Informal finance in low-income countries.* Boulder, Colo., U.S.A.: Westview Press.

Adesina, A., J. Chianu, and D. Mbila. 1997. *Property rights and alley farming technology adoption in West and Central Africa.* Paper presented at Workshop on Property Rights, Collective Action, and Technology Adoption, International Center for Agricultural Research in the Dry Areas (ICARDA), Aleppo, Syria, November 22–25, 1997.

Agrawal, A., and C. Gibson. 1997. Community, resources, and development: Beyond enchantment and disenchantment. Indiana University, Bloomington, Ind., U.S.A. Photocopy.

Agarwal, B. 1994. *A field of one's own: Gender and land rights in South Asia.* Cambridge: Cambridge University Press.

Ahluwalia, M. 1997. Representing communities: The case of a community-based watershed management project in Rajasthan, India. *IDS Bulletin* 28 (4): 23–35.

Anderson, C. L., L. Locker, and R. Nugent. 2000. Microcredit, social capital, and common pool resources. Presented at "Constituting the Commons," the eighth annual conference of the International Association for the Study of Common Property, Bloomington, Ind., U.S.A., May 31–June 4, 2000.

Arnold, J. E. M., and W. Stewart. 1989. Common property resource management in India: A desk review. Report for the Asian Environment and Social Affairs Division and the India Agriculture Division. Washington, D.C.: World Bank.

Ashby, J. A., E. B. Knapp, and H. M. Ravnborg. 1998. Involving local organizations in watershed management. In *Agriculture and the environment: Perspectives on sustainable rural development,* ed. Ernst Lutz. Washington, D.C.: World Bank.

Athukorala, K., and M. Zwarteveen. 1994. Participatory management: Who participates? *Economic Review* 20 (6): 22–25.

Bahduri, A. 1973. A study in agricultural backwardness under semi-feudalism. *Economic Journal* 83 (329): 120–137.

Baland, J.-M., and J.-P. Platteau. 1995. *Does heterogeneity hinder collective action?* Cahiers de la Faculté des Sciences Économiques et Sociales 146. Namur, Belgium: Centre de Recherche en Economie du Développment, Facultés Universitaires Notre-Dame de la Paix.

———. 1996. *Halting degradation of natural resources: Is there a role for rural communities?* Oxford: Clarendon Press.

———. 1998. Wealth inequality and efficiency in the commons. Part 2, The regulated case. *Oxford Economic Papers* 50: 1–22.

Bardhan, P. K. 1979. Agricultural development and land tenancy in a peasant economy: A theoretical and empirical analysis. *American Journal of Agricultural Economics* 61 (1): 48–56.

Barrows, R., and M. Roth. 1990. Land tenure and investment in African agriculture: Theory and evidence. *Journal of Modern African Studies* 28 (2): 265–297.

Behnke, R. H. 1994. Natural resource management in pastoral Africa. *Development Policy Review* 12 (1): 5–27.

Berger, M., and M. Buvinic. 1989. *Women's ventures: Assistance to the informal sector in Latin America.* West Hartford, Conn., U.S.A.: Kumarian Press.

Berry, S. 1988. Property rights and rural resource management: The case study of tree crops in West Africa. *Cahiers des Sciences Humaines* 24 (1): 3–16.

Bhatia, B. 1992. Lush fields and parched throats: The political economy of groundwater in Gujarat. *Economic and Political Weekly* 27 (51-2): A-142–170.

Bhole, L. M., and R. V. Bhavani. 1995. Grameen Bank of Bangladesh: A model for financing rural development. *International Journal of Development Banking* 13: 35–46.

Blyn, G. 1983. The Green Revolution revisited. *Economic Development and Cultural Change* 31 (4): 705–725.

Boserup, E. 1965. *The conditions of agricultural growth.* New York: Aldine.

Bromley, D. W., and M. M. Cernea. 1989. The management of common property natural resources: Some conceptual and operational fallacies. World Bank Discussion Paper 57. Washington, D.C.: World Bank.

Brouwer, R. 1992. Common goods and private profits: Traditional and modern communal land management in Portugal. Paper presented at the "Inequality and the Commons" conference of the International Association of Common Property, Washington, D.C., September 17–20, 1992.

Bruce, J. 1988. A perspective on indigenous land tenure systems and land concentration. In *Land and society in contemporary Africa,* ed. R. E. Downs and S. P. Reyna.

Hanover, N.H., U.S.A., and London: University of New Hampshire and University Press of New England.

————. 1993. Do indigenous tenure systems constrain agricultural development? In *Land in African agrarian systems*, ed. T. J. Bassett and D. E. Crummey. Madison, Wisc., U.S.A.: University of Wisconsin Press.

Carney, J. 1988. Struggles over crop rights and labor within contract farming households in a Gambian irrigated rice project. *Journal of Peasant Studies* 15 (3): 334–349.

————. 1992. *Contract farming and female rice growers in The Gambia*. Network Paper 15. London: Overseas Development Institute.

Carter, M. R., K. Wiebe, and B. Blarel. 1991. Tenure security for whom? Differential impacts of land policy in Kenya. LTC Research Paper Number 106. Madison, Wisc., U.S.A.: Land Tenure Center, University of Wisconsin.

Chambers, R., N. C. Saxena, and T. Shah. 1989. *To the hands of the poor: Water and trees*. New Delhi: Oxford and IBH.

Chen, M. A. 1983. *A quiet revolution: Women in transition in rural Bangladesh*. Cambridge, Mass., U.S.A.: Schenkman.

————. 1989. The working women's forum: Organizing for credit and change in Madras, India. In *Seeds: Supporting women's work in the Third World*, ed. A. Leonard. New York: Feminist Press.

Cheung, S. N. S. 1970. The structure of a contract and the theory of a non-exclusive resource. *Journal of Law and Economics* 13 (1): 49–70.

Cleaver, F. 1998. Incentives and informal institutions: Gender and the management of water. *Agriculture and Human Values* 15 (4): 347–360.

Coase, R. H. 1960. The problem of social cost. *Journal of Law and Economics* 3 (October): 1–44.

Cohen, J. 1980. Land tenure and rural development in Africa. In *Agricultural development in Africa*, ed. R. Bates and M. Lofchie. New York: Praeger.

Coward, E. W., Jr. 1986. Direct or indirect alternatives for irrigation investment and the creation of property. In *Irrigation investment, technology, and management strategies for development*, ed. K. W. Easter. Boulder, Colo., U.S.A.: Westview Press.

Davis, L. E., and D. C. North. 1971. *Institutional change and American economic growth*. London: Cambridge University Press.

de Janvry, A. 1979. Comment. In *Economics and the design of small farmer technology*, ed. A. Valdez, G. Scobie, and J. Dillon. Ames, Ia., U.S.A.: Iowa State University Press.

Demsetz, H. 1967. Toward a theory of property rights. *American Economic Review* 57 (2): 347–359.

Dorner, P. 1972. *Land reform and economic development*. Kingsport, Tenn., U.S.A.: Kingsport Press.

Drijver, C. A., J. C. J. van Wetten, and W. T. de Groot. 1995. Working with nature: Local fishery management on the Logone floodplain in Chad and Cameroon. In *Local resource management in Africa*, ed. J. P. M. van den Breemer, C. A. Drijver, and L. B. Venema. West Sussex, U.K.: John Wiley.

Economist. No title. March 29, 2001.

Ensminger, J. 1997. Changing property rights: Reconciling formal and informal rights to land in Africa. In *The frontiers of the new institutional economics,* ed. J. N. Drobak and J. V. C. Nye. San Diego: Academic Press.

Erenstein, O., and P. C. Iniguez. 1997. The adoption of conservation tillage in a hillside maize production system in Motozintla, Chiapas. NRG Paper 97-01. Mexico City: International Maize and Wheat Improvement Center (CIMMYT).

Eyzaguirre, P. B. 1988. Competing systems of land tenure in an African plantation economy. In *Land and society in contemporary Africa,* ed. R. E. Downs and S. P. Reynas. Hanover, N.H., U.S.A.: University Press of New England.

Fafchamps, M., and B. Minten. 1998. *Relationships and traders in Madagascar.* Markets and Structural Studies Division Discussion Paper Number 24. Washington, D.C.: International Food Policy Research Institute.

FAO (Food and Agriculture Organization of the United Nations). 1985. *Women and developing agriculture.* Women in Agriculture Series Number 1. Rome.

Farmer, B. H. 1977. *Green revolution? Technology and change in rice growing areas of Tamil Nadu and Sri Lanka.* London: Macmillan.

————. 1986. Perspectives on the "Green Revolution" in South Asia. *Modern Asian Studies* 20 (February): 175–199.

Feder, G., and R. Noronha. 1987. Land rights, systems, and agricultural development in Sub-Saharan Africa. *World Bank Research Observer* 2 (2): 143–169.

Feder, G., and T. Onchan. 1987. Land ownership security and farm investment in Thailand. *American Journal of Agricultural Economics* 69 (2): 311–320.

Feder, G., T. Onchan, Y. Chalamwong, and C. Hongladaron. 1988. *Land policies and farm productivity in Thailand.* Baltimore, Md., U.S.A.: Johns Hopkins University Press.

Folbre, N. 1997. Gender coalitions: Extrafamily influences on intrafamily inequality. In *Intrahousehold resource allocation in developing countries: Models, methods, and policy,* ed. L. Haddad, J. Hoddinott, and H. Alderman. Baltimore, Md., U.S.A.: Johns Hopkins University Press.

Fortmann, L. 1988. The tree tenure factor in agroforestry with particular reference to Africa. In *Whose trees? Proprietary dimensions of forestry,* ed. L. Fortmann and J. W. Bruce. Boulder, Colo., U.S.A.: Westview Press.

Fortmann, L., and D. Rocheleau. 1985. Women and agroforestry: Four myths and three case studies. *Agroforestry Systems* 2 (4): 253–272.

Fortmann, L., C. Antinori, and N. Nabane. 1997. Fruits of their labors: Gender, property rights, and tree planting in two Zimbabwe villages. *Rural Sociology* 62 (3): 295–314.

Foss, P. O. 1960. *Politics and grass: The administration of grazing on the public domain.* Seattle, Wash., U.S.A.: University of Washington Press.

Frankel, F. R. 1976. *India's Green Revolution: Economic gains and political costs.* Princeton, N.J., U.S.A.: Princeton University Press.

Freebairn, D. K. 1995. Did the Green Revolution concentrate incomes? A quantitative study of research reports. *World Development* 23 (2): 265–279.

Freudenberger, M. 1994. *Tenure and natural resources in The Gambia: Summary of research findings.* Land Tenure Center Research Paper. Madison, Wisc., U.S.A.: University of Wisconsin.

Galaty, J. G. 1994. Rangeland tenure and pastoralism in Africa. In *African pastoralist systems: An integrated approach*, ed. E. Fratkin, K. A. Galvin, and E. A. Roth. Boulder, Colo., U.S.A.: Lynne Rienner.

Ghose, A. K., and A. Saith. 1976. Indebtedness, tenancy and the adoption of new technology in semi-feudal agriculture. *World Development* 4 (April): 305–320.

Gilles, J. L., and K. Jamtgaard. 1981. Overgrazing pastoral areas: The commons reconsidered. *Sociologica Rurales* 21 (2): 129–141.

Grabowski, R. 1990. Agriculture, mechanization, and land tenure. *Journal of Development Studies* 7 (1): 43–53.

Griffin, K. 1972. *The Green Revolution: An economic analysis.* Geneva: United Nations Research Institute for Social Development.

———. 1974. *The political economy of agrarian change.* London: Macmillan.

Gupta, A. K. 1987. Why poor people do not cooperate: A study of traditional forms of cooperation and implications for modern organisations. In *Policies and practices of social research*, ed. G. C. Wanger. London: Allen and Unwin.

Hansmann, H. 1988. Ownership of the firm. *Journal of Law, Economics, and Organization* 4 (2): 267–304.

———. 1990. The viability of worker ownership: An economic perspective on the political structure of the firm. In *The firm as a nexus of treaties*, ed. M. Aoki, B. Gustaffson, and O. E. Williams. London: Sage.

Harrison, P. 1987. *The greening of Africa.* London: Paladin Grafton.

Hazell, P. B. R., and C. Ramasamy. 1991. *The Green Revolution reconsidered: The impact of high-yielding rice varieties in South India.* Baltimore, Md., U.S.A.: Johns Hopkins University Press.

Hazell, P., and S. Wood. 2000. From science to technology adoption: The role of policy research in improving natural resource management. *Agriculture, Ecosystems and Environment* 82 (1–3): 385–393.

Hitchcock, R. K. 1980. Tradition, social justice and land reform in Central Botswana. *Journal of African Law* 24 (1): 1–34.

Hogg, R. 1987. Settlement, pastoralism, and the commons: The ideology and practice of irrigation development in Northern Kenya. In *Conservation in Africa: People, policies, and practice,* ed. D. Anderson and R. Grove. New York: Cambridge University Press.

Hopkins, J., S. Scherr, and P. Gruhn. 1994. Food security and the commons: Evidence from Niger. International Food Policy Research Institute, Washington D.C. Photocopy.

Jodha, N. S. 1986. Common property resources and the rural poor in dry regions of India. *Economic and Political Weekly* 21, July 5: 1169–1181.

———. 1988. Institutional aspects of range resource management in the arid zone of India. Paper presented at the Third International Rangeland Congress, November 7–11, New Delhi.

———. 1992. *Common property resources: A missing dimension of development strategies.* World Bank Discussion Paper 169. Washington, D.C.: World Bank.

Johnson, O. E. G. 1972. Economic analysis, the legal framework, and land tenure systems. *Journal of Law and Economics* 15 (1): 259–276.

Katon, B. M., R. S. Pomeroy, and A. Salamanca. 1997. *The marine conservation project for San Salvador: A case study of fisheries co-management in the Philippines.* Paper presented at "Workshop on Property Rights, Collective Action, and Technology Adoption," November 22–25, International Center for Agricultural Research in the Dry Areas, Aleppo, Syria.

Kerr, J., with G. Pangare, V. L. Pangare, and P. J. George. 2000. *An evaluation of dryland watershed development projects in India.* Environment and Production Technology Division Discussion Paper 68. International Food Policy Research Institute, Washington, D.C.

Keya, G. A. 1991. Alternative policies and models for arid and semi-arid lands in Kenya. In *When the grass is gone: Development intervention in African arid lands*, ed. P. T. W. Baxter. Uppsala, Sweden: Scandinavian Institute of African Studies.

Kilkelly, K. 1986. Women's roles in irrigated agricultural production systems during the 1985 yala season: Parakrama Samudra Scheme and Giritale Scheme, Polonnaruma District. Report for the U.S. Agency for International Development, Colombo, Sri Lanka.

Kirk, M. 1988. Technological innovations and changes in agrarian structures: The diffusion of animal traction in Cameroon and Togo. *Quarterly Journal of International Agriculture* 27 (1): 52–63.

Knox, A., B. Swallow, and N. Johnson. 2001. Conceptual and methodological lessons for improving watershed management and research. CAPRi Policy Brief 3. Washington, D.C.: International Food Policy Research Institute.

Kurien, J. 1995. Collective action for common property resource rejuvination: The case of people's artificial reefs in Kerala State, India. *Human Organization* 54 (2): 160–168.

Lastarria-Cornheil, S. 1997. Impact of privatization on gender and property rights in Africa. *World Development* 25 (8): 1317–1333.

Lawry, S. W. 1989. Tenure policy toward common property natural resources in Sub-Saharan Africa. *Natural Resource Journal* 30 (2): 403–421.

Leach, R. 1961. *Pul Elya, a village in Ceylon: A study of land tenure and kinship.* Cambridge: Cambridge University Press.

Lipton, M., with R. Longhurst. 1989. *New seeds and poor people.* Baltimore, Md., U.S.A.: Johns Hopkins University Press.

Lynam, J. 1994. Sustainable growth in agricultural production: The links between production, resources and research. In *Opportunities, use, and transfer of systems research methods in agriculture to developing countries: Proceedings of an international workshop on systems research methods in agriculture in developing countries,* ed. P. Godsworthy and F. Penning de Vries. Boston: Kluwer.

Maggs, P., and J. Hoddinott. 1997. *The impact of change in common property resource management on intra-household allocation.* Food Consumption and Nutrition Division Discussion Paper 34. International Food Policy Research Institute, Washington, D.C.

Mahendraraja, S. 1981. *Water resource optimisation in small dams in Sri Lanka.* Canberra: Australian National University.

Mayoux, L. 1993. Integration is not enough: Gender inequality and empowerment in Nicaraguan agricultural co-operatives. *Development Policy Review* 11 (1): 67–89.

McCarthy, N. 2002. Production risk and common-pool resources: Impact on externalities, profits, and welfare. Submitted to *Economic Development and Cultural Change.*

Mearns, R. 1996. Community, collective action and common grazing: The case of post-socialist Mongolia. *Journal of Development Studies* 32 (3): 297–339.

Meinzen-Dick, R. S. 1996. *Groundwater markets in Pakistan: Participation and productivity.* Research Report 105. Washington, D.C.: International Food Policy Research Institute.

Meinzen-Dick, R. S., L. R. Brown, H. S. Feldstein, and A. R. Quisumbing. 1997. Gender, property rights, and natural resources. *World Development* 25 (8) 1303–1315.

Meinzen-Dick, R. S., L. A. Jackson, and T. A. White. 1996. Conceptual framework: System-wide program on property rights and collective action. International Food Policy Research Institute, Washington, D.C. Photocopy.

Migot-Adholla, S. E., G. Benneh, F. Place, and S. Atsu. 1994. Land, security of tenure, and productivity in Ghana. In *Searching for land tenure security in Africa,* ed. J. W. Bruce and S. Migot-Adholla. Washington, D.C.: World Bank.

Neef, A., and F. Heidhues. 1994. The role of land tenure in agroforestry: Lessons from Benin. *Agroforestry Systems* 27 (2): 145–161.

Ngaido, T., and M. Kirk. 2001. Collective action, property rights, and devolution of rangeland management: Selected examples from Africa and Asia. In *Collective action, property rights, and devolution of natural resource management: Exchange of knowledge and implications for policy,* ed. R. Meinzen-Dick, A. Knox, and M. Di Gregorio. Feldafing, Germany: Zentralstelle für Ernährung und Landwirtschaft.

Noronha, R. 1985. *A review of the literature on land tenure systems in Sub-Saharan Africa.* World Bank Report ARU 43. Washington, D.C.: World Bank, Agriculture and Rural Development Department.

North, D. 1990. *Institutions, institutional change, and economic performance.* Cambridge, U.K.: Cambridge University Press.

———. 1992. Institutions, ideology, and economic performance. *Cato Journal* 11 (3): 477–488.

Nugent, J. B. 1993. Between state, markets and households: A neoinstitutional analysis of local organizations and institutions. *World Development* 21 (4): 623–632.

Oakerson, R. J. 1992. Analyzing the commons: A framework. In *Making the commons work: Theory, practice, and policy,* ed. D. W. Bromley. San Francisco: Institute for Contemporary Studies Press.

Okali, C. 1983. *Cocoa and kinship in Ghana: The matrilineal Akan.* London: Routledge and Kegan Paul.

Olson, M. 1971. *The logic of collective action.* Cambridge, Mass., U.S.A.: Harvard University Press.

Ostrom, E. 1990. *Governing the commons: The evolution of institutions for collective action.* Cambridge, U.K.: Cambridge University Press.

———. 1994. *Neither market nor state: Governance of common-pool resources in the twenty-first century.* IFPRI Lecture 2. Washington, D.C.: International Food Policy Research Institute.

Otsuka, K., and F. Place. 2001. *Land tenure and natural resource management: A comparative study of agrarian communities in Asia and Africa,* ed. K. Otsuka and F. Place. Baltimore, Md., U.S.A.: Johns Hopkins University Press.

Pearse, A. 1980. *Seeds of plenty, seeds of want.* Oxford: Clarendon Press.

Pender, J. L., and J. M. Kerr. 1998. Determinants of farmers' indigenous soil and water conservation investments in semi-arid India. *Agricultural Economics* 19 (1–2): 113–125.

Picardi, A. C. 1974. A systems analysis of pastoralism in the West African Sahel. In *Framework for evaluating long-term strategies for the development of the Sahel-Sudan Region*, Annex 5. Cambridge, Mass., U.S.A.: Center for Policy Alternatives, Massachusetts Institute of Technology.

Pinstrup-Andersen, P., and P. Hazell. 1985. The impact of the green revolution and prospects for the future. *Food Reviews International* 1 (1): 1–25.

Place, F., and P. Hazell. 1993. Productivity effects of indigenous land tenure systems in Sub-Saharan Africa. *American Journal of Agricultural Economics* 75 (1): 10–19.

Quiggan, J. 1993. Common property, equality, and development. *World Development* 21 (7): 1123–1138.

Quisumbing, A. R., E. Payongayong, J. B. Aidoo, and K. Otsuka. 2001. Women's land rights in the transition to individualized ownership: Implications for tree resource management in western Ghana. *Economic Development and Cultural Change* 50 (1): 157–182.

Rasmussen, L., and R. S. Meinzen-Dick. 1995. *Local organizations for natural resource management: Lessons from theoretical and empirical literature.* Environment and Production Technology Division Discussion Paper 11. International Food Policy Research Institute, Washington, D.C.

Rocheleau, D. 1988. Women, trees, and tenure: Implications for agroforestry. In *Whose trees? Proprietary dimensions of forestry,* ed. L. Fortmann and J. W. Bruce. Boulder, Colo., U.S.A.: Westview Press.

Rocheleau, D., and D. Edmunds. 1997. Women, men, and trees: Gender, power, and property in forest and agrarian landscapes. *World Development* 25 (8): 1351–1371.

Rosegrant M., and P. Hazell. 1999. *Transforming the rural Asian economy: The unfinished revolution.* Hong Kong: Oxford University Press for the Asian Development Bank.

Roth, M., J. A. Cochrane, and W. Kisamba Mugerwa. 1993. *Tenure security, credit use, and farm investment in the Rujumbura pilot land registration scheme, Rukungiri District, Uganda.* Land Tenure Center Research Paper 112. Madison, Wisc., U.S.A.: University of Wisconsin.

Roth, M., J. Unruh, and R. Barrows. 1994. Land registration, tenure security, credit use, and investment in the Shebelle region of Somalia. In *Searching for land tenure security in Africa,* ed. J. W. Bruce and S. E. Migot-Adholla. Washington, D.C.: World Bank.

Roth, M., K. Wiebe, and S. Lawry. 1993. Land tenure and agrarian structure: Implications for technology adoption. In *Proceedings of a workshop on social science research and the CRSPs: June 9–11, 1992, University of Kentucky, Lexington, KY.* Washington, D.C.: U.S. Agency for International Development.

Runge, C. F. 1986. Common property and collective action in economic development. *World Development* 14 (5): 623–635.

Sarin, M. 1995. Regenerating India's forests: Reconciling gender equity with joint forest management. *IDS Bulletin* 26 (1): 83–91.

Sarin, M., and R. Khanna. 1993. Women organize for wasteland development: A case study of SARTHI in Gujarat. In *Women and wasteland development in India*, ed. A. M. Singh and N. Burra. New Delhi: Sage.

Scandizzo, P. L. 1979. Implications of sharecropping for technology design in Northeast Brazil. In *Economics and the design of small-farmer technology*, ed. A. Valdez, G. Scobie, and J. Dillon. Ames, Ia., U.S.A.: Iowa State University Press.

Scherr, S. J., and P. Hazell. 1994. Sustainable agricultural development strategies in fragile lands. Environment and Production Technology Division Discussion Paper 1. International Food Policy Research Institute, Washington, D.C.

Schlager, E., and W. Blomquist. 1998. Resolving common pool resource dilemmas and heterogeneities among resource users. Paper presented at "Crossing Boundaries," the seventh annual conference of the International Association for the Study of Common Property, June 10–14, Vancouver, British Columbia, Canada. <http://www.indiana.edu/~iascp/Final/schlager.pdf>.

Schroeder, R. 1993. Shady practice: Gender and political ecology of resource stabilization in Gambian garden/orchards. *Economic Geography* 69 (4): 349–365.

Shipton, P. 1988. The Kenyan land tenure reform: Misunderstandings in the public creation of private property. In *Land and society in contemporary Africa,* ed. R. E. Downs and S. P. Reynas. Hanover, N.H., U.S.A.: University Press of New England.

Swallow, B. 1994. *The role of mobility within the risk management strategies of pastoralists and agro-pastoralists.* London: Sustainable Agricultural Programme of the International Institute for Environment and Development.

Swallow, B., R. Meinzen-Dick, T. Williams, and T. Anderson White. 1997. *Multiple functions of common property regimes.* Environment and Production Technology Division Workshop Summary Paper 4. Washington, D.C.: International Food Policy Research Institute.

Swynnerton, R. J. M. 1954. *A plan to intensify the development of African agriculture in Kenya.* Nairobi: Government Printer.

Tang, S. Y. 1992. *Institutions and collective action: Self- governance in irrigation.* San Francisco: Institute of Contemporary Studies Press.

Thompson, G. D., and P. N. Wilson. 1994. Common property as an institutional response to environmental variability. *Contemporary Economic Policy* 12 (July): 10–21.

Toulmin, C. 1992. Herding contracts: For better or worse? *ILEIA Newsletter* 8 (3): 8–9.

Uphoff, N. 1986. *Improving international irrigation management with farmer participation: Getting the process right.* Boulder, Colo., U.S.A.: Westview Press.

van Koppen, B. 2000. Gendered water and land rights in construction: Rice valley improvement in Burkina Faso. In *Negotiating water rights*, ed. B. Bruns and R. Meinzen-Dick. New Delhi: Vistaar.

van Koppen, B., and S. Mahmud. 1995. *Woman and water pumps in Bangladesh: The impacts of participation in irrigation groups on women's status.* Wageningen, The Netherlands: Department of Irrigation and Soil and Water Conservation, Wageningen Agricultural University.

Vedeld, T. 1997. Village politics: Heterogeneity, leadership, and collective action among Fulani of Mali. Doctor Scientiarum thesis, Agricultural University of Norway, As, Norway.

von Braun, J., and P. J. R. Webb. 1989. The impact of new crop technology on the agricultural division of labor in a West African setting. *Economic Development and Cultural Change* 37 (3): 513–534.

Vosti, S. A., and T. Reardon. 1997. *Sustainability, growth, and poverty alleviation: A policy and agroecological perspective.* Baltimore, Md., U.S.A.: Johns Hopkins University Press.

Wade, R. 1988. *Village republics.* Cambridge, U.K.: Cambridge University Press.

Waller, R., and N. W. Sobania. 1994. Pastoralism in historical perspective. In *African pastoralist systems: An integrated approach*, ed. E. Fratkin, K. A. Galvin, and E. A. Roth. Boulder, Colo., U.S.A.: Lynne Rienner.

White, T. A., and C. F. Runge. 1994. Common property and collective action. Lessons from cooperative watershed management in Haiti. *Economic Development and Cultural Change* 43 (1): 1–41.

————. 1995. The emergence and evolution of collective action: Lessons from watershed management in Haiti. *World Development* 23 (10): 1683–1698.

Wood, G. D., and R. Palmer-Jones. 1990. *The water sellers: A cooperative venture by the rural poor.* West Hartford, Conn., U.S.A.: Kumarian.

Yoder, R. 1994. *Locally managed irrigation systems: Essential tasks and implications for assistance, management transfer, and turnover programs.* Colombo, Sri Lanka: International Irrigation Management Institute.

Zeller, M. 1996. *Determinants of repayment performance in credit groups: The role of program design, intra-group risk pooling, and social cohesion in Madagascar.* Food Consumption and Nutrition Division Discussion Paper 13. International Food Policy Research Institute, Washington, D.C.

3 Assessing the Relationships between Property Rights and Technology Adoption in Smallholder Agriculture: Issues and Empirical Methods

FRANK PLACE AND BRENT SWALLOW

This chapter aims to provide researchers and policy analysts with a better understanding of the key issues and guidelines for conducting research on the relationships between property rights and technology adoption in smallholder agriculture. The primary target group for this chapter consists of researchers who have advanced training in microeconomic theory and statistics but are not specialists in property rights per se. An important secondary target group is policy analysts who review empirical studies and draw lessons for policy design.

The study of property rights and technology is complicated in several respects. First, defining and measuring property rights and tenure security present challenges. There is now general agreement that tenure security is related to a number of rights over land and other resources that may or may not be vested in individuals. But there is no general agreement about how rights should be measured, aggregated, or otherwise manipulated to derive quantifiable measures of tenure security.

Second, researchers can have several different reasons for undertaking a study of the relationship between property rights and technology adoption. Each reason may have different implications for methodology. Perhaps the most common reasons are:

1. providing input into discussions of property rights policy;
2. defining recommendation domains for existing technologies or those under development;

The authors of this chapter have many intellectual debts. Frank Place and Brent Swallow have learned about property rights and technology adoption over the past 10 years by working with more colleagues than can be listed here. Their collective contributions to our understanding of the issues addressed in this chapter are greatly appreciated. The need for this particular chapter was identified at the CAPRi workshop "Property Rights, Collective Action, and Technology Adoption," hosted by ICARDA in Aleppo, Syria, in November 1997. We received constructive comments on earlier drafts of the chapter from Peter Hazell, Keijiro Otsuka, and Jean-Marie Baland. Ruth Meinzen-Dick and Anna Knox provided helpful comments and ideas throughout the chapter's considerable gestation period.

3. identifying traits that will make new technology attractive to farmers;
4. assessing the impacts of technology on objectives such as production and poverty alleviation; and
5. identifying groups (such as women) that may not be able to adopt a technology because of the property rights institutions.

Objective 1 suggests the need for a good dialogue between researchers and policymakers (local or national) to ensure that the study will have a positive impact on the policy formulation process. The other objectives imply closer collaboration with applied researchers, development institutions, and farmers themselves.

How researchers define property rights variables and model the causes and consequences of property rights also differ across the five objectives. For objective 1 the results must have policy relevance. That is, the analysis must involve variables that policymakers understand and can influence through the policy instruments under their control. A clear structural model in which the effects of the policy variables can be distinguished from other variables is required. This structural model also needs to show the linkages between property rights and the other important outcome variables. Policymakers are likely to be interested in the effects of property rights on technology adoption, productivity, sustainability, equity, and income. To fully address objectives 4 and 5 the researcher also needs a structural model that isolates the impacts of individual variables. On the other hand, a cost-effective predictive model is needed to achieve objectives 2 and 3. The research, extension, and development agencies that use the research outputs will be most interested in identifying and measuring the variables that can guide them in targeting new technologies. In that case they may be most interested in proxy variables that are easy to measure.

The third challenge concerns the difficult theoretical and empirical issues involved in such analyses. Some of the major issues are:

1. defining the technology, including the spatial and temporal dimensions of the costs, benefits, and scale of adoption;
2. identifying the dimensions of property rights that have the greatest effects on technology adoption;
3. selecting the appropriate level or levels of observation and analysis—plot, individual, farm, and community;
4. reducing potential biases in sampling;
5. accounting for the endogenous determination of property rights;
6. controlling for the confounding effects of property rights with other explanatory variables correlated with property rights; and
7. making appropriate interpretations of the empirical results.

As a result of these complicating factors, there have been several different approaches to empirical testing of the links between property rights and technology adoption. By synthesizing and evaluating previous studies, this chapter seeks to benefit those who wish to undertake or interpret empirical research in the future. This chapter does not develop a particular structural model of the relationship between property rights and technology adoption. Instead, it draws upon models that have been recently developed by analysts such as Feder and Feeny (1993) and Sjaastad and Bromley (1997).

The remainder of the chapter briefly delineates the boundaries within which this review is organized, reviews key issues pertaining to modeling and conceptualizing technology adoption and property rights variables, and discusses the relationships between them. It then discusses specific data collection and measurement issues and addresses some key aspects associated with analyses and interpretation of findings.

Scope and Definitions

To enable this review to be tractable and thus useful, we have deliberately put some boundaries around different dimensions of the review.

Technologies

This chapter will focus on the intensity of adoption and management of technologies by individuals for use on agricultural land. Agricultural land includes home gardens, fields, fallow lands, and grazing lands. Collective adoption of technologies is not considered here.

Property Rights

Property rights considered here are the rights of individuals to benefit streams produced from agricultural land (including all natural resources on the land). We review literature relating to both customary and formal (such as statutory legal) tenure systems that affect smallholder farmers. This discussion includes the situations of legal pluralism in which customary and statutory legal systems overlap.

Topical Scope

The review concentrates on methods for empirical analysis rather than theoretical modeling. Attention is given, however, to the links between theory and empirical analysis.

Geographic Scope

The methods reviewed should be relevant to smallholder agriculture in developing countries, especially where there is insecure social and legal support for customary and formal rights.

Modeling and Hypotheses

As already noted, the type of structural model that is developed to guide an empirical study depends upon the purpose of the study. Some of the questions that need to be considered when developing a structural model are:

- What characteristics of a technology suggest a relationship with property rights?
- What aspects of technology adoption and use are most important to model and test?
- What dimensions of property rights are important in the adoption decision?
- How are property rights expected to affect technology adoption?
- How is technology adoption hypothesized to affect property rights?
- Are property rights variables correlated with other variables that affect adoption?
- What are the most important social-spatial scales for the problem at hand?

What Characteristics of a Technology Indicate a Relationship with Property Rights?

The nature of the technology or investment will affect the hypothesized relationships between technology adoption and property rights. Technologies whose cost and benefit streams are of very short duration will be less affected by property rights than those whose benefit streams are lengthier. Thus, a land manager who faces a high probability of losing her rights to land may still use fertilizer on her crops. Other types of investments, though of a longer-term nature, may be undertaken if the costs of investment are very low. This may be the case with the direct sowing of a small number of trees. For many other types of investment, such as terracing, fencing, water harvesting, windbreaks, and medium-term fallowing, property rights are expected to have greater effects on incentives. The extent of those effects will depend on the degree of insecurity. However, the effect of insecure tenure is not necessarily pervasive. High expected profits can overcome the negative incentives that result from insecure property rights.

The type of technology also affects whether or not it may have an impact on property rights. Tree planting is widely cited as an investment that confers strong land rights to individuals (Fortmann and Bruce 1988; Snyder 1996; Baland et al. 1999; Suyanto et al. 1999). Fallowing, on the other hand, is a type of land investment that may weaken land rights. This may be because land that is left uncultivated can be perceived as excess to household needs and thus become subject to claims by other extended family members (Place and Otsuka 2001a). Investments in water wells and pumps may confer a high degree of exclusivity over the water resource. Investments in fruit trees, however, may be subject to a myriad of secondary use rights by community members. Many other types of investments may have little effect on property rights, particularly those with short duration.

What Aspects of Adoption Are Important to Model and Test?

A few remarks about what constitutes "technology" and "adoption" are appropriate at this point. Technology is often used broadly to encompass physical/ biological structures and objects as well as management practices. Most often, researchers are interested in the adoption of specific technology components (such as fertilizer) or integrated technological packages (such as high-yielding crop varieties with fertilizer). However, it may be more important to study the traits or functions of these technologies. For example, rather than analyzing the adoption of all types of improved maize varieties or a particular variety, a study could be designed to examine the adoption of all short-duration maize varieties. Similarly, one might wish to study the adoption of trees, not by species, but by grouping together all species that farmers use to enhance soil fertility. Grouping criteria will depend on one's hypothesis about what function of a particular technology constitutes the underlying rationale for adoption.

Generally, it is difficult to identify exactly when a technology has been adopted. Researchers instead often record current use of the technology. This approach may be unsatisfactory for new technologies farmers may be merely experimenting with or in areas where projects have had a strong influence and may have provided incentives for farmers to use particular technologies. Informal discussions and qualitative research can identify whether these issues are important in the study area. If so, additional questions could be added to formal surveys to distinguish among different types of users.

Technology adoption is often measured by a single binary variable: the technology is present or absent on a farm at a particular time. A binary variable may be adequate for assessing farmer investment in, for example, traditional water wells. Traditional water wells have five special characteristics that lend themselves to this present/absent measurement. First, farmers are quite familiar with traditional wells and thus are relatively certain about the associated payoffs and risks. This situation implies that farmers are willing to make full rather than partial investments. Second, farmers are usually not given any external incentive to invest in a traditional well, so it is safe to assume the investment is demand driven. Third, traditional wells are indivisible. A farmer cannot choose to invest in half a well. Fourth, traditional wells do not normally require complementary inputs in order to be functional and thus are independent of constraints associated with other technologies. Lastly, once they have been built, wells exist for a long time, compared with technologies like crop varieties that come and go.

However, researchers are usually interested in technologies that differ from traditional water wells in one or more of those four characteristics. First, researchers are often interested in technologies that are under development or have been recently made available to farmers. In those cases, it may be important to explore the farmers' knowledge and information about the technology. Does the farmer have accurate information about the technology? Are there systematic biases that limit access to information by certain types of farmers (such as women, migrants, and minority ethnic groups)? Decision-tree modeling may be appropriate for separating the effects of information from the effects of property rights (Gladwin et al. 1997).

Second, new technologies are often made available to farmers in developing countries through some type of adaptive research, extension, or development project. In that case, it is important to consider the amount of discretion that the farmer exercises over the investment. Erroneous and misleading results can result from studies that confuse adoption with acquiescence to the wishes of researchers or extension workers. Some farmers also test or use a technology solely because they wish to copy other villagers or to obtain intangible benefits such as prestige from visits by researchers. If possible, it is preferable to restrict studies of adoption behavior to farmers who do not have direct contact with such projects. If not, then researchers should endeavor to account for this potential effect in the analysis.

Third, it is often necessary to quantify the intensity of technology adoption beyond simple presence or absence of the technology on the farm. Trade-offs usually arise between the benefits and costs of more refined measurement of the intensity of technology adoption. For example, the adoption of trees can be measured by the number of trees per farm, the density of trees per hectare, the number of particular species or types of trees per hectare, or the standing biomass of trees per hectare, among others. Where investments are divisible and relatively easy to make (like trees), a binary assessment of adoption may fail to detect important variation in technology adoption. In this case further narrowing of the technology (say to certain species of trees) or quantification is essential.

Fourth, farmers often adopt components of technology packages in a stepwise manner, with some components necessarily predating others. In that case the absence of a technology at a particular time may be unrelated to farmer plans to adopt the technology at a future time. Equally, the absence of a technology at a particular time does not mean that the farmer has never used the technology. Again, decision tree modeling may be appropriate for understanding farmers' strategies vis-à-vis the technology. The collection of historical data is thus valuable and may be warranted in some cases, such as when there are clear relationships between technologies, links between farming systems and technologies, or links between household life cycle and technology traits. If indeed the duration is more relevant than the current presence of a technology, this would suggest the use of survival or hazard models that deal explicitly with temporal issues. In addition, complementary relationships between technologies would suggest the use of models that account for these relationships (such as multinomial logits).

What Dimensions of Property Rights Affect Adoption?

The literature suggests that the three important dimensions of property rights are exclusivity, security, and transferability. The exclusivity dimension refers to the way that relationships among potential right holders are defined. Under open access, no one has rights or duties. Under common property, rights are defined to coexist for an identified group, with other groups or individuals having duties to respect those rights. Under communal property, rights of ownership are vested in groups, but rights of usufruct and limited rights of transfer may reside with individual households. Under private property, individuals or households may enjoy rights to the exclusion of others. Private property does not, however, necessarily imply a high degree of exclusion. In Africa, it is common for people to have secondary rights to the livestock feed, firewood, and water produced on private land.

Place, Roth, and Hazell (1994) describe key components of tenure security to be freedom from interference from outside sources, continuous use, and ability to reap the benefits of labor and capital invested in the resource. Embedded in this description are three dimensions of land rights: breadth, duration, and assurance. Breadth refers to the types of rights held. Generally the more rights held, the more secure those rights. Households with rights to alienate (dispose of) land or to make long-term improvements on land would be considered more secure than those with only use rights to land. Certain rights, however, such as the right to bequeath, are often critical to motivate long-term investment. Some rights may be indicative of larger bundles of rights. For example, someone who holds the right to sell may automatically hold the right to rent out. Duration refers to the length of time over which the individual or group may enjoy specific rights. Assurance refers to the ability of individuals to exercise their rights. Despite adequate breadth and duration of rights, assurance may be lacking where overlapping rights exist or where there is weak enforcement of rights.

Transferability refers to the ability of the right holder to transfer rights over the resource to others. Primary examples of this include the ability to select heirs and bequeath land, the ability to rent or lease land or trees to others temporarily, and the ability to alienate an asset. Transferability is valuable because it increases the ability to raise cash through sale or rental of the property (and through credit) and by allowing farmers to endow heirs with key assets.

How Are Property Rights Hypothesized to Affect Technology Adoption?

It is generally accepted that, at least in Sub-Saharan Africa, there are both direct and feedback relationships between property rights and technology adoption. First, the property rights that govern the use of a particular plot of land will affect farmers' adoption and use of technology on that land. Second, the adoption and use of technology has feedback effects on property rights. Some of these feedbacks occur within a prevailing property rights institution. Others put pressure on the property rights institution to change. This section is concerned with the direct effects of property rights on technology adoption, and the following section is concerned with the feedback effects.

EXCLUSIVITY.   Property rights that are generally regarded as being "private" may confer rights to individuals, nuclear families, or lineages. Private property rights may also be encumbered by secondary rights or public restrictions. It is generally hypothesized that the degree of exclusivity has a positive effect on the incentive to produce, invest in, and adopt technology. The greater the exclusivity, the greater the incentive to adopt technologies that are fixed to the land. Thus, for example, institutionalized seasonal grazing of farmland (lack of exclusivity) may discourage certain types of investment such as the planting of perennial crops. However, free-grazing livestock may well encourage investment in fencing and adoption of nonpalatable plants and trees. Also, Baland and Platteau (1996) suggest that there may be circumstances in which less exclusive land rights may help people to pool the risks associated with new innovations or technologies.

SECURITY.   Feder and Feeny (1993) distinguish different possible effects of insecure property rights on technology adoption. First, rights of short duration provide a direct disincentive for farmers to undertake investments in land. Similarly, when the breadth or assurance of rights is inadequate, local rules may not protect an individual's claim to benefits from investments. This situation has often been noted in the case of women, who lack rights to undertake long-term investments (with regard to trees, see Kerkhof and May 1988, McLain 1992; Place 1995; Mugo 1999). Whether breadth or assurance is hypothesized to be linked to technology adoption depends upon the specific technology/property rights context, such as the payback period of the technology. Second, insecure property rights will increase the relative price of long-term assets to land and thus reduce the capital intensity of farming.

TRANSFERABILITY.   The transferability of land rights, including through rental, bequest, temporary and permanent gift, and sale, may affect technology adoption in three ways. First, restrictions on transferability may reduce the incentives of current residents to adopt technologies likely to generate benefits beyond their likely tenure. For example, if an elderly man cannot pass a piece of land to his heirs, then he will probably exploit existing trees rather than plant new trees. In this case there is a clear interaction between property rights and life cycle of the household. Second, restrictions on transferability are likely to reduce the market exchange of land and thus may affect the efficiency of land allocation. Households with the most incentive to undertake investments on certain land types will thus have limited access to that land. As a consequence, it might be expected that land that is purchased might receive more investment than others. At a community level, one would expect a greater level of technology adoption in communities where rights to sell land were more prevalent.

Third, restrictions on transferability will reduce the possible use of land as collateral. In theory, land is the most important collateral asset in rural areas. It is only valuable to potential lenders, however, to the extent that it can be sold by lenders to third parties in case of default. In many parts of Sub-Saharan Africa, it is difficult to sell land, particularly to people from outside the community. As already noted, the importance of specific transfer rights in a given area depends on whether such rights are exercised.

How Is Technology Adoption Hypothesized to Affect Property Rights?

Two possible types of feedback effects occur between technology adoption and property rights. First, an existing property rights institution may provide a farmer with different types of property rights to a particular plot of land (in terms of exclusivity, security, and transferability) depending upon their investment in that plot. For example, qualitative studies have documented the ability of certain investments, such as in land clearing and tree planting, to enhance tenure security (for example, Snyder 1996; Quisumbing et al. 1999). The expectation of more secure property rights may thus stimulate farmers to undertake certain investments (for Uganda see Place and Otsuka 2001a and Baland et al. 1999; for Burkina Faso see Braselle, Gaspart, and Platteau 1998). More research is needed to assess the temporal duration of this effect and to assess the aspects of tenure security that can be expected to change following such investments.

Second, the adoption of certain types of technology may result in pressure on property rights institutions to change. For example, recognition of investment in trees has induced changes in tenure rules in Uganda and Zambia. In eastern Zambia the adoption of improved fallows by a few thousand farmers prompted the paramount chief to pass a new bylaw that prohibits free grazing of livestock (Paramount Chief 1998). In Kabale, Uganda, secondary grazing rights continue, but there are now strict fines for damage to young trees planted by households. The introduction of certain technologies can also modify rights of women over resources. For instance, women who were not allowed to plant timber and pole trees by their husbands were allowed to plant trees for soil fertility in Uganda, as these were considered to be different types of trees (Two Wings Agroforestry Group 1996).

If property rights variables are likely to be treated as dependent variables, then one must try to identify variables that would influence changes or differences in observed values and plan for the collection of those data. Furthermore, if property rights and technology variables influence each other, then it is important to construct an appropriate structural model to account for these relationships. This task can be complicated by multiple scale considerations. For example, property rights institutions may prevail at the level of a community or ethnic group whereas technology adoption may be an individual decision. This situation may call for the integration of community and household level studies. Whether at multiple or single scales, multiple-equation systems should be specified. In a simultaneous system one must identify, measure, and include variables that can help to identify the equations. Often, this effort comes down to identifying an explanatory variable that explains only one of the dependent variables. We reexamine this topic later in this chapter.

Are Property Rights Variables Correlated with Other Variables That Affect Adoption?

There are strong theoretical reasons to believe that some property rights variables are correlated with other variables that may be directly related to technology adoption. At an individual level, women and men may differ systematically with respect to the ways they can acquire rights to land and the subsequent rights they enjoy to this land. For instance, women may tend to rely more on temporary land acquisitions and therefore have less secure rights to land than men. In this case a tenure variable related to acquisition or land rights may capture other gender-differentiated impacts. Other variables that may be related to property rights variables at the plot or household level might be wealth (for example, wealthier households may have stronger rights to land), soil fertility (purchased parcels may be of better quality), and distance from house to parcel (closer parcels may be more secure). At the community level, there may be systematic relationships between property rights and population pressure and distance to market. Theory suggests that individualization of land rights strengthens under greater population pressure and proximity to developing markets by virtue of heightened competition for land and higher returns brought on by better access to markets. The presence of such correlations suggests more complicated structural models with multiple equations. Strategies for sampling and data collection will have to be modified accordingly.

If multicollinearity is anticipated, then it is important to explore theoretically the relationships between property rights and other explanatory variables. Otherwise, misspecification of the model can lead to erroneous conclusions about the importance of individual variables. For example, it may be that the effect of gender on technology is transmitted entirely through indirect effects on farm size and tenure security. If this is the case, then the inclusion of gender, farm size, and tenure security in a single equation model would show gender to be insignificant. But if a structural model was well thought out, the effect of gender might emerge as significant in a reduced form regression. Adjusting the original model will likely imply the collection of additional variables that might be used to help identify equations of a more complex model. All these concerns are lessened, however, if the objective is only a predictive model. In this case, identifying inexpensive variables associated with adoption takes priority over teasing out the causal relationships among individual variables.

Are There Dimensions of the Problem That Are Resolved at Different Social-Spatial Scales (Plot, Individual, Farm, Community)?

With respect to social and spatial scales, two dimensions are important. The first pertains to the right holders and the second to the resource unit. Right holders could be individuals, households, pastoralists, user groups, communities, and the like. Resource units could be individual trees, wells, and various land units such as forests, pastures, agricultural parcels, or fields within parcels. No single unit of observation is either best or even appropriate to address all tenure issues. The best unit or units of observation will vary according to the particular issue under study. Most of the empirical studies dealing with property rights and technology adoption use households or individual household members as key right holders and land parcels or fields as the main resource for which property rights are examined.

How can one best select the appropriate units? Perhaps it is best to indicate the types of cases where the standard practice of using the household right holder/land parcel resource combination may not be the most appropriate. One is the issue of how the rights of women may affect technology adoption. Using the household as the key right holder unit will allow the researcher to be able to compare only the cases of female-headed and male-headed households. Obtaining information for all male and female adults within a household is the most effective way to look at intrahousehold distinctions (see Golan 1994; Mugo 1999). Moreover, women's rights over land may not be identical across the entire farm. Women may enjoy more secure rights over some specific plots of land than over others. Researchers must understand these subtleties before analyzing the more complex tenure issues. Other cases requiring special attention to the unit of observation are those where trees must be differentiated according to species or function, higher-level tenure variables are uniform for many households within a defined area, landholdings are fragmented, or resources are shared by households.

Though these cases suggest that there may be a superior strategy for selecting units of observation, it should be stressed that conducting analyses at multiple units of observation can yield different insights into the property rights–technology adoption relationships. In some cases, the use of a single observational unit may lead to erroneous conclusions. For example, a farm-level analysis could mask many important relationships taking place on different land parcels or fields where rights may differ. On the other hand, focusing only on the smaller units can sometimes cause one to lose sight of the broader implications of tenure on household-level decisionmaking. For instance, many studies have found negative relationships between rented parcels and investment in technology using household parcel–level analyses. However, such analyses may obscure the effect that renting land might have on enabling households to make longer-term plans on their owned parcels, for instance. There-fore, one should always consider whether the units of observation selected will lead to unambiguous answers to the key questions being studied.

The most common right holder studied in property rights studies is the household. These studies begin with the assumption that most decisions con-cerning agricultural investment and technology adoption are made at the house-hold level, normally by the head of household. As a result, property rights over a specific resource are treated as uniform for the household, bearing the prop-erty rights of the household head. These approaches are well accepted in the literature and are therefore generally well founded to study certain issues. For example, focusing on the rights of the household head in a study of how the right to sell land affects technology adoption is quite sensible. Other members of the household or community cannot initiate sales. In such studies, the most common resource units are farms or plots. It is now well recognized that in many rural settings, households may acquire more than one plot of land using different methods of acquisition. Furthermore, the rights of a particular house-hold member over these plots could differ. Therefore, it is now routine to col-lect property rights information at plot level.

Studies at the individual (that is, household member) level are intended primarily to look at the implications of gender on technology adoption. One of the key differences between males and females is their control of and access to resources and the benefits streams they produce. Thus, these studies often look at gender differences in methods of land acquisition and rights to land and then relate these differences to resource management in general and technology adoption in particular. Studies that account for individual difference also often recognize that property rights arrangements may differ across plots. For in-stance, wives may have more control over decisions in one plot than on the rest of the farm, and property rights studies may focus on whether this asymmetry leads to difference in technology adoption.

Studies at the community level are rare, in large part because agricultural land is managed directly by smaller units and as such the smaller units are purer observational units. Another reason may be related to measurement problems: how can one accurately measure technology adoption at the community level? What property rights variables are appropriate at the community level, and which can be measured? Increasingly, however, researchers are recognizing the power of such studies (Pender, Scherr, and Durón 1998; Baland et al. 1999; Suyanto, Tomich, and Otsuka 1999; Place and Otsuka 2000). Community-level studies are ideal for examining property rights aspects that tend not to vary over smaller units or areas. Those that may be linked to ethnicity, such as grazing practices, land acquisition methods, and the rights of women, may be quite vari-able across communities but vary little within communities. Community-level studies enable researchers to study wider areas for less financial cost. The draw-back is that compromises must be made in the precision of data. Moving to higher levels of aggregation brings even more difficulties in conceptualizing meaningful variables for technology adoption and property rights. Often the aggregation of very diverse intranational variables renders a national-level analysis weak. Some innovative work has taken place at the national level, however, at least in formulating property rights variables (for example, Deacon 1994).

Data Collection and Measurement

In collecting data some iteration between individual and group interviews and between qualitative and quantitative research techniques is usually appropriate. Qualitative techniques are used to identify priority issues for study, determine the population to be considered in the study, identify variables for stratifying the population, identify local definitions of property rights, determine the sensitivity of the questions, and interpret quantitative results. Quantitative techniques (including quantification through participatory techniques) are used to validate qualitative results, statistically test hypotheses, estimate elasticities, and prioritize policy and action steps.

Population and Sampling Strategy

Several issues must be considered early in a study of property rights and technology adoption. Once a specific technology is defined, it is important to define the population from which a sample may be drawn for further analysis. Then a sampling scheme must be devised. Finally, one must decide whether to georeference the observations drawn in order to be able to relate observations at different spatial locations and scales.

POPULATION. Identifying the population on which to base a sample for a study of a property rights and technology adoption study can be challenging. It is a smaller concern when the study is focused on the adoption or impact of a specific technology. In that case the researcher must define the population from within the feasible adoption domain (for example, an area surrounding the points of technology dissemination). Such a sample of communities and households will include different degrees of adoption, allowing a researcher to examine the relationship between technology and property rights from either direction. It is a greater difficulty for a researcher who wishes to identify representative property rights systems, because detailed information about property rights is not generally available across large areas. Further, there can be peculiar property rights institutions based on ethnicity, and these conditions will affect the degree to which specific empirical results may be generalized. Nonetheless, a great deal of dispersed qualitative information about property rights systems is available and can be exploited to assist in developing study populations. Rather than being overwhelmed with the nuances distinguishing different property rights systems, researchers may find it more fruitful to classify specific characteristics or incentives in delineating pathways for extrapolating results.

SAMPLING.   Once the population is defined, the next step is to develop a sampling scheme. Among the first issues to address is that of unit of observation. Given that this is the focus of the earlier section on social-spatial scales, this discussion is postponed to the corresponding empirical section on measuring property rights at aggregate levels. Regardless of the unit of observation, when the purpose of the study is to examine factors affecting technology adoption or impact, it is essential to have a sufficient number of adopter and nonadopter outcomes in the sample. From a statistical perspective, ensuring a reasonable number of cases for each outcome improves the ability to find statistical and reliable links between factors and different outcomes by reducing standard errors and influence of outliers.

Whether the sampling procedure should be random or stratified depends on the size of intended sample and the distribution of technology. If a very large sample is planned (say, more than 1,000), then a random sample might produce sufficient numbers of adopters and nonadopters, even if adoption rates are relatively low, say between 10 and 20 percent. More frequently, studies can only afford smaller samples in the range of 100–200 households. For technologies used by a large proportion of the population, a random sample of households or individuals may suffice. For new technologies with limited exposure, however, stratification of specific geographical areas, if not households themselves, may be necessary. Nonrandom sampling will lead to oversampling of areas where the technology has been introduced. The implications of this approach on interpretation and extrapolation are important and are discussed in a later section.

Most studies of technology adoption have not stratified households on the basis of property rights variables. The first reason is that it is not always possible to obtain sufficient information on property rights with which to stratify. Second, if property rights variables are endogenous, such stratification can lead to econometric complications such as model misspecifications and omitted variable biases. Third, important categories of property rights will be automatically included if the sample is sufficiently large and not too narrow geographically. An indirect way to obtain a representation of different tenure arrangements would be to stratify on the basis of ethnic group and population pressure or any other variable that is available and is related to property rights variables (see, for example, Place and Otsuka 2001b; Baland et al. 1999). Where such techniques are inadequate and secondary data are not available, rapid censuses have been found to be helpful in generating sampling frames based on tenure variables (for example, Place and Otsuka 2001b).

GEOREFERENCING.   Georeferencing is a technique for improving the ability to relate locations of study units to one another and to other phenomena in the landscape, such as towns or roads. To the extent that aggregations of phenomena and distances to key physical or manmade structures are important in creating incentives for behavior, analyses can be improved by using georeferencing. Georeferencing should definitely be used in community-level studies, where primary data collection can be easily linked to other variables likely to differ across communities. Georeferencing may be less important for studies at lower levels (because information on other variables may be too coarse to vary at these levels), but an exception is the creation of variables of aggregation (pockets of like households, areas of similar land characteristics) or measures of dispersion (fragmentation of household plots). A cost-benefit analysis of georeferencing should be undertaken as part of the planning of the study.

Measurement of Technology Adoption

First, we consider the identification of "real" adoption. This is especially relevant to the Consultative Group on International Agricultural Research (CGIAR), which faces pressure to demonstrate impact from its research. Farmers may undertake rather lengthy experimental processes before deciding whether to adopt a technology. An understanding of recent technology expansion is helpful in distinguishing testers from adopters. An adopter may be one who has expanded the level of use over a number of years. Spending some time to understand these differences is most critical for researchers unfamiliar with an area or technology.

The most common way of measuring technology adoption is through the use of a binary variable indicating its current presence or not on a particular plot. This method leaves unanswered questions about how the technology found its way onto the field. Was it demand driven, or were farmers rewarded for trying it? This approach also crudely places observations into one of two categories and may group households with quite dissimilar behavior. For instance, a household that has planted 1 tree may be treated as equal to the household that has planted 1,000 trees. A binary measure works better for larger, more indivisible investments such as a well or the formation of a bench terrace. Whether one uses simple binary measures or more quantitative assessments, it is important to verify that willful investments were made. Variants on binary measurements involve incorporating evidence of prior expansion or willingness to expand in the future into criteria for adoption (see, for example, Manyong and Houndekon 2000).

If investment levels are well distributed, a binary measure results in considerable loss of information. As a consequence, the statistical relationship between property rights and investment may differ fundamentally in the cases of binary and quantitative measure of investment. Likewise, it becomes more difficult to isolate the impact of property rights from other possible explanatory variables. Another concern emerges in regression analysis. Because property rights variables are themselves often represented by discrete variables, regression models may not converge. This probability increases the more unbalanced are the frequencies of adoption and property rights.

When measuring technology adoption, it is often easy to scale up to higher levels. For instance, with a measure of plot-level technology adoption, a similar variable can be created at a household level or a community level (given that suitable sampling methods were employed). Thus a binary plot-level variable on adoption of terraces can be aggregated to form a community variable on the percentage of plots or households with terraces.

Quantifying the level of adoption is used in some cases (see Lin 1991; Adesina and Zinnah 1993; and Bellon and Taylor 1993 for examples). Some examples of quantifying adoption would be the meters of similar types of conservation strips, meters of live fencing, and area under a particular tree crop. Quantifying adoption raises challenges, however, including evaluating the quality of the technological investment. A terrace bund formed by earth, vegetative strips, and stone is technically superior to that formed by earth alone. In this case a comparison of "meters under terrace" would not provide an appropriate measure of intensity of adoption. Some investments are more easily quantified, such as the number of trees planted, but here too quantifying can become costly if there are many different tree species to condition upon and within each species, many different dates of planting. There are trade-offs between precision and cost. Certain cases suggest that further precision is more important. If property rights are expected to have specific impacts, say on a particular type of tree rather than on trees in general, then all trees cannot be grouped together. This is true in the case of timber trees in Uganda (Place 1995). On the other hand, one should not mine the data to find any type of relationship. Focusing on narrow definitions rather than the bigger picture can lead to erroneous conclusions.

If the duration of an investment or the date of investment is important to measure, it is usually relatively easy to collect at the plot or household level. For some types of technologies, such as the use of a particular crop variety or management practice, it may become more difficult. In conducting community-level surveys, finding average dates of adoption is virtually impossible. Instead, one might need to settle for first dates of technology adoption, which is achievable, though average duration among those who adopt is more easily understood. A survey could thus be modified to indicate not only whether a technology is present or not, but also whether it had ever been present and when. This type of survey can provide the information necessary to investigate adoption rates between two points in time (such as in Knudsen 1991 and Fischer, Arnold, and Gibbs 1996) or the sequential adoption of related technologies or components (such as in Feder 1982).

Two additional points are relevant here. First, a technology that is observed may well have been inherited (especially something such as tree crops), and it is crucial to understand what was already present on the land at the time of inheritance. For example, measuring only the current stock of trees may produce perverse effects. A farmer with a relatively high current level may in fact have inherited a much larger number of trees and reduced his density. Meanwhile, another farmer with a low current number of trees could have started with none and planted all those observed. Second, if technology adoption had in fact taken place several years before the survey, it may be wise to attempt to match property rights and other explanatory variables as much as possible to the conditions at the time of adoption.

Measurement of Property Rights

The concepts of exclusivity, security, and transferability are often captured empirically through various measures of rights to resources. To capture exclusivity, surveys have asked whether households or individuals need to seek approval or notify particular individuals, groups, or authorities outside of the household before exercising a right (see Migot-Adholla et al. 1991). Excludability may also be proxied by collecting information about the extent of secondary rights to resources. This factor is pertinent for community-level surveys to gain an understanding of the general level of excludability of rights. The particular context of the technology–property rights issue will suggest the most appropriate types of rights or approval mechanisms.

Security has been approached in several different ways. One common way is to capture the breadth or number of rights held by individuals (Migot-Adholla et al. 1991; Besley 1995; Hayes, Roth, and Zepeda 1997; Braselle, Gaspart, and Platteau 1998). Others have identified hierarchies of land rights and then measured the presence or absence of key land rights (Migot-Adholla et al. 1991; Hayes, Roth, and Zepeda 1997; Baland et al. 1999). This approach is appropriate if, from the perspective of the respondents, some rights are more important than others or if possession of more powerful rights implies possession of many less powerful rights (Schlager and Ostrom 1992). Another common approach is to use the method of acquisition or local tenure categories as a proxy for tenure security (Matlon 1994; Gavian and Fafchamps 1996; Ayuk 1997; Adesina 1997; Manyong and Houndekon 2000). Normally, purchased land is hypothesized to be most secure and rented and leased land the least secure, with other types of acquisitions lying somewhere in between. Some studies have endeavored to differentiate categories that contain a large proportion of cases. For instance, Lawry and Stienbarger (1991) and Adesina (1997) distinguished between divided and undivided inheritance acquisition methods. Likewise, Place and Otsuka (2001b) distinguished four different inheritance patterns among patrilineal and matrilineal ethnic groups in Malawi. A few studies have asked farmers directly about their perceptions of the risks of losing land (for example, Kisamba-Mugerwa and Barrows 1989). Informal discussions in the study area assist greatly in identifying important tenure security groupings.

Transferability is almost always measured either by the right to sell or rent land or by the presence of land title (Feder et al. 1988). Whether these are useful variables to distinguish different degrees of transferability can be evaluated by obtaining information about the prevalence of land market transactions. For example, if few land sales take place, it is not clear that the right to sell is linked strongly to transferability per se. Information about rights to sell and rent can be obtained rather easily, but care should be taken to understand the degree to which individuals can make free and independent decisions. Often extended families or elders must approve sales. In some societies land must first be offered to members of one's extended family before it can be placed on the open market. The presence of land title or any other formal document (such as purchase agreement) is also easy to enumerate. In the case of title, because updating land registers following land transfers is often an endogenous choice of farmers, titles to land are sometimes outdated, remaining in the name of the previous owner, often the father. The separation between title holder and user may not mean much in terms of tenure security, but it may have an important implication for the ability of the user to transfer land.

One group of variables is often described as constituting components of land tenure, though these variables are not directly linked to security or rights. These are variables that describe landholding patterns, such as plot size, farm size, distance between homesteads and plots, and fragmentation (or scattering) of plots. For the size variables, the data collection issue is the accuracy of farmer estimates. In areas where land surveys have been done, their knowledge is normally quite accurate. In other areas errors in estimation may be significant. It is advisable to collect information on total farm size and to check this with information on (or direct measurements of) individual plots or fields. Distance between the homestead and specific plots is fairly easy to collect, whether by space (such as kilometers) or time (such as minutes of walking time). Growing population pressure has led to increasing fragmentation of farm holdings in some areas. Farmers might therefore operate one or more inherited plots, one or more purchased plots, and one or more rented plots at the same time. Farm fragmentation as a variable could be measured by the number of plots or by more sophisticated measures that take into account the size of plots or the distances between them (for instance, dispersion indices can be used; see Blarel et al. 1992).

While these proxies of tenure security are important in understanding the fundamental links between property rights and technology adoption (see Haugerud 1989; Blarel et al. 1992; Place and Hazell 1993; and Carter, Wiebe, and Blarel 1994), they are often not variables over which formal policymakers have direct influence. Analysis may be quite important for additional legal property rights instruments. For instance, a relevant research issue would be how the issuance of formal titles to land affects investment and agricultural productivity. The impact of title has been tested by several authors (Feder et al. 1988; Roth, Cochrane, and Kisamba-Mugerwa 1994; Pinckney and Kimuyu 1994; Alston, Libecap, and Schneider 1996; Place and Migot-Adholla 1998) and reviewed by Atwood (1990). Other legal instruments that have appeared in empirical research include contracts with the state and with other farmers through tenancy (Gavian and Ehui, Chapter 5, this volume).

Three issues regarding the method of data collection are of particular relevance to property rights studies. First, some types of topics or questions are believed to be quite sensitive to respondents. Researchers should investigate this possibility in informal discussions. Considering the wide variety of information on property rights reported in the literature, however, such concerns do not appear to be widely validated. Second, articulating concepts of tenure security and rights in questionnaires is not straightforward. For instance, there may be confusion over the distinction between what rights may be exercised and what rights are commonly exercised. This distinction is problematic for both enumerators and respondents, and researchers should prepare for considerable training on these topics. Third, not all types of respondents are equally informed on property rights issues. Often, it is the male head of household who is best able to respond about household-level rights and details of acquisition methods. In fact, if the head is a male, the wife may not be willing to divulge detailed information about property rights. On the other hand, in studies of individual household members' rights, researchers should seek responses from the particular individuals concerned rather than accepting responses from a single respondent. The same principles apply in community studies; it is important to identify respondents with appropriate knowledge of the subject while still capturing the varied viewpoints of different stakeholders.

Timing of Study Relative to Time Periods of Adoption and Realization of Payoffs from Adoption

The different reasons for conducting a study of property rights and technology adoption can imply different timings for the study. Organizations that wish to identify recommendation domains or desirable traits of new technology can benefit greatly from studies conducted during early stages of technology dissemination. The feedback from these studies can prevent wasted resources. Studies that are geared toward influencing policy are best served by allowing technology development and transfer processes to mature for a longer period. In studying the impact of technology, it is beneficial to implement studies at different times. Early studies can identify improvements and feed them back into the research process, whereas late studies can give better assessments of overall impact. In all cases, it is important to be sure that farmers are beyond an early testing phase.

If a study seeks to look at the influence of technology adoption on property rights change, then a longer time frame is clearly warranted since such institutions cannot be expected to change rapidly. Moreover, it may be that only after widespread technology adoption would there be sufficient pressure on institutions to change.

Measuring the Feedback of Technology Adoption on Property Rights

If technology adoption is expected to affect property rights variables, a couple of important data collection issues arise. First, it is best to be able to document a change in property rights from one point in time to another. For a plot, this change might be measured from the time of acquisition or the period just before the adoption of technology to the current period. The variables selected to represent property rights must not be static (so method of plot acquisition would not be appropriate) and must be relatively easily recalled by respondents. The second issue concerns the ability to distinguish the property rights–technology adoption link from the technology adoption–property rights link. To some extent distinguishing these links means understanding the temporal processes involved. But there may be several distinct processes. Therefore, at a statistical level it is important to identify variables that might affect one of the links but not the other so as to be able to identify the parameters associated with the different directional relationships.

Variables may affect adoption, property rights, or both. Examples of variables affecting adoption only are

- household size, size of family labor force, and certain plot biophysical characteristics (plot size, slope).

Those affecting property rights only are

- ethnic group, leadership, and community political variables.

Those affecting both are

- farm size, marital status of household, age of head, and gender of head.

These variables and their effects are not fixed or defensible in all cases. They must be developed for the particular situation under study.

Data Collection When Explanatory Variables Are Expected to Be Correlated

When correlations between property rights and other explanatory variables are probable, then adjustments to data collection may be in order. Examples include land titles and farm size (Carter, Wiebe, and Blarel 1994) and gender and mode of land acquisition (de Zeeuw 1997; Manyong and Houndekon 2000). One of the best ways to distinguish the influence of the property rights variable or variables from others is through sampling strategies. The goal is to have sufficient variation in the sample to produce an adequate number of cases contrary to the systematic correlations (for example, women with strong rights or low populated areas with strong rights). It is best to deal with this issue through stratification. It can be exorbitantly costly, however, to design a sampling frame to achieve this stratification. One remedy is to increase the size of the sample in order to increase the number of different interactions among the independent variables. Increasing the sample size has long been known as one of the best ways to mitigate against multicollinearity problems. If multicollinearity is recognized only at the data analysis stage, another option is to do some informal, quick, and inexpensive data collection to distinguish real driving factors from symptomatic variables (for example, to solicit expert opinion from key informants from a village). If all these methods are unavailable, then the researcher can apply some of the econometric techniques available to deal with multicollinearity, such as ridge regression (Goldberger 1990).

Measuring Property Rights at More Aggregate Levels of Observation

The section reviewing measurement of property rights at the plot and household levels showed that at the purest level of specific resource and specific right holder, it is possible to make detailed assessments and precise measurements of property rights. At higher levels, such as a community, information will be collected from spokespersons on behalf of the community, leading to some fundamental differences in the quality of information. The information will be less detailed—for example, averages will be reported and the rich variation in property rights systems will be lost. Reporting may also be less accurate. Thus, some property rights arrangements could be reported as much more important than they actually are. Collecting reliable information at the community level can be challenging. It is, of course, good practice to interact with individuals or groups of different characteristics to be able to assess the variety of tenure arrangements. Older people will be the key resource people for obtaining historical information. In some cases, it may be necessary to build up community-level property rights variables from rapid surveys of households in order to be assured of reliable data (Suyanto, Tomich, and Otsuka 1999). Participatory tools may be used to help obtain more precise property rights variables. For instance, for variables that are highly related to spatial location (such as extent of commons or area under a broad tenure regime such as customary versus estate), respondents might be able to draw boundaries on maps, allowing for more accurate assessment of the importance of different tenure arrangements. If the boundaries are subsequently stored in a geographic information systems (GIS) database, the tenure variables can be linked to a host of other information similarly stored (Place and Otsuka 2000).

Analysis and Interpretation

This section explores alternative statistical and econometric techniques, as well as the interpretation of the results for research and policy.

Statistical analysis has at least three important components:

- investigation of the statistical significance of a relationship;
- investigation of the importance of a relationship and its interpretation;
- extrapolation of results to affect policy.

These components are discussed in the following subsections.

Analysis

Multivariate regression techniques are almost always preferred over simpler univariate or bivariate analyses in the statistical investigation of the property rights–technology adoption link. Property rights are often associated with other plot and household characteristics, so simple comparisons of adoption under different property rights will likely bias the strength of the relationship. Technology adoption is almost always in the form of a limited dependent variable. Where it is binary, a logit or probit regression model is appropriate. Where adoption values may take many positive values (such as level of adoption), a tobit model is normally appropriate. If adoption is measured by proportion of area under the technology, truncated models should be used instead. Maddala (1983) provides a highly readable introduction to these cases, while other authors (such as Greene 1993) may provide more accessible treatments of the underlying econometrics.

Two complications to this methodological approach are the observance of multiple technologies and the endogeneity of property rights. Many studies of technology adoption find several technologies of interest. In many cases, clear conceptual relationships exist between different technologies—for example, terracing and tree crops, zero grazing and improved fodder, and water wells and fencing. When the number of individual technologies is small, or if some grouping of technologies can be made, a multinomial logit regression analysis can be used. If there is a large number of technology variables, most studies have resorted to an assumption of independence between them and have used single equation models. Simultaneous models involving limited dependent variables are not yet well developed and are not used in this literature. A study by Hayes, Roth, and Zepeda (1997), though, applied a two-stage procedure to tease out the indirect effects of land rights on productivity through their effects on investment.

When property rights both affect technology adoption and are affected by technology adoption, a simultaneous equation model is appropriate. If the property rights and technology adoption variables are continuous, then the three-stage least-squares estimation method can be used. This is rarely the case, however. For limited dependent variables, single equation methods for handling endogeneity (such as two-stage least-squares) have been used and techniques such as bootstrapping have been employed to correct for the resulting biases in estimated standard errors of coefficients (Braselle, Gaspart, and Platteau 1998; Baland et al. 1999). The treatment of simultaneous equations consisting of limited dependent variables is neither well developed in this literature nor in other applications.

An additional complication in the development of simultaneous models is that property rights and technology adoption are not always measured at the same unit of observation, a requirement in simultaneous equation models. For example, land rights may be measured at a parcel level, while adoption of livestock technologies might be a farm-level variable. Similar difficulties have been noted in developing analytical methods for examining the effect of land titling (parcel level) on crop productivity (field level) or use of credit (farm level) (Place and Migot-Adholla 1998).

Nonetheless, simpler, noneconometric techniques are preferable in some instances. One is where investments show little variation in a plot- or household-level survey. For this situation econometric models for qualitative variables do not always work and are not always appropriate. Sometimes simpler decision trees (diagrammatic descriptions of relationships among discrete choice variables) can explain a substantial proportion of the different outcomes. For example, it may be that nearly all sloped land is terraced whereas hardly any flat land is terraced. A simple decision tree can show the patterns of these recursive relationships more clearly and powerfully than can econometric results.

Interpretation

When faced with a situation where the majority of technologies are not found to vary much, researchers may be tempted to aim their attention on those few that do lend themselves to further analysis. This approach is of course legitimate. When making conclusions, however, researchers must remember to re-examine the totality of investments. For instance, if property rights are found to affect one or two types of land investment, but five other similar investments were found to be present on nearly all fields or farms, what is the appropriate conclusion? The role of property rights will be overstated if only those investments exhibiting variation across the observational units are considered.

Finding a statistically significant result on a property rights variable is not the end of the analysis. Evaluating the magnitude of the coefficient is the second step in ascertaining whether or not a variable has a significant impact on technology adoption. Since property rights variables are often binary in nature, the size of the coefficient will directly reflect the impact of observing or not observing the specific property rights variable.

As explained earlier in this chapter, the results should be interpreted in light of the objectives of the study. If the study is based on a stratified sample using adoption of the technology as a criterion, then this objective must be kept in mind when interpreting marginal impacts. For instance, the sample rate of adoption will be overstated in such a purposeful sample and thus so will the marginal impact of explanatory variables.

Finally, it may be wise in some instances to bring property rights variables into interaction with others to improve understanding. For example, the effects of property rights may manifest themselves in different ways in different circumstances. Rights of sale may be important in only periurban areas, so causing this property rights variable to interact with another indicating periurban location or not can help clarify the circumstances under which the property rights effect holds.

Providing Input into Policy Discussions

The finding that property rights may affect technology adoption does not necessarily suggest changes to the property rights systems. It may be much simpler and more effective to alter certain characteristics of the technologies to enhance their adoptability under existing property rights. There are other reasons to pause before making policy recommendations from such studies. While case studies may have direct policy relevance at the study site, the wider policy relevance of the research depends on the ability to draw wider implications from the study. Do the conclusions hold for more aggregated spatial scales? Are the conclusions based on a comprehensive evaluation of the impacts of property rights or only on certain impacts (such as efficiency only or equity only)? Such questions are critical, for there are costs associated with property rights change.

If properly done, recommendations can be useful to policymakers who have influence at the study site or sites. Most researchers, however, hope that their results could have influence well beyond the boundaries of their study sites. Working against ease of extrapolation is that property rights systems are complex, influenced by varying customary practices, formal rules and institutions, and hosts of intervention organizations, such as development agencies. Thus, types of land acquisition methods and rights over resources may be uniquely defined within local areas. To find a basis for comparison and extrapolation, it may be necessary to find common characteristics of rights and acquisition methods. For example, what might be defined as renting may actually differ significantly from site to site. Components of the rental method of accessing land, such as the formalization of the agreement, duration, relationship between transactors, and payment and other considerations exchanged are the types of variables that can be used to reconcile types of acquisitions across sites. It may well be that one or more of these components of renting are more important for technology adoption than the more aggregate and blunt "renting" variable.

Because property rights systems are fundamental to the pursuit of economic growth, equity, and sustainability, studies that focus only on the property rights–technology adoption link are generally modest in their policy recommendations. Analyses of policy implications could be strengthened in two ways. First, it is often presumed that more incidence of a technology is better, but the links between technology adoption and the wider goals of economic growth, equity, and sustainability are not often clearly elaborated. Second, the sequencing of complementary property rights interventions or of property rights and other policy options is not usually explored. These extensions could add considerable policy value to research in this area.

Dealing with the Complexity of Property Rights and Technology Adoption

This review covered several conceptual and empirical aspects associated with the study of the relationships between property rights and technology adoption in smallholder agriculture. Most of the discussion stems from the chapter's general point that the study of property rights and their effects is very complex. There is complexity in conceptualizing the important aspects of property rights and, once defined, in measuring them. Further complications in the study of property rights and their relationships with technology adoption arise because the different reasons for undertaking such studies lead to different research methodologies. Finally, property rights are often dynamic and related to other variables, including technology adoption, so the isolation and quantification of direct and indirect effects between property rights and other variables is complicated from an empirical point of view. This chapter has briefly referred to a number of other studies that attempt to deal with portions of this complexity. The main recommendation of this chapter is that researchers review this body of research before launching new studies on property rights and their relationships with agricultural technology adoption.

References

Adesina, A. 1997. Land and tree property rights, and farmers' investment in alley farming in Cameroon. Paper presented at "Workshop on Property Rights, Collective Action, and Technology Adoption," November 22–25, International Center for Agricultural Research in the Dry Areas, Aleppo, Syria.

Adesina, A., and M. Zinnah. 1993. Technology characteristics, farmers' perceptions, and adoption decisions: A tobit model application in Sierra Leone. *Agricultural Economics* 9 (4): 297–311.

Alston, L., G. Libecap, and R. Schneider. 1996. The determinants and impact of property rights: Land titles on the Brazilian frontier. *Journal of Law, Economics, and Organization* 12 (1): 25–61.

Atwood, D. 1990. Land registration in Africa: The impact on agricultural production. *World Development* 18 (5): 659–671.

Ayuk, E. 1997. Adoption of agroforestry technology: The case of live hedges in the central plateau of Burkina Faso. *Agricultural Systems* 54 (2): 189–206.

Baland, J.-M., and J.-P. Platteau. 1996. *Halting degradation of natural resources: Is there a role for rural communities?* Oxford: Clarendon Press.

Baland, J.-M., F. Gaspart, F. Place, and J.-P. Platteau. 1999. Poverty, tenure security, and access to land in central Uganda: The role of market and non-market processes. Centre de recherches sur l'économie développement, Namur, Belgium. Photocopy.

Bellon, M., and J. E. Taylor. 1993. "Folk" soil taxonomy and the partial adoption of new seed varieties. *Economic Development and Cultural Change* 41 (4): 763–786.

Besley, T. 1995. Property rights and investment incentives. *Journal of Political Economy* 103 (5): 913–937.

Blarel, B., P. Hazell, F. Place, and J. Quiggin. 1992. The economics of farm fragmentation: Evidence from Ghana and Rwanda. *World Bank Economic Review* 6 (2): 233–254.

Braselle, A.-S., F. Gaspart, and J.-P. Platteau. 1998. Land tenure security and investment incentives: Further puzzling evidence from Burkina Faso. Centre de recherches sur l'economie developpement, Namur, Belgium. Photocopy.

Carter, M., K. Wiebe, and B. Blarel. 1994. Tenure security for whom? Differential effects of land policy in Kenya. In *Searching for land tenure security in Africa*, ed. J. Bruce and S. Migot-Adholla. Dubuque, Ia., U.S.A.: Kendall/Hunt.

Deacon, R. 1994. Deforestation and the rule of law in a cross-section of countries. *Land Economics* 70 (4): 414–430.

de Zeeuw, F. 1997. Borrowing of land, security of tenure, and sustainable land use in Burkina Faso. *Development and Change* 28 (3): 583–595.

Feder, G. 1982. Adoption of interrelated agricultural innovations: Complementarity and the impacts of risk, scale, and credit. *American Journal of Agricultural Economics* 64: 94–101.

Feder, G., and D. Feeny 1993. The theory of land tenure and property rights. In *The economics of rural organization: Theory, practice, and policy,* ed. K. Hoff, A. Braverman, and J. E. Stiglitz. Washington, D.C.: World Bank.

Feder, G., T. Onchan, Y. Chalamwong, and C. Hongladaron. 1988. *Land policies and farm productivity in Thailand.* Baltimore, Md., U.S.A.: Johns Hopkins University Press.

Fischer, A., A. Arnold, and M. Gibbs. 1996. Information and the speed of innovation adoption. *American Journal of Agricultural Economics* 78 (4): 1073–1081.

Fortmann, L., and J. W. Bruce. 1988. *Whose trees? Proprietary dimensions of forestry.* Boulder, Colo., U.S.A.: Westview Press.

Gavian, S., and M. Fafchamps. 1996. Land tenure and allocative efficiency in Niger. *American Journal of Agricultural Economics* 78 (2): 460–471.

Gladwin, C., K. L. Buhr, A. Goldman, C. Hiebsch, P. E. Hildebrand, G. Kidder, M. Langham, D. Lee, P. Nkedi-Kizza, and D. Williams. 1997. Gender and soil fertility in Africa. In *Replenishing soil fertility in Africa*, ed. R. J. Buresh, P. A. Sanchez, and F. Calhoun. SSSA Special Publication 51. Madison, Wisc., U.S.A.: Soil Science Society of America.

Golan, E. 1994. Land tenure reform in the peanut basin of Senegal. In *Searching for land tenure security in Africa*, ed. J. Bruce and S. E. Migot-Adholla. Dubuque, Ia., U.S.A.: Kendall/Hunt.

Goldberger, A. 1990. *A course in econometrics.* Cambridge: Harvard University Press.

Greene, W. 1993. *Econometric analysis.* 2nd ed. New York: Macmillan.

Haugerud, A. 1989. Land tenure and agrarian change in Kenya. *Africa* 59 (1): 61–90.

Hayes, J., M. Roth, and L. Zepeda. 1997. Tenure security, investment and productivity in Gambian agriculture: A generalized probit analysis. *American Journal of Agricultural Economics* 79 (2): 369–382.

Kerkhof, P., and V. May. 1988. Sex roles in agroforestry in Kakamega. *Appropriate Technology* 15 (1).

Kisamba-Mugerwa, W., and R. Barrows. 1989. *Land tenure and agricultural development in Uganda.* Madison, Wisc., U.S.A.: Makerere Institute for Social Research and the Land Tenure Center.

Knudsen, M. 1991. Incorporating technological change in diffusion models. *American Journal of Agricultural Economics* 73: 724–733.

Lawry, W. S., and M. D. Stienbarger. 1991. *Tenure and alley farming in the humid zone of West Africa: Final report of research in Cameroon, Nigeria, and Togo.* LTC Research Paper 105. Madison, Wisc., U.S.A., and Ibadan, Nigeria: University of Wisconsin and International Livestock Centre for Africa.

Lin, J. 1991. Education and innovation adoption in agriculture: Evidence from hybrid rice in China. *American Journal of Agricultural Economics* 73: 713–723.

Maddala, G. 1983. *Limited dependent and qualitative variables in econometrics.* New York: Cambridge University Press.

Manyong, V., and V. Houndekon. 2000. Land tenurial systems and the adoption of *mucuna* planted fallows in the derived savannas of West Africa. CAPRi Working Paper Number 4. Washington, D.C.: International Food Policy Research Institute.

Matlon, P. 1994. Indigenous land use systems and investments in soil fertility in Burkina Faso. In *Searching for land tenure security in Africa*, ed. J. Bruce and S. E. Migot-Adholla. Dubuque, Ia., U.S.A.: Kendall/Hunt.

McLain, R. 1992. *Recommendations for a new Malian forest code: Observations from the Land Tenure Centre's study of land and tree tenure in Mali's fifth region.* LTC Research Paper 109. Madison, Wisc., U.S.A.: University of Wisconsin.

Migot-Adholla, S. E., P. Hazell, B. Blarel, and F. Place. 1991. Indigenous land rights systems in Sub-Saharan Africa: A constraint on productivity? *World Bank Economic Review* 5 (1): 155–175.

Mugo, F. 1999. The effects of fuelwood demand and supply characteristics, land factors, and gender roles on tree planting and fuelwood availability in highly populated rural areas of Kenya. Ph.D. diss., Department of Natural Resources, Cornell University, Ithaca, N.Y., U.S.A.

Paramount Chief. 1998. Personal communication. October 8.

Pender, J., S. J. Scherr, and G. Durón. 1998. *Pathways of development in the hillsides of Honduras: Causes and implications for agricultural production, poverty, and sustainable resource use.* Plenary paper presented at the American Agricultural Economics Association International Conference on Agricultural Intensification, Economic Development, and the Environment, July 31–August 1, Salt Lake City, Utah, U.S.A.

Pinckney, T., and P. Kimuyu. 1994. Land tenure reforms in East Africa: Good, bad, or unimportant? *Journal of African Economies* 3 (1): 1–28.

Place, F. 1995. *The role of land and tree tenure on the adoption of agroforestry technologies in Zambia, Burundi, Uganda, and Malawi: A summary and synthesis.* Madison, Wisc., U.S.A.: University of Wisconsin Land Tenure Center.

Place, F., and P. Hazell. 1993. Productivity effects of indigenous land tenure systems in Sub-Saharan Africa. *American Journal of Agricultural Economics* 75 (1): 10–19.

Place, F., and S. E. Migot-Adholla. 1998. Land registration and smallholder farms in Kenya. *Land Economics* 74 (3): 360–373.

Place, F., and K. Otsuka. 2000. Population pressure, land tenure, and tree resource management in Uganda. *Land Economics* 76 (2): 233–251.

———. 2001a. Customary and private land management in Uganda. In *Land tenure and natural resource management: A comparative study of agrarian communities in Asia and Africa,* ed. K. Otsuka and F. Place. Baltimore, Md., U.S.A.: Johns Hopkins University Press for the International Food Policy Research Institute.

———. 2001b. Population, land tenure, and natural resource management: The case of customary land area in Malawi. *Journal of Environmental Economics and Management* 41: 13–32.

Place, F., M. Roth, and P. Hazell. 1994. Land tenure security and agricultural performance in Africa: Overview of research methodology. In *Searching for land tenure
security in Africa*, ed. J. Bruce and S. E. Migot-Adholla. Dubuque, Ia., U.S.A.:
Kendall/Hunt.

Quisumbing, A. R., E. Payongayong, J. B. Aidoo, and K. Otsuka. 1999. *Women's land
rights in the transition to individualized ownership: Implications for the management of tree resources in Western Ghana*. Food Consumption and Nutrition Division Discussion Paper 58. Washington, D.C.: International Food Policy Research
Institute.

Roth, M., J. Cochrane, and W. Kisamba-Mugerwa. 1994. Tenure security, credit use,
and farm investment in the Rujumbura pilot land registration scheme, Uganda. In
Searching for land tenure security in Africa, ed. J. Bruce and S. E. Migot-Adholla.
Dubuque, Ia., U.S.A.: Kendall/Hunt.

Schlager, E., and E. Ostrom. 1992. Property rights regimes and natural resources: A
conceptual analysis. *Land Economics* 68 (3): 249–262.

Sjaastad, E., and D. W. Bromley. 1997. Indigenous land rights in Sub-Saharan Africa:
Appropriation, security, and investment demand. *World Development* 25 (4): 549–
562.

Snyder, K. A. 1996. Agrarian change and land-use strategies among Iraqi farmers in
Northern Tanzania. *Human Ecology* 24 (3): 315–340.

Suyanto, S., T. P. Tomich, and K. Otsuka. 1999. Agroforestry management in Sumatra.
International Centre for Research in Agroforestry, Bogor, Indonesia. Photocopy.

Two Wings Agroforestry Group. 1996. Personal communication. June 14.

4   The Role of Tenure in the Management of Trees at the Community Level: Theoretical and Empirical Analyses from Uganda and Malawi

FRANK PLACE AND KEIJIRO OTSUKA

In most of Sub-Saharan Africa long-term economic growth hinges upon sustaining and improving the productivity of the natural resource base. Policymakers must face the challenge of identifying appropriate pathways for the use and management of natural resources in their jurisdictions and sets of policies that will steer their constituents toward these pathways. Unfortunately, policymakers in Sub-Saharan Africa have little information about the dynamic processes that have led to current land use patterns and to related effects on the stock of natural resources and their productivity.

With respect to tree resources, empirical research has only recently begun to identify important driving forces behind household decisions to plant trees on farms (Dewees 1995; Patel, Pinckney, and Jaeger 1995; Place 1995; Scherr 1995). Another body of research centers on understanding changes in forested areas at the national and international levels (Deacon 1994; Capistrano and Kiker 1995; Kahn and McDonald 1995). A third scale or observational level that is particularly lacking in empirical research might be called the community or landscape level (exceptions are Cline-Cole, Main, and Nichol 1990 for 2 sites in Nigeria and Southgate, Sierra, and Brown 1991 for 11 sites within Ecuador). Given a sample of sufficient size, this level could offer unique insight into the factors whose magnitudes are often constant across observations in household studies from a given village but whose aggregated averages are too crude across observations at a national level. Examples include land tenure institutions, which govern the use and allocation of land and natural resources; the degree of market access, which determines the structure of

The authors would like to acknowledge the strong empirical research efforts of colleagues in Uganda (Joe Ssenteza, Emmanuel Buyinza, and Jutta Breyer) and in Malawi (Redge Masupayi, Ken Neils, Vincent Mkandawire, and Bob Green). We also wish to thank the Government of Japan and the Rockefeller Foundation for providing financial support to the project. Lastly, we also thank the Japan International Cooperation Agency, the Department for International Development (United Kingdom), and the Biomass Project (Uganda) for generous assistance in making available remote sensing.

market-driven derived demands for these resources; and population pressure, which is considered the key variable affecting the choice of farming systems in the economic literature since Boserup (1965).

This chapter will first endeavor to develop an analytical approach to improve understanding of the relationship between tenure and other factors on tree resource management at the community level. Second, the chapter will provide new evidence about how communities in the case study countries of Uganda and Malawi have managed their land and tree resources and what factors seemed most important in their decisions. This information is valuable to policymakers who continue to struggle with the twin objectives of alleviating poverty in the short run and preserving the natural resource base in the long run so that future generations may have access to high-quality income-generating assets.

This chapter comprises six sections. The first introduces the key issues concerning the determinants of tree cover change and elaborates on important analytical issues. The second section discusses tenure systems in Uganda and Malawi. The following sections describe the study sites for the community-level analysis of tree cover change and present theoretical and econometric models for land use and tree cover change in Uganda and Malawi. Next the chapter discusses the results from the econometric analyses and finally offers key conclusions and implications of the study.

Important Analytical Issues in the Study of Tree Management

Conceptual Issues with Respect to Changes in Tree Stocks

Trees serve many different purposes for households and communities. Ideally, therefore, one should analyze households' and communities' different tree-planting and management strategies, which may be determined by unique processes and factors. The task of classifying tree management strategies is complicated, however, by the many species and niches of agroforestry systems and by their multipurpose nature. These differences are all the more difficult to identify at the community level, where different households may adopt similar tree species in similar configurations for different purposes. Although identifying these differences is important, we do not address such subtleties in this section. For the remainder of this section, we refer to the stock of tree resources per unit area as "tree cover" and to tree establishment, management, and harvesting systems as "tree management strategies."

One distinguishing feature that separates trees from other types of long-term land improvements is that tree cover can grow and shrink without human interference, through, for instance, natural regeneration, fire, and disease.[1] That

---

1. This capacity is not true of all species or of all purposeful tree systems, such as timber plantations.

is, in addition to purposeful management of tree resources, there is a "biological supply side," implying that one cannot equate the *presence* of trees with *investment* in trees. Increases in tree cover could simply result from neglect of the land by a land manager.

Another unique aspect of trees is their link with land tenure. First, in Sub-Saharan Africa an investment of labor in clearing communal woodland was historically a necessary condition in establishing private rights to land (Ault and Rutman 1979; Noronha 1985; Bruce 1988). Second, in many societies tree planting was seen as a way of establishing long-term rights to land (Fortmann and Bruce 1988). Third, certain tree species carry with them tenurial implications, such as those customarily used for boundary demarcation or others viewed as "communal" trees (many types of indigenous fruit trees, for example).

These observations have implications for our analysis of investment in tree strategies. First, household-level analyses are useful for understanding specific tree management objectives and strategies, whether the focus is on the household or the community level. Second, careful attention must be paid to the treatment of tenure variables in the context of tree management. Some tenure variables cannot be viewed as exogenous given their strong links to trees. For instance, the duration of rights to land may be related to prior tree-planting efforts.

Conceptual Issues with Respect to Trees at the Community Level

Tree cover and tree strategies are found across virtually all tenure and land use systems on a landscape.[2] Thus the study of tree cover, to be comprehensive, must cover an entire spectrum of landscapes and key decisionmakers managing the different lands.

The reason for this is that the patterns of tree cover and the tree management strategies observed differ across tenure and land use systems. For instance, tree cover density tends to be lower on agricultural land and higher on other land use types such as forest and woodland. In the case of tenure systems, regardless of the degree of management of common pool resources, the vast proportion of tree planting is found on private agricultural land. Furthermore, trees in different locations are linked by complementary and substitution relationships because many of the tree products desired by households can be obtained by trees located anywhere on the surrounding landscape.[3]

Added to this complexity is the fact that tenure and land use systems are often dynamic. Thus, changes in tree cover are the result of complex interactions of changes in tenure, changes in land use, and changes in tree densities on

---

2. The use of "tenure system" in this context is taken to be a broad classification such as "private" or "communal" within a customary tenure regime. A land use system may be agriculture, woodland, bushland, forest, or wetland, among others.

3. Restricted or limited rights of access to farmland, nonfarmland, and trees on these lands will affect the degree to which possibilities for complementarity or substitution exist.

each tenure/land use niche. It is vitally important to take these different processes into account for they have their own driving forces and critical actors. For example, decisions on tree density on agricultural land may be purely an individual choice.

The tenure conversion process by which the individual acquired his or her farm, however, may have involved others, such as state authorities, local authorities, clan leaders, and extended family members.

In summary, studies of tree cover change for the purpose of addressing issues of biomass supply must include the different types of land uses and tenures found across the landscape.[4] Past studies that have focused solely on the implications of forest land for biomass supply have limited usefulness. Furthermore, the different niches must be analyzed in an integrated manner owing to the interactions of trees and other production systems. Lastly, it is crucial in models of tree cover changes to distinguish among the different processes affecting tree cover change.

Conceptual Issues with Respect to Tenure at the Community Level

Numerous studies at the farm level have been able to conceptually define and empirically measure several important tenure variables affecting farmer incentives. These variables include those related to the nature of landholdings (such as farm size), the nature of land rights, the duration of land rights, and the possession of formal tenure documents, among others. In comparison, there is little understanding of tenure factors at the community level. How can the diverse set of institutions within a community be effectively aggregated and captured? At very broad levels, major legal tenure systems such as customary, freehold, and state systems can be viewed as exogenous. Many other tenure variables are likely to be endogenous at the community level. For instance, customary systems may differ in a number of ways, including the degree of individualization (the extent to which rights are held by families as opposed to the state or communal authorities), exclusivity, and property inheritance patterns.

Conceptual Issues with Respect to Land Use and Tenure Conversion
at the Community Level

The dominant types of conversions have been tenure conversions from nonprivate to private and land use conversions from nonagriculture to agriculture land uses. While the two types of conversions are clearly related, we first discuss each separately beginning with tenure conversion.

The major tenure conversion in Sub-Saharan Africa has been toward privatization of land rights in arable areas (Noronha 1985; Migot-Adholla et al.

---

4.   For certain objectives (such as measuring biodiversity or the presence of fauna), studying the changes to forests alone may be sufficient.

1991). In the literature, this change has been linked to population growth and commercialization of agriculture (Migot-Adholla and Bruce 1994). Three factors, however, limit the rate of conversion. First, a household cannot cultivate unlimited land area, and local customs (for meeting equity objectives) may not allow the conversion of an area larger than what can be cultivated by the household. Second, there may be transaction costs associated with converting land that stem from the community's desire to maintain woodlands, wetlands, and the like for reasons of equity, risk reduction, or long-term productivity. These costs are likely to increase with the proportion of land already converted. Third, these benefits from woodlands may also generate collective action for management of woodland resources that could impose restrictions on conversion of land.

Whether or not land use is changed before, during, or after a tenure conversion is an empirical issue and depends on the relative profits and associated risks of different activities, as well as access to capital and other resources. Tenure change may be preconditioned on land use change where chiefs may require conversion to agriculture (often specifically to food crop production) as a prerequisite for allocating land. Such a condition is embedded in a strong adherence to equity motives over commercialization considerations. While land use can change from crop-based agriculture to other land uses, this change is not widely observed except for allocation of fields to woodlots, pastures, or long fallows. It is equally rare to observe endogenous conversion from private tenure to other types of tenure.

Background on Case Study Countries of Uganda and Malawi

Uganda and Malawi were selected as case studies for two primary reasons. First, they are part of a multicountry study examining the role of tenure on tree resource management that also included Ghana, Indonesia, Japan, Nepal, and Viet Nam (Otsuka and Place 2001). The set of seven countries was selected to represent a range of different tenure regimes. Second, Uganda and Malawi were selected from among a handful of candidates because of the availability of aerial photographs from different dates (so that changes in tree resource stocks could be evaluated).

Uganda is a landlocked country of about 19 million people, of which slightly less than 90 percent reside in rural areas. The average ratio of rural population to cultivable land for all of Uganda is 88 per square kilometer and ranges between 51 and 319 in the districts containing our study sites (World Bank 1993). Langdale-Brown (1960) estimated dense forest area to be greater than 25,000 square kilometers in the mid-1920s and greater than 11,000 square kilometers in 1958. In 1990 estimated tropical high forest area was reduced to 7,000 square kilometers, representing about 3 percent of land area (World Bank 1993). The annual rate of deforestation (including all types of natural forests) was estimated to be about 0.9 percent between 1980 and 1990 (World Bank

1994). The loss of tree cover jeopardizes key ecosystem services and basic provision of wood products. It is estimated that about 90 percent of cooking and heating energy comes from wood (World Bank 1996).

Malawi has a similar rural-based population with large variations in density across regions. Like other countries in Sub-Saharan Africa, Malawi has experienced a significant change in its landscape cover. Although reliable figures are hard to come by, the Forestry Department estimated the annual deforestation rate to be 1.3 percent per year in the 1980s (World Resources Institute 1994). This rate has raised concern about the future supply of fuelwood and other tree products and environmental services (French 1986; Hyde and Seve 1993; Dewees 1995). Much of the deforestation is believed to be linked to conversion of *miombo* woodlands (the open woodland ecosystem of southern Africa) into agricultural land. This conversion involves expansion onto steep slopes and other fragile lands in many cases. Per capita food production has declined over the 1980s and early 1990s. Moreover, Bojo (1994) presents data showing high soil erosion rates and the subsequent high costs to the Malawian economy, which depends heavily on agriculture (World Bank 1995).

Tenure Systems in Uganda

Across our study sites in Uganda, several land tenure systems were prevalent before 1975, and despite the de jure nationalization of all land in that year, the same tenure systems are recognized both in the perceptions of the population and in formal land tenure reform debates. The most widespread of the tenure regimes is customary land tenure, which is virtually the only tenure system operating in our eastern and northern sites. Customary lands in these sites were traditionally governed by clans that allocated plots of land to members. By the early 1900s households had settled on lands in many of the sites and acquired strong permanent rights to specific parcels (Bazaara 1992). In some areas power shifted from clans to chiefs following colonial intervention, but in 1966 the Ugandan government formally abolished kingdoms. All customary systems follow patrilineal rules of descent, and in our study region inheritance is the most common method of land acquisition.

In the Buganda region of central Uganda, the major tenure system is the *mailo* tenure system. Vast tracts of land given to notables and elites by the colonialists beginning in the early 1900s were known as private *mailo* land. Owners, lacking labor to till such large land areas and seeking status in the community, received fees, rents, or other payments (such as shares of output) by settling tenants (*kibanja*) on their land. Landlords' powers to evict tenants were subsequently restricted in a 1928 law that required full compensation for any investments tenants had made. Later the 1975 land reform abolished all rents. Although only *mailo* owners may acquire titles to land, many tenants have strong rights over the land they occupy, including the right to bequeath.

Today some *mailo* owners occupy and farm their land; in many areas, however, tenants make up the overwhelming majority of occupants.

Other nonallocated land in the Buganda region was initially classified as Crown Land and included land considered "waste." During the reign of traditional rulers, this land was loosely administered by chiefs and was akin to customary land, although Muhereza (1992) describes the management of many of these areas as resembling open access. Settlers on these lands face tenure security risks owing to the allocation of leaseholds to wealthy individuals and elites. In some highly publicized cases, these new settlers have evicted families (renamed "squatters") who had occupied the land for several generations. It is difficult to know how many evictions have occurred, but the local populations are well aware of them. Because of the increased potential for conflict over rights to these lands, we distinguish them from the customary areas in the eastern and northern sites and refer to such land as "public" land.

Tenure Systems in Malawi

Although three major tenure systems prevail in Malawi—state, estate, and customary—our study sites are almost wholly from the customary tenure sector, and this chapter will focus only on this tenure system.[5] The customary sector consists mainly of smallholders. A key distinction here is between matrilineal and patrilineal ethnic groups. When land was abundant, both systems vested land in chiefs and village headmen. The village headmen in turn would cede rights over specific tracts of land to families and family leaders. New lands could be opened through requests to family leaders and village headmen.

In the matrilocal cum matrilineal system practiced by the Chewa and Yao in our study sites, husbands moved to live in the wife's village and land traditionally passed from mother to daughter or from family leader to female family members (Mkandawire 1983/84). The couple often resided permanently in the wife's village.[6] We found, however, that traditional matrilocal and matrilineal practices were being circumvented by households who relocated to the husband's villages or to new villages.

A patrilineal (and patrilocal) system, common in the north of Malawi, is similar to those elsewhere in Sub-Saharan Africa in that men claim landownership and can pass on all land and property to their children. Married couples reside permanently in the husband's village. It has been customary among the Ngoni and Tumbuka at our sites to favor sons over daughters in inheritance practices.

---

5. The customary sector is estimated to occupy about 70 percent of land area. For more information on the state and estate tenure systems see Dickerman and Bloch (1991).

6. This system is akin to matrilineal systems observed in some parts of Asia, such as Sumatra (Otsuka, Suyanto, and Tomich 1997). A matrilineal system in which the couple resides in the husband's village was rare in our sites.

The various modes of transfer and tenure arrangements might have different incentives on farm and tree management owing to differences in tenure security. Two types of situations are of concern with respect to the tenure security of males in our sample areas.

The first is where husbands intend to reside in the wife's village on a temporary basis, favoring a move elsewhere when they increase their land rights. A second case concerns rights to land following death or divorce of a spouse. Upon divorce, the husband must leave the wife's village, and similarly, following the death of the wife, the husband's rights to residence are not at all guaranteed (traditionally, he would be expected to return to his village). In each of these cases, the husband is likely to increase activities that enhance short-term returns at the expense of long-term returns.

The customary sector includes both private and communal lands. The communal lands are held by the clan or village headman and are reported to be virtual open-access resources, with few rules on user group membership or use rates (Coote, Luhanga, and Lowore 1993a,b). One notable exception is the Village Forest Area system initiated in the 1920s and recently rekindled by the Forestry Department, in which communities demarcate woodland areas to be placed under special management rules (which are always conservation oriented). To date, Village Forest Areas are few in number and those in operation are small in size.

Methodology and Description of Study Sites

Sampling

The sampling units chosen in both countries reflected units defined by the respective governments. In Uganda the sampling unit was a parish, which is the smallest administrative unit for which georeferenced boundaries are known (they average 30 square kilometers in size). In Malawi the unit selected was a census enumeration area, and the average was 12 square kilometers in size. The boundaries of both parishes and enumeration areas were created by the governments to encompass villages and to contain roughly similar sizes of population. The administrative areas are thus smaller in areas of high population density and larger in areas of low population density. We found that in Uganda a parish often contained five or six villages and in Malawi a census enumeration area contained two or three villages. The group surveys therefore sought representation from multiple villages.

For the purposes of the study, the selection of sites required variation in land tenure systems, variation in population density, and availability of aerial photographs. The last criterion was not constraining in the case of Malawi, where countrywide aerial photographs are available for several dates, including the early 1970s and the mid-1990s. In Uganda the coverage of aerial photography from the late 1940s to the early 1960s is extensive, whereas aerial photography from the late 1980s to the mid-1990s is highly selective. The widest recent air photo coverage was a wide strip north of Lake Victoria and south of Lake Kyoga starting from the Kenyan border in the east up to Kiboga District in the west.

A second factor considered in sampling was the tenure system. In Uganda this factor is relatively easy to account for because the major tenure systems have well-known boundaries that correspond closely to current district boundaries. Similarly, in Malawi we ensured variation in customary tenure system (patrilocal versus matrilocal) by sampling across different geographical regions.

The sampling procedure did not explicitly account for the final variable of concern, population density, because we believed that sufficient variation would emerge by following a random selection process based on geographical stratification. After stratifying by 11 districts in Uganda and by 4 broad regions in Malawi, we drew samples randomly.[7] In Uganda we selected 64 parishes for study from the districts of Kiboga, Luwero, Mukono, Kamuli, Iganga, Tororo, Mbale, Kumi, Lira, and Apac. In Malawi we analyzed 57 enumeration areas more or less in equal numbers from the north (Mzuzu Agricultural Development Division [ADD]), north-central (Kasungu and Salima ADD), south-central (Lilongwe and Mchinji ADD), and south (Machinga and Blantyre ADD).

Data Collection

The data for this study came from three primary sources. The land use cover and tree density data were generated entirely from aerial photos and satellite imagery that were checked in the field. The variables hypothesized to affect land use and tree cover were obtained either from secondary sources or from socioeconomic field surveys. Following discussions about the data sources and methods of data acquisition, mention will also be made about the analytical methods used.

Measurement of Variables

Land use cover data were acquired from a combination of aerial photography and satellite imagery in Uganda, and exclusively from aerial photography in Malawi. Tree cover estimates could only be obtained from aerial photography. Thus, in Malawi the number of sampling units for land use and tree cover change are identical, while in Uganda land use figures are available for a greater number of parishes than are tree density figures.

---

7. Exceptions were urban centers and state-protected areas that were excluded. In Uganda we also excluded extremely large parishes (of over 150 square kilometers) because we thought we could not obtain reliable field information for such sizes. This excluded less than 2 percent of parishes.

In both countries, remote sensing data were acquired for two distinct periods of time. In Uganda, we used photos from eight different flight contracts were used and these were flown between 1948 and 1961. Almost all photos used, however, were taken between 1957 and 1961. The recent aerial photography used here covered 42 parishes and was taken in 1995. In Malawi, aerial photographs were used for both periods of assessment (1971–73 and then 1995). The year for which we collected information on initial conditions of explanatory variables, such as population density, was 1960 for Uganda and 1971 for Malawi.

LAND USE COVER.   A classification scheme was developed to describe land use cover. Agricultural land includes all land for which a discernible field pattern could be detected with a whole complex of covers ranging from crops, fallows, grazing patches, and clusters of trees and woodlots. Wooded land was divided into four types: plantations, tropical forests, woodlands, and bushlands. Although data were collected for each type, in our analyses plantations and forests were grouped together, as were woodlands and bushlands. Remaining land was further disaggregated into grasslands, wetlands, urban land, barren land, and water. More details for land use and tree cover classifications can be found in Breyer (1996).

TREE COVER.   Forests either were closed (100 percent tree cover) or slightly degraded (80–100 percent cover). Four subclasses of woodland/bushland and wetlands were distinguished based upon tree and shrub crown (or canopy) cover. Using woodlands as an example, open woodland has a crown cover density between 2 and 20 percent. Medium woodland has a crown cover density between 20 and 40 percent. Dense woodland has a crown cover between 40 and 60 percent. And finally very dense woodland has a crown cover density between 60 and 80 percent. For agricultural land, a different tree cover methodology was used. In Uganda we decided to sample agricultural land areas, calculate the proportion of area under tree cover in each sample area, and then take the average of the samples as an indicator of aggregate tree canopy cover in agricultural land within a parish. In Malawi we mapped agricultural tree cover according to ranges of cover, but bounds were much tighter than for non-agricultural land (for example, 0–2 percent, 2–10 percent, 10–20 percent, and 20–40 percent).

EXPLANATORY VARIABLES.   A field survey was administered at each of the sites (parishes or census enumeration areas) to collect information on hypothesized explanatory variables and to provide additional information about the characteristics of woody vegetation. The survey was administered to groups (comprising elders, local leaders, and extension agents, among others) in each site and generally took three to four hours to complete. The survey included sections on proximity of the site to markets and infrastructure; demographic variables; farming systems and livestock holdings; common tree species and characteristics; tree management interventions and markets for tree products; and tenure regimes and associated rights to land and trees. To the extent possible, questions distinguished the base year situation from the current (1995–96) situation.

Unique to Uganda was the participatory drawing of broad tenure boundaries (that is, between customary, *mailo*, public, and leasehold tenure regimes) within parishes overlaid on remote sensing images. We planned a similar approach in Malawi but found that customary tenure occupied all land in nearly all sites. Because of the complexity of cultural practices and tenure systems in Malawi, we also implemented a household- and plot-level survey to better assess key variables such as patterns of residence and mode of land acquisition. Other explanatory variables were taken from secondary sources. These variables include population, average annual rainfall, soil type, soil texture, and elevation.

Descriptive Information

GENERAL DESCRIPTION OF SITES. Table 4.1 displays the means of important explanatory factors hypothesized to affect land use and tree cover change. The set of sites in Uganda and Malawi show considerable similarity in terms of population density, population growth, and distance to tarmac. One notable difference concerns rainfall: the Malawian sites were significantly drier than those in Uganda. Although a distinct drier zone encompasses the northernmost sites in Uganda, most of the Ugandan sites are in favorable agricultural zones with two rainy seasons. It is important to mention that each of the variables exhibited a high degree of variation across sites within a country. Many different cropping systems are found in the Ugandan sample—banana, coffee, maize, and sorghum to name a few. The Malawian sites, on the other hand, are unified by their emphasis on maize. Cases of pest, disease, and drought have occurred in both countries, but perhaps the most noteworthy event affecting the

TABLE 4.1 Means of some key explanatory variables

Variable	Uganda	Malawi
Population density (persons per square kilometer)	79 (1960)	65 (1971)
Annual growth of population (percentage)	4.5	4.1
Distance from site to major city (kilometers)	181	120
Distance from site to tarmac (kilometers)	25	25
Average annual rainfall (millimeters)	1,230	915
Percentage of land in customary tenure	50.2	100.0
Percentage of land in *mailo* tenure	39.4	. . .
Percentage of plots acquired through the wife's family	0	46.0

SOURCES: IFPRI-ICRAF survey, 1996; MFEP (1992); FAO (1984); Green and Mkandawire (1997).

use of land was the Ugandan war of the 1980s, which, among other things, led to displacement of people in some of the sites.

TENURE VARIABLES.   As already mentioned, the study areas had three main types of tenure regimes whose boundaries remained fixed throughout the study period in Uganda. Customary land was found in 37 (58 percent) of the parishes. Customary land covered the entire parish area in 30 parishes, and it occupied about 50 percent of all land in the study area. The *mailo* land tenure system was found in 29 (45 percent) parishes and comprised 39 percent of all land area in the study. In 34 percent of *mailo* areas, virtually all *mailo* owners were resident, whereas the remaining two-thirds had moderate to high levels of absentee ownership. Public land was found in 24 (38 percent) parishes, occupying about 10 percent of total land area.

In all tenure categories individual rights to plant trees and to cut non-timber trees were ubiquitous. The only tree right to exhibit much variation concerned the right to cut timber trees, which reflected differences in awareness of the legal protection for these species. As for land rights, in only a few cases was the unrestricted right of sale noted. Nearly all of these cases were in *mailo* land (where 55 percent of parishes reported prevalence of unrestricted rights). On the other hand, the unrestricted right of sale was not common in any of the customary land areas surveyed or in 15 of 16 public land areas. Free grazing, and hence less exclusive rights to land, was reported for 32 percent of customary areas, 66 percent of *mailo* areas, and 42 percent of public lands. The higher percentage within the *mailo* tenure category may reflect the fact that large and often absentee owners are unable to enforce exclusion rights and that it is mainly on the larger *mailo* farms where supplies of such communally used resources are found.

In Malawi the major difference between customary tenure systems was in the pattern of land inheritance. Over 90 percent of all sampled parcels were acquired from parents, with about 46 percent determined to have been through the wife's side of the family. The prevalence of matrilineal inheritance systems is strongest in the south, weakest in the north where patrilineal systems dominate, and moderate in the transitional north-central zone. The Chewa, a traditional matrilineal and matrilocal group, was the most prevalent group, found in 48 percent of enumeration areas. In our sample other matrilocal or matrilineal groups were a majority in 30 percent of enumeration areas, whereas patrilineal groups were the most prevalent in 23 percent of enumeration areas.

Further questions regarding land rights and markets produced little variation in response. For instance, not one purchase of land occurred among the 570 households surveyed, and none of the communities surveyed recognized the right of sale. Likewise, little variation arose in groups' responses to questions on other land and tree rights.

LAND USE COVER AND ITS CHANGE.   For discussion purposes, the land use cover classifications have been grouped into agriculture, forest or

TABLE 4.2 Land use in Ugandan and Malawian sites at two points in time (percentage of land under each land use category)

Country/land use		
Uganda	1960	1995
Agriculture	57	70
Woodland/bushland	28	18
Forest/plantations	4	2
Wetland/grassland	11	10
Malawi	1971–73	1995
Agriculture	52	68
Woodland/bushland	33	19
Forest/plantations	1	1
Wetland/grassland	14	13

SOURCES: IFPRI-ICRAF survey, 1996; Green and Mkandawire (1997); Breyer (1996).

plantation, woodland, or bushland, and wetland. The figures in the tables are simple averages across observational units (parishes or enumeration areas).[8]

Table 4.2 shows the broad land use patterns as of 1960 and 1995 across 64 parishes in Uganda. Agriculture was the most widespread land use in 1960 and in 1995. The share of land under agriculture increased over the period from 57 percent to 70 percent.

The increase in agriculture came largely at the expense of woodland and bushland, whose share fell from 28 percent to 18 percent during the same time period. Forested land also saw its share cut in half over the period from 4 percent to 2 percent. On the other hand, wetland and grassland area remained fairly constant at 11 percent in 1960 and 10 percent in 1995. Some wetlands are difficult to convert because of perennial waterlogging.

In Malawi, the data on land use change paint a similar picture as in Uganda, though the change seems to have occurred more rapidly (Table 4.2). The share of land in agriculture increased over the 1971–95 period from 52 percent to 68 percent across all study sites. There was substantial variation in the change in the share of agricultural land among the study sites, with the range being from +73 percent to –32 percent. This expansion came almost exclusively at the expense of woodlands and bushlands, whose share of land area fell from 33 percent to 19 percent. The remaining land use categories remained nearly constant: wetlands at around 14 percent and forests at around 1 percent.

---

8. Using a weighted aggregation, the proportion of land under agriculture would be lower since the sampling units for which the share of agriculture is low are generally larger (because of the relationship to relatively low population density). The same logic applies to our estimates of tree cover.

TABLE 4.3 Tree cover in Ugandan and Malawian sites for two
points in time (percentage of land under tree canopy cover)

Country/land use		
Uganda	1960	1995
Agriculture	23	28
Forest	97	97
Woodland/bushland	44	42
Wetland	17	17
Aggregate	31	31
Malawi	1971–73	1995
Agriculture	2	2
Nonagriculture	24	17
Aggregate	17	10

sources: IFPRI-ICRAF survey, 1996; Green and Mkandawire (1997); Breyer
(1996).

TREE COVER AND ITS CHANGE.   Table 4.3 shows the simple average tree cover canopy across sample sites in 1960 and 1995 in Uganda. The
proportion of area under trees has remained nearly constant at 31 percent.[9]
Movements in aggregate tree cover change are influenced by two key processes: change in land use and change in tree density on particular land uses.
Because agriculture has traditionally had less tree cover than woodlands and
bushlands, the change in land use has reduced aggregate tree cover. Tree cover
densities on the specific land use categories have also changed. The most im-
pressive increase was found on agricultural land. Our samples found that
whereas in 1960 the average proportion of area under trees was 23 percent, in
1995 the proportion had increased to 28 percent.

Average tree cover on woodlands and bushlands decreased slightly from
44 percent to 42 percent. Tree cover density on forested land (see the definition
given earlier) was unchanged at 97 percent and that on wetlands was unchanged
at 17 percent. Given these changes, the contribution of agricultural land to total tree canopy (taking into consideration the proportion of area and tree density) increased from 35 percent in 1960 to 58 percent in 1995.

Table 4.3 also displays some summary statistics pertaining to tree canopy cover across the enumeration areas in Malawi. In 1972 the average canopy
cover was estimated to be about 17 percent, but the median was much lower,
at 9 percent. By 1995 tree cover had fallen to 10 percent (the median being only

---

9.   Recall that data on tree cover are from 42 parishes rather than the full 64 used for land
use change. The tree cover data exclude the northern districts of Apac, Lira, and Kumi that would
be expected to have a lower tree density because of their dryness.

3 percent). Significant differences in tree cover arise according to whether the primary land use was agricultural or not. Table 4.3 shows that tree canopy cover on agricultural land was very low in the sites, estimated to be only around 2 percent in both years. This level of cover has remained virtually constant in 80 percent of the sites. Tree cover in nonagricultural areas was much higher but has shown a more marked decline. From a level of about 24 percent in 1971, tree cover in nonagricultural areas dropped to 17 percent. As many as 44 sites experienced a decrease in nonagricultural land tree cover, whereas 9 showed an increase.

Theoretical and Econometric Models of Tree Cover Change at the Community Level

Theoretical Framework and Hypotheses

As mentioned in the introduction, we are concerned with two types of decisions: decisions concerning the choice of land use system and decisions concerning the management of trees within the resulting land uses. We hypothesize that land use choice is linked primarily to two key factors: the expected profits from alternative land uses and the costs (ease) of conversion from one land use to another.[10] We now analyze these decisions in Uganda and Malawi under the assumption that households and communities have two land uses available to them: agriculture and woodland. More detailed theoretical models are developed for Uganda and Malawi in Place and Otsuka (2000) and Place and Otsuka (2001), respectively.

Uganda has three types of tenure systems in which to analyze land use and tree cover decisions. On customary land, evidence shows that the use of woodlands is virtually open access. Consequently, expected profits from woodlands are low, and conversion to private tenure and agriculture offers substantial benefits. Moreover, conversion is not restricted by tenure institutions that follow the common rules of accommodating land demands from new households and rewarding the conversion of land with stronger individual rights to land.

The case of *mailo* land is quite different, principally because of the restrictions on tenancies that have arisen from land tenure policy and resulting distortions on land use. *Mailo* owners now have strong incentives not to "lease" land to tenants. Because land is unevenly distributed in *mailo* areas (some relatively large landowners still remain), the restrictions on leasing or renting, along with possible inefficiencies of crop production due to labor supervision

---

10. Considerations of risks (such as climatic risk) may play a more important role if individuals are risk averse.

costs (as found in Asia; see Hayami and Otsuka 1993), tend to preserve un-cultivated areas such as woodlands or grazing lands.

Leasing or renting could equally have emerged on customary land, but the relatively equitable distribution of land did not provide the necessary incentives for this to occur. This situation reinforces the tendency for the proportion of agricultural land to be lower on *mailo* land than on customary land. In the case of public land, conversion to agricultural land has been regulated to some degree by the state. Thus we hypothesize that, other things being equal, the rate of conversion to agricultural land is higher on customary land than on *mailo* and public land.

Incentives to invest in tree resources will be affected by the degree of tenure security, both before investment (Besley 1995) and as it rises after investment. Individual land rights are strongest on private *mailo* lands owned by resident owners who usually manage their lands directly and have both incentives and capacity to manage land and tree resources intensively. *Mailo* tenants also have strong planting rights with the exception of a few high-value timber trees. Although individual rights are relatively weak within the customary system, we expect that the planting of trees will increase land rights in the customary tenure system. Therefore, we hypothesize that tree densities are higher on *mailo* and customary land than on public land where uncertainty and tenure insecurity are in evidence. We also hypothesize that within *mailo* land, areas managed by resident owners have greater tree density than those managed by absentee owners, as the latter have less control over the disposition of trees.

In Malawi, as in Uganda, there are few management rules regulating the use of woodlands. Thus woodlands tend to be open access, which means that individuals have incentives to degrade or convert woodlands whenever they can gain short-term profit by doing so. In comparing the incentives for degrading or converting land in matrilocal with those in patrilocal households, one factor appears overriding. Because husbands in patrilocal households have greater security of tenure (in many, but not all cases), they will have higher expected profits from agriculture than their matrilocal counterparts. Thus, given that men are the primary decisionmakers regarding land use, we hypothesize that incentives for conversion are greater among patrilocal households.

We expect that where tenure security for males is greater, men choose more sustainable land use systems. In our case this fact implies greater investment in tree planting or preserving tree resources in patrilocal than in matrilocal systems. Because open access seems to prevail in woodlands throughout Malawi, however, we anticipate that such differences will be observed only on agricultural land. Thus for woodlands our hypothesis is that there are no significant differences in tree cover under the different customary systems. In the case of agricultural land, we were unable to test the hypothesis because there was hardly any variation in tree cover change on agricultural land (this result itself suggests that residence patterns have had little impact on tree cover on agricultural land).

Econometric Testing

Although expected profits feature as a key factor in our framework, we have no way of directly measuring the profits of alternative activities. Instead, we use proxies to reflect prices and productivity and include tenure variables to proxy for the probability of realizing expected returns. Prices are determined by relative factor endowments and market access, which are captured by population density, proportion of land under agriculture in base year, distance to paved road, and distance to major urban center. Productivity is captured by environmental variables such as soil type and annual rainfall.

In Uganda tenure refers to the three broad tenure regimes found in the study sites: *mailo*, public, and customary tenure. Specifically, the proportions of land under each of two tenure categories were used as explanatory variables (the third tenure category is the base case for comparison). These tenure measures can be reasonably considered exogenous to the communities. Some further distinctions within these categories, such as the degree of individualization of rights or the degree of absentee ownership in *mailo* tenure, are also tested.

In Malawi the tenure variable is the proportion of plots acquired through the wife's family and as such is an index of the importance of the matrilocal system. This variable could be treated as endogenous because communities and families have some latitude in determining land acquisition methods. We do include this as a dependent variable in a single-equation model and present the results. Using this variable, actual or predicted, in second-stage regressions on land use change, tree cover change, or yield change resulted in insignificant coefficients in all cases. We found, however, that by specifying an interaction between the tenure variable and the geographic (and therefore ethnic) zone, we obtained some interesting results. Unfortunately, it is difficult to endogenize the interaction terms through estimation. Thus the tenure variables are assumed to be exogenous, and in all cases we estimate the equations independently. In Malawi we also estimated the three natural resource management equations simultaneously using three-stage least squares. Those results are essentially the same as the two-stage results reported here.

The econometric models tested are shown in Table 4.4.

Empirical Findings

Before turning to the specific findings, we should emphasize that the explanatory power of the models is very high. In Malawi adjusted *R*-squared measures ranged from .52 to .80 in most equations, and in Uganda the same values ranged from .52 to .72. There were also several significant variables in each equation, and we now discuss these in more detail.

TABLE 4.4 Econometric models tested and methods applied

Model tested	Method applied
Uganda	
Land use change = f (tenure, profit indicators, productivity indicators)	OLS, 64 observations
Tree cover change in agricultural land = f (tenure, profit indicators, productivity indicators)	OLS, 42 observations
Tree cover change in nonagricultural land = f (tenure, profit indicators, productivity indicators)	OLS, 67 observations (from 42 sites)
Malawi	
Proportion of plots acquired through matrilineal ties = f (profit indicators, productivity indicators)	Two-stage least squares, 57 observations
Tree cover change in nonagricultural land = f (tenure, profit indicators, tree characteristics, yield change, land use change)	Two-stage least squares, 57 observations
Land use change = f (tenure, profit indicators, productivity indicators, tree cover change, yield change)	Two-stage least squares, 57 observations

Uganda

The results in Table 4.5 show that the type of land tenure regime affects the change in agricultural land share. Customary tenure is positively related (in comparison with public land) to agricultural land conversion in all models. This result could imply the existence of weak indigenous institutional management of lands in which land clearing is not regulated. It could, however, also indicate a purposeful strategy on the part of indigenous institutions to respond to demands for agricultural land by its ever-increasing constituents. There is no significant difference in land use change between *mailo* and public tenure systems in any of the models. This finding may be related to the fact that individual owners (on *mailo* land) and the government (on public land) exercise some control over conversion of these lands.

Population variables were extremely important in explaining land use change. Increased agricultural land share was linked to higher population growth and higher population density, the latter at a nonlinear decreasing rate. The coefficient on the 1960 share of agricultural land was negative and very strong; this result is expected because at higher share levels, the potential for additional expansion is less. Distance to a paved road was positively and sig-

TABLE 4.5 Two-stage least squares independent regression models for Uganda

Variable	Change in share of agricultural land	Tree cover change on agricultural land	Tree cover change on nonagricultural land
Constant	.012	.523**	−.837**
	(0.71)	(2.21)	(−3.12)
Share of custom-	.181**	0.47	−.052
ary tenure	(2.08)	(0.69)	(−1.00)
Share of *mailo*	.026	.187*	−.011
tenure	(0.28)	(1.91)	(−0.27)
1960 population	.0020**	.00035	.0010
density	(2.52)	(0.32)	(0.88)
1960 population	−.000003**	.0000003	−.000003**
density squared	(−1.96)	(0.29)	(−2.49)
Population growth	0.33**	−.0127	.065**
(predicted value)	(2.00)	(−0.65)	(2.79)
Number of dry	.0008	.00001	.0055**
days	(0.90)	(0.01)	(3.76)
Sandy soil		−.129**	.181**
		(−2.85)	(3.40)
Distance to paved	.0022**	−.0028**	.0028**
road	(2.60)	(−2.64)	(2.29)
Distance to	−.00002	.0002	−.0004
Kampala	(−0.07)	(0.43)	(−1.20)
1960 share of	−.651**	−.362**	.356**
agriculture land	(−7.67)	(−3.26)	(2.90)
1960 agricultural		−.971**	−.291*
tree cover		(−6.41)	(−1.93)
1960 nonagricul-		−.076	−.520**
tural tree cover		(−0.76)	(−5.29)
Coffee important		.063	
crop		(1.45)	
Adjusted *R*-squared	.59	.72	.52

SOURCE: IFPRI-ICRAF survey, 1996, and authors' calculations.

NOTE: Numbers in parentheses are *t*-statistics.

**—significant at 5 percent level.

*—significant at 10 percent level.

nificantly related to increased agricultural land share in all cases, probably because land near main roads was already converted before 1960.

Table 4.5 also shows the results from the tree cover change regression on agricultural and nonagricultural land respectively. Among tenure variables, the main effect found was that tree cover change on agricultural land was positively related to *mailo* tenure (compared with public land). Positive tree cover change was also stronger on *mailo* land dominated by resident owners than by absentee owners (results not shown in the table). These results support our hypothesis that the highly individual rights to land and trees on *mailo* land (compared with public land) lead to greater incentives for long-term investment in trees, especially where *mailo* owners are resident. No other tenure variables were statistically significant. This finding indicates, among other things, that trees on nonagricultural land are managed similarly under different tenure systems.

Population density and population growth had much less impact on tree cover change than on land use change. The exception was the positive and statistically significant relationship between predicted population growth and tree cover on nonagricultural land. The reason for this result is not apparent, but the variable may be picking up the effect of the 1980–86 war, which may have simultaneously ravaged vegetation cover and lowered population growth in these sites.[11] This finding indicates that although increased population unambiguously leads to conversion of land to agriculture, the effect of population on tree cover or its change on agricultural or nonagricultural land is ambiguous.

Although several other results are statistically significant, we highlight only three. Distance from a paved road was negatively related to the change in agricultural tree cover but positively related to the change in tree cover on nonagricultural lands. Although both results together suggest that in areas near paved roads, incentives for exploiting trees are greater, only on agricultural land, where tenure is individualized, has this incentive led to improved long-term tree management. The coffee variable was not significant, showing that tree cover change did not depend exclusively upon increased coffee plantings, although these certainly contributed to improved tree cover. Lastly, the strong negative signs on the 1960 tree cover variables reveal that individuals and communities are induced to react to the increasing scarcity value of trees by planting and protecting tree resources.

Malawi

The first column of Table 4.6 shows the results of a regression model explaining the prevalence of the matrilocal system. Prevalence of the matrilocal system was found to be related to the southern zone, the non-Chewa matrilineal groups, closer proximity to paved roads, and further distance from major cities. These results show that the non-Chewa groups are more likely than the Chewa to retain their traditional matrilineal practices and differentiate themselves from patrilocal groups. The Chewa, especially in the north-central zone, are more likely to change these practices. In areas more remote from major cities, tradi-

---

11. Indeed the effect disappears when a dummy variable for parishes strongly affected by the war is included. The war dummy itself was not significantly related to land use or tree cover change when included.

tions appear to be better maintained. Proximity to roads has the opposite effect of proximity to cities and is difficult to explain. Interestingly, neither population pressure nor population growth had a significant impact on the pace of change in traditional inheritance practices.

Both tenure and population density had statistically significant impacts on land use change. Conversion of woodlands into agricultural land was accelerated in patrilocal areas relative to matrilocal areas, but in the southern region only. Within the southern region, more patrilocal practices indicate areas experiencing more profound changes to the traditional system. Thus greater change in the traditional tenure system is associated with greater land use conversion.

Population density has the expected positive but diminishing effect on the rate of conversion of woodlands to agricultural land. Population growth, however, was not significantly related to conversion. The initial share of agricultural land was negatively related to conversion as expected. The initial log of maize yield was significant and had a positive effect on conversion, also as expected. Greater conversion to agriculture is associated with faster loss of nonagricultural tree cover. This situation would be anticipated if the resulting loss in tree cover lowered profits of woodlands relative to profits from conversion to agriculture.

The change in woodland tree density is found to be related to tenure but not in the manner hypothesized. In the northern region more matrilocal systems led to faster decline in tree cover. In the north-central region, however, the presence of matrilocal systems appears to increase tree cover. Tenure did not play a role in the more densely settled southern region. A consistent explanation for this result is that faster loss of trees is associated with the influx of migrant groups—the matrilineal groups into the patrilineal north and the patrilineal groups into the Chewa-dominated north-central region. The influx of migrants may make the creation and enforcement of conservation rules more difficult.

The proportion of land under Village Forest Areas had a positive effect on tree cover change (as seen in smaller decreases in tree cover). Respondents identified Village Forest Areas as specially managed areas, implemented with the assistance of the Forest Department. Since our surveys suggested that these areas are very small, the presence of a Village Forest Area may also proxy for a broader interest in managing tree resources. The change in tree density was strongly and negatively related to the initial period tree cover, suggesting that change is more rapid when the scarcity value is lower. Tree cover loss was found to be more severe in areas farther from major cities. This result is contrary to expectations but may simply mean that woodlands nearer to cities were cleared before 1970 (as would be expected under virtual open-access conditions). Tree density loss has been greater in the north-central region, which is characterized by estate development and high wood demands for tobacco drying and curing. Loss of tree density has also been greater in the southern region, where demand for wood for fuel and shelter is acute.

TABLE 4.6 Two-stage least squares regressions for extent of matrilineal system, land use change, and tree cover change in Malawi

Varible	Extent of matrilineal system	Change in share of agricultural land	Tree cover change on nonagricultural land
Constant	−13.762	−.919*	.406*
	(−1.22)	(−1.84)	(1.74)
North-central zone	−.039	−.099	−.441**
	(−0.24)	(−0.70)	(−3.46)
Southern zone	.309**	−.081	−.423**
	(2.16)	(−0.56)	(−4.78)
Percentage of population	.0002		.0004
of main ethnic group	(0.10)		(0.93)
1970 population density	.007	.011*	.002
	(1.19)	(1.95)	(0.46)
1970 population	−.00003	−.00005*	−.00001
density squared	(−1.04)	(−1.65)	(−0.50)
Log of distance to	−.061**	−.011	.003
tarmac	(−2.32)	(−0.61)	(0.25)
Log of distance from	.065*	.028	−.026**
tarmac to major city	(1.94)	(1.14)	(−2.52)
1970 log of yield		.108**	
		(2.01)	
1970 share of land in	−.006	−.588**	−.109
agriculture	(−0.03)	(−3.00)	(−0.93)
1970 woodland tree			−.748**
cover			(−6.06)
1970 census area tree		−.272	
cover		(−0.59)	
Proportion of trees that			.045
coppice well			(1.37)
1970 percentage of			.002**
Village Forest Area			(2.83)
to total area			
Log of trees planted by			−.001
external projects			(−0.23)
1970 percentage of		.002*	.0004
households with		(1.66)	(0.84)
cattle			
Mean altitude		.00009	
		(0.98)	
Average years since	.007		
plots acquired	(1.23)		
Chewa ethnic group	−.126		
	(−1.37)		

TABLE 4.6 *Continued*

Varible	Extent of matrilineal system	Change in share of agricultural land	Tree cover change on nonagricultural land
Patrilineal ethnic groups	−.201** (−2.66)		
Percentage of plots acquired by women in north zone		−.419 (−1.15)	−.569** (−4.35)
Percentage of plots acquired by women in north-central zone		−.011 (−0.07)	.179* (1.89)
Percentage of plots acquired by women in south zone		−.158* (−1.66)	.044 (0.63)
Population growth[a]	.022 (0.59)	.020 (0.67)	.003 (0.15)
Change in woodland tree cover[a]		−.780** (−1.99)	
Change in yield[a]		.107 (1.18)	−.112** (−2.82)
Change in share of agricultural land[a]			−.143 (−1.25)
Adjusted *R*-squared	.59	.46	.69

SOURCE: IFPRI-ICRAF survey, 1996, and authors' calculations.

NOTES: Numbers in parentheses are *t*-statistics. Regressions are corrected for heteroscedasticity.

**—significant at 5 percent level.

*—significant at 10 percent level.

[a] Fitted values from first stage instrumental variable regression used.

Summary and Implications

Our data show that, given current conditions and institutions, conversion of land to agricultural use will continue. In Uganda the effect is mitigated significantly by relatively high tree densities on farms. Aggregate tree cover was the same in 1960 and 1995. In Malawi tree cover on farms is very low with little change. Off-farm, there is evidence of significant depletion as tree cover declined by about 33 percent between 1972 and 1996. Thus off-farm sources continue to provide a substantial amount of tree products to households and have not been replaced by agroforestry systems on farms.

What may contribute to the differences between Uganda and Malawi? A number of factors may play a role. First, there is likely more competition for land from crop enterprises in Malawi, where farmers must produce all their food crops in a single rainy season. Second, the coffee and banana systems found in many of the Ugandan sites are highly suited to integration with trees. Third, most types of vegetation grow better in Uganda thanks to favorable ecological conditions. Fourth, until very recently, Malawian farmers had a single parastatal source for all agricultural inputs. While this arrangement proved adequate for providing the inputs necessary for maize production, it offered virtually no other options for farmers, including tree seed. Such factors appear to play a stronger role than tenure factors.

To increase the tree resource base, the most promising strategy is to support tree planting in agricultural land. This strategy is compatible with farmers' incentives, as land rights are generally well established on agricultural land. Our analysis suggests that infrastructure policy can also play a catalyzing role in changing the stock of tree resources. Connection to markets enhanced agricultural tree cover in Uganda, yet they reduced tree cover on nonagricultural land. In Malawi distance to roads had a neutral effect on tree cover. The impact of infrastructure development is therefore not clear in these countries but should call into question the assumption that it will necessarily have deleterious effects on the environment.

On nonagricultural land prescriptions are less clear. Certainly, more effort is required to create awareness of the value of woodlands and to strengthen local institutional arrangements for their management. But our sites did not appear to offer good examples of such institutions.

What are some research implications? First, assessing tree cover in nonforested land is more difficult than on forested land but will be increasingly important to do. Second, one must be cautious in interpreting the results on tree cover. Tree cover may not be a good proxy of biomass and certainly cannot be used to make inferences on biodiversity. Hence, this single measure should not be overused as a proxy to assess natural resource management performance. Third, we have established no link between tree cover and social welfare. It may well be that some communities are better off after some tree cover loss, whereas others are better off after some tree cover increase.

As for our understanding of the role of tenure factors, the different approaches taken present clear trade-offs. We have selected numerous sites in order to have sufficient variation in tree cover assessments and to ensure adequate degrees of freedom to disentangle the effects of many mitigating factors. A consequence of the large sample size was the cost of obtaining in-depth information about social and economic variables at the community level. Nevertheless, we believe that the marriage of remote sensing data with primary and secondary socioeconomic and ecological data proved to be very powerful in explaining changes in land use and tree cover. These types of marriages between disciplines should be pursued.

References

Ault, D. E., and G. L. Rutman. 1979. The development of individual rights to property in tribal Africa. *Journal of Law and Economics* 22 (2): 163–182.

Bazaara, N. 1992. Land policy and the evolving forms of land tenure in Masindi District, Uganda. Centre for Basic Research Working Paper 28. Centre for Basic Research, Kampala, Uganda.

Besley, T. 1995. Property rights and investment incentives. *Journal of Political Economy* 103 (5): 903–937.

Bojo, J. 1994. The cost of land degradation from a national perspective: An assessment of African evidence. Paper presented at the Eighth International Soil Conservation Conference, New Delhi, India, December 4–8.

Boserup, E. 1965. *The conditions of agricultural growth: The economics of agrarian change under population pressure.* London: George Allen and Unwin.

Breyer, J. 1996. Land use cover change in central Uganda. Report prepared for International Food Policy Research Institute and International Centre for Research in Agroforestry, Nairobi, Kenya.

Bruce, J. 1988. Is indigenous tenure a development constraint? Land Tenure Center, University of Wisconsin. Photocopy.

Capistrano, A. D., and C. F. Kiker. 1995. Macro-scale economic influences on tropical forest depletion. *Ecological Economics* 14 (1): 21–29.

Cline-Cole, R. A., H. A. Main, and J. E. Nichol. 1990. On fuelwood consumption, population dynamics, and deforestation in Africa. *World Development* 18 (4): 513–527.

Coote, H., J. Luhanga, and J. D. Lowore. 1993a. *Community use and management of indigenous forests in Malawi: The case of chemba village forest area.* FRIM Report Number 93006. Zomba, Malawi: Forestry Research Institute of Malawi.

————. 1993b. *Community use and management of indigenous forests in Malawi: The case of three villages in the Blantyre City Fuelwood Project Area.* FRIM Report No. 93007. Zomba, Malawi: Forestry Research Institute of Malawi.

Deacon, R. 1994. Deforestation and the rule of law in a cross-section of countries. *Land Economics* 70 (4): 414–430.

Dewees, P. 1995. Trees on farms in Malawi: Private investment, public policy, and farmer choice. *World Development* 23 (7): 1085–1102.

Dickerman, C., and P. Bloch. 1991. *Land tenure and agricultural productivity in Malawi.* LTC Paper 143. Madison, Wisc., U.S.A.: Land Tenure Center.

FAO (Food and Agriculture Organization of the United Nations). 1984. *Agroclimatic data for African countries south of the equator.* Rome.

Fortmann, L., and J. Bruce. 1988. *Whose trees? Proprietary dimensions of forestry.* Boulder, Colo., U.S.A.: Westview Press.

French, D. 1986. Confronting an unsolvable problem: Deforestation in Malawi. *World Development* 14 (4): 531–540.

Green, R., and V. Mkandawire. 1997. Land relations and management of trees in Malawi: Land use change determination. Research report prepared for International Food Policy Research Institute and International Centre for Research on Agroforestry, Nairobi, Kenya.

Hayami, Y., and K. Otsuka. 1993. *The economics of contract choice: An agrarian perspective.* Oxford: Clarendon Press.

Hyde, W., and J. Seve. 1993. The economic role of wood products in tropical deforestation: The severe example of Malawi. *Forest Ecology and Management* 57 (2): 283–300.

Kahn, J. R., and J. A. McDonald. 1995. Third-world debt and tropical deforestation. *Ecological Economics* 12: 107–123.

Langdale-Brown, I. 1960. *The Vvegetation of Uganda.* Research Division, Uganda Department of Agriculture, series 2, no. 6. Kampala.

MFEP (Uganda Ministry of Finance and Economic Planning). 1992. *The 1991 population and housing census (District summary series).* Entebbe.

Migot-Adholla, S. E., and J. Bruce. 1994. Introduction: Are indigenous African tenure systems insecure? In *Searching for land tenure security in Africa,* ed. J. Bruce and S. E. Migot-Adholla. Dubuque, Ia., U.S.A.: Kendall/Hunt.

Migot-Adholla, S. E., P. Hazell, B. Blarel, and F. Place. 1991. Indigenous land rights systems in Sub-Saharan Africa: A constraint on productivity? *World Bank Economic Review* 5 (1): 155–175.

Mkandawire, R. 1983/84. Customary land, the state, and agrarian change in Malawi: The case of the Chewa peasantry in the Lilongwe Rural Development Project. *Journal of Contemporary African Studies* 3 (1/2): 109–128.

Muhereza, E. F. 1992. Land tenure and peasant adaptations: Some reflections on agricultural production in Luwero District, Uganda. Centre for Basic Research Working Paper 27. Centre for Basic Research, Kampala.

Noronha, R. 1985. *A review of the literature on land tenure systems in Sub-Saharan Africa.* World Bank Report Number ARU 43. Washington, D.C.: World Bank, Agriculture and Rural Development Department.

Otsuka, K., and F. Place. 2001. *Land tenure and natural resource management: A comparative study of agrarian communities in Asia and Africa.* Baltimore, Md., U.S.A.: Johns Hopkins University Press for the International Food Policy Research Institute.

Otsuka, K., S. Suyanto, and T. Tomich. 1997. Does tenure insecurity discourage tree planting? Agroforestry management in Sumatra. International Food Policy Research Institute, Washington, D.C. Photocopy.

Patel, S. H., T. C. Pinckney, and W. Jaeger. 1995. Smallholder wood production and population pressure in East Africa: Evidence of an environmental Kuznets curve? *Land Economics* 71 (4): 516–530.

Place, F. 1995. *The role of land tenure in the adoption of agroforestry in Burundi, Uganda, Zambia, and Malawi: A summary and synthesis.* Land Tenure Center Report. Madison, Wisc., U.S.A.: Land Tenure Center.

Place, F., and K. Otsuka. 2000. Population pressure, land tenure, and tree resource management in Uganda. *Land Economics* 76 (2): 233–251.

———. 2001. Population, tenure, and natural resource management: The case of customary land area in Malawi. *Journal of Environmental Economics and Management* 41 (1): 13–32.

Scherr, S. 1995. Economic factors in farmer adoption of agroforestry: Patterns observed in western Kenya. *World Development* 23 (5): 787–804.

Southgate, D., R. Sierra, and L. Brown. 1991. The causes of tropical deforestation in Ecuador: A statistical analysis. *World Development* 19 (9): 1145–1151.

World Bank. 1993. *Uganda: Agriculture.* World Bank Country Study. Washington, D.C.

———. 1994. *World development report 1994.* Washington, D.C.

———. 1995. *World development report 1995.* Washington, D.C.

———. 1996. *African development indicators for 1996.* Washington, D.C.

World Resources Institute. 1994. *World resources 1994–95.* New York: Oxford University Press.

5 Measuring the Production Efficiency of Alternative Land Tenure Contracts in a Mixed Crop-Livestock System in Ethiopia

SARAH GAVIAN AND SIMEON EHUI

Many agricultural policy decisions in Sub-Saharan Africa are affected by the belief that land must be privatized or that people should have exclusive and secure rights on their lands (such as titled lands). An important argument in favor of land reforms is that farmland held under exclusive and secure land rights is more productive than farmland held under other forms of land rights. If this argument is true then reforms that involve titling lands or individualizing land rights should improve production efficiency. The hypothesized greater production efficiency of privatized lands, however, may be an illusion if other public policies, such as provision of rural infrastructure, promotion of market efficiency, dissemination of information about new technologies, and access to credit, are not in place (Atwood 1990). From a public policy viewpoint, better information on the true relative efficiency of farmlands under different tenure contracts would provide a better indication of how land tenure systems affect resource use and thereby the overall productivity of farming operations. If we can measure the relative efficiency of alternative land tenure systems, we can then determine the productivity gains possible through land reforms. If land tenure arrangements are major sources of productivity differences, then efforts to develop technologies will be secondary to land reform policies.

Although the question of relative production efficiency of indigenous land rights is central to a discussion of land reform in Sub-Saharan Africa, there is relatively little rigorous empirical research because of a lack of adequate disaggregated data. With the exception of few studies (Place and Hazell 1993; Besley 1994; Bruce, Migot-Adholla, and Atherton 1994; Gavian and Fafchamps 1996; Hayes, Roth, and Zepeda 1997), the subject has not benefited from rigorous empirical analysis. Further, most studies have covered only areas of rain-fed agriculture. Questions remain about the suitability of indigenous land rights for irrigated farming, extensive pastoral and livestock-based systems, and communal forestry areas (Place and Hazell 1993).

This chapter was previously published as Gavian and Ehui (1998) and is reproduced with permission from Elsevier Science. The authors thank Charles F. Nicholson, Mohammad Jabbar, and two anonymous referees for very helpful comments and suggestions.

The objective of this chapter is to determine the relative production efficiency of alternative land tenure arrangements and the sources of differences in productivity levels using Ethiopia as a case study. In 1974 the country nationalized rural lands, redistributing land use rights "to-the-tillers" but maintaining landownership in the hands of the state. Land sales were outlawed. Tenancy relations, such as sharecropping and renting, were prohibited. In recent years the country has lifted restrictions on informal land transactions, and farmers currently have an array of formal and informal means of obtaining land. The varying degrees of security and rights associated with these arrangements make Ethiopia appropriate for a case study of differences in productivity with land tenure.

The current study differs in several ways from similar studies by Place and Hazell (1993), Besley (1994), Gavian and Fafchamps (1996), and Hayes, Roth, and Zepeda (1997). First, it focuses on a farming system in which livestock not only contribute 40 percent of the country's agricultural gross domestic product, but also provide most of the power for plowing and threshing. Second, the data used for the analysis were highly detailed, based on repeated short-term (three-day) recall and actual measured yields, rather than end-of-season recall and qualitative measures. Unlike most other studies, actual labor hours per plot were collected. Finally, where most studies have attempted to gauge efficiency from econometric estimation of reduced-form production functions, this analysis relies on the concept of interspatial total factor productivity (TFP) as defined by Denny and Fuss (1980, 1983). The TFP method is well suited to the complexity and diversity of smallholder farming because it summarizes across fields with varying inputs and outputs. The use of TFP methods permits comparisons across systems with multiple outputs. Thus while controlling for differences in input levels, it is possible to examine differences in the output of land under different tenure arrangements. The TFP method does not isolate the impact of long-term investment. It rather focuses on allocation of variable input levels.

Land Tenure Issues in Sub-Saharan Africa

Despite the large body of literature, the degree to which prevailing land tenure contracts constrain agricultural productivity in Sub-Saharan Africa is unresolved. Some authors argue that informal contractual tenure arrangements (such as tenancy or sharecropping) and other forms of indigenous land tenure rights result in an inefficient allocation of resources as well as reduced incentives to improve agricultural lands (Hayami and Otsuka 1993). The argument is that land tenure arrangements that assign land rights either to the community or to a landlord rather than to the principal land user discourage investment in land improvements. Individual farmers without secure private rights may not be able to fully claim the returns on their investments in land or attached to land. Informal contractual tenure arrangements may fail to promote investments required for conservation. Accordingly, reforms such as the privatization of land rights, the abolition of sharecropping, and land redistributions are viewed as policy instruments that can improve agricultural productivity (Dorner 1977; Ip and Stahl 1978; Harrison 1987; Hayes, Roth, and Zepeda 1997).

Other authors, however, argue that the form of land tenure has little bearing upon allocative efficiency and attribute the poverty of the agricultural sector in Sub-Saharan Africa to agricultural factor endowments and public policies other than land tenure. This second school of thought cites evidence that indigenous tenure arrangements are dynamic and evolve in response to factor price changes. They argue that privatization of land rights, whereby farm households acquire a complete set of transfer and exclusive rights over land, occurs with increases in population pressure and agricultural commercialization (Cohen 1980; Boserup 1981; Noronha 1985; Feder and Noronha 1987; Pinckney and Kimuyu 1994; Platteau 1996). Place and Hazell (1993) found that land rights were not significantly related to yields in Ghana, Kenya, and Rwanda, thus undermining the common view that land rights constrain agricultural productivity. They further concluded that lack of access to credit, insufficient human capital, and labor shortages adversely affect investment decisions more than insecurity of tenure. Gavian and Fafchamps (1996) tested whether traditional land tenure systems allocate land efficiently and whether insecurity affects the manner in which households allocate manure (a short- to medium-run land improvement strategy) among their fields. They found evidence that tenure insecurity incites farmers to divert soil-enhancing resources to more secure fields whenever possible. On the other hand, they found no significant relationships between manuring and whether or not local customs allowed land sales.

The Conceptual Framework

Most productivity analyses are based on partial productivity measures such as yield per hectare (land productivity) or output per person (labor productivity). Such productivity measures can be misleading if considerable input substitution occurs as a result of widely differing input prices due to market imperfections. Although partial productivity measures provide insights into the efficiency of an input in the production process, they mask many of the factors accounting for observed productivity growth or differentials.

A conceptually superior way to estimate productivity—and therefore efficiency—is to measure total factor productivity. TFP is defined as the ratio of aggregate outputs to aggregate inputs used in the agricultural production process. There are two basic approaches to the measurement of productivity: the growth accounting approach, which is based on index numbers, and the parametric approach, which is based on an econometric estimation of production, cost, or profit functions. In this chapter, we use the index number approach for three reasons. First, with the index number approach, detailed data with many input and output categories can be used regardless of the number of observations over time. Therefore no problems of degrees of freedom or statistical reliability arise in working with small samples. Second, there is no need to aggregate outputs into a single index, and we thus avoid input-output separability assumptions. Finally, under certain technical and market conditions, the econometric and index number approaches are found to be equivalent. Advances in growth accounting theory have shown that nonparametric methods do indeed impose an implicit structure on the aggregate production technology (Ohta 1974; Diewert 1976, 1981; Denny, Fuss, and May 1981).

The major difficulty with the index number approach is to derive aggregate output and input measures that represent the numerous outputs and inputs involved in most production processes. Earlier approaches to TFP used a Laspeyres or Paasch weighting system, in which base period prices were used as aggregation weights. The Laspeyres or Paasch indexing procedure is inexact, however, except when the production function is linear and all inputs are perfect substitutes in the relevant range (Christensen 1975; Diewert 1976). The most popular indexing procedure is the Divisia index, which is exact for the case of homogenous translog functions (Capalbo and Antle 1988). The translog function does not require inputs to be perfect substitutes, but rather permits all marginal productivities to adjust proportionally to changing prices. Hence the prices from both production systems being compared enter the Divisia index to represent the differing marginal productivities. There have been relatively few applications of this approach in the context of farming systems. Ehui and Spencer (1993) have used the Divisia approach to TFP to measure the sustainability and economic viability of alternative farming systems in Nigeria.

Assume that the agricultural process in land held under tenure system i at time t can be represented by the production function:

$$Q_{it} = F(X_{it}, T_{it}, D_i) \qquad (1)$$

where Q_{it} is the output level on a plot under tenure system i at time t, $\{X_{it}\}$ is a vector of factor inputs, T_{it} is an index of technology, and $\{D_i\}$ is a vector of dummy variables for every tenure system other than the reference base system.[1] T_{it} and $\{D_i\}$ denote also intertemporal and interspatial efficiency difference indicators. Equation (1) assumes that the production function in each tenure system has common elements as well as differences resulting from the tenure arrangement, which are maintained by the additional argument D.

Suppose that we wanted to know the difference between the level of output on land held under tenure system i at time s and land held under tenure sys-

---

1. This section is based on Denny and Fuss (1980, 1983).

tem o at time t. Application of Diewert's (1976) quadratic lemma[2] to a logarithmic approximation of (1) gives:

$$
\begin{aligned}
\Delta \ln Q &= \ln Q_{is} - \ln Q_{ot} \\
&= \frac{1}{2} \sum_k \left[\frac{\partial \ln F}{\partial \ln X_k} \Big|_{x_k = x_{kis}} + \frac{\partial \ln F}{\partial \ln X_k} \Big|_{x_k = x_{kot}} \right] [\ln x_{kis} - \ln x_{kot}] \\
&= \frac{1}{2} \left[\frac{\partial \ln F}{\partial D_i} \Big|_i + \frac{\partial \ln F}{\partial D_i} \Big|_o \right] [D_i - D_o] \\
&= \frac{1}{2} \left[\frac{\partial \ln F}{\partial \ln T} \Big|_{T - T_{is}} + \frac{\partial \ln F}{\partial \ln T} \Big|_{T - T_{ot}} \right] [\ln T_{is} - \ln T_{ot}] \qquad (2)
\end{aligned}
$$

Let us define the interspatial (that is, tenure) effect as:

$$
\theta_{io} = \frac{1}{2} \left[\frac{\partial \ln F}{\partial D_i} \Big|_i + \frac{\partial \ln F}{\partial D_i} \Big|_o \right] [D_i - D_o] \qquad (3)
$$

and the intertemporal effect as:

$$
\mu_{st} = \frac{1}{2} \left[\frac{\partial \ln F}{\partial \ln T} \Big|_{T - T_{is}} + \frac{\partial \ln F}{\partial \ln T} \Big|_{T - T_{ot}} \right] [\ln T_{is} - \ln T_{ot}] \qquad (4)
$$

Constant returns to scale and perfect competition in input and output markets implies that $(\partial \ln F / \partial \ln X_k) = s_k$, where the term s_k represents the cost share for the kth input. Using these assumptions, we can rewrite (2) as:

$$
\Delta \ln Q = \frac{1}{2} \sum_k [S_{kis} + S_{kot}][\ln X_{kis} - \ln X_{kot}] + \theta_{io} + \mu_{st} \qquad (5)
$$

From equation (5) the output differential across tenure systems and time periods may be broken down into a factor intensity effect, a tenure system effect, and an intertemporal effect.

Let A denote the land input. Equation (5) can be rewritten as:

$$
\Delta \ln \left(\frac{Q}{A} \right) = \frac{1}{2} \sum_{k \neq A} [S_{kis} + S_{kot}] \left[\ln \left(\frac{X_{kis}}{A_{is}} \right) - \ln \left(\frac{X_{kot}}{A_{ot}} \right) \right] + \theta_{io} + \mu_{st} \qquad (6)
$$

---

2. Diewert's (1976) quadratic lemma basically states that if a function is quadratic, the difference between the function's values evaluated at two points is equal to the average of the gradient evaluated at both points multiplied by the difference between the points:

$$
F(Z^1) - F(Z^0) = \frac{1}{2} [F(Z^1) + F(Z^0)]^T (Z^1 - Z^0)
$$

where $F(Z^r)$ is the gradient vector of F evaluated at Z^r, $r = 0,1$.

where $\Delta \ln(Q/A)$ denotes the change in land productivity levels.[3] The first expression on the right-hand side of (6) denotes the weighted sum of differences in the level of factor intensities. Let us define this expression as:

$$\rho_{io} = \frac{1}{2} \sum_{k \neq A} [S_{kis} + S_{kot}] \left[\ln\left(\frac{X_{kis}}{A_{is}}\right) - \ln\left(\frac{X_{kot}}{A_{ot}}\right) \right] \qquad (7)$$

The difference in land productivity can therefore be decomposed into three effects: (1) a factor intensity effect ρ_{io}; (2) a tenure system effect (θ_{io}), and (3) an intertemporal effect (μ_{st}). If we want to measure the production efficiency levels across tenure systems at a given point in time (where $t = s$), we rearrange the terms to isolate the tenure effect:

$$\theta_{io} = \left[\ln\left(\frac{Q}{A}\right)_i - \ln\left(\frac{Q}{A}\right)_o \right] - \frac{1}{2} \sum_{k \neq A} [S_{ki} + S_{ko}] \left[\ln\left(\frac{X_{ki}}{A_i}\right) - \ln\left(\frac{X_{ko}}{A_o}\right) \right] \qquad (8)$$

The expression θ_{io} is the Tornqvist-Theil approximation (Tornqvist 1936; Capalbo and Antle 1988) to the change in productivity levels due to the type of tenure contract at a particular point in time. The difference in the TFP of two systems is a function of differences in land productivities and factor intensities. Factor intensities are the weighted sum of differences in the level of variable inputs applied per unit of land.

In the case of multiple outputs, the Tornqvist-Theil quantity index can also be used to aggregate the various outputs into a single index:

$$\left[\ln\left(\frac{Q}{A}\right)_i - \ln\left(\frac{Q}{A}\right)_o \right] = \frac{1}{2} \sum_j [r_{ji} + r_{jo}] \left[\ln\left(\frac{Q_j}{A_j}\right)_i - \ln\left(\frac{Q_j}{A_j}\right)_o \right] \qquad (9)$$

where r_{ij} and r_{io} denote the jth output revenue share in systems i and o, respectively. Q_j denotes the jth output level.

Equation (8) indicates that there are two components that contribute to any observed differences in TFP. First are changes in the level of land productivity. This is the major component underlying TFP differentials. Second are changes in factor intensities. TFP is therefore the residual, or the portion of change in output levels not explicitly explained by changes in input levels. Increases in factor intensities may occur, however, without any increases in TFP. Changes in TFP levels and factor intensities are not independent, but they are of different significance. Increases in TFP will occur if land productivity increases proportionally more than increases in factor intensity levels. But increases in land productivity that are due to increases in factor intensities are qualitatively

---

3. Dividing by A is the equivalent of presenting agricultural data on a per unit area basis (for example, per hectare or acre). The final TFP figures are the same whether or not land is used as a numeraire, but the interpretation of the components does not correspond to those described in equation (8).

(although not quantitatively) less significant than changes in TFP. Indeed land productivity will increase if a farmer applies more purchased inputs. Unless there are improvements in the use of these inputs, this increase will be a change in factor intensity and not TFP. It is clear that with TFP changes, in contrast to factor intensity differentials, the farmer's capability to produce more with the same resources has improved.[4]

Study Area and Data Collection

Since 1975 all rural lands in Ethiopia have been owned by the government in the name of the people. Lands were nationalized in a countrywide campaign, expropriated from both large landlords and small peasant farmers alike. Control over this precious resource was given to the representatives of lowest level of government, the Peasant Association (PA). PA officials periodically redistributed land between households based primarily on family size. To be eligible for land at the time of the next distribution, a farmer was required to register with the Peasant Association at age 18 or when he married.[5] When the transitional government of Ethiopia took power in 1991, it imposed a moratorium on land distributions until such time as a new land policy was formulated. Although the Constitution of 1994 reiterated the inability of private citizens to own or sell land, it remained vague on the question of land distribution. To this day, this policy has yet to be clarified, although some regions of the country have undertaken or are planning rural land redistributions.[6] The International Livestock Research Institute (ILRI) conducted a study in 1994 to present evidence on ways farmers in the Ethiopian highlands gain access to land and the production and management strategies they use to cultivate and maintain that resource.

Study Area

The study area was selected from one of the most productive regions of the country, the Arsi zone of Oromia region. Four Peasant Associations in the Tiyo

---

4. Although this study focuses on only one time period, the general expression shown in equation (6) can be specialized to provide a comparison of the rate of growth of productivity due to technical change for a particular system over time ($D_i = D_o$ and $s = t+1$):

$$\mu_{t+1,t} = \left[\ln\left(\frac{Q}{A}\right)_{t+1} - \ln\left(\frac{Q}{A}\right)_t \right] - \frac{1}{2}\sum_{k \neq A}[S_{k,t+1} + S_{kt}]\left[\ln\left(\frac{X_{k,t+1}}{A_{t+1}}\right) - \ln\left(\frac{X_{kt}}{A_t}\right)\right]$$

$\mu_{t+1,t}$ measures the intertemporal TFP of a production system over two periods. It is the Tornqvist-Theil approximation to the change in productivity levels due to technical change.

5. The original law did not distinguish between men and women. In practice, however, women are usually registered as independent PA members and allocated land in their names when, for some reason, they could not depend on their spouse for land, as with widows, divorcees, and wives in polygamous marriages.

6. For a more thorough description of the recent evolution of land tenure legislation in Ethiopia, see Girma and Asfaw (1996).

woreda (district)—Abichu, Bilalo, Ketar Genet, and Mekro Chebote—were selected for their varying altitudes and thus mix of crop and livestock activities. A census carried out in March 1994 provided a sampling frame for classifying households based on their official access to state lands. Households classified as PA members were those that had received at least one crop or pasture field from the government. The second tenure class was made up of households that had not yet acquired either crop or pastureland from the government (NPA) but were farming land acquired from their PA neighbors through various informal contracts. The census indicated that in the total farming population of 1,671 households, 83 percent were PA members and the other 17 percent were not. To determine the appropriate sample size for both the PA and non–Peasant Association (NPA) samples, the Weyman procedure (Cochrane 1963) was applied to gauge the variability of the key agricultural variables in the census data by tenure class. Based on these results, a random sample of 161 households was selected from the census list, composed of 115 PA and 46 NPA households.

These households controlled 510 crop fields from which a final sample of 317 crop fields was selected. Each of the sampled crop fields was subdivided where necessary into plots, where a plot was defined as a distinct management unit owing to the farmer's choice to plant a unique crop or intercrop there. Not only were crops such as barley, wheat, and teff,[7] distinguished from one another, but so too were the subvarieties within these categories. Some fields were made up of only one plot, while others had as many as 10 plots. The sampled crop fields contained 477 separate plots for which input and output data were collected.

Input data were collected on all inputs used on each plot during the main 1994 growing season (from April to December 1994). These were collected twice weekly by asking the farmer to recall activities on that particular plot during the past three days. Data included labor time (by source, gender, age, and field operation), as well as the quantities of traction (oxen and tractors), seed, fertilizers, pesticides, and herbicides employed. The prices of all purchased inputs were likewise recorded at this time.

Output data were gathered on the total quantity of all cereals, pulses, and residues harvested from each plot on the field. Enumerators weighed the full amount of off-take after threshing and winnowing operations.

In a separate survey, the prices of all crops and residues were collected in each of the two major rural markets frequented by farmers from these PAs: Asella and Ketar Genet markets. Twice monthly, enumerators recorded prices from three samples of each crop species and subvariety found on the sampled plots.

---

7. *Eragrostis tef.*

Description of Land Contracts in the Survey Region

There are many arrangements under which farmers gain access to crop land in Ethiopia. As already stated, the only official contract is with the government, through the PA. Numerous informal contracts also exist unofficially between farmers without involving the PA. Whereas patterns of land transactions vary greatly between regions of the country, the results of our census showed that in 1994 in Tiyo *woreda*, 76 percent of all fields were allocated by the PA. The remaining 24 percent were farmed under some sort of informal contract between farmers.

NPA farmers relied solely on informal contracts, whereas PA farmers relied on both formal contracts with the government and informal contracts between themselves. The census indicated that more than one-fifth of the PA households exported, or contracted out, one of their fields, and about the same proportion imported, or contracted in, at least one field. A very small proportion (2 percent) both imported and exported land, perhaps to lessen the distances they had to walk to their fields. More than half of the PA households farmed only the lands they had been allocated by the PA.

Based on differences in the nature of these contracts—in terms of duration, rights, and costs—we have grouped fields into four categories: PA-allocated, rented, sharecropped, and borrowed.

PA fields are those that were allocated directly to the farmer by PA officials. Because no farmer has a permanent, legally defensible claim to land, even PA contracts have a fairly short-term duration. PA-allocated fields are held longer, however, and have a greater range of rights than the informally contracted fields. The average PA-allocated field had been used by the current farmer two and a half to four times longer than the average contracted field (depending on the type of contract). Furthermore, the duration of the current contract on PA-allocated fields was indefinite, whereas most contracted fields had only one-year contracts (Table 5.1).

Most farmers on PA-allocated fields felt able to exercise most of the usufruct rights shown in Table 5.1. About one-fifth believed they could not build wells, stone bunds, or permanent fences of metal or stone, but these responses may reflect their desire rather than their right (the distinction is difficult to make to farmers because the concept of rights is rather abstract). In contrast, farmers on the informally contracted fields felt substantially more restricted in all activities except the right to choose the crop they planted. Structural changes, fallowing, and subcontracting out the land were less possible for farmers with informal land contracts.

Although PA members were required to pay taxes, that tax was unrelated to amount of crop- or pastureland they received. In 1994 PA members were taxed 22 Ethiopian birr (EB) per household, which, at an average holding of about 2.9 hectares, equals about 7.5 EB per hectare (or $US1.20 per hectare). Essentially, therefore, PA-allocated lands were free.

TABLE 5.1 Frequency and nature of land contracts in the Arsi zone in Ethiopia

	PA-allocated fields	Informally contracted fields		
		Rented	Sharecropped	Borrowed/gift
Share of contracts for cropped fields users (%)	83	5	4	7
PA member households	100	18	76	64
Landless households	0	83	24	36
Number of years field used by current farmer	8	2	3	3
Duration of current contract (%)	100	100	100	100
One year	0	91	63	16
Two years	0	6	7	2
Three or more years	0	0	7	0
Permanent/indefinite	100	3	23	81
Proof of contract (% of fields)	100	100	100	100
None required	0	27	77	96
Witnesses required	100	8	0	0
Written contract	0	65	23	4
Share of fields for which user holds the following rights (%)				
Unrestricted crop choice	100	100	100	97
Fallow for one year	96	87	33	16
Fallow for more than one year	95	64	8	13
Plant trees	92	75	12	19
Install a well or pump	77	75	12	19
Build stone bunds	79	82	37	35
Build fence from natural materials	93	89	34	55
Build fence from stone or metal	79	68	14	32
Share out	98	64	53	6
Rent out	97	62	44	6
Lend out	96	61	45	6
Bequeath out	99	68	34	6

SOURCE: ILRI Field Management Survey: Rights Survey.

Rented fields are those for which a fixed cash sum is paid—usually in advance—by the tenant to the landholder. The renter-tenant pays for all inputs and reaps all benefits (or losses) of his cropping activities. Of the informally contracted fields, rented fields have the shortest leases. The average renter operated under a one-year agreement that was less often extended than agreements established by borrowers or sharecroppers (as indicated by the number of years the field had actually been used in Table 5.1). As on all informally contracted fields, the range of use and modification rights was more restricted on rented fields than it was on PA-allocated fields. Compared with the users of other types of contracted fields, however, renters had the broadest range of rights. They also were the most likely to have a written contract. The average cost of renting a field in the survey area was 352 EB per hectare in 1994 (US$56 per hectare). Rented fields made up about 8 percent of all cropped lands in Tiyo *woreda* in 1994 and 33 percent of the area's contracted fields.

Sharecropped fields involve a commitment by both partners to share the costs of the inputs and the benefits of the outputs.[8] Sharecropped fields were held somewhat longer than rented fields, with 23 percent under long-term agreements and an average holding time of three years (Table 5.1). The reverse is true in terms of rights; the considerably more restricted range of rights on sharecropped than rented fields reflects the lack of autonomy for the share-tenant in this partnership. In the survey year the cost of the sharecropped contract was two and a half times greater than that of rented fields. After deducting the landholder's share of all labor and inputs from his or her share of the outputs, the average cost of a sharecropped contract was 935 EB per hectare (US$148 per hectare).[9] Sharecropped fields made up 4 percent of all cropped lands in Tiyo *woreda* in 1994 and 17 percent of the area's contracted fields.

Borrowed and gift fields are those the landholder gives to the user free of charge. Borrowed fields are lent for a defined period, whereas gift fields are usually given for a longer but indefinite period (that is, until the next land distribution). Both types of fields are almost always given by relatives, usually by parents who give out part of their holdings to their newly married family members. As offspring or relatives of the landholder, many of these farmers contributed labor to the landholders' fields. These contributions were difficult to monitor and have not been valued here. Because the basic attributes of gift and borrowed fields are very similar, they have been combined and analyzed as a unit (borrowed/gift). The duration of the average borrowed/gift contract came closest of all the three informal contracts to the PA-allocated fields, with fully 81 percent of users operating under a long-term arrangement (Table 5.1). Borrowed/gift fields had an average holding time of three years, and as relatives, the two parties rarely required a written document. The range of rights, how-

---

8. *Equl* and *Siso* are local names of the two most common contracts, meaning equal sharing and two-thirds share, respectively (from the tenant's point of view). Under either contract, the share-tenant provides most of the labor. In spite of these simplified names, there are numerous permutations on these arrangements, based on the specific endowments of the two contracting partners.

9. Note that 1994 was a good crop year in the Arsi zone, and therefore the cost of the average share contract was higher than usual.

ever, was quite restricted, roughly the same as sharecropped fields, more restricted than rented fields, and much more restricted than PA-allocated fields. As with shared fields, these restrictions represented the partnership underlying the borrowing arrangement, in this case between family members. Borrowed/gift arrangements were fairly common, making up 12 percent of all cropped lands and half of all contracted fields in 1994.

Defining Security

Theory suggests farmers will be reluctant to invest in insecure fields. But the concept of security is complex and elusive, depending on the farmer's subjective assessment of the political and legal climate. Bruce, Migot-Adholla, and Atherton (1994) describe security in terms of the formal duration of rights, the protection of rights, and the robustness of rights. The analysis by Place and Hazell (1993) employs qualitative variables to represent tenure security in terms of bundles of transfer rights: limited (cannot be permanently transferred), preferential (can be bequeathed or given), and complete (can be sold). Besley (1994) measures land tenure security in terms of two variables: the number of transfer rights the farmer can exercise without approval from the family members and the number of transfer rights for which such approval is needed.

In this study we define land tenure security as a combination of the expected longevity of the contract and the breadth of rights to carry out a range of field-related activities. Because none of the tenure contracts is long term or alienable and nearly all farmland is under exclusive control only for the duration of the growing season (becoming open to grazing animals in the dry season), the definition of security is necessarily relative. The four tenure arrangements in this study have been ranked from 1 to 4 based on the information presented in Table 5.1 in terms of (1) duration (a combination of past holding and current contract length), (2) use rights (planting, fallowing), (3) modification rights (trees, wells, fences, bunds), and (4) transfer rights (share, rent, lend, bequeath). A ranking of 4 indicates that the given tenure arrangement was superior to all the other arrangements on the particular measure; conversely a ranking of 1 indicates that tenure arrangement ranked lowest. Where there was no notable difference between two categories, an equal score was granted (Table 5.2).

This ranking procedure permits us to order the land tenure arrangements in terms of declining security: PA, rented, shared, and borrowed. Although PA-allocated lands are not "secure" in a truly long-term sense, the security offered by the government is necessarily greater than what farmers can offer each other under renting, sharecropping, and borrowing contracts. Furthermore, most farmers on PA-allocated lands claim the right to undertake important investments (modifications to the field) or transfers, whereas farmers on informally contracted fields feel unable to undertake major improvements to fields. Generally, renters have less security but a wider range of rights than either share-

TABLE 5.2 Relative ranking of security of land tenure arrangements in the Arsi zone in Ethiopia

	PA-allocated fields	Informally contracted fields		
		Rented	Sharecropped	Borrowed/gift
Duration	4	1	2	2
Use rights	4	3	2	2
Modification rights	4	3	2	2
Transfer rights	4	3	2	1
Total	16	10	7	6

NOTE: Based on the data on contract duration and rights displayed in Table 5.1, the land contracts have been ranked from 1 (least secure) to 4 (most secure). The sum of these rankings is given in the row entitled "Total" and represents a qualitative measure of tenure security.

croppers or borrowers. What distinguishes the latter two groups is the stiff price tag paid by sharecroppers in kind to the landholder.

Transforming the Production Data

For the purposes of this analysis, we hypothesize the different types of land contracts to have different effects on the structure of production in the region. We have conducted pair-wise comparisons between those lands allocated by the government (that is, PA-allocated) and each type of land received under an informal farmer-to-farmer arrangement (that is, rented, sharecropped, or borrowed lands).

To have an adequate number of observations in each field tenure class, we have restricted the analysis to wheat, barley, and legume plots, which constitute 82 percent of the plots surveyed.

Within each generic crop category (that is, wheat, barley, and legume), farmers distinguished numerous subvarieties.[10] Because not all subvarieties were found in each tenure system, grains were aggregated into three categories—wheat, barley, and legumes—and all crop residues were grouped together. Likewise, because not all inputs were used in each of the four tenure systems, more generic input categories have been formed: human labor, power (oxen and tractor), chemicals (fertilizer and herbicides), and seed.

Given that the different tenure arrangements had multiple and dissimilar crop outputs and inputs, it was necessary to aggregate the varying inputs and outputs into meaningful categories to permit application of the Tornqvist-Theil indexing procedure, as shown in equations (8) and (9). Implicit output indexes

---

10. Because these distinctions were not made by trained agronomists, we refrain from calling these cultivars.

of wheat, barley, and legumes were calculated by dividing the total value of all output by the price index obtained by weighting the individual output prices by the revenue share of each crop. A corresponding input quantity index for labor, power, chemicals, and seed was computed as the ratio of total expenditures in each input category to the weighted price index of that input. The latter was measured as an index of all prices of individual input prices weighted by the cost share of each input.

All inputs and outputs enter the calculations on a per hectare basis; land enters the model with a quantity value of one along with the associated per hectare price for each tenure category. This method of including land as a numeraire permits the output and input components to be interpreted as land productivity and factor intensity, respectively, as shown in equation (8).

The prices used for these models were derived from several sources. Output and seed prices were drawn from the twice-monthly survey of retail prices in the two major markets in the area. Based on the observation that most farmers market their crops in the three months following harvest, the December through February price average was used to represent output prices. Based on the similar observation that seeding is carried out in May and June, the average of the market prices for these months was used to represent the value of seed, whether purchased or reserved from last year's stock. Prices for purchased inputs such as fertilizers, herbicides, pesticides, and tractor power were derived from averages cited by farmers in the course of the production survey. Pricing unpurchased inputs such as human and animal labor was more difficult. Although there is a labor market, hired labor made up only 7 percent of total labor time. For the purposes of the TFP computations, all labor was valued at the market rate, disaggregated by activity where there were significant differences in daily wages. Assuming the opportunity cost of most household labor is not as high throughout the growing season as the wage rate for labor hired at peak periods, this method most likely overstates the labor component of total input costs. (Analyses to test the sensitivity of the results to this method indicated that using the hired labor rate did not distort the final results.) Because the market for animal labor is even thinner than that for human labor,[11] it was impossible to gather good data for this input. The final prices used were derived from key informant interviews.

Productivity Estimates

Table 5.3 shows the average TFP levels for each of the three informal contracts (rented, shared, and borrowed lands) relative to the PA-allocated land tenure type. TFP levels were lower for these contracts relative to the PA-allocated

---

11. When farmers need additional animal power, they tend to swap between themselves.

TABLE 5.3 Total factor productivity, land productivity, and factor intensities by tenure arrangement in the Arsi zone in Ethiopia

	PA-allocated fields	Informally contracted fields		
		Rented	Sharecropped	Borrowed
Total factor productivity	1.00	.90	.87	.84
Land productivity	1.00	.96	.91	.92
Wheat	1.00	1.12	1.21	.95
Barley	1.00	.88	.78	.95
Legumes	1.00	.96	.98	1.03
Residues	1.00	1.01	.99	.99
Factor intensity	1.00	1.06	1.05	1.10
Labor	1.00	1.00	.99	.98
Power	1.00	1.01	.99	1.01
Chemicals	1.00	1.04	1.06	1.10
Seed	1.00	1.01	1.01	1.01

arrangement. Borrowed lands had the lowest TFP levels, producing 16 percent less output than the PA-allocated lands using the same input bundle. The shared lands were 13 percent less efficient than the PA-allocated lands, whereas rented lands were only 10 percent less efficient.

The land productivity levels for informally contracted fields were also lower than for PA-allocated fields. The gap was smaller, however, than the gap in TFP levels because of the relatively high levels of factor intensity on informally contracted fields. The higher levels of inputs (labor, power, chemicals, and seed) applied to informally contracted fields increased the level of land productivity but not the level of TFP. For example, the factor intensity level on borrowed land was 10 percent higher than the PA-allocated lands, but the TFP level was 16 percent lower.

Although equation (8) provides an excellent framework for decomposing the change in TFP into its various components, we can also express the changes in the levels of inputs as a percentage of the change in land productivity. Table 5.4 indicates that differences in most input levels between the informally contracted lands and PA lands were positive, whereas differences in land productivity were negative, thus resulting in a negative change in TFP levels for all lands under informal contracts. Chemical inputs (fertilizers and herbicides) were the major contributor to higher levels of inputs for all the informal contracts, whereas the contributions of animal power, human, and seed remain roughly the same. The increase in the level of chemicals was inversely proportional to the degree of land tenure security as defined earlier. The more insecure the land, the more farmers applied chemical inputs. The largest increase (10 percent) was for borrowed lands. TFP was not the source of land productivity dif-

TABLE 5.4 Sources of productivity differences: Informally contracted fields relative to PA-allocated fields in the Arsi zone in Ethiopia

	Rented fields	Sharecropped fields	Borrowed/gift fields
Differences in TFP from PA-allocated fields (percentage points)	−10	−13	−16
Land productivity	−4	−9	−8
Total factor intensity	6	5	10
Labor	0	−1	−2
Power	1	−1	1
Chemicals	4	6	10
Seed	1	1	1
Differences in TFP from PA-allocated fields as a percentage of the difference in land productivity	250	144	200
Total factor intensity	−150	−56	−125
Labor	0	11	25
Power	−25	11	13
Chemicals	−100	−67	−125
Seed	−25	−11	−13

ferences in the lands under informal tenure contracts compared with the PA-allocated land. The declines in TFP differentials were 250 percent, 144 percent, and 200 percent higher than the declines in land productivity for the rented, shared, and borrowed lands, respectively.

The high input intensities, combined with low land productivity ratios and thus low TFP, indicate that the capacity of rented, shared, and borrowed lands to produce more output was not hampered by underinvestment in variable inputs due to land insecurity. Rather than applying fewer inputs, as the common view would suggest, farmers on informally contracted fields applied more inputs, in particular more chemical fertilizers. There are several reasons for this high input/low output combination on informally contracted fields. First, informally contracted fields may have poor soil quality. Although data on the physical description of these fields failed to show a significant difference in slope or erosion on the informally contracted fields, there was some evidence of differences in soil type. Borrowed fields were less likely to be found on the rich black soils that characterize much of the Ethiopian highlands. (More precise assessments of soil quality were not done.) Furthermore, borrowers almost always received their land from their fathers, who shared a piece of their limited PA-allocated holdings. Dependent on their fathers' generosity for this free land, borrowers were thus stuck with what they are given, as compared with renters and sharecroppers who had more bargaining power to search for better land. Many reported not finding land until well into the plowing season. To the extent that landholders may continually contract out the same plot year after year (to different farmers), the inherent quality of those plots may have been low. It is thus possible that the quality of all informally contracted fields, and especially borrowed fields, was lower than PA fields.

Second, land-importing farmers may use labor inefficiently. As young adults, borrowers usually have strong obligations to contribute labor to the family farm. Additionally, they tend not to own the oxen needed to plow their borrowed fields. Although they use the same amount of total human and animal days per hectare as PA farmers, they do so by relying on labor and oxen exchanges, after tending to family fields. Such inputs are likely to be somewhat less effective. Thus the TFP efficiency gap is likely due to youth and poor soil quality rather than tenure insecurity.

Conclusions

The reform of land policies in Sub-Saharan Africa has received much attention in recent years. Many authors believe that farmland held under indigenous or informal land contracts in Sub-Saharan Africa is formed less efficiently than that held under title or individualized land rights (for example, owner cultivation). Others argue that indigenous tenure arrangements have little bearing on crop productivity because they are dynamic and evolve in response to changes in land values. This debate will continue as long as there is insufficient empirical evidence to support the arguments. Using plot-level data and the concept of interspatial total factor productivity, this analysis determined the relative production efficiency of four alternative land tenure arrangements prevailing in Ethiopia. There are no privately owned lands in Ethiopia to use as a standard; thus we focused on lands formally allocated by the government (PA-allocated lands), as well as those informally exchanged between farmers (rented, shared, and borrowed lands). Lands allocated by the government were the most secure because farmers had relatively greater duration and a greater range of rights on them compared with the informal tenure arrangements.

The results of our study show that although the production efficiency of farming differed by tenure contract, the differences were relatively small and not attributable to the use of fewer variable inputs as a result of insecurity. Informally contracted lands were relatively less productive than the PA-allocated lands. Borrowed lands were the least productive, followed by shared lands and rented lands. As shown in the conceptual framework in this chapter, TFP is a function of both land productivity and factor intensities. The land productivity levels for informally contracted lands were lower than unity, but the factor intensities levels were greater than unity, indicating that overall lower levels of

TFP were due to increases in the quantities of factor inputs without corresponding increases in land productivity (Table 5.4). Further decomposition of the factor intensity levels identified chemical inputs as the major source of differences. Because of the relatively high use of chemical inputs on less-secure fields, we suggest that important factors other than tenure contributed to the low productivity levels of farming operations, such as soil quality, farmer endowments, and farmer experience. In other words productivity determines tenure instead of vice versa. Thus there seems to be little evidence to say that changing tenure arrangements per se will change productivity unless it can also change soil quality and farmer experience. Although this study uses a different method from most analyses of agricultural productivity and property rights, it supports the conclusions of those who argue that land tenure does not constrain productivity at the current level of development in Sub-Saharan Africa. The results of the study suggest that the government should assess farmers' demand for formalization of informal tenure contracts.

References

Atwood, D. 1990. Land registration in Africa: The impact on agricultural production. *World Development* 18 (5): 659–671.

Besley, T. 1994. *Property rights and investment incentives: Theory and evidence from Ghana.* Research Program in Development Studies, Princeton University, Princeton, N.J., U.S.A. Photocopy.

Boserup, E. 1981. *Population and technological change.* Chicago: University of Chicago Press.

Bruce, J. W., S. E. Migot-Adholla, and J. Atherton. 1994. The findings and their policy implications: Institutional adaptation or replacement. In *Searching for land tenure security in Africa,* ed. J. W. Bruce and S. E. Migot-Adholla. Washington, D.C.: World Bank.

Capalbo, S. M., and J. M. Antle, eds. 1988. *Agricultural productivity measurement and explanation.* Washington, D.C.: Resources for the Future.

Christensen, L. R. 1975. Concepts and measurement of agricultural productivity. *American Journal of Agricultural Economics* 57 (5): 910–915.

Cochrane, W. G. 1963. *Sampling techniques.* 2d ed. New York: John Wiley and Sons.

Cohen, J. 1980. Land tenure and rural development in Africa. In *Agricultural development in Africa,* ed. R. Bates and M. Lofchie. New York: Praeger.

Denny, M., and M. Fuss. 1980. Intertemporal and interspatial comparisons of cost efficiency and productivity. Working Paper 8018. Toronto: Institute for Policy Analysis, University of Toronto.

————. 1983. A general approach for intertemporal and interspatial productivity comparisons. *Journal of Econometrics* 23 (3): 315–330.

Denny, M., M. Fuss., and J. D. May. 1981. Intertemporal changes in regional productivity in Canadian manufacturing. *Canadian Journal of Economics* 14 (3): 391–406.

Diewert, W. E. 1976. Exact and superlative index numbers. *Journal of Econometrics* 4 (2): 115–145.

————. 1981. The economic theory of index numbers: A survey. In *Essays in the theory and measurement of consumer behaviour in honour of Sir Richard Stone,* ed. A. Deaton. London: Cambridge University Press.

Dorner, P. 1977. *Land reform and economic development.* Kingsport, Tenn., U.S.A.: Kingsport Press.

Ehui, S., and D. Spencer. 1993. Measuring the sustainability and economic viability of tropical farming systems: A model from Sub-Saharan Africa. *Agricultural Economics* 9 (4): 279–296.

Feder, G., and R. Noronha. 1987. Land right systems and agricultural development in Sub-Saharan Africa. *World Bank Observer* 2 (2): 143–169.

Gavian, S., and S. Ehui. 1998. Measuring the production efficiency of alternative land tenure contracts in a mixed crop-livestock system in Ethiopia. *Agricultural Economics* 20: 37–49.

Gavian, S., and M. Fafchamps. 1996. Land tenure and allocative efficiency in Niger. *American Journal of Agricultural Economics* 78 (2): 460–471.

Girma, T., and Z. Asfaw. 1996. *Land tenure structure and development in Ethiopia: A case study of 10 peasant associations in Wara Jarso, Ethiopia.* Paper presented at the Sub-regional Workshop on Land Tenure Issues in Natural Resources Management, sponsored by The Sahara and Sahel Observatory, Natural Resource Management Programme. Economic Commission for Africa, Addis Ababa, March 11–15.

Harrison, B. 1987. *The greening of Africa.* London: Paladin Grafton Books.

Hayami, Y., and K. Otsuka. 1993. *The economics of contract choice.* Oxford: Clarendon Press.

Hayes, J., M. Roth, and L. Zepeda. 1997. Tenure security, investment, and productivity in Gambian agriculture: A generalized probit analysis. *American Journal of Agricultural Economics* 79 (2): 369–382.

Ip, P. C., and C. W. Stahl. 1978. Systems of land tenure, allocative efficiency, and economic development. *American Journal of Agricultural Economics* 60 (1): 19–28.

Noronha, R. 1985. *A review of the literature on land tenure systems in Sub-Saharan Africa.* World Bank Report ARU 43. Washington, D.C.: World Bank, Agriculture and Rural Development Department.

Ohta, N. 1974. A note on the duality between production and cost functions: Rate of return to scale and rate of technical progress. *Economic Studies Quarterly* 25 (1): 63–65.

Pinckney, T. C., and P. K. Kimuyu. 1994. Land tenure reforms in East Africa: Good, bad, unimportant. *Journal of African Economies* 3 (1): 1–28.

Place, F., and P. Hazell. 1993. Productivity effects of indigenous land tenure systems in Sub-Saharan Africa. *American Journal of Agricultural Economics* 75 (1): 10–19.

Platteau, J.-P. 1996. The evolutionary theory of land rights as applied to Sub-Saharan Africa: A critical assessment. *Development and Change* 27 (1): 29–86.

Tornqvist, L. 1936. The Bank of Finland's consumption price index. *Bank of Finland Monthly Bulletin* 10: 1–8.

6 Land Tenure and the Adoption of Agricultural Technology in Haiti

GLENN R. SMUCKER, T. ANDERSON WHITE,
AND MICHAEL BANNISTER

Experts commonly cite Haiti's complex land tenure system as a key constraint—sometimes *the* key constraint—to agricultural intensification and rural development. Because a majority of parcels are informally divided and the formal system for administering tenure is ineffective, the conventional wisdom holds that Haiti's tenure system constrains peasant investment and adoption of technology. Such arguments correspond to prevailing property rights theory, as represented by Boserup (1965) and Demsetz (1967), that private, individualized tenure is the most efficient in situations of land scarcity. These claims have led to calls for national cadastral survey and titling programs to update the formal land tenure system and unleash the rural sector (see USAID 1985; FAO 1991, 1995; World Bank 1991; IDB 1992; MARNDR 1992; Victor 1993; APAP 1995; Nathan 1995; FAO/INARA 1997). At least one pilot cadastre and titling program has been established, and major new investments in land reform are under consideration. The empirical evidence, however, suggests that the informal system has evolved in response to other pertinent factors and is reasonably efficient from a peasant perspective.

The findings described in this chapter support Baland and Platteau's (1998) claim that prevailing property rights theory underappreciates three important variables: the role of the state, social capital, and the distributional concerns of local people. The evidence suggests that land scarcity in Haiti is acute, and labor—in simple, aggregate terms—is in abundant supply; however, access to labor remains a critical issue for most Haitian peasants. In this rural context of extreme cash scarcity, labor serves as the primary medium of exchange. Access to labor is, on the margin, more important than access to land.

This evidence challenges the proposition that direct interventions to reform tenure—especially large-scale cadastral survey and titling—should be a priority for rural Haiti. Instead, more fundamental reforms must first be addressed. Furthermore, the evidence shows that peasant social relations support agricultural intensification even in the absence of formalized property rights and titles.

The purpose of this chapter is to contribute clarity to the debate by reviewing and interpreting the body of literature concerning relationships between land tenure and the adoption of technology in rural Haiti. The chapter first summarizes the modern context of peasant production and Haiti's statutory and customary tenure systems. It then reviews the results of previous studies on tenure and technology adoption, including a recent national household survey on food security commissioned by the U.S. Agency for International Development (BARA 1996a,b, 1997) and analyzed by the World Bank (Wiens and Sobrado 1998). Next, the chapter presents important new data from the Pan American Development Foundation agroforestry impact survey (Bannister 1998a,b) and concludes with a discussion of findings, including implications for theory and future research.

The Context of Peasant Production

In 1804 Haiti became the New World's second republic and the world's first nation of free citizens to achieve independence from Europe. (Unlike the United States, Haiti abolished slavery from its inception as an independent state.) A colonial social structure based on acute class stratification set the stage for Haiti's postindependence evolution as a deeply divided society.[1] After 1804 the masses of former slaves established themselves as independent freeholders—a reconstituted peasantry.[2] Peasant society emerged as largely self-regulating to cope with geographic isolation, exclusion from the political system, exploitative market relations, regressive taxes, and the virtual absence of state investment in the rural sector. Haitian peasants created a complex network of local institutions to ensure social security and channel access to land, labor, and capital.[3]

Historically, peasant agriculture has been Haiti's primary economic activity. An estimated 59 percent of Haiti's population is rural—one of the highest rates in the region.[4]

---

1. See Leyburn (1966), Mintz (1974), and Farmer (1994) for reviews of colonial history and implications for national development; James (1963) and Saint-Louis (1970) on the Haitian revolution; and Lundahl (1979, 1983, 1992), Fass (1988), Trouillot (1990), and Cadet (1996) on Haiti's political economy and poverty.

2. Mintz (1974) coined the term "reconstituted peasantry" and identified the antecedents of peasant production strategies under the slave plantation regime of colonial Saint-Domingue. See Leyburn (1966) and Moral (1961) for the historical origins and early evolution of Haitian society and Lundahl (1979) for economic history including the role of land.

3. On rural institutions see Bastien (1985), Barthélémy (1989, 1996), Murray (1977), Smucker (1983a), and Woodson (1990). See Lundahl (1992) on the informal system of social security in Haiti, and SACAD and FAMV (1993a,b, 1994) on peasant agricultural strategies.

4. Demographic data are based on population projections estimated at 7,630,997 in 1998. The most recent national demographic survey (see Cayemittes et al. 1995) was undertaken by the Enquête Mortalité, Morbidité et Utilisation des Services (EMMUS-II) of the Institut Haitien de l'Enfance (1994/95). This survey estimated the rural population at around 63 percent in 1993 and

Most farmers in Haiti are mountain peasants with farm units composed of several dispersed field plots. Recent national surveys confirm that the vast majority of peasants continue to be owner-operators by purchase or inheritance (see Table 6.1); however, average landholdings are small, fragmented, and generally of poor quality.[5]

Land, labor, and social relations are the most important assets of the household economy. Peasants actively manage kin ties, fictive kinship (godfatherhood), patron-client relations, and other special relationships as social capital that can be leveraged for access to land, labor, and capital. Cash resources are extremely scarce; farm strategies tend to be labor intensive. Land is the most significant tangible asset and serves as a powerful fulcrum for access to labor and capital resources. Farmers are acutely aware of micro-site variations, such as topography and soils, and actively diversify land portfolios and cropping patterns to manage risk and spread out harvest cycles.

As a strategy for survival, most peasants tend to focus on reducing risk rather than maximizing production. Managing a peasant household's stock of social capital is the key element of this strategy.[6]

Recent surveys show that 81 percent of rural households fall below the poverty line.[7] This alarming level of poverty reflects a precipitous decline in Haitian agriculture. Production per capita has dropped 33 percent since 1980, and agriculture's contribution to gross national product dropped from 47 percent in the 1970s to 24 percent in 1996.[8] This abrupt decline coincides with

---

decreasing due to outmigration and rapid urban growth, around 4 percent annually in the capital city.

5. See Zuvekas (1978) for available census data. According to national census data of 1971, the average size of peasant holding is less than 1.5 hectares and the average plot size is less than 0.8 hectare. The census data on farmland and its distribution may not be reliable. The census data do not recognize mixed-status categories or distinguish production units from landholding units. Nevertheless, the census data are indicative of the fragmentation and small size of peasant farms. The recent USAID survey, interpreted by Wiens and Sobrado (1998), found that more than 90 percent of farmers have access to land and that two-thirds own land through either purchase or inheritance. The average farm size is about 1.7 hectares and these farms are composed of an average of 3.7 dispersed plots. Farmers average only 0.6 hectare of good or mixed-quality soil.

6. The literature on Haitian peasants includes numerous references to risk management, agricultural strategies focused on survival issues and food security, and the importance of retaining a diversity of plots, cultigens, and income sources. See Moral (1961), Zuvekas (1978), Smucker (1983a,b), Ehrlich et al. (1985), Kermel-Torres and Roca (1993), SACAD and FAMV (1994), BARA (1997), Gagnon (1998), and Wiens and Sobrado (1998).

7. See Wiens and Sobrado (1998) on the USAID food security baseline survey (BARA 1996a, 1996b, 1997). They find 67 percent of households surveyed below the indigency line, 81 percent below the poverty line, and only 28 percent of food consumed by peasants as self-produced. The indigency line is defined as the local cost of reaching the minimum nutritional standard of 2,240 calories daily per capita, set by the Food and Agriculture Organization of the United Nations (FAO), with a diet that matches the food expenditure percentages of the average sample household.

8. See USAID (1997) among others. This document also reports a decline of 33 percent in the number of calories consumed per person per day since 1980. Further, agriculture's share of

TABLE 6.1 Distribution of modes of access to land

Source	Ownership[a]	Purchased	Divided inheritance	Undivided inheritance	Rented	Sharecropped	Other
			(percentage of parcels in each category)				
Wiens and Sobrado (1998)[b]	65.5	32.4	33.1	7.5	8.4	11.9	6.6
Bannister (1998)[c]	53.2	38.5	14.7	21.0	12.6	10.0	3.3
USAID (1995)[d]	58.2	38.6	19.7	14.0	12.1	5.5	10.2
ADS II (1988)[e]	61.0	—	—	13.0	9.0	9.0	7.0
Zuvekas (1978)[f]	60.0	—	—	—	14.3	14.4	11.1

NOTE: Tenure categories as defined here include direct access to land by virtue of ownership and indirect access through tenancy.

[a] Ownership is defined as "purchased" plus "divided inheritance" plots. Purchased and divided inheritance categories do not distinguish formal from informal transactions and may not have updated title.

[b] Data source: USAID food security survey—a nationwide, area-frame baseline survey of 4,026 households (BARA 1996a, 1996b, 1997).

[c] Data source: PADF/PLUS agroforestry impact study—a nationwide, area-frame survey of 5,658 plots and 1,540 households. The category of "other" includes leasehold on state lands and plots controlled by a land "manager" for absentee landlords.

[d] Data source: Interim Food Security Information System (IFSIS)—a nationwide, area-frame sample of 5,000 agricultural parcels. In this survey the "other" category includes "gift" (1.32 percent) and "other arrangements" (8.87 percent).

[e] Data source: Agricultural Development Support Project (ADS II 1988)—a nationwide, area-frame sample of 1,307,000 parcels. In this survey the "other" category includes "rental from state" (4 percent), "without title" (2 percent), and "other" (1 percent). The "ownership" category includes "purchased" and "divided inheritance" lands.

[f] Data source: Institut Haïtien des Statistiques (IHS)—a nationwide census of 1,484,385 plots. In this survey the "other" category includes "rental from state" (3.8 percent).

acute land scarcity, the closing of the agricultural frontier, and prolonged political and economic crisis in Haiti since the mid-1980s. The agricultural sector is significantly decapitalized, and public investment in rural infrastructure is limited. A shortage of off-farm employment opportunities heightens the extent of rural poverty. Despite recent efforts to decentralize and democratize the economy and the state, reform efforts have yet to make a palpable difference in rural areas. The peasantry remains in a state of chronic and growing crisis.[9]

The Land Tenure System

Origins

In 1804 the new Haitian state acquired immense holdings by confiscating French colonial estates and asserting state ownership of all unclaimed lands. Informally, newly freed slaves established themselves as independent agriculturists in areas of weak government control. Victor (1993) estimates that over a third of Haiti's present territory was settled outside of government control. Between 1807 and 1817, President Pétion distributed 150,000–170,000 hectares to some 10,000 beneficiaries (Moral 1961, 27–41). Land distribution in Haiti today remains significantly more egalitarian than elsewhere in the Caribbean and Latin American region (Zuvekas 1979; Lundahl 1997).

Ownership, Law, and Custom

The literature on Haitian land tenure is based primarily on local community studies, old census data, especially the census of 1971, and other more recent survey data. Community studies include research in widely dispersed areas of the country, lowland plains, and mountain communities. A review of the literature suggests that categories of access to land are fairly standard throughout most of rural Haiti. The duality of formal and informal systems is applicable in all regions of the country.[10]

Identifying characteristics of Haitian land tenure include the following: (1) individual, private property is the rule, (2) peasant smallholders predominate over large holdings, (3) the majority of peasant farmers are owner-operators of their own land, (4) peasant farms are composed of several noncontiguous parcels, (5) most peasants are simultaneously landlords and tenants, (6) land is

---

total export value fell from around 60 percent in the 1970s to less than 10 percent by the end of the 1980s.

9. See World Bank (1998). For a review of the economics of long-term rural decline, see Lundahl (1979, 18): "The Haitian peasant sector is caught in a downward spiral of circular and cumulative causation which slowly depresses the standard of living among the peasants."

10. See Zuvekas (1978), Ehrlich et al. (1985), Bloch, Lambert, Singer, and Smucker (1988), Victor (1993), and FAO/INARA (1997).

readily bought and sold without updating title, (7) inherited land is divided equally among all children of the deceased, (8) farm holdings are built up over the course of a lifetime, then divided and dispersed (Oriol 1996; Bloch, Lambert, Singer, and Smucker 1988).

Land tenure categories discussed in this chapter are categories of access rather than strictly legal categories based on title or lease contracts. These access categories include direct access to land by virtue of ownership and indirect access through various forms of tenancy or usufruct. Table 6.1 summarizes overall distribution of agricultural plots by direct and indirect modes of access. A farmer may own, rent, and sharecrop several plots. Therefore, it is important to distinguish farm operations (land use) from the proprietary base (land ownership and control).[11]

Haitian peasant holdings are firmly grounded in the concept of private property. Peasant landownership originates from formal and informal purchase, inheritance, and gifts. According to national surveys, peasant owner-operators own 37 percent of all agricultural parcels by purchase, 23 percent via divided inheritance, and 15 percent via undivided inheritance (averages based on Table 6.1).[12] Other forms of access derive from a variety of arrangements including usufruct, nonformalized gifts of land, preinheritance, plots controlled by land managers for absentee landlords, and leasehold on state land.

In keeping with the profound dualism of Haitian society, land tenure arrangements are marked by two parallel systems—one legal and the other customary.[13] In practice the two systems are interactive and constitute a type of legal pluralism rather than two discrete systems.[14] Statutory (legal) land transactions and entitlement rely heavily on documents prepared by notaries and updated surveys. In general, peasant land transactions reflect skepticism of notaries, land surveyors, and virtually all agents of the state including the judiciary.

In the customary system people make land available in response to family obligations, special ties to fictive kin (godparenthood), and various forms of clientship (such as labor relations, personal loans, banking of favors). Normatively, kinship groups have an obligation to make land available to all family

---

11. See Wiens and Sobrado (1998), Bannister (1998a), Bloch, Lambert, Singer, and Smucker (1988), and Block, Smucker, and McLain (1988).

12. The findings of FAO/INARA (1997), Oriol (1996), Wiens and Sobrado (1998), and Bannister (1998a) are consistent with earlier findings. See Zuvekas (1979) for an earlier compilation of studies demonstrating ownership.

13. See Montalvo-Despeignes (1976), Bloch, Lambert, Singer, and Smucker (1988), Victor (1989, 1993), and MARNDR (1992), on the dualism of law and custom and for reviews of Haitian land law.

14. See Benda-Beckmann (1995, 322) for a definition of legal pluralism drawn from legal anthropological studies: " the simultaneous existence of multiple normative constructions of property rights in social organizations (legal pluralism)."

members. Informal (customary) tenure arrangements among peasant farmers tend to be self-regulatory. Peasant farmers occasionally update title to inherited land, but ownership rights stem primarily from kinship ties and transactions not regulated by law. Most farmers hold land by extralegal agreements, but owners of informally divided inheritance plots may also refer back to master deeds three or four generations removed (Murray 1977; Barthélemy 1996).

There is a lively land market among peasants in Haiti. Land sales are driven by consumption and the need for cash. In addition to its value as a basic factor of production, land is held as a store of value or insurance fund for crisis, illness, burial, ceremonial obligations, schooling, or outmigration (FAO/INARA 1997; Murray 1977).

The recent FAO/INARA study estimates that 95 percent of land sales in rural Haiti avoid the formalities prescribed by Haitian law. Some evidence suggests that updated title is more common in irrigated zones or periurban areas subject to high rents and speculative land values. Still, farmers make every effort to avoid, diminish, or postpone notarial fees, survey costs, taxes, and other charges for land registration and updated title.[15] From a peasant perspective, avoiding surveys also diminishes the risk of land loss due to the possible revisions of current plot lines to conform to old master deeds. In the Haitian context of legal pluralism, formal title is not necessarily more secure than informal arrangements, although it is demonstrably more expensive and considerably less flexible than the informal system.[16]

In general, patterns of inheritance redistribute family land with the passing of each generation. In both law and custom, all recognized children have equal rights to a share of parental landholdings. The mechanism of inheritance tends to maintain egalitarian distribution of land; however, subdivision also perpetuates fragmentation and diminished plot size over time. With high population growth, the size of farm units and individual plots has diminished dramatically since the nineteenth century. The effects of fragmentation are mitigated by outmigration, consolidation of shares (usually by men since women commonly marry out and move away from the family land base), and customary restrictions against selling inherited land to outsiders (non-kin) (Barthélemy 1996). Customary norms assure potential access to land by all members of the family, but the system rewards family members who stay on the land rather than migrating or marrying outside the community. Co-heirs who remain on the land assume control of absentee shares and consolidate adjoining shares of inheritance into larger blocks of land. Co-heirs and kinfolk have priority for land

---

15. See Bruce and Migot-Adholla (1994) for reports of such practices in Africa.
16. See Moral (1961), Murray (1977), Smucker (1983a), Victor (1989), Bloch, Lambert, Singer, and Smucker (1988), McLain, Stienbarger, and Sprumont (1988), Oriol (1996), FAO/INARA (1997, Chapter 5.4), and FAO/IDB (1998, 24).

purchase. Long-standing sharecroppers or leaseholders also enjoy priority over others for the opportunity to purchase (Smucker 1983b).

A striking feature of the system is the prevalence of undivided family inheritance land, which retains its legal status as a single block of land even when subdivided by custom, usually without updating titles. Once divided by custom, these shares are readily bought and sold informally among heirs. Consequently, the percentage of legally undivided family inheritance is undoubtedly higher than shown in national census and survey data. Land access categories in Table 6.1 include both statutory and customary forms of land purchase or inheritance and do not distinguish between them.

As illustrated in Table 6.1, about 10 percent of all agricultural plots are accessed via rental agreements and 10 percent via sharecropping agreements. Most sharecroppers are not solely dependent on sharecropping. Peasants generally view sharecropping as a favor to the tenant since land and cash are both scarce. Paying rent in cash is commonly viewed as a favor to the landlord—perhaps a relative faced with a heavy burden of funeral debt. Some tenants retain continuous access to rented or sharecropped land for many years. Others rent land for shorter periods when the tenant's own holdings are in fallow or otherwise occupied (McLain, Stienbarger, and Sprumont 1988).

In the customary system, people also make land available by usufruct, especially to kinfolk. Usufruct may be limited to specific rights such as the right to harvest particular trees or bushes (coffee, fruit), grazing, or agricultural use for a single growing season. Usufruct may also take the form of preinheritance plots with the understanding that the beneficiary will cover the giver's eventual burial costs. Some inheritance land remains undivided—even informally—for several generations. In such cases co-heirs and their descendants may retain joint use rights to house sites, wood lots, pasture, or ceremonial sites (Smucker 1983a; Barthélemy 1996; Oriol 1996).

Leaseholders and squatters on state land are a significant exception to the rule of private property. Oriol (1993) calculates the number of state leaseholders at around 35,000, or roughly 5 percent of rural households and 10 percent of agricultural land.[17] Peasant leaseholders on state lands treat their leases as though they were private property—buying, selling, renting, sharecropping, and inheriting their lease rights by customary agreements.[18]

---

17. ADS II (1988) estimates 4 percent of agricultural parcels under state leasehold. Victor (1993) notes that estimates of state land vary from 100,000 to 300,000 hectares. There are no verifiable inventories of farmers on state lands or the amount of state land.

18. See Bloch, Lambert, Singer, and Smucker (1988) and author interviews (Smucker and Delatour 1979; Smucker and Smucker 1979) with leaseholders on the offshore island of La Gonave and the Northwest Department.

Land Tenure Security

In this context of legal pluralism, with the prevalence of informal modes of access to land, what ultimately defines land tenure security and insecurity? From a juridical perspective, clear and defensible title derives ultimately from the state. Clear title should presumably ensure long-term access to land, freedom to alienate the asset, and freedom from the threat of eviction. As a corollary, juridical insecurity exists when the landowner or land user lacks the necessary legal status (clear title, lease) or the institutional means (court system, law enforcement) to enforce property and leasing rights.

By these measures, peasant farmers in Haiti do not enjoy land tenure security. This juridical insecurity stems from contradictions in land law and weak institutions of enforcement. First, most peasant landholdings are not covered by updated title. This situation is due in large part to the high transaction costs. Second, those with updated title cannot adequately defend their rights in a court of law.[19]

Field studies show there is a generalized peasant distrust of the law and a primary reliance on social relations and customary arrangements to ensure access to land. Most peasants are aware of procedures for formalizing landownership and value updated title to land, particularly if they wish to sell land to non-kin. However, customary arrangements are standard in virtually all peasant households.

Peasants may also turn to the formal system when the informal system proves unable to resolve conflicts over inheritance or rightful ownership. This course of action is prohibitively expensive for most peasant households and tends to be a recourse of last resort in managing land conflict (see Murray 1978; Smucker 1983a). Recent research on land conflicts adjudicated by the courts has concluded that the courts are often unable to arrive at a definitive judgment and that the judicial apparatus is generally unable to enforce its judgments (FAO/INARA 1997). The same study also found that the judicial system actively generates land conflict and insecurity[20] and that most peasants are virtually excluded from due process by the inaccessibility of courts. There are no courts in Haiti's 565 rural sectional jurisdictions, and only a small number of courts are authorized by law to judge land disputes. The lower courts most

---

19. Clear title does not provide protection from intervention by powerful outsiders, land invasions to reclaim lost land, or the takeover of unoccupied land, usually in the aftermath of changes in government (Moral 1961; FAO/INARA 1997). Such incursions, however, are more commonly reported on state lands, periurban zones, irrigated zones, or sites with speculative value.

20. See Chapter 2, La sécurité foncière et ses garants: "il n'y a en Haïti aucune garantie ou sécurité foncière opposable à tous" (FAO/INARA 1997, 35). Chapter 3, La gestion des conflits: droits et propriété et tribunaux: "Le dysfonctionnement des institutions préposées à assurer la sécurité foncière . . . est générateur d'insécurité foncière et producteur de conflits fonciers, violents ou larvés" (p. 7).

accessible to peasants have very limited formal authority over land disputes. FAO/INARA notes that the courts are interminably slow, corrupt, and politicized. Therefore, broad-based reforms and a viable system of justice are essential preconditions for land tenure security.[21]

Haiti today lacks a comprehensive, operative system for recording landownership. Victor (1993) supports the cadaster as an essential tool in reforming the system but notes that Haitian laws on cadaster have never been implemented and that cadaster projects have generally failed. The government together with foreign agencies or investors has carried out cadastral surveys as an element of project investment or agroindustry. This approach has sometimes had the effect of excluding peasant smallholders (FAO/INARA 1997).

Local cadasters were undertaken in irrigated zones of Haiti's Gonaives Plains (1974–79) and the Artibonite Valley (1950s, 1980, 1982). In these cases physical cadasters were undertaken with the promise of land reform, but delivery of title to peasants never materialized (Victor 1993). Landowners within the perimeters of these local cadasters have commonly made a choice not to register subsequent land transactions despite the offer of free registration. There is some evidence of success in the use of physical cadasters to regulate water rights—an approach based on water users within an irrigated perimeter— regardless of tenure status (Hauge 1984).

Poverty is itself an important source of land tenure insecurity. In a cash-starved peasant economy, farmers find it difficult to expand their land base by purchase and are not inclined to invest scarce savings to update title. Although subdivision gives each member of the next generation a stake in the land, this is a two-edged sword. People are guaranteed a social safety net and means for survival, but for most people the land base is inadequate to meet basic livelihood needs and necessitates heavy reliance on agricultural day labor and other intermittent sources of income. By redistributing the wealth in land, the system neutralizes poverty by sharing it.

In a context of high risk within the statutory system, it is hardly surprising that peasants rely heavily on extralegal measures of accessing land. The customary system offers a more manageable level of risk. Customary arrangements are more reliable and embody lower financial and transaction costs. They are flexible and adapted to daily realities of peasant decisionmaking. For the vast majority, the informal system assures at least minimal access to land—the pivotal asset of peasant livelihood. Peasants use mixed patterns of tenure to defray labor costs, ensure cash flow, and meet social obligations based on kinship ties or patron-client relations. Finally, the customary system is locally controlled and addresses household imperatives to manage risk, enhance social security, and set aside an insurance fund.

---

21. See FAO (1995) and FAO/INARA (1997), especially Chapters 2 and 3, cited earlier.

In essence, the prevailing customary system addresses peasant concerns about secure tenure through stability of access, rather than tenure security via title. Assured access is largely dependent on kinship status and one's personal stock of social capital.[22]

Technology Adoption and Tenure

Given the mix of formal and informal procedures for accessing land in Haiti, do peasants feel secure enough to adopt agricultural technologies and invest in their land? This section first reviews the results of previous studies on tenure and the adoption of agricultural technologies and then presents new evidence from the agroforestry impact survey conducted by the Pan American Development Foundation.

Results from Previous Studies

NATIONAL FOOD SECURITY BASELINE SURVEY. Between 1994 and 1996 USAID funded a national-level survey on food security that included questions on land tenure, adoption of agricultural technologies, inputs, production, demography, and nutrition.[23] This survey of 4,026 households generated the most comprehensive set of household data of the 1990s and the only national-level data relating tenure, adoption, and productivity. Wiens and Sobrado (World Bank 1998) analyzed the data to better understand the dynamics of rural production and poverty. Only the findings related to tenure will be reported here.

First, Wiens and Sobrado examined simple correlations between tenure type and agricultural practices. Five types of land access—purchased, inherited-and-divided, rented, sharecropped, inherited-and-undivided—were tested against four types of practices—cropping pattern, degree of crop diversification, input intensity, and the adoption of soil conservation techniques. Wiens and Sobrado tested the partial correlations while holding area cultivated and area of good or mixed-quality soil constant, as these variables may be associated with particular tenure patterns and may mask other relationships if not held constant.

---

22. See Murray (1978, 1979), Bloch, Lambert, Singer, and Smucker (1988), Locher (1988), and SACAD and FAMV (1993a,b). McLain, Stienbarger, and Sprumont (1988) collected data on length of occupancy for all tenure types, finding a high incidence of lengthy periods of tenure even for short-term forms of tenure.

23. Under the sponsorship of the U.S. Agency for International Development, three nongovernmental organizations (NGOs)—CARE, the Adventist Development and Relief Agency (ADRA), and Catholic Relief Services (CRS)—conducted the food security baseline survey, each in a different region of the country. The Bureau of Applied Research in Anthropology (BARA), University of Arizona, analyzed and published the findings. For the detailed reports, see BARA (1996a,b, 1997).

As judged by partial correlation coefficients with $p \leq .05$, they found no significant relationships between tenure and agricultural practices tested, except for sharecropping. Sharecropping was positively correlated with the proportion of agricultural output represented by corn, rice, and chickens and negatively associated with growing vegetables and other cash crops. Sharecropping was not negatively associated with purchased input but was negatively associated with the practice of fallowing.

Next Wiens and Sobrado prepared a regression to predict crop output per hectare using data on 2,922 farms. Though the regression was highly significant, again, variables indicating tenure types were not significant except for sharecropping, which was found to be negatively related. In addition, they found that sharecropping had productivity levels 72 percent of the average.

Finally, Wiens and Sobrado tried to determine the characteristics of "successful" peasants. They defined these as those who worked at least 0.3 hectare and had relatively high levels of crop productivity and household expenditures. They prepared a logistic regression to determine the probability of being successful or not. Again, the distribution of tenure types was not significantly different between the successful and unsuccessful peasants at $p < .1$. Successful peasants had no different access to their land than did unsuccessful peasants. This finding corroborated another result from the entire sample of households: farmers own (including access via purchase, divided, and undivided inheritance) approximately two-thirds of all land worked regardless of income level. Wiens and Sobrado concluded that tenure was not generally a constraint on technology adoption or on production and increases in income. Their findings on sharecropping were consistent with interpretation of sharecropping as a mutually advantageous practice to mitigate risks on marginal land.

LOCAL-LEVEL PROJECT STUDIES. Perhaps the majority of agricultural and natural resource management projects have focused on technology transfer and proposed a relatively short menu of technologies to peasants in contrast to broader-based rural development projects.[24] Some of these projects have assessed the relationship between tenure and technology adoption.[25]

The most pertinent study was Smucker (1988), which carried out field research and summarized findings from six community studies assessing factors affecting peasant planting of project tree seedlings. The study found that peasants preferred to plant on purchased and divided inheritance lands; however, they regularly planted on undivided inheritance lands and other short-term forms of tenure. In some communities with less purchased land available, the major-

---

24. See White and Jickling (1992) on offering a limited menu of technologies in rural development projects.

25. Murray (1978) and Zuvekas (1978) reviewed the literature on tenure and found no conclusive links between tenure constraints and failure to adopt.

ity of trees were planted on undivided inheritance lands (Buffum 1985). In all six communities, peasants planted trees on rented and sharecropped plots in addition to owned plots. In a separate but related survey Conway (1986) surmised that planting trees on undivided land was a strategy to enhance individual claims to specific portions of jointly inherited land.

After reviewing the evidence from Conway (1986) and six community studies, Smucker (1988) concluded that peasants expressed a clear but far from exclusive preference for adoption on purchased and divided tenures. These findings corroborated those of a similar study assessing correlations between tenure and adoption of soil conservation methods (Pierre-Jean and Tremblay 1986). Smucker surmised that, although the tenure system as a whole was characterized by insecurity, this limitation was commonly overcome by personal ties and obligations and did not prevent peasants from planting trees on a broad range of tenure types.

In the area of Les Anglais in southern Haiti, McLain, Stienbarger, and Sprumont (1988) carried out land tenure research and tested for tree cover, tenure categories, and length of occupancy. They noted a strong correlation between length of occupancy and degree of tree cover regardless of tenure category—including trees on typically short-term tenures such as sharecropping. The finding that tenure categories and length of occupancy were not significantly correlated suggests that sharecropping and rental arrangements were renewed regularly and provided uninterrupted access comparable to long-term categories of tenure. The FAO/INARA study in nine different agroecosystems lends some support to this finding (1997).

White and Runge (1994, 1995) assessed the collective adoption of watershed management in multiowner watersheds of Maïssade. The study asked two questions: (1) what factors were associated with individual choice to participate in the collective management activity; and (2) what factors were associated with the emergence of watershed management regimes? White and Runge found no significant difference between the tenure status of participant and nonparticipant groups and no significant difference in the distribution of tenure types in successful and unsuccessful watersheds.

The emergence of successful watershed regimes was explained by two factors: significant economic gain from the action, and a critical mass of social capital derived from labor exchange practices and the existence of producer groups. Both conditions were necessary, and neither sufficient.

In a context where labor commonly substitutes for cash as a medium of exchange, White and Runge concluded that labor in times of need was effectively more important than cash or tenure. The need for labor and the social organization of labor diminished the potential for disputes over tenure. The authors further concluded that land title or tenure type was not the key factor, but rather the degree to which individuals were incorporated in a nexus of enduring and well-adapted personal and social relations (White and Runge 1995).

The sum of local-level project evidence suggests that farmers make investment decisions based on their perception of prospects for long-term access to a plot—regardless of its tenure status, including investments that actively enhance their prospects for long-term access. This finding suggests that perceived stability of access to land—via stability of personal and social relationships—is a more important determinant of technology adoption than mode of access.

New Evidence: The PADF Impact Study

The Pan American Development Foundation (PADF) implements the Productive Land Use Systems (PLUS) project financed by USAID. This agroforestry extension project provides plant materials and technical assistance to interested farmers and has reached 100,000 hillside farmers since 1992. In 1996 PADF carried out an impact survey of PLUS farmers that included information on land tenure and adoption of agroforestry practices (Bannister 1998a,b). Survey conclusions may not characterize all Haitian farmers; however, comparison with household data reported by Wiens and Sobrado (1998) suggests that both samples represent similar populations in terms of access to land and soil fertility.[26]

The survey collected data on all plots worked or owned by 1,540 peasant households, for a total of 5,663 plots, and additional information on 2,295 plots having project-inspired agroforestry practices, including site characteristics, crop yields, technician observations, and farmer perceptions of agroforestry practices adopted. The sample represented 5.6 percent of the 27,728 farmers who had adopted project technologies before January 1, 1995. The survey was repeated in the spring of 1998 with 931 farmers (1 percent of eligible farmers) and 1,658 plots.

TENURE AND PLOT CHARACTERISTICS.   Bannister tested for correlations between tenure and plot distance from the residence, area, topographic position, slope, elevation, erosion, and farmer perception of soil fertility. Farmers had purchased 49 percent of residential plots, 35 percent of nearby plots, and 37 percent of distant plots.[27] Among plots visited by technicians, share-

---

26. The number of persons per household is the same (5.78 for Wiens and Sobrado, 5.6 for PADF), but other characteristics of the household are somewhat different. PADF households contained on average 54 percent males, with 85 percent of heads of household being male. The corresponding percentages for the Wiens and Sobrado sample were 49 and 72 percent, respectively. The average percentage of heads of household having six or fewer years of school was 58 percent for Wiens and Sobrado but 85 percent for the PADF sample. The average size of the total holdings per household was 1.7 hectares for PADF and 1.78 hectares for Wiens and Sobrado. Of this total, the PADF households averaged 1.26 hectares owned (purchased plus inherited), and 0.59 hectare in good or mixed soil quality. The corresponding numbers for Wiens and Sobrado were 1.20 hectares and 0.62 hectare, respectively. Purchased plot area accounted for 37 percent of PADF households' total area and 32 percent of the Wiens and Sobrado households' total area. The largest 1 percent of farms occupied 8 percent of the total area for PADF and 10 percent of the total area for Wiens and Sobrado.

27. A 3 by 5 cross tabulation, Pearson's chi-square, *p*-value .000.

TABLE 6.2 Soil fertility by tenure category

Tenure	Farmer's evaluation of soil fertility			Number of plots
	Low	Medium	High	
	(percentage of plots)			
Purchased	14	37	49	948
Divided inheritance	13	45	42	324
Undivided inheritance	19	38	43	482
Sharecropped	18	38	44	189
Rented	22	41	38	284

NOTE: Pearson's chi-square p-value for the 3 by 5 cross tabulation is .001.

cropped plots were somewhat more distant than plots in other tenure categories.[28] Purchased plots averaged 0.53 hectare, significantly larger than divided, undivided, and sharecropped plots. This finding suggests that buying and selling markets have worked against the poor.[29]

The survey found no significant differences between tenure types in terms of elevation, topographic position, slope, or severity of erosion.[30] There were statistically significant differences in soil fertility (see Table 6.2). A higher percentage of purchased plots were in the high fertility category compared with other plots, and there was no evidence of use of organic fertilizers on purchased plots.[31]

TENURE AND THE ADOPTION OF AGROFORESTRY TECHNOLOGIES. Sampled farmers had installed project technologies on 41 percent of available plots and reported significant yield increases.[32] Crop yields were measured by technicians in farmers' plots during a series of case studies conducted in January 1995 (Lea 1995a,b). Increases of 70 percent in sorghum yield were noted

---

28. Kruskall-Wallis test, p-value .000.

29. Kruskall-Wallis test, p-value .000.

30. A 3 by 8 cross tabulation, Pearson's chi-square, p-value .694.

31. Soil fertility was described for each visited plot on a five-point qualitative scale by the farmer being interviewed, with 1 being very infertile and 5 very fertile. Responses were recoded into the three categories shown in Table 6.2. These categories are apparently the same as those used in the Wiens and Sobrado study. In the PADF study, however, fertility information was collected only for the subset of household plots actually visited. The Wiens and Sobrado study obtained fertility information for all plots in the household but did not compare it with tenure status.

32. The PADF impact survey asked farmers questions regarding the differences in crop yield they attributed to the presence of soil conservation structures, but the authors do not consider these recall responses reliable. Haitian farming systems contain a large number of crops, harvest is sometimes done in stages and in small amounts, new crops are sometimes planted owing to the improved microclimate created by soil conservation structures, and there was confusion about whether or not the question referred to crops in the alleys or crops grown within the structures themselves.

TABLE 6.3 Technology adoption on project plots by tenure category, 1996 survey

Tenure	Hedgerow	Crop band	Rock wall	Gully plug	Trees[a]	Top grafting	Number of plots
			(percentage of project plots)				
Purchased	54	6	29	19	55	11	948
Divided inheritance	59	4	29	11	47	12	324
Undivided inheritance	63	4	27	16	51	9	482
Sharecropped	68	2	32	16	23	4	189
Rented	67	3	36	16	23	4	284
p-value[b]	.000	.033	.078	.017	.000	.000	

NOTES: Percentages for rows do not total 100 because most plots had more than one project practice.

[a]Trees seedlings raised by the farmer with project assistance and planted on the plot during 1995.

[b]Pearson's chi-square significance for the 2 by 5 cross tabulation for each practice.

in hedgerow gardens and increases of 60 to 120 percent in rock wall gardens in controlled experiments on adjoining plots.

Overall, the impact survey indicates that farmer decisions to adopt new technologies are correlated with several plot characteristics in addition to tenure. Table 6.3 shows the percentage of project plots in each tenure category. Hedgerows, which are relatively easy to install, are the most commonly adopted technology. This finding may reflect a strategy of risk minimization when trying a new practice or fulfilling project requirements to install soil conservation measures. Undivided inheritance, sharecropped, and rented plots have higher adoption rates for hedgerows than purchased or divided inheritance.

The opposite is true for crop bands, gully plugs, trees, and top-grafting. For those technologies, the highest adoption rates are found in plots with purchased or divided inheritance plots. This situation is likely attributable to the high value of perennial food crops in crop contour bands (pineapple, plantain, sugarcane) and the economically important crops planted in soil collected by gully plugs (plantains, taro). Also, the value of tree products increases over time, so farmers need to protect their rights to harvest. For rock walls, the highest adoption rates are found on rented and sharecropped plots, but the differences are not significant.[33]

The 1998 survey shows adoption by tenure category for all plots controlled by participating households (see Table 6.4). Adoption rates are somewhat different from those of Table 6.3, but in general they confirm the previous findings. Notably, percentages of soil fertility (Table 6.2) and soil conservation practices (Tables 6.3 and 6.4) are quite similar across different tenure types. This finding suggests that it does not make sense for extension programs to target technologies toward or away from any particular tenure type.

Although not a project intervention, the presence of mature trees on a plot represents an important form of technology adoption. Bannister assessed the correlation between tenure and mature trees per hectare and found significant differences: there were more trees on purchased and divided inheritance plots (Table 6.5).[34] These results could indicate a preference for investing in land with long-term over short-term tenure. They may also suggest a pattern of asserting ownership claims by planting and maintaining trees on undivided plots. A similar analysis found more mature trees per hectare on plots with higher fertility (Bannister 1998b).

The correlation between technology adoption and soil fertility (Table 6.6) is as important as the relation between adoption and tenure status. This result is perhaps to be expected since tenure status and soil fertility are also related

---

33. Level of significance of 95 percent.
34. The visiting technician counted all trees on the plot, either planted with project assistance or otherwise, having a breast-height diameter greater than 10 centimeters.

TABLE 6.4 Technology adoption on all household plots by tenure category, 1998 survey

Tenure	Hedgerow	Crop band	Rock wall	Gully plug	Trees[a]	Top grafting	Number of plots
			(percentage of all household plots)				
Purchased	24	5	15	8	36	4	1,382
Divided inheritance	19	4	12	7	33	4	517
Undivided inheritance	29	2	13	7	34	2	688
Sharecropped	28	3	8	4	20	2	299
Rented	23	2	16	4	16	3	432
p-value[b]	.002	.004	.011	.044	.000	.086	

NOTE: Percentages for rows do not total 100 because most plots had more than one project practice.

[a]Tree seedlings raised by the farmer with project assistance and planted on the plot during 1997.

[b]Pearson's chi-square significance for the 2 by 5 cross tabulation for each practice.

TABLE 6.5 Number of adult trees per hectare by tenure category

Tenure	Number of trees per hectare	Number of plots
Divided inheritance	103c	324
Purchased	88c	946
Undivided inheritance	69d	481
Sharecropped	61d	189
Rented[a]	56d	283

NOTE: Kruskall-Wallis test, *p*-value .000; numbers followed by the same letter are not different at the 95 percent level of probablity (multiple comparisons done by paired Mann-Whitney tests with Bonferroni correction).

[a]Private rental; does not include leasehold on state land.

(Table 6.2); however, farmer assessments of fertility also appear to integrate other productive factors not measured by laboratory analysis of soil nutrient levels.[35]

Tables 6.3, 6.4, and 6.6 show that tenure and soil fertility are both associated with adoption in parallel fashion. Technologies (crop contour bands, gully plugs, trees, top-grafted fruit trees) more common on purchased and divided inheritance plots are also more common on fertile plots. Conversely, hedgerows are less common on purchased and divided inheritance plots and more common on infertile plots.

Bannister's evidence does not allow clear separation of the relative influence of tenure and fertility on adoption; therefore, it is not possible to determine which is more important in a particular decision to adopt new technology. Bannister's analysis (1998b) finds no association between tenure status and differences in management.[36] Although overall analysis of PADF data shows that the mode of access to land is an important variable, the data show no definitive relationship between tenure status and adoption.

---

35. PADF had soil analyses performed on a randomly selected subset of 175 plots, 35 in each of the five qualitative categories, to determine if there was a relationship between farmers' perception and amount of soil nutrients as measured in the laboratory. Soils rated as fertile had a lower pH, more potassium, and more organic carbon than those rated as infertile. Since the difference in pH was very small, however, and potassium was abundant in both classes of soils, the difference in organic carbon was the most interesting result. There were no statistically significant relationships between the laboratory fertility findings and farmer's qualitative perception of soil depth, degree of "heat" (on a qualitative hot/cold scale) of the soil, or the severity of erosion found in the garden.

36. Technicians evaluated the management quality of hedgerows, crop contour bands, rock walls, and gully plugs. Observations were made on the percentage of rows well managed, the percentage of rows poorly managed, the number of breaches larger than 25 centimeters per 100 meters, and whether or not the farmer repaired the breaches. The statistical tests found no significant tenure-related differences in management for any of the agroforestry technologies promoted by the project.

TABLE 6.6 Technology adoption on fertile and infertile plots, 1996 survey

Soil fertility	Hedgerow	Crop band	Rock wall	Gully plug	Trees	Top grafting	Number of plots
			(percentage of plots)				
Fertile plots	54	6	33	19	48	12	1,032
Infertile plots	64	3	27	15	44	7	1,263
p-value[a]	.000	.007	.001	.026	.036	.000	

NOTE: Fertile plots are those with soils in the top two categories of the 1 to 5 point fertility scale; infertile plots are those with soils in the bottom three categories.

[a]Pearson chi-square significance for the 2 by 2 cross tabulations.

Conclusions

There Is No Definitive Relationship between Tenure and Adoption by Peasants

A broad range of studies on Haitian peasant agriculture and tenure find no simple and definitive relationship between tenure status and willingness to adopt agricultural technology. Levels of investment are quite similar across tenure types. Important exceptions to the general rule include the following: (1) other things being equal, peasants prefer to plant and graft trees on purchased or divided inheritance lands, and (2) peasants prefer to adopt certain soil conservation techniques—particularly hedgerows—on parcels with shorter-term tenures such as rental or sharecropping, perhaps to strengthen their claims or rights of access to that land or perhaps to reduce the risk of adopting the new technology. Notably, these two preferences are far from exclusive, and peasants frequently plant trees and establish hedgerows on all types of tenure. This finding supports the basic contention that tenure is not the preeminent criterion for overall investment, though it may influence the type of investment.

Approximately 60 percent of all agricultural parcels are purchased or divided inheritance plots (see Table 6.1); therefore, tenure is not a constraint for adopting technologies with long time horizons such as tree planting or grafting on the majority of parcels in Haiti. The various studies also suggest that tenure is not a constraint to agricultural intensification and soil conservation on the vast majority of parcels. Agricultural research and extension services are available, however, to only a small fraction of Haitian households. Despite continuously high peasant demand for agroforestry extension, Haiti's most significant effort to date reached just 25 percent of all peasant households over a 10-year period and then ceased.[37] Peasants continued to plant trees spontaneously in the wake of this outreach program albeit on a smaller scale. The key constraint to wider adoption and continued extension services was not land tenure but funding levels and the absence of a permanent institutional base for extension.

Local-level studies suggest that certain other factors are at least as important as tenure in peasant decisions to adopt. These factors include the relative size and fertility of available plots, proximity of plots to a farmer's residence, stability of access to land, and the quality of local social capital resources (such as kinship and other special ties and obligations, traditional rotating labor and credit groups, and grassroots peasant organizations). Where stocks of social capital are high, peasants are willing to adopt technology on short-term tenures including leasehold and sharecropping. This finding also holds for adoption of

---

37. This effort consisted of the Agroforestry Outreach Project (AOP) and the Agroforestry II (AF II) projects funded by USAID between 1981 and 1991 and implemented by the Pan American Development Foundation and CARE (see Smucker and Timyan 1995).

complicated watershed management regimes in degraded watersheds with many owners.

The importance of these factors sheds light on the alleged preeminence of tenure as a constraint and the fundamental importance of social capital in agricultural development. These results also suggest that development agents should give a higher priority to assessing and strengthening local social capital resources rather than updating title to land.

Because findings from these studies derived from studying the adoption patterns of those who are integrated into peasant society and influenced by traditional peasant social and cultural relations, their implications may not apply to farmers occupying the modern, capital-intensive agricultural sector. Conclusions drawn in this chapter pertain primarily to traditional, peasant smallholders.

Peasants Are Preoccupied More by Political and Economic Insecurity Than Insecure Tenure or Title

For most peasants in Haiti, the basic source of insecurity is poverty, not tenure. The agrarian poor are preoccupied above all with protecting themselves in a broader context of political and economic insecurity.[38] This insecurity goes far beyond land tenure and the normal risks of rain-fed agriculture on degraded sites. The pivotal constraints on peasant investment are political and economic uncertainty and the growing scarcity of productive land. Formal instruments of land registration, title, and the judicial process have high transaction costs and are not transparent, credible, or affordable.

Therefore, the peasantry's first line of defense is access to land via kinship ties and other social capital resources in order to enhance personal security. Peasant incentives to update title will remain weak unless there is progress in solving underlying sources of insecurity, including an agricultural sector in severe crisis and the absence of credible recourse in a court of law. Haiti's informal land tenure system provides a degree of social security to peasants via flexible and affordable land transfer and tenancy. The system prioritizes concerns for stability of access, food security, and risk management over particular modes of access to land.

Policymakers Should Focus on the Rural Sector and Broader Judicial Reforms Rather Than Tinker with the Tenure System

The sum of evidence suggests that Haiti's land tenure situation is largely compatible with smallholder agricultural development. Furthermore, rural poverty and technological stagnation are due to fundamental constraints other than

---

38. Political uncertainty includes but is much broader than the elections cycle or its absence. Peasant farmers have historically been excluded from the national political system, and the Haitian state has been deeply marked by a predatory character, few public services, especially in rural areas, and very limited protection of the rights of citizens.

tenure. These constraints are driven by the paucity of investment in human and social capital and rural infrastructure, lack of investment in agricultural research and extension, deficits in capital and credit markets, lack of off-farm labor opportunities, a dysfunctional judiciary, and disenfranchisement of the rural majority.

In general the evidence suggests that intensification and landscapewide rehabilitation will not be achieved simply by diffusing a limited range of technologies, whose economic and environmental impact tend to be marginal. Rather, smallholder agriculture in Haiti has successfully intensified where fundamental constraints are alleviated and where indigenous social capital has diminished peasant insecurity. Ultimately, formal land tenure insecurity is a subset of the generalized insecurity that peasants experience in their dealings with the legal system and the state. Land law reform is certainly needed, but premature investment in national cadastre and titling amounts to tinkering on the margins of a historically corrupt judicial system. At the very least, a legitimate and functioning system of justice is an essential precondition for land tenure security and title reform. Cadastre and titling programs also need to build on local demand and be implemented at the local level in conjunction with action that expands access to credit markets for obtaining and investing in land. Otherwise, titling programs run the risk of undermining the goals of enhanced tenure security and agricultural intensification.

Titling programs could prove useful in the long run, once peasants have gained an active voice in the political system and peasant rights are better protected in the law and related formal institutions. In the meantime, in order to address rural poverty and modernize the agricultural sector, policymakers should focus on the fundamentals and the creation of an enabling environment for change.

References

ADS II (Agricultural Development Support II). 1988. Preliminary results of the national agricultural survey in Haiti: First Agricultural Season (February–July 1987). University of Arkansas, Winrock International, and Haitian Ministry of Agriculture, Report 56. U.S. Agency for International Development, Port-au-Prince, Haiti. Photocopy.

APAP (Agricultural Policy Analysis Project). 1995. Haiti agribusiness assessment. Agricultural Policy Analysis Project, Phase III. U.S. Agency for International Development, Port-au-Prince, Haiti. Photocopy.

Baland, J.-M., and J.-P. Platteau. 1998. Division of the commons: A partial assessment of the new institutional economics and land rights. *American Journal of Agricultural Economics* 80 (August): 644–650.

Bannister, M. 1998a. Description of PADF/PLUS households and their gardens: Findings of the 1995 PADF/PLUS impact survey. PADF/PLUS Working Paper 1. Pan American Development Foundation, Port-au-Prince, Haiti. Photocopy.

————. 1998b. The relationship of plot characteristics to agroforestry adoption and management: Findings of the 1995 PADF/PLUS impact survey. PADF/PLUS Working Paper 2. Pan American Development Foundation, Port-au-Prince, Haiti. Photocopy.

BARA (Bureau of Applied Research in Anthropology). 1996a. A baseline study of livelihood security in Northwest Haiti. Conducted in collaboration with CARE/ Haiti and the Interim Food Security Information System. University of Arizona, Tucson. Photocopy.

————. 1996b. A baseline study of livelihood security in the southern peninsula of Haiti. Conducted in collaboration with Haiti Catholic Relief Services and the Interim Food Security Information System.University of Arizona, Tucson. Photocopy.

————. 1997. A baseline study of livelihood security in the departments of the Artibonite, Center, North, Northeast and West. Conducted in collaboration with the Adventist Development and Relief Agency and the Interim Food Security Information System. University of Arizona, Tucson. Photocopy.

Barthélemy, G. 1989. *Le pays en dehors: Essai sur l'univers rural haïtien.* Port-au-Prince, Haiti: Editions Henri Deschamps.

————. 1996. *Dans la splendeur d'un après-midi d'histoire.* Port-au-Prince, Haiti: Editions Henri Deschamps.

Bastien, R. 1985. *Le paysan haïtien et sa famille.* Paris: Editions Kathala.

Benda-Beckmann, F. von. 1995. Anthropological approaches to property law and economics. *European Journal of Law and Economics* 2(4): 309–336.

Bloch, P., G. Smucker, and R. McLain. 1988. Workshop on land tenure issues in watershed management. A report on workshop proceedings, October 3–8, Camp-Perrin, Haiti. Land Tenure Center, University of Wisconsin, Madison, Wisc., U.S.A. Photocopy.

Bloch, P., V. Lambert, N. Singer, and G. Smucker. 1988. *Land tenure issues in rural Haiti: Review of the evidence.* LTC Research Paper 94. Madison, Wisc., U.S.A.: Land Tenure Center, University of Wisconsin.

Boserup, E. 1965. *The conditions of agricultural growth: The economics of agrarian change under population pressure.* London: Allen and Unwin.

Bruce, J. W., and S. E. Migot-Adholla, ed. 1994. *Searching for land tenure security in Africa.* Dubuque, Ia., U.S.A.: Kendall

Buffum, W. 1985. Three years of tree planting in a Haitian mountain village: A socioeconomic analysis. Haiti Agroforestry Outreach Project. Pan American Development Foundation, Port-au-Prince, Haiti. Photocopy.

Cadet, C. 1996. *Crise, pauperisation et marginalisation: Dans l'Haïti contemporaine.* Port-au-Prince, Haiti: United Nations Children's Fund (UNICEF).

Cayemittes, M., A. Rival, B. Barrère, G. Lerebours, and M. Gédéon. 1995. Enquête mortalité, morbidité et utilisation des services (EMMUS-II), Haïti 1994/95. Institut Haïtien de l'Enfance, Pétionville, Haiti, and Macro International Inc., Calverton. Md., U.S.A. Photocopy.

Conway, F. 1986. Synthesis of socioeconomic findings about participants in the USAID/ Haiti Agroforestry Outreach Project. University of Maine Agroforestry Research Project. U.S. Agency for International Development, Port-au-Prince, Haiti. Photocopy.

Demsetz, H. 1967. Toward a theory of property rights. *American Economic Review* 57 (May): 347–359.

Ehrlich, M., F. Conway, N. Adrien, F. LeBeau, L. Lewis, H. Lauwerysen, I. Lowenthal, Y. Mayda, P. Paryski, G. Smucker, J. Talbot, and E. Wilcox. 1985. *Haiti country environmental profile: A field study*. Port-au-Prince, Haiti: U.S. Agency for International Development.

Farmer, P. 1994. *The uses of Haiti*. Monroe, Me., U.S.A.: Common Courage Press.

Fass, S. 1988. *Political economy in Haiti: The drama of survival*. New Brunswick, N.J., U.S.A.: Transaction Books.

FAO (Food and Agriculture Organization of the United Nations). 1991. Agricultural technology development project: Initiating project brief. 116/91 CP-HAI 21 PB. Rome.

———. 1995. Agricultural sector review and identification of projects: Sector report. Vols. 1 and 2. 75/95, TCP-HAI 23. Rome.

FAO/IDB (Food and Agriculture Organization of the United Nations/Inter-American Development Bank). 1998. Etude socio-économique d'une aménagement hydroagricole: Canal André aux Gonaives et d'un futur périmetre à Gilbert, près de Mirebalais. Document de Travail 1. Haïti Projet d'intensification agricole. Report 97/014 IDB-HAI. Inter-American Development Bank, Port-au-Prince, Haiti. Photocopy.

FAO/INARA (Food and Agriculture Organization of the United Nations/Institut National de la Réforme Agraire). 1997. Définir une politique agro-foncière pour Haïti: Eléments d'orientation. TCP-HAI-4553. Port-au-Prince, Haiti. Photocopy.

Gagnon, G. 1998. *Food security issues in Haiti: The challenges of poverty reduction*. Vol. 2, *Technical Papers*. Report No. 17242 HA. Washington, D.C.: World Bank.

Hauge, A. B. 1984. Factors in irrigation management in Haiti and the potential of water users associations. U.S. Agency for International Development, Port-au-Prince, Haiti. Photocopy.

IDB (Inter-American Development Bank). 1992. Haiti: Agricultural sector review. Port-au-Prince, Haiti. Photocopy.

James, C. L. R. 1963. *The black jacobins: Toussaint Louverture and the San Domingo revolution.* New York: Random House.

Kermel-Torres, D., and P.-J. Roca. 1993. Bilan prospectif d'une agriculture de survie. In *La république haitienne: État des lieux et perspectives*, ed. G. Barthélémy and C. Girault. Paris: ADEC-Karthala.

Lea, J. D. 1995a. Revised report of rockwall case study results: Memo to CARE, PADF, and USAID. U.S. Agency for International Development, Port-au-Prince, Haiti. Photocopy.

———. 1995b. Hedgerow case study results from winter harvest 94–95: Memo to CARE, PADF, and USAID. U.S. Agency for International Development, Port-au-Prince, Haiti. Photocopy.

Leyburn, J. G. 1966. *The Haitian people.* New Haven, Conn., U.S.A.: Yale University Press.

Locher, U. 1988. *Land distribution, land tenure, and land erosion in Haiti*. Paper presented at the Twelfth Annual Conference of the Society for Caribbean Studies, July 12–14, High Leigh Conference Centre, Hoddesdon, Hertfordshire, U.K.

Lundahl, M. 1979. *Peasants and poverty: A study of Haiti.* London: Croom Helm.

————. 1983. *The Haitian economy: Man, land, and markets.* London: Croom Helm.

————. 1992. *Politics or markets: Essays on Haitian underdevelopment.* London: Routledge.

————.1997. Income and land distribution in Haiti: Some remarks on available statistics. *Journal of Interamerican Studies and World Affairs* 38 (2/3): 109–126.

MARNDR (Ministère de l'Agriculture, des Ressources Naturelles et du Development Rural). 1992. Réforme agraire en Haiti: Problématique et perspectives. Port-au-Prince, Haiti. Photocopy.

McLain, R. J., D. M. Stienbarger, and M. O. Sprumont. 1988. *Land tenure and land use in southern Haiti: Case studies of the Les Anglais and Grande Ravine du Sud watersheds.* LTC Research Paper 95. Madison, Wisc., U.S.A.: Land Tenure Center, University of Wisconsin.

Mintz, S. W. 1974. *Caribbean horizons.* Chicago: Aldine.

Montalvo-Despeignes, J. 1976. *Le droit informel haitien.* Paris: Presses Universitaires de France.

Moral, P. 1961. *Le paysan haïtien: Etude sur la vie rurale en Haiti.* Port-au-Prince, Haiti: Les Editions Fardin.

Murray, G. 1977. The evolution of Haitian peasant land tenure: A case study in the agrarian adaptation to population growth. Ph.D. diss., Columbia University, New York.

————. 1978. Land tenure, land insecurity, and planned agricultural development among Haitian peasants. Report for U.S. Agency for International Development. USAID, Port-au-Prince, Haiti. Photocopy.

————. 1979. Terraces, trees, and the Haitian peasant: Twenty-five years of erosion control in rural Haiti. Report for U.S. Agency for International Development. USAID, Port-au-Prince, Haiti. Photocopy.

Nathan Associates. 1995. Haiti: Analysis of legal and regulatory framework for trade and investment. Latin America and Caribbean Trade and Investment Development Project. Report for U.S. Agency for International Development. USAID, Port-au-Prince, Haiti. Photocopy.

Oriol, M. 1993. La mauvaise gestion des terres de l'état. In *La République Haitienne, Etat des lieux et perspectives,* ed. G. Barthélémy and C. Girault. Paris: ADEC-KARTHALA.

————. 1996. Structure foncière, réforme agraire et agro-foncière: Concepts et réalités. In *Conjonction* 200 160–162. Port-au-Prince, Haiti: L'Institut Français en Haïti.

Pierre-Jean, L., and A. Tremblay. 1986. Premier bilan d'une méthode d'approche de lutte antiérosive sur l'amélioration des systèmes de cultures en sols basaltiques (La Vallee de Jacmel, Haiti). *Recherche et Développement Rural* 2(2): 11–15.

SACAD (Systèmes Agraires Caribéens et Alternatives de Développement) and FAMV (Faculté d'Agronomie et de Médecine Veterinaire). 1993a. *Paysans, systèmes et crise: Travaux sur l'agraire haitien.* Vol. 2, *Stratégies et logiques sociales,* ed. D. Pillot. Point-à-Pitre, Guadeloupe, and Port-au-Prince, Haiti: SACAD, Université des Antilles et de la Guyane, and FAMV Université d'Etat d'Haiti.

————. 1993b. *Paysans, systèmes et crise: Travaux sur l'agraire haitien.* Vol. 1, *Histoire agraire et développement,* ed. A. Bory and F. Michel. Port-au-Prince, Haiti: SACAD, Université des Antilles et de la Guyane, FAMV Université d'Etat d'Haïti.

————. 1994. *Paysans, systèmes et crise: Travaux sur l'agraire haitien.* Vol. 3, *Dynamique de l'exploitation paysanne,* ed. A. Bellande and J. Paul. Point-à-Pitre, Guadeloupe, and Port-au-Prince, Haiti: SACAD, Université des Antilles et de la Guyane and FAMV Université d'Etat d'Haïti.

Saint-Louis, R. 1970. *La présociologie haïtienne: Haïti et sa vocation nationale (Eléments d'ethno-histoire haïtienne).* Ottawa: Editions Lemeac.

Smucker, G. 1981. Trees and charcoal in Haitian peasant economy. U.S. Agency for International Development, Port-au-Prince, Haiti. Photocopy.

————. 1983a. Peasants and development politics: A study in Haitian class and culture. Ph.D. diss., New School for Social Research, New York. Ann Arbor, Mich., U.S.A.: Text-fiche.

————. 1983b. Supplies of credit among Haitian peasants. Development Alternatives, Inc., Washington, D.C. Photocopy.

————. 1988. Decisions and motivations in peasant tree farming: Morne-Franck and the PADF cycle of village studies. Proje Pyebwa, Pan American Development Foundation, Port-au-Prince, Haiti. Photocopy.

Smucker, G., and L. Delatour. 1979. Food aid and the problem of labor-intensive rural development. U.S. Agency for International Development, Port-au-Prince, Haiti. Photocopy.

Smucker, G., and J. N. Smucker. 1979. HACHO and the Community Council Movement. U.S. Agency for International Development, Port-au-Prince, Haiti. Photocopy.

Smucker, G., and J. Timyan. 1995. Impact of tree planting in Haiti: 1982–1995. Haiti Productive Land Use Systems Project, South-East Consortium for International Development and Auburn University, Petion-Ville, Haiti. Photocopy.

Trouillot, M.-R. 1990. *Haiti: State against the nation: The origins and legacy of Duvalierism.* New York: Monthly Review Press.

USAID (U.S. Agency for International Development). 1985. *Haiti country environment profile: A field study.* Port-au-Prince, Haiti.

————. 1997. USAID strategy to improve food security in Haiti. Prepared for USAID/Haiti by LAC TECH II. Port-au-Prince, Haiti. Photocopy.

Victor, J.-A. 1989. *Sur la piste de la réforme agraire.* Port-au-Prince, Haiti: L'Imprimeur II.

————. 1993. La réforme agraire à l'envers. In *La République haïtienne: Etat des lieux et perspectives,* ed. G. Barthélemy and C. Girault. Paris: ADEC-Karthala.

White, T. A., and J. Jickling. 1992. *An economic and institutional analysis of soil conservation in Haiti.* Environment Department Divisional Working Paper 1992-33. Policy and Research Division, Environment Department. Washington, D.C.: World Bank.

White, T. A., and C. F. Runge. 1994. Common property and collective action: Lessons from cooperative watershed management in Haiti. *Economic Development and Cultural Change* 43 (1): 1–41.

————. 1995. The emergence and evolution of collective action: Lessons from watershed management in Haiti. *World Development* 23 (10): 1683–1698.

Wiens, T., and C. Sobrado. 1998. Rural poverty in Haiti. In *Haiti: The challenges of poverty reduction.* Poverty Reduction and Economic Management Unit and Caribbean Country Management Unit, Latin American and the Caribbean Region. Report 17242 HA. Washington, D.C.: World Bank.

Woodson, D. G. 1990. Tout moun se moun men tout mounn pa menm: Micro-level sociocultural aspects of land tenure in a northern Haitian locality. Ph.D. diss., University of Chicago, Chicago.

World Bank. 1991. *Haiti: Agricultural sector review.* Washington, D.C.

————. 1998. *Haiti: The challenges of poverty reduction.* Poverty Reduction and Economic Management Unit and Caribbean Country Management Unit, Latin American and the Caribbean Region, Report 17242 HA. Washington, D.C.

Zuvekas C. 1978. Land tenure, income, and employment in rural Haiti: A survey. Working Document Series, Haiti. Sector Analysis Internalization Group. International Development Staff. Washington, D.C.: U.S. Department of Agriculture. Photocopy.

————. 1979. Land tenure in Haiti and its policy implications: A survey of the literature. *Social and Economic Studies* 28 (4): 1–30.

7 Tribes, State, and Technology Adoption in Arid Land Management in Syria

JONATHAN RAE, GEORGE ARAB, THOMAS NORDBLOM, KHALIL JANI, AND GUSTAVE GINTZBURGER

Arid rangelands dominate the countries of West Asia and North Africa (WANA). Syria, at the eastern end of the Mediterranean, is better endowed with arable lands than most countries in the region, but still just over half its area, or 10.2 million hectares, falls below the 200-millimeter isohyet and is designated as *badiah,* or steppe, where cultivation is outlawed. In the steppe the majority of people are tribally organized and dependent on a migratory pastoral or agro-pastoral economy in which extensive customary systems facilitate mobility and natural resource management. For much of this century, however, migratory pastoralists have been blamed for being the key instigators of land degradation. Most WANA states won their independence after World War II and pursued policies of nation building and economic growth, neither of which carved out a role for tribes or migratory pastoralism. Not only did states generally perceive the tribes and their mobility as divisive and unstable elements in fledgling nations, but they also saw customary grazing practices as archaic, inefficient, and environmentally exploitative. The tribes were seen as political and environmental threats that, if not eliminated, would undermine the new states and stifle economic growth.

With the assistance of the Food and Agriculture Organization of the United Nations (FAO) and other aid agencies, many WANA states sidestepped and sought to suffocate customary practices and to "green the desert" with the introduction of national rangeland management. Coming in the early years of independence for many of the WANA countries, the dominance of this paradigm had considerable influence on the direction and evolution of state institutions responsible for steppe management. This chapter looks specifically at Syria and examines how national policy over the past 40 years has affected the institutions governing range management, as well as how the overlap and interface of the Syrian government and customary legal systems have shaped the history of shrub technology transfer in the Syrian steppe.

Rangeland Degradation: Models and Empirical Evidence

Theoretical Models Applying to Rangelands

The characterization of moving tribes as creators of desert conditions has a long history among people of the settled areas in the region and further afield (Bietenholz 1963; Ibn Khaldun, translated in Issawi 1987). Hardin (1968) described a rationale for this position in his influential paper "Tragedy of the Commons." He considered the perspective of a rational herder with private ownership of livestock in a pastoral society that is reliant on pastures open to all. Herders would follow the incentive to increase the number of their herd because they would receive direct benefit but bear only a share of the costs resulting from the delayed impact of their action. Each herder is "locked into a system that compels him to increase his herd without limit—in a world that is limited" (Hardin 1968, 1243). According to tragedy theorists, effective property rights and rational rangeland management is not possible without strong state involvement. This theory has formed the rationale for state governance over rangelands and other natural resources in many developing countries.

State programs to assess, manage, or increase the productivity of steppe areas are also based on a model of how the steppe ecosystem functions. Predominant in rangeland management science for much of this century has been the range succession model, which derives from plant ecology (Westoby, Walker, and Noy-Miller 1989). It assumes that the livestock sector operates in environments that are largely stable, where weather variability is limited to a narrow range and therefore inconsequential for long-term outcomes. The model supposes that a given rangeland continually returns to a single persistent state (the climax) of vegetation in the absence of grazing. By producing changes in the opposite direction, grazing pressure arising from a set stocking rate can slow or halt the successional tendency, producing an equilibrium in vegetation levels. This theory has guided the principles of the western ranching system, which were subsequently introduced in many parts of Sub-Saharan Africa and WANA to supplant customary practices. These included private rights to graze, rotational or paddock grazing systems, the establishment of water points to spread grazing pressure, the setting of a universal stocking rate, and the reseeding or replanting of the range with grasses and shrubs.

Empirical Evidence

Although claims of degradation in Syria are widespread, only limited inventories and no long-term studies of the steppe flora have been carried out. Nonetheless, numerous references in the literature attest to the "degraded" nature of the vegetation. A synthesis of range reports through the mid-1950s concluded that "without exception, range management specialists and ecologists have stressed that the range grazing of the steppe and semi desert regions of Syria . . . is progressively deteriorating as a result of overgrazing" (FAO 1956, 3). A 1985 study of the Syrian rangelands by the Arab Center for the Studies of Arid Zones and Dry lands suggested that unpalatable shrub species have become "dominant in large areas of the steppe" (ACSAD 1992, 7). It went on to estimate that 25 percent of the steppe is affected by wind erosion to one degree or another, while water erosion affects around 6 percent of the area. Furthermore, almost all relevant publications issued from the International Center for Agricultural Research in the Dry Areas (ICARDA), which is based in Aleppo, are premised on the assumption of widespread degradation in the Syrian steppe (Rae 1999). Yet evidence exists to the contrary.

An unpalatable shrub associated with a degraded steppe in Syria and neighboring regions is the spiny *Noaea mucronata*. An ecological study carried out by Deiri (1990) under the auspices of ICARDA found *Noaea* ubiquitous in the Aleppo steppe, masking the heterogeneity of climate and soil. Apparently, dominance of *Noaea* in some areas is a relatively new phenomenon here (Sankary 1982) and elsewhere (Zakirov 1989; Noy-Mier 1990). Deiri and others have assumed that this shift in floral composition is the result of overgrazing for lack of good management and that with a reduction in grazing pressure a climax community dominated by the palatable shrub *Salsola vermiculata* would return (Sankary 1982; Deiri 1990). The link between cause and effect, however, is not adequately demonstrated.

Indeed, the basis of an alternative interpretation comes from grazing trials carried out by the FAO and the Steppe Directorate in the 1960s at the Wadi al-'Azib research station in the Aleppo steppe. Over a three-year period, three sites were fenced off with a different stocking rate in each (trial A allocated 9 hectares per sheep; B, 6 hectares; and C, 4.5 hectares). No sizable differences in average meat production per animal were reported between the three treatments. As for the vegetation, it was noted that plant density "fluctuated more between years than between stocking rate treatments" (FAO 1966, 9), suggesting climate determines productivity more than grazing does. The reported vegetation change was, however, unexpected. Spininess in plants is usually interpreted as an anti-grazing adaptation, and it has often been recorded that spiny plants increase under heavy grazing but give way once protected (Noy-Mier 1990). In treatment C, with the highest stocking rate there was a "reduction" in the spiny variety *Noaea*, whereas in treatment A, with the lowest stocking rate, *Noaea* "increased greatly in density" (FAO 1967, 23). Neither this report nor an earlier one in 1966 allude to the cause of this vegetation change; *Noaea* is just described as "a spiny, undesirable shrub" (FAO 1967, 23).

An explanation for the expansion of *Noaea* under reduced grazing pressure is given by another study in the Negev and Jerusalem deserts (Noy-Mier 1990). During certain periods on the open range, *Noaea* are exposed to heavy pressure from herbivores selecting for the rare green material. Even though spines and other types of protection save the plants from local extinction,

Noy-Mier asserted they are insufficient to outweigh grazing pressure and are therefore among the first plants to benefit when an area is protected.

The crucial difference between *Noaea mucronata* and other shrubs is its extended growing period. Heavy grazing at either end of the green season disadvantages *Noaea,* but when such grazing pressure is relieved the extended growing period becomes an advantage. When camels are removed from the near steppe, the pressure in late spring and summer is largely removed. Also, whereas as recently as 30 years ago almost all herders wintering on the near steppe (November–February) sustained their flocks entirely from grazing,[1] today almost none do. Instead they feed their sheep on hand feed generally imported from the settled areas.[2] Thus, rather than being due to overgrazing, the shift to *Noaea mucronata* is a result of changes in the composition of livestock grazing the steppe coupled with the adoption and widespread use of hand feed for winter—something encouraged by the state following the 1958–61 drought (Lewis 1987).

Conclusions like this bring into question the validity of the range succession model in arid environments. Whereas the model predicts that rainfall cycles combined with sustained grazing pressure will keep range vegetation in equilibrium, it is now thought that where droughts or other episodic events are a feature, population fluctuations hinder plants and herbivores from establishing closely linked interactions and succession is abbreviated or nonexistent (Behnke, Scoones, and Kerven 1993; Scoones 1994). This realization that equilibrium conditions are not met in many instances has led to the development of an alternative paradigm centered around two models: the nonequilibrium model, which deals with population dynamics in uncertain environments; and the state-and-transition model (Westoby, Walker, and Noy-Mier 1989). In contrast to the linear succession model, it is argued that rangeland dynamics can be more accurately described by a set of discrete states of vegetation with discrete transitions between them, triggered by natural events, like floods, drought, or fire, either alone or in combination with herbivore activity.

Objectively apportioning responsibility for perceived or actual changes in steppe vegetation composition is therefore difficult. Grazing inevitably has an impact on shrub communities, but the nature of this impact is unclear, particularly when causes arise from a conjunction of other factors in addition to grazing. Indeed, some speculate that the landscape may in some sense be "adapted"

---

1. Van de Veen estimates that 58 percent of the Syrian sheep population, or 3.8 million head, wintered in the steppe grazing only shrubs, among them *Noaea mucronata* and *Haloxylon articulatum* (FAO 1967).

2. In an in-depth two-year study on animal diets of 129 herds frequenting the Aleppo steppe, 98 percent of feed needs came from hand feeding, and the remainder from crop residues. No steppe grazing was reported during the winter months (Wachholtz 1996). Perversely, pressure is relieved on the steppe to the advantage of *Noaea.*

to grazing pressure. That is, either less-resistant shrub species have been eliminated long ago or the species in these communities have adapted to grazing pressure. There is even some evidence to suggest that a certain amount of grazing pressure on arid rangelands maintains or even enhances floral species diversity (Olsvig-Whittaker et al. 1993; Perevolotsky 1995). In the case of the transition to *Noaea mucronata,* it seems likely that this was actually brought about by a reduction in grazing during critical times of the year.

Performance of Technologies Aimed at Improving Rangeland Conditions

Atriplex Shrub Technology

Despite the lack of a clear consensus on the best model for predicting the extent and causes of rangeland degradation, the Syrian government, aided by international research and development institutions, has undertaken several measures to bring about a change in rangeland management for the stated purpose of improving environmental outcomes. Actions have reflected a persistent adherence to "tragedy of the commons" and rangeland succession models. They span from centralizing the governance and enforcement of rangeland management to introducing new technologies designed to enhance the quantity and quality of rangeland vegetation. This section will discuss shrub and plantation technologies that have been developed, extended, and often imposed on herders occupying the Syrian steppe. Despite more than 50 years of technological efforts, however, technology uptake has lagged far behind expectations. The following sections elaborate on the institutional changes preceding and accompanying technical solutions that demonstrate the important role played by customary institutions in steppe management and shed light on the underlying reasons for the lack of adoption success.

From its creation in 1961, the Steppe Directorate of the Syrian government was given responsibility for range management, range and pasture research, management and expansion of government wells, and organization of emergency feed during times of drought. With the assistance of the FAO, the Steppe Directorate embarked on a highly centralized range management initiative, setting the tenor for all future interventions. Part of this initiative included trials to identify rain-use-efficient, edible plants to revegetate the steppe and act as a drought feed store. This step was deemed necessary because, although the successional model predicted natural regeneration toward a climax community, climatic variability and the unpredictable recurrence of devastating droughts meant that natural regeneration could be a long time coming. Shrub planting would fill this temporal gap, check soil erosion, and provide a source of animal feed during drought. The trials concluded in the late 1960s recommending *Atriplex,* a shrub species already favored by range managers elsewhere around the world, most notably Australia, South Africa, and the United States (Le Houerou 1995).

Le Houerou, one of the most influential people involved in rangeland management and rehabilitation in the WANA region over the past 30 years, describes the planting of *Atriplex* species as "one of the most efficient ways to reclaim [arid lands], if not the only one" (Le Houerou 1992, 107). The shrubs can prevent wind and water erosion and are efficient users of water (McKell 1975). They could also serve as a feed reserve in years of drought. There are around 400 species of *Atriplex* in the world, most in midlatitude temperate, subtropical, and Mediterranean zones. Though many *Atriplex* species exist in the Mediterranean region, their use in arid land stabilization and rehabilitation began with the introduction of the Australian variety *Atriplex nummularia* into Tunisia in the last years of the 19th century (McKell 1975). The introduction of this and other varieties from Australia continued after World War I in Morocco and Tunisia. By the 1950s *Atriplex* was being recommended for steppe rehabilitation in FAO circles, and beginning in the 1960s introductions took place throughout the WANA region and further afield. Although many trials of nonindigenous species showed limited promise, Omar Draz, FAO's chief adviser to the Syrian government on rangeland issues, conducted trials in 1968–69 with *Atriplex nummularia* that produced successful outcomes in an agricultural district of Aleppo (FAO 1974).

With the support of Draz and a wider scientific consensus for the technology, the Syrian authorities initiated programs to transfer *Atriplex* onto the steppe. The history of this intervention in Syria can conveniently be divided into two phases: (1) encouraging and later obliging agropastoralists to plant a part of their area with *Atriplex;* and then (2) establishing government-run fodder shrub plantations from 1987. The first phase envisaged that agropastoralists would forgo barley cultivation over a portion of their licensed steppe area and plant *Atriplex* in its place. In hindsight poor adoption rates for *Atriplex* were a foregone conclusion. Barley is nutritious and palatable, and postharvest stubble can be used for grazing. During drought it can be grazed in situ. By contrast, it can take between three and five months for sheep grazing *Atriplex* to get used to consuming and digesting it. Oxalates in the plant are potentially toxic to some ruminant microorganisms and can form stones in the urinary tract (Goodchild and Osman 1993). Furthermore, to compensate for the high salt content of the plant, the animal must drink between 6 and 12 liters of water a day (depending on the heat of the day), twice the normal levels (Le Houerou 1992; Nordblom et al. 1995). Moreover, *Atriplex* does not fit comfortably in the bedouin farming system. The "proper" time to harvest most *Atriplex* used in Syria is late summer and early autumn, a period when most sheep are grazing nutritious cotton residues in the settled areas (Wachholtz 1996). Not surprisingly, only a fraction of those cultivating in the steppe actually planted *Atriplex,* and of those all but a handful maintained their private plantation. With the shrubs gone, the majority of agropastoralists again cultivated barley (Leybourne et al. 1993).

The Plantation Approach

The poor success of government initiatives to encourage or require private adoption of range technology led directly to the plantation concept. Here, the government effectively privatizes an area of steppe with a trench, plants the enclosure with shrubs, and after a period of establishment permits range users restricted access under contract and on payment of a grazing fee. The idea is not unique to Syria. Since 1980, 470,000 hectares have been taken for plantations in Tunisia, 133,000 hectares in Iran, and 33,000 hectares in Algeria, and there are many others (World Bank 1995). In Syria the plantations have been at the heart of state intervention in the steppe since the late 1980s and by 2000 occupied 220,000 hectares.

The plantation concept came after a generation of frustrated state intervention in rangeland management and technology transfer. It represented a significant step against the tide of devolution in natural resource management elsewhere, and instead advocated centralization as a solution for sustainable development in arid regions. The actual presence of the plantations on the steppe, coupled with the fact the state had tilled and planted the land (that is, invested), brought the formal legal system and state authorities into direct conflict with the customary land tenure system like never before.

Plantations are supposedly located where Steppe Directorate officials judge the steppe to be degraded. Only private steppe land (approximately 2 percent) cannot be included within a plantation; all other land (including cultivated fields and cooperative pastures) is technically state land and can therefore be appropriated, despite the fact that customary institutions have governed land tenure for centuries. Once the site and size are determined, a committee is appointed within the Ministry of Agricultural and Agrarian Reform (MAAR) to produce a technical and economic feasibility study for the proposed plantation.[3] Socioeconomic or environmental impact assessments are not regularly carried out. If the committee gives its approval, the MAAR provides financial support for establishing the plantation.

After a period of shrub establishment averaging five years, the plantations are opened under contract for use during restricted periods, generally a couple of months each in the winter and spring. Enforcement of plantation rules is the prime responsibility of the Steppe Directorate, but the rules themselves are decided on at the provincial level by the Agricultural Council[4] and hence vary. The following rules, however, are broadly applicable. The carrying capacity of all

---

3. The committee is composed of an agricultural economist, a geologist, and representatives from the provincial departments of the MAAR and the Steppe Directorate.

4. The Agricultural Council is chaired by the provincial governor and includes provincial heads for Agriculture, Finance, the Ba'th Party, and the Peasants' Union.

the plantations was set at three head-of-sheep per hectare in 1995 and has not changed since. In line with the succession model of plant ecology, if the Steppe Directorate officials believe that grazing is insufficient in a particular season, access to the plantations is delayed, truncated, or denied completely. Firewood collection, camping, milking, and watering are prohibited in the plantations during leasing. A deposit on the contract is also required in some provinces, including Aleppo, and where this is the case each contract is clearly designated an allotted area. The cost to a herder for a spring contract is harmonized across the country, at 125 Syrian lira (SL) (US$2.25) per hectare per month.

> On the frontline of plantation rule enforcement are year-round resident guards. Those caught trespassing in Aleppo province are fined 5,000 SL, the equivalent of around $100 or the price of a two-year old ewe. The official number of trespassers prosecuted in the country since the plantations were first opened in 1995 is estimated around a thousand, the vast majority of them reportedly at two plantations in the Aleppo steppe.[5]

Technological Outcomes, Rangeland Management, and Institutions

Syrian authorities have sought to transfer shrub technology to the steppe through a variety of institutional arrangements, all of which have discounted customary land tenure and property rights. The underlying premise for the state approach is rooted in the "tragedy of the commons" model of pastoral society, which hinges on the assumption of noncooperating herders and eventual degradation.

While many researchers and rangeland scientists implicate government policy itself for the decline of customary systems, a pervasive perception is that the system is unable to adapt to changing socioeconomic conditions (FAO 1967; World Bank 1995; Ngaido 1997). Customary systems in Syria, as elsewhere, have been perceived as being unable to regulate pasture use in the face of pressures from increasing human and animal populations and a diminishing range area. Some have felt that the organizational and institutional basis on which the customary system relies is in a process of irreversible decline as an inevitable consequence of modernization (United Nations 1955; Abu Jaber 1966). That is, tribes weaken as they become superfluous in the presence of a maturing and ubiquitous judiciary and civil administration system.

Research on customary control and access systems in Syria is noticeable for its absence. The tribes have been identified as the cause of degradation by a process of deductive reasoning from ecology and political science theories. This belief is reinforced by policymakers' ambivalent attitudes toward migratory groups. Herders' resistance to adoption of technologies and institutions

---

5. Paraphrased conversation with staff at Steppe Directorate headquarters, Palmyra, July 4, 1999.

imposed by government authorities is poorly understood and often attributed to irrational behavior. A more accurate understanding of the institutions governing rangeland management and the incentives underlying adoption behavior necessitates a detailed appreciation of the customary system, state centralization, capitalist penetration, and the evolution of these institutions in Syria during the 20th century.

Property Rights in Syria: A Historical Overview

Modern-day Syria is a relatively new phenomenon. It was originally carved out of two Ottoman provinces after World War I and placed under French mandatory rule before the country won its independence in 1944. A judicial-political division, called the "steppe line," was inherited by the French and subsequently by the nationalists. It was first defined in state law in 1870 by a centralizing Ottoman government that wished to encapsulate and subject the moving camel- and sheep-rearing tribes of the desert interior. Within the steppe line, the Syrian state recognized the authority of customary law and courts in regulating the activities of tribal society, including land tenure issues. What amounted to a state within a state remained ostensibly unchanged following independence, but it was an obvious anathema to a fledgling nation, and within 14 years of independence customary law and tribes were formally abolished and the steppe areas nationalized. This move was of historic importance for it was the last legislation to deal specifically with the tribes and marked the final act in the long struggle by central governments to eliminate the tribes and *shaykhs* as rivals to their own power and jurisdiction.

Key to understanding property rights in Syria is the concept of legal pluralism. For a long time the formal legal system of the state, the *qanun*, coexisted with tribal customary law, '*urf*. Whereas the *qanun* is by definition written, the '*urf* is largely unwritten. Often the *qanun* has confirmed existing local custom, as custom is recognized as one of the sources of Islamic law, *shari'a*, itself a pillar of the *qanun* (Heyd 1973). The moving tribes were rarely subject to *qanun* before 1958. Among them customary law prevailed in all matters including marriage, divorce, homicide, and property rights. These tribal legal institutions have been described as "remarkable for their sophistication, and a central feature of the culture" (Stewart 1995, 1).

The question of property rights in the steppe area was of little concern to the authorities before the 1940s. Historically, the government's principal interest in rural property rights has been in regulating and taxing cultivation. The authority of the state has broadly correlated with the extent of cultivation, and both have waxed and waned at various times in history. Cultivation's most recent expansion began in the 1840s with impetus from world trade and later a growing domestic human population. For a century this expansion was mostly accommodated within the steppe line, particularly south of Aleppo City and the

Euphrates River. Rising international and local demands were also encouraging expansion of sheep numbers in the steppe. These two forces of expanding cultivation and growing sheep numbers converged along the margins of the steppe in the early 1940s, raising land scarcity and precipitating dramatic developments in both the statutory and customary land tenure systems.

The Statutory Tenure System

In Islamic law the uncultivated steppe was categorized *mawat*, or dead land, and this type of land was prevalent in Syria until the 1950s. On *mawat* land the state claimed no taxes and all persons could "cut for fuel and for building—or collect herbage—without anyone being able to prevent him" (Ottoman Land Code 1858, taken from Heyd 1973). As for cultivation, Sunni jurists considered vivification of *mawat* land as desirable and an activity to be encouraged (Maktari 1971), although the state retained the right to demand consent before cultivation in lieu of a fee. This said, such consent was largely academic in the steppe before state expansion in the late 19th century and was never fully enforced thereafter. In the first years of independence (1952), the state abolished prescriptive rights and the ancient category of *mawat,* and all such land was reclassed as state land (*amlak dawlah*). *Mawat* was seen as a legitimization of open access and the destructive habits that open access in principle engenders among resource users.

Nationalization not only underscored the state's authority to regulate land use, but also provided the state a tool with which to further reduce tribal power. The law, however, failed to make a material impact until 1958, when the sway of customary law among the tribes was officially abolished and a government more bent on state-led steppe development, the Socialist Ba'th Party, came to power in 1963. They originally espoused "pragmatism and evolutionism within the national framework" (Abu Jaber 1966) and advocated the dispersal and sedentarization of moving tribes in order that individual loyalty could be redirected toward national goals. The Ba'thist constitution states:

> Nomadism is a primitive social state. It decreases the national output and makes an important part of the nation a paralyzed member and an obstacle to its development and progress. The party struggles for the sedentarization of nomads by the grants of land to them [and] for the abolition of tribal custom (Article 43).

The abolition of tribal rights coincided with the start of a severe drought (1958–61) that destroyed herds on an unprecedented scale. According to official estimates 80 percent of the camel population was killed, while the sheep population dropped from 6 million in 1957 to 3.5 million in 1961 (FAO 1967). The single most important government response to the drought was the establishment of the Steppe Directorate within the MAAR to take on range management and alleviate the impact of future droughts. With virgin cultivable land in the country now thought to be exhausted, the state redirected considerable state resources to steppe management and animal husbandry in the hopes of stabilizing and expanding meat production. FAO had charged that overgrazing, the absence of grazing control mechanisms, the expansion of cultivation, and the uprooting of shrubs had together "resulted in the grazing capacity of the steppe being seriously depleted" (FAO 1973, 5). These factors, along with the current breeding system and the region's susceptibility to drought, were implicated in adversely affecting the nation's terms of trade and balance of payments, since livestock meat and grains tended to be exported at low prices and imported at high prices.

With the guiding principles of import substitution and food security through self-sufficiency, the authorities devised a four-point plan for steppe development with assistance from the FAO, the impact of which continues to be felt today. It proposed to regenerate the steppe through controlled grazing, increase local production of forage, create feed supplies to meet emergencies caused by drought, and improve sheep fattening. Their target was 11 million sheep by 1985, which would contribute to a desired increase in per capita meat consumption and at the same time continue the valuable export trade for which there was a large demand in neighboring countries (FAO 1967). To fulfill these ambitious objectives, the Steppe Directorate began research in shrub technology for range rehabilitation and in 1968 initiated a rotational grazing scheme within a cooperative model termed Hema, designed to supplant the tribal system. Although Hema was inspired by a perceived indigenous mechanism of controlled grazing, in fact it showed little resemblance to the indigenous system. The stringency of Hema cooperative rules, the corruption of cooperative structures for political ends, and the government's inability to supply credible grazing management institutions and structures undermined the cooperative approach.

The Customary Tenure System

The prevailing assumption that the tribal system was inadequate to manage steppe resources supposedly stems from the tribes' failure either to adapt their institutions to changing socioeconomic conditions or to resist suppression by a nationalist state. Examining the case of tribes and land tenure in the northern region of the Syrian steppe reveals an alternative history for the customary system. Indeed, there is clear indication of an evolving, resilient customary system, one that has not only endured repression by the state but also obliged government authorities to resume a positive and active role in its institutions.

All Arab tribal individuals belong to a particular tribe, which imparts an authenticity of descent and a quality of honor that sets them apart from nontribal society (Hourani 1991; Dresch 1993). Individual families form larger groups, called *'quam* (singular: *qom*), the fundamental organizing units within a tribe. A collection of *'quam* forms a maximal lineage or clan, called *fakhdh*. Families within a clan rely on group collective action and commonly hold water and pastures together (Wilkinson 1983). Generally, a council of elders guides the clan, and in many instances there is a well-respected individual among them, a *mukhtar* or *wajih*, who can speak for the group as a whole. A tribe is much larger, often comprising several villages or herding groups. Common to many tribes and clans is the ethnopolitical ideology of patrilineal descent or shared ancestry. The language of common descent does not necessarily reflect fact but is better understood as a metaphor for signifying notions of closeness (LaBianca 1990). In the wider region most tribes also have had long histories of a specific territorial identity.[6]

Tribal society has a wealth of social capital—the social relations and norms embedded in the structures of their society that regulate interactions. Relationships do change over time, but given that individuals involved in any of these social structures engage in repeated interactions, each relationship is guided by expectations of predictable behavior, leading to trust and reciprocity. Such trust underpins the customary land tenure system and its flexibility. The fact that the state has had to take overt actions to break up customary systems and as yet remains unable to do away with them attests to the strength and utility of these social capital networks.

A group associated with a territory holds the exclusive right to invest in land, such as through digging a well, building a house, or cultivating a field. They also hold the right to graze and exclude others, but given the nature of an arid environment and the size of any one territory, herders inevitably need to maintain flexible, reciprocal arrangements with other groups to maintain mobility. Hence, social capital is a critical ingredient upholding such arrangements and assuring mutual compliance. Events that transpired at the turn of the 20th century in the Aleppo steppe illustrate the important role played by such adaptive customary institutions in the face of resource competition.

Before the arrival of trucks, the broad region in which a tribe migrated throughout the year was (and sometimes still is) known as the *dirah*. It represented a functional area of habitual use composed of water holes and associated pastures to which the group held rights. In drought years when parts or all of a *dirah* were affected, families, groups, or larger parts of a tribe sought water and pastures through social networks in the *dirah* of other tribes.

At the turn of the 20th century, the Aleppo steppe was dominated by two neighboring sheep-herding tribes, the Hadidiyin and the Mawali, and a powerful camel-herding tribe called the Sba'ah. The size of the *dirah* depended on the herding animal, with camel herders having substantially larger *dirah* and venturing deeper into the desert then their brethren, the sheep and goat herders. These latter herders were restricted by the water dependency of their animals

6. For the Sinai, see Stewart (1986); for Yemen, see Dresch (1993); Hourani (1991).

to the desert fringes where water sources were more frequent and plentiful. The Sba'ah spent their winter and early spring around the wells of Wadi Hauran and its environs in modern-day western Iraq, 500 kilometers southeast of the Aleppo steppe line. In spring the Sba'ah migrated to the Aleppo steppe, where they stayed the summer, occupying water points and pastures just vacated by the sheep-herding tribes, the Hadidiyin and the Mawali. There, they traded with the settled areas and grazed their animals on steppe shrubs largely unpalatable to sheep. This complementary and nonexclusive use of water and pastures between the sheep- and camel-rearing tribes has an ancient history in the region, with rights to waters and pastures in the near steppe and the time windows on seasonal movement acknowledged in a written tribal treaty signed in the last years of the Ottoman Empire (1907–18) (Zakrya 1947).

This agreement lasted until the 1940s. In the meantime, cultivation in Syria trebled to 2.1 million hectares, sheep numbers also trebled to 3.4 million head, while camels started to give way to tractors and trucks (Widmer 1936; Issawi and Dabezies 1951). Sba'ah households were adapting to the changing demands in the marketplace. Whereas they owned no sheep in 1920, they reportedly held some 80,000 10 years later (HCRF 1930). Because all three tribes now had sheep in large numbers but still broadly lacked the ability to truck water, conflict arose between Sba'ah and the old sheep-herding tribes over water and pastures in the near steppe during winter and spring months.

Together with an expansion of agriculture, the rising sheep numbers demanded changes in the customary land tenure system, at least in the near steppe. Of immediate concern to the Hadidiyin, the Mawali, and the Sba'ah was an untangling of their overlapping *dirah* in the near steppe and the establishment of discrete tribal territories as a basis for access rights to natural resources. Once this goal was achieved, they could undertake investment in either water or agriculture without risk of intertribal disputes. To facilitate this shift, the disputing tribes sought an agreement through customary channels and under the auspices of the state. By far the most important of such agreements was the Damascus tribal treaty of 1956, which divided more than 500,000 hectares of the Aleppo steppe among the three tribes, although preexisting claims to water and pasture were kept intact. The political process used in this treaty, and other similar ones before and after it, was based on tribal custom.

In 1958, when Syria formally abolished the role of customary law and structures, the Damascus treaty and others like it were automatically annulled. The authorities assumed full responsibility for rangeland management, placing it with the Steppe Directorate from 1961. Nevertheless, customary institutions continued to exert authority over rangeland management and tribal control. Documented evidence shows that substantial cooperation to regulate control and access to steppe resources persisted among herders from different tribes, despite the hostile political environment, including a significant level of tribal corporate activity in protecting rights.

Following the abolition of tribal rights in 1958, large numbers of the Sba'ah left Syria for Saudi Arabia. With most of Sba'ah gone, Ghanatsah (a faction of the Hadidiyin) took the opportunity to reoccupy and claim for themselves a portion of the treaty lands called Abu al-Naytel and Dayl'. They went unchallenged for more than a decade, but in 1974 Muharrab al-Rakan, a son of the supreme shaykh of Sba'ah, "and the members of Sba'ah represented by him" (SAR 1975, 1) returned to Syria and immediately laid a claim on the Abu al-Naytel well and the lands of Dayl'.

Ghanatsah took the matter to the state authorities. The head (*mudir*) of the Palmyra administrative district carried out preliminary consultations with the disputing tribes and visited the questioned site. The "final meeting" (SAR 1975) to resolve the problem was convened on February 10, 1975. The decision went in favor of Ghanatsah, and the old mutual border from the 1956 treaty was adjusted to the new agreement. The legal precedent for the decision was adverse possession—that is, undisputed occupation of property for a given period of time becomes the property of the occupant.

Six years later, the situation flared up again when Muharrab attempted again to extend his area of control by cultivating his shared border with Ghanatsah in an area referred to as the "airport." This was land Ghanatsah believed was theirs. Another round of resolution talks was held. The settlement reached went again in favor of Ghanatsah. Muharrab was allowed to reap his crop "as he had ploughed and planted it" (SAR 1981, 1), but afterward the land would revert to Ghanatsah.

This agreement, like many others,[7] was extraordinary considering the Ba'thist constitution and ideology. The decision had been reached with the full participation of the state authorities. As far as the written law was concerned, the disputed land was state land and, since it was not part of a cooperative, was technically open to all Syrian citizens and their livestock. Although the *shaykhs'* intermediary roles were formally terminated in 1958, two decades later little had changed in practice. Indeed, customary institutions remain the principal mechanism regulating access to steppe resources on a day-to-day basis, while the state continues to implicitly recognize and endorse tribal customary rights and practices, with high officials and party cadres guaranteeing agreements and signing documents in the name of the state. It is important to note, however, that the Steppe Directorate of the Ministry of Agriculture, with statuary responsibility for steppe resource management, was not involved in this particular agreement. It was seen instead as a political not a land management problem per se.

---

7. Additional post-1958 documented territorial treaties have come to light. The dates of these agreements include 1962, 1983, 1989, and 1992.

Conflicts between Statutory and Customary Tenure on the Plantations

The overlap of tribal territories at least partially explains the problem of violations of plantation rules of access in Aleppo. Both plantations discussed here form a group of four located on lands held by the Abraz clan of the Hadidiyin.

A guard at one of these plantations reported that he had turned over for prosecution no fewer than 200 Abraz herders in five years, in addition to the "many others caught but not charged" (conversation with the guard, Maraghah, Syria, June 21, 1999). Faysal, the *shaykh* of Abraz, puts the total number of Abraz prosecuted at 370. Evidence from official communications on a proposed fifth plantation in the Abraz area strongly suggests that appropriation of land for the plantations was causing serious pasture shortages for the clan. Upon hearing of the proposed plantation in early 1995, Faysal wrote to the Aleppo governor:

> Once these lands are annexed and the said plantation is established . . . we would no longer have lands for our sheep to graze. We were moved from 'Ein al-Zarqah and Maraghah where two plantations were established. To the north of us is the al-Haib tribe—with whom we have a bloody dispute—[and consequently] we are not welcome on their pasture. Moreover, the establishment of the plantation would cause hundreds of herders to move away, many of whom have houses in the area (Al-Nuri 1995).

As a result the proposed plantation was abandoned, although the reason given was that the site was in fact "one of the good sites in our steppe in terms of plant cover" (Al-Nuri 1995). This episode demonstrates that past decisions about plantation location failed to assess the implications of customary land tenure and the inevitable impact the change would have on local range uses.

It is an unwritten rule within the Steppe Directorate that local herders and clans have the right of first refusal on plantation leases, despite formal claims that the steppe and the plantations are open to all. Problems of who can have access to a plantation do not generally arise when the site is located entirely within a particular clan territory. When the plantation border cuts across tribal territories, however, or unwelcome groups from far afield attempt to purchase a lease on a local plantation, then the incongruence of tenure systems can result in some serious problems. Of the four plantations under study by ICARDA in 1996, two plantations fell wholly within clan territories but the other two did not. In the latter, disputes over access between neighboring groups resulted in considerable difficulties for the authorities.

Such was the case when two clans, Bu Hasan and Jimlan (both of the Hadidiyin tribe), attempted to gain access to the plantation and establish de facto possession of land that was originally part of three tribal territories belonging to the Bu Salah of Abraz, the Twimat of Ghanatsah, and the Ma'atah, all three of which are also part of the Hadidiyin. In the previous two leasing seasons, the plantation had been leased predominately by the Bu Salah, Abraz, which had also secured the vast majority of leases for that season. The only other group to have grazed the plantation in previous seasons was that led by members of Bu Kurdy (Ghanatsah), whose territory abutted the reserve to the north, and they were there again in 1996. When Bu Hasan and Jimlan also lodged requests for licenses, all applications were approved. Both Bu Kurdy and Bu Salah, however, believed that Jimlan and Bu Hasan had no right to any leases on the plantation, as their tribal grazing grounds at Hrabjah were unaffected by the plantation. They took their grievance to the plantation guard, who canceled Jimlan's and Bu Hasan's leases on the spot.

Aggrieved, Jimlan and Bu Hasan took their protest to the authorities, reiterating the formal position that any Syrian could legally take out a lease. The Hama governor went with the heads of the provincial Steppe Directorate and the Peasants' Union[8] office to Abu al-Fayad to settle the dispute. The resolution went in Jimlan and Bu Hasan's favor. The authorities hired a local tractor and plowed a boundary line within the plantation to separate the disputing parties. As compensation, Bu Salah and Bu Kurdy were released from all plantation rules: firewood could henceforth be collected, sheep numbers would be unregulated, and camping, watering, and milking could take place in the plantation. The head of the Steppe Directorate protested strongly against the decision but was ultimately unsuccessful in changing it. Within a few days, instead of the 22,000 sheep paid for by the Bu Salah and the Bu Kurdy groups, there were now 40,000 in the plantation. The plantation was shut down after three weeks.

Conclusions and Policy Implications

The previous discussion demonstrates the value of customary institutions supportive of herder mobility, reciprocal arrangements with respect to resource use, and intertribal conflict resolution mechanisms when it comes to rangeland management. Contrary to popular belief that they have broken down and disappeared, many customary institutions in Syria remain strong and continue to be influential in the property rights domain. Their inherent flexibility means they are usually better suited to the prevailing nonequilibrium environment of the Syrian rangelands than are the rigid statutory laws and inappropriate technologies imposed by the state. Imposition of technologies will not succeed unless tribal land tenure and institutions are taken into account. Customary institutions represent a superior foundation for an integrated and inclusionary

---

8. The Peasants' Union is an arm of the ruling Ba'th Party and took control of cooperatives from the MAAR in 1974.

resource management system. The continuing existence of these institutions contradicts Hardin's assumption of the inability of resource users to coordinate their actions to avert overexploitation. It is not possible to prove that these customary methods are environmentally sustainable since ecological studies based on the new paradigms in the field have yet to be conducted. But what these institutions do represent are the foundations of a sustainable system that reduces transaction costs and affords local legitimacy.

Past policies centralizing rangeland management were founded on misplaced assumptions about the physical dynamics of the steppe environment as well as the capacity of herders to cooperate with one another and regulate their use of pastoral resources. Shrub technologies like *Atriplex* have proven ill suited to livestock as well as incompatible with herders' socioeconomic realities. Plantations likewise conflict with mobility objectives and customary land tenure, fueling the incidence of tribal conflict. In contrast to this failed top-down approach are the enduring customary institutions whose sensitivity to the physical and social environment and inherent legitimacy have enabled them to overcome statutory abolition, even to the extent of obliging the authorities to recognize customary agreements.

With a fresh understanding of arid environments and the customary system, there are new opportunities for rangeland management in Syria. Tribes no longer represent a political threat as they once did, but they do represent irreplaceable social capital. With doubts raised about imported shrub technologies, plantations, and steppe policy more broadly, existing tribal systems offer a solid foundation on which to build an effective and efficient administration of steppe management and conservation. The task that now faces the authorities in Syria and elsewhere in the region is to respond to this latent opportunity and enter into a genuine partnership with the steppe users for the management and conservation of steppe resources.

References

Abu Jaber, K. 1966. *The Arab Ba'th Socialist party: History, ideology, and organization.* Syracuse, N.Y., U.S.A.: Syracuse University Press.

ACSAD (Arab Center for the Studies of Arid Zones and Dry Lands). 1992. Desertification in Syria. In *World atlas of desertification*, ed. N. Middleton and D. Thomas. London: Edward Arnold.

Al-Nuri, Faysal. 1995. Letter to H.E. The Governor of Aleppo from Faysal al-Nuri and companions on behalf of the Abraz tribe, February 13.

Behnke, R., I. Scoones, and C. Kerven. 1993. *Range ecology at disequalibrium: New methods of natural variability and pastoral adaptation in African Savannas.* London: Overseas Development Institute.

Bietenholz, P. 1963. *Desert and Bedouin in the European mind: Changing conceptions from Middle Ages to the present day.* Extramural Studies Board. Khartoum: University of Khartoum.

Deiri, W. 1990. Contribution a l'étude phyto-écologique et de la potentialité pastorale en Syrie aride. M.Sc. thesis, Institut de botanique, Université de Montpellier.

Dresch, P. 1993. *Tribes, government, and history in Yemen.* Oxford: Clarendon Paperbacks.

FAO (Food and Agriculture Organization of the United Nations). 1956. Report to the government of Syria on a program for improvement in sheep breeding and management. Number 571. Rome.

———. 1966. *Report to the Steppe Directorate: Grazing trial, Wadi al-'Azib Range and Sheep Experiment Station 1963–1966.* Rome.

———. 1967. *Report to the government of Syria on range management and fodder development.* Number TA2351 PL:TA/43. Rome: United Nations Development Programme/FAO.

———. 1973. *Terminal report: Syria 002.* Intergovernmental Committee, 24th Session, October 3–9, 1973, p. 14. Rome.

———. 1974. *Report to the government of the SAR on range management and fodder development.* SYR/58/011. Rome.

Goodchild, A., and A. Osman. 1993. Value of *Atriplex halimus* and *Salsola vermiculata* foliage as supplements for barley straw. In *1992 ICARDA annual report,* Pasture, Forage and Livestock Program. Aleppo: International Centre for Agricultural Research in the Dry Areas (ICARDA).

Hardin, G. 1968. The tragedy of the commons. *Science* 162: 1243–1248.

HCRF (Haut-Commisariat de la République Francaise and Direction du Service des Renseignements du Levant). 1930. Les tribus nomades et semi-nomads des états du Levant places sous mandat français. Beirut: Imp. Jeanne d'Arc.

Heyd, U. 1973. *Studies in old Ottoman law.* Oxford: Clarendon Press.

Hourani, A. 1991. Tribes and states in Islamic history. In *Tribes and state formation in the Middle East,* ed. P. Khoury and J. Kostiner. London: IB Tauris.

Issawi, C. 1987. *An Arab philosophy of history: Selections from the Prolegomena of Ibn Khaldun of Tunis (1332–1406).* Cairo: American University in Cairo Press.

Issawi, C., and C. Dabezies. 1951. Population movements and population pressure in Jordan, Lebanon, and Syria. *Midland Memorial Fund Quarterly* 29 (4).

LaBianca, O. 1990. *Sedentarization and nomadization: Food system cycles at Hesban and vicinity in Transjordan.* Berrien Springs, Mich., U.S.A.: Andrews University Press.

Le Houerou, N. 1992. The role of saltbush (*Atriplex spp.*) in arid land rehabilitation in the Mediterranean Basin: A review. *Agroforestry Systems* 18 (2): 107–148.

———. 1995. Drought-tolerant and water-efficient trees and shrubs ('trubs') for rehabilitation of tropical and subtropical arid lands. Photocopy.

Lewis, N. 1987. *Nomads and settlers in Syria and Jordan, 1800–1980.* Cambridge: Cambridge Middle East Library.

Leybourne, M., F. Ghassali, A. Osman, T. Nordblom, and G. Gintzburger. 1993. The utilization of fodder shrubs (*Atriplex* spp., *Salsola vermiculata*) by agro-pastoralists in the north Syrian steppe. In *1993 ICARDA annual report,* Pasture, Forage and Livestock Program. Aleppo: International Centre for Agricultural Research in the Dry Areas (ICARDA).

Maktari, A. 1971. *Water rights and irrigation practices in Lahj: A study of the application of customary and Shari'ah law in southwest Arabia.* Cambridge: Cambridge University Press.

McKell, C. 1975. Shrubs: A neglected resource of arid lands. *Science* 187: 803–809.

Ngaido, T. 1997. *Land tenure issues and the development of rangelands in Syria: Appraisal mission for the Badia rangeland development project in Syria.* Rome: International Fund for Agricultural Development.

Nordblom, T., G. Arab, A. Osman, A., and G. Gintzburger. 1995. *Survey of Bedouin groups with contracts to graze the government rangeland plantations at Maraghah, Aleppo Province, Syria.* Regional symposium on integrated crop-livestock systems in the dry areas of West Asia and North Africa. Aleppo: International Centre for Agricultural Research in the Dry Areas (ICARDA).

Noy-Mier, I. 1990. Responses of two semiarid rangeland communities to protection from grazing. *Israel Journal of Botany* 39 (4): 431–442.

Olsvig-Whittaker, L., P. Hosten, M. Shochat, and E. Shochat. 1993. Influence of grazing on sand field vegetation in the Negev desert. *Journal of Arid Environments* 24 (1): 81–93.

Perevolotsky, A. 1995. *Conservation, reclamation and grazing in the northern Negev: Contradictory or complementary concepts.* ODI Pastoral Network Paper 38a. London: Overseas Development Institute.

Rae, J. 1999. Tribe and state: Rangeland management in the Syrian steppe. Ph.D. thesis, University of Oxford, Oxford, U.K.

Sankary, A. 1982. *Flora of the Syrian steppe.* Aleppo: University of Aleppo.

SAR (Syrian Arab Republic). 1975. The minutes of meeting to resolve dispute over al-del'a al-gharbieh between Muhurrab Rakan al-Murshed, the representative of Sba'ah tribe, and the members of Ghanatsah tribe [Hadidiyin], represented by Faysal al-Sfuk. Office of Chief, Secret Police. Homs: Homs Provincial Administration.

———. 1981. Minutes of a meeting between Sba'ah and Ghanatsah over the lands of al-Del'a al-Gharbien. Ministry of Interior.

Scoones, I. 1994. *Living with uncertainty: New directions in pastoral development in Africa.* London: Intermediate Technology Publications.

Stewart, F. 1986. *Bedouin boundaries in central Sinai and the southern Negev.* Wiesbaden, Germany: Otto Harrassowitz.

———. 1995. Texts in Bedouin law. Unpublished copy of cases recorded in southern Sinai, the Social Studies Center. Blaustein Center for Desert Research, Sede Boqer, Israel.

United Nations. 1955. *Progress in land reform.* New York: United Nations Economic and Social Council.

Wachholtz, R. 1996. *Socio-economics of Bedouin farming systems in dry areas of Northern Syria.* Stuttgart-Hohenhiem, Germany: Wissenschaftsverlag Vauk KG.

Westoby, M., B. Walker, and I. Noy-Mier. 1989. Opportunistic management for rangelands not at equilibrium. *Journal of Range Management* 42 (4): 266–274.

Widmer, R. 1936. Population. In *Economic organization of Syria,* ed. S. Himadeh. New York: AMS Press.

Wilkinson, J. 1983. Traditional concepts of territory in southeast Arabia. *Geographical Journal* 149 (3): 301–315.

World Bank. 1995. *North Africa and Iran: Rangelands development in arid and semiarid areas, strategies and policies.* Washington, D.C.: World Bank.

Zakirov, P. 1989. Grazing problems in Iraq: Problems of desert development. *Problemy Osvoeniia Pustyn'* 4: 58–63.

Zakrya, A. 1947. *Tribes of al-sham.* Damascus: Dar al-Fekr.

8 Land Dispute Resolution in Mozambique: Evidence and Institutions of Agroforestry Technology Adoption

JON D. UNRUH

Nonadoption of natural resource management technologies frequently occurs in an environment lacking in functioning institutions, viewed as legitimate and workable by the parties concerned, for resolving land tenure disputes. The frequency, severity, and perception of land conflict and the character of land dispute resolution institutions have a fundamental influence on the resource access arrangements and tenure security necessary for technology adoption. Because all societies experience land disputes, the formation or evolution of customs or rules pertaining to legitimate evidence of rights to property is important to tenure security and resource access. If the availability and legitimacy of evidence change, then the associated property rights institutions will also change, with implications for technology adoption. This situation is especially the case if the resource technology is also regarded as evidence.

This chapter presents a study undertaken in postwar Mozambique that explores how cashew agroforestry has on the one hand strengthened claims to land during a period of significant dislocation. On the other hand, its potential as a productive technology has been weakened by its role as one of the few forms of evidence in land tenure disputes that continues to have widespread legitimacy.

The study compares clusters of villages in three different provinces of Mozambique in order to explore: (1) the incidence and nature of land tenure conflicts, (2) the types of evidence used to resolve those conflicts along with their corresponding availability and legitimacy, (3) the complex interactions between property rights and cashew agroforestry, and (4) the tensions existing between customary and statutory law concerning property rights. The chapter also considers alternatives that have the potential to enable the evolution of dispute resolution and property rights institutions as well as further the adoption of cashew agroforestry in Mozambique, particularly in light of recent reforms in land legislation.

The Recent History of Mozambique

The War, Rural Reintegration, and Land Tenure

The recent 16-year civil war in Mozambique dislocated approximately 6 million people (primarily small-scale agriculturalists) from land resources that they are now reclaiming. This return comprises the largest reintegration of refugees and displaced persons in the history of Africa. Although the war officially ended in 1992, the population's lack of confidence about the actual end to the conflict delayed moves back into agriculture (USCR 1993). As a result, the United Nations expected to continue its resettlement activities in Mozambique until the year 2000 (Lauriciano 1995).

Resource tenure issues are increasingly coming to the fore as populations respond to what they perceive to be lasting peace and make decisions about returning to areas of origin or migrating elsewhere and reengaging in agriculture. Many demobilized and dislocated smallholders have returned to find their lands occupied by others, resulting in significant numbers of land disputes (Galli 1992; Willett 1995). At the same time rural households are expanding areas under cultivation with each successive season as farmers bring areas long under fallow due to the war back into cultivation (USAID 1996). Further complicating access to land are large-scale recovery efforts to rehabilitate whole agricultural sectors, such as cashew and livestock production. These efforts involve free or greatly subsidized saplings and animals, which are then connected to the landscape in some fashion and are frequently used to claim land.

All land belongs to the state in Mozambique. Because the state has limited capacity to exercise authority over land, however, there is considerable ambiguity over exactly what rights individuals, communities, and the state have. Even if the national land tenure framework operated perfectly and the necessary enforcement capacity existed, it would not be able to resolve the complicated land conflicts emerging in postwar Mozambique. The central issue is less the lack of a surveying service and an official agency of coordination and arbitrage than the legitimacy of existing services with the competence and accountability to solve land conflict problems for different groups (Tanner and Monnerat 1995). Although recent political change increasingly recognizes the legitimacy of local, customary authority structures, the land law in place at the end of the war did not recognize customary tenure systems and therefore denied community access rights to land not currently under cultivation. The land law also failed to recognize customary decisions that resolve conflicts between smallholders and customary evidence in disputes with largeholders who use the formal land tenure system. Thus lands incorporated in fallow systems, forest extraction, grazing, and land otherwise held by communities are recognized as vacant and are vulnerable to occupation by commercial land interests able to get title, resulting in widespread land disputes (Tanner and Monnerat 1995).

One of the features of postwar land tenure in Mozambique is that agricultural reintegration for many small-scale producers has begun with an initial dependence on locations where the most fertile land, perennial water supplies, infrastructure, markets, relief services, and physical security are present together. Migration to such areas occurred throughout and after the war, with food-insecure migrants coming into conflict with long-term customary residents. Large land interests are also most interested in acquiring property in these agronomically endowed, or "critical resource," areas. At least 9 million hectares of land have been awarded through the formal land tenure system to concessions for farming, hunting, tourism, and mining activities. Virtually all these concessions overlap with settlements of smallholders, who were not part of formal land allocation decisions. These 9 million hectares occupy the highest-quality land of the 35 million hectares of arable land, including all the major river basins and land near infrastructure and towns (Moll 1996). This situation has generated further conflict between migrants, in-place communities, and concession holders, in an environment where property rights (including dispute resolution) institutions are problematic.

Cashew Agroforestry in Mozambique

Since the introduction of cashew trees to Mozambique by the Portuguese during the colonial era, the tree has become established in approximately one-third of the surface area of the country. In the early 1970s Mozambique was the world's largest producer of cashew nuts in shell, and cashew was the primary export commodity. Cashew trees exist largely on smallholder land in Mozambique, in groves and intermixed in cropping patterns with cassava, cowpea, maize, and groundnuts (CCL 1994). Planting and maintaining new trees is a fundamental aspect of cashew agroforestry, as is removing older nonproducing trees to create space in closed canopy groves and tree-crop associations.

The war and the associated collapse of the rural economy led to a significant change in cashew agroforestry (CCL 1994). Older trees were not removed, existing producing trees were not maintained (pruned, brush cut away from beneath trees), and perhaps most important, new trees were not planted over large areas of the country as populations were dislocated and transport, marketing, and processing of cashew were disrupted (Finnegan 1992; CCL 1994).

A recent national cashew tree population survey found very low numbers of trees less than 15 years old in all areas. Only 10–15 percent of the cashew tree population are in younger age classes (0–5, 6–10 years), with 20–30 percent between 16 and 25 years old and 60–70 percent over 25 years of age (CCL 1994). Studies indicate that cashew production begins to decline after year 20 (FAO 1987; MOA/SSTC 1989). A significant percentage of the younger trees that do exist appear to be self-seeded from the large stock of neglected adult trees (CCL 1994), meaning that their spatial placement is not optimized for an agroforestry system. Thus a primary challenge in Mozambique is the adoption (or postwar readoption) of tree replacement strategies and techniques, and hence the development of a renewed role for agroforestry in natural resource management.

Methodology

In order to consider how evidence in land conflicts operates for and between smallholders, largeholders, and migrants, Unruh (1997) carried out social surveys in two critical resource areas and a control area in the northern part of the country in 1996. The idea was to compare the role of different forms of evidence (and customs and norms regarding evidence) in land dispute resolution.

The data for the study were gathered in the provinces of Nampula and Cabo Delgado in northern Mozambique (Figure 8.1). A social survey was carried out with 521 households in 21 villages, distributed in three sets of seven villages each. Two of these sets were situated in agronomically endowed, or "critical resource," locations, where fertile soils, perennial water, markets, infrastructure, and transport are fairly close together and thus are also locations most favored by large landholder interests. The third set of seven villages was dispersed within Nampula province in areas much less agronomically endowed and not in critical resource areas; this set acts as a control.

Households within the villages of Nampula were selected according to a stratified random sampling, whereby all households of each village were divided according to their relationship with large landholding cotton producers and then randomly selected. Smallholder proximity to cotton production is the largest source of smallholder versus largeholder land conflict in Nampula (Tanner 1996). Control village households were also stratified according to their participation and nonparticipation in a CARE oilseeds project and randomly selected.[1]

Critical Resource Areas and the Control

Tables 8.1, 8.2, and 8.3 provide a look at some of the more relevant differences between the three village sets. Generally, those occupying the critical resource areas (especially Montepuez) are in a more constrained and problematic situation regarding land tenure. The number of migrants is higher, land conflicts and land loss due to conflicts are more of a problem, agricultural investments (such as field bunding, fertilizer, fences) are lower, but surprisingly years of education is higher (Table 8.1). In general, high values for tenure security are more

---

1. This study was part of a larger study dealing with land tenure and food security, as these topics related to largeholder cotton interests that operated in these areas. Although this subsequent stratification is not directly relevant to the present land tenure study, the subsample adequately represents households in noncritical resource areas.

FIGURE 8.1 Study areas in Mozambique

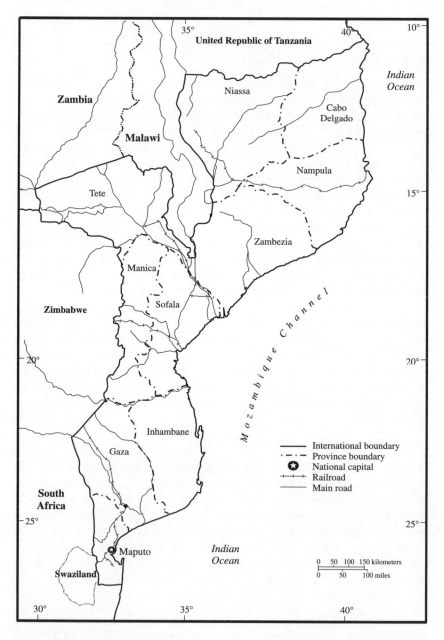

NOTE: The boundaries and names shown on this map do not imply official endorsement or acceptance by the United Nations.

TABLE 8.1 Summary of selected variables for the three village sets

Variables	Control set	Monapo set	Montepuez set
Migrants (percentage)	10	23	73
Average number of land conflicts per household	0.21	0.53	0.49
Households reporting that smallholders lose land in the area (percentage)	23	34	88
Households perceiving land conflicts as a problem (percentage)	64	91	92
Household perceiving arrival of outsiders to obtain land as a problem for the community (percentage)	16	39	66
Education (total years for household)	1.4	6.5	7.4
Farm investments (average number)	5.5	5.2	2.4

SOURCE: Unruh (1997).

frequent in the control, while the critical resource sites have fewer respondents that are tenure secure (Table 8.2). Conflict resolution between smallholders using the customary tenure regime is regarded as more "unjust" in critical resource areas, as is land conflict resolution between smallholders and large-holders using the formal system (Table 8.3).

Significant differences exist between village sets at the 0.05 level, with the exception of between Monapo and Montepuez for "Perception of land conflicts as a problem," and between the control and Montepuez for "Farm investments."

TABLE 8.2 Tenure security in the three village sets

Tenure security index	Control set	Monapo set	Montepuez set
		(percentage of respondents)	
Low: 8–15	10	27	50
Medium: 16–21	34	45	43
High: 22–30	56	28	7

SOURCE: Unruh (1997).

NOTE: For land tenure security, an index was derived using 21 variables from the survey, including the general perception of land conflict (4 variables); land loss and possibilities for losing land, including the role of title in land loss (8 variables); land lending (3 variables); and investment in land (6 variables). These variables were scaled, so that greater values indicated less presence and severity of land conflict, less land loss and preoccupation over land loss, more lending, and more investment. The values for the variables were added to give a scaled index for overall tenure security for each household. The index ranges from 8 to 30, with higher values indicating greater tenure security. Means for the tenure security index for the Montepuez (15.8) and Monapo (18.2) critical resource areas are significantly different from the control (21.4), and from each other, at the 0.05 level.

TABLE 8.3 Legitimacy of land dispute resolution for smallholders

Village set	Very just	Just	Unjust
	(percentage of village set's sample)		
Resolution between smallholders using the customary system[a]			
Control	85	12	3
Monapo	59	38	3
Montepuez	29	53	17
Resolution between smallholders using the statutory legal tenure system			
Control	52	43	4
Monapo	50	46	4
Montepuez	47	47	7
Resolution between smallholders and largeholders using the statutory legal tenure system[a]			
Control	24	44	33
Monapo	14	31	55
Montepuez	13	17	71

SOURCE: Unruh (1997).

[a]Values between village sets are significantly different at the 0.05 level.

Cashew Agroforestry Trees as Evidence

TREES AND LAND TENURE.   In the developing world, economically valuable trees are among the most common and valuable forms of customary evidence for claiming "ownership" of land (Fortmann and Riddell 1985; Raintree 1987). This fact is underscored by the restriction on tree planting by certain groups, such as women, tenants, and migrants, for fear that they would establish long-term or stronger claims to land, and the failure of agroforestry programs that do not take into account this important custom regarding valuable trees. Trees, by their enduring nature, can be evidence that lands in fallow are still "owned." This function is important because land laws, including Mozambique's, often stipulate that land is declared "abandoned" if uncultivated for more than a certain number of years, frequently a duration much shorter than an adequate fallow period.

In Mozambique, cashew tree tenure plays a large role in property rights institutions for smallholders, including land conflict resolution. Forces associated with the war and the disconnect between customary, migrant, and formal tenure have acted to put even greater weight on older cashew trees compared with other forms of evidence. There are important relationships between this evidence role and the continued adoption and maintenance of cashew agroforestry. The remainder of this section examines the relative importance of cashew trees as evidence. The subsequent two sections consider the two primary forces that shape the availability and legitimacy of cashew and other forms of evidence. The final three sections look at cashew agroforestry's effect on property rights, factors important to the evolution of nonagroforestry evidence and institutions, and recent changes in the formal law to acknowledge forms of customary evidence.

CASHEW EVIDENCE IN THE THREE VILLAGE SETS. For the three village sets in the study, the presence of cashew and other valuable trees is the single most important piece of evidence for defending or asserting rights to land, regardless of the average number of trees per smallholder. For the control, Monapo, and Montepuez samples, 86, 93, and 90 percent of respondents, respectively, identified cashew trees as important evidence with respect to the occupation and "ownership" of land. These were the greatest percentages for any form of evidence (from a total of 30 forms) (Table 8.4). When asked if having trees provided a "guarantee" against loss of land, the percentages were also quite high: 99, 99, and 94 percent for the control, Monapo, and Montepuez samples, respectively (Table 8.5). The number of smallholders actually owning trees, however, was much lower: 59, 69, and 16 percent of the control, Monapo, and Montepuez samples. The average number of trees owned in the three samples was also low: 25, 39, and 3 for the control, Monapo, and Montepuez samples (Table 8.5). Thus whereas nearly all households consider trees as quite valuable evidence, many did not actually possess the evidence, and in Montepuez very few possessed significant numbers of trees. One way to interpret this result is that it may indicate the degree to which customs and norms that respect cashew trees as evidence are in place after the war, compared with other forms of evidence. Montepuez illustrates that even in situations where institutions regarding property rights are most disrupted (Tables 8.1–8.3), the norms regarding agroforestry trees as legitimate evidence are nonetheless operative.

Because this evidentiary role of agroforestry trees strengthens property rights and tenure security, it should theoretically provide incentives to further invest in cashew agroforestry (adoption). As the following sections illustrate, however, several factors significantly complicate this investment, with repercussions for property rights.

The War: Dislocation and Agricultural Disruption

The dislocations and disruptions attending the war have had significant impacts on land tenure evidence in two ways: (1) creating and maintaining an age-gap in agroforestry trees, and (2) making other forms of evidence less available and legitimate.

TABLE 8.4 Social, cultural-ecological, and physical evidence of landownership in the three village sets

Evidence list	Control set	Monapo set	Montepuez set
	(percentage of respondents mentioning form of evidence)		
Social evidence			
Village elders	13	10	0
Local leaders	25	10	0
Local organization	3	0	
Testimony of family	16	11	0
History of occupation	7	2	0
Knowledge of community area	3	0	0
Testimony of neighbors	36	45	3
History of economic trees	1	2	1
Cultural-ecological evidence			
Trails	4	3	1
Cemeteries	3	7	1
Location roads	4	0	0
Sacred areas	1	3	0
Ruins, old village	3	0	0
Economic trees	86	93	90
Tombs	15	7	0
Field boundaries	3	2	15
Location of old crops	0	0	1
Physical evidence			
Local terrain differences	5	5	4
Very large trees	11	5	48
Location of mountains	4	6	5
Termite hills	5	5	28
Rivers	8	11	28
Soil type	31	26	61
Near cotton land	0	3	0
Boulders	1	5	1
Location of hills	0	1	8

SOURCE: Unruh (1997).

The Tree Age-Gap

The dislocation of 6 million people had a direct effect on tree planting and the removal of older, non-producing trees. Migrants residing on others' land were prevented by their hosts from planting or removing trees because it would be seen as a land claim. Because the areas where migrants settle tend to be relatively crowded, it would likely be known who cut the trees. It would thus seem

TABLE 8.5 Summary of variables regarding agroforestry trees as evidence in the three village sets

Variable	Control set	Monapo set	Montepuez set
Agroforestry trees as important evidence (percentage of respondents)	86	93	90
Average number of trees per household	25	39	3
Planning to plant trees (percentage of respondents)	32	25	10
Possess trees (percentage of respondents)	59	69	16
Trees provide a "guarantee" of not losing land (percentage of respondents)	99	99	94

SOURCE: Unruh (1997).

NOTE: Between-village average values are significantly different at the 0.05 level between all three village sets for "Average number of trees per household"; between the control and Monapo for "Agroforestry trees as important evidence"; and between Montepuez and the other two sites for both "Planning to plant trees" and "Possess trees."

wiser for migrants to attempt borrowing or renting arrangements with local inhabitants, rather than attempt to overtly undermine their claims. For migrants cultivating land with no clear ownership, the temporary nature of their residence deterred tree planting.

Even for communities not dislocated, the war and resulting food security problems meant that the agricultural time horizons of many small-scale producers were reduced considerably, effectively precluding tree planting in favor of cultivating much quicker-producing annual crops. At the same time older trees near the end of production were not removed, as they frequently still provided small amounts of cashew for food-insecure agriculturalists.

The control set was the village set with the greatest percentage of respondents planning to plant cashew trees in the coming year, the lowest number of migrants from elsewhere, and the greatest tenure security (Tables 8.5, 8.1, and 8.2). For all three village sets the percentage of migrants is inversely related to the percentages of those intending to plant cashew trees and the level of tenure security (Tables 8.1, 8.5, and 8.2). The fact that Montepuez has the highest level of migrants and the fewest cashew trees may suggest why tenure security is lowest and the perception of unjust dispute resolution is highest.

The frequency and severity of land conflict also influences the cashew age-gap. Key informant interviews in the three village sets revealed that smallholders in areas where conflicts are a large problem (Monapo and Montepuez, Table 8.1) are especially reluctant to remove older trees because of their greater evidence value (as indications of long-term occupation) over seedlings and saplings, which can be easily pulled up. An additional constraint to new tree planting is that as more smallholders lose land in the course of disputes (different from dislocation due to the war), they must then rent out or borrow land from other smallholders, again discouraging planting.

Availability of Nontree Evidence

During the war many agricultural areas were repeatedly occupied and abandoned at different times and by different groups. This pattern obscured, confused, and made less accessible or inaccessible many forms of evidence related to human occupation of the landscape, particularly nontree evidence. This is perhaps most notably the case where migrants presently make up a significant proportion of the local population. Not only has the legitimacy of social evidence been weakened by dislocation, but it has also affected the comparative importance and legitimacy of other forms of evidence like agroforestry that provide a clear indication of history of occupation.

In order to ascertain differences in evidence availability between the three village sets, forms of evidence were first categorized as social, cultural-ecological, and physical. Social evidence is oral or testimonial evidence provided by or confirmed by others in the community that demonstrates occupation and ties individuals and households to their local communities. Social evidence also corroborates other social, as well as physical and cultural-ecological, evidence. Cultural-ecological evidence is defined as the physical pieces of evidence that exist because of human activity on the landscape, such as agroforestry trees, current and old field boundaries, and cemeteries. This evidence demonstrates occupation and corroborates social evidence and some other forms of cultural-ecological evidence. Physical evidence is defined as naturally occurring terrain features that are easily observable to anyone, and knowledge of physical evidence demonstrates familiarity with an area but corroborates no other category of evidence.

These three categories of evidence vary considerably in their utility. Social and cultural-ecological evidence is much more meaningful than simply an individual's knowledge of where pieces of physical evidence (such as rivers, fallen trees, depressions, and termite hills) are located because knowledge of the location of naturally occurring terrain features is readily observable by anyone. It is the combination of social evidence with cultural-ecological evidence that is most valuable in constructing an argument for a claim to land in a dispute. This is because cultural-ecological evidence corroborated by social evidence constitutes the connection between the physical signs of land occupation due to human presence and the social aspects, which tie individuals to communities (such as inheritance of land and networks of lending land). Such social evidence is at the heart of the definition of land tenure, which Middleton (1988, ix) describes as "a system of relations between people and groups expressed in terms of their mutual rights and obligations with regard to land."

Table 8.4 compares the percentage of the village set samples favoring different forms of evidence. What is most striking are the differences in social and physical evidence for the three village sets, especially between the control and Montepuez. Social evidence is largely lacking in the Montepuez set in favor of naturally occurring physical evidence, in contrast to the other two sets. This result indicates the high preference for evidence that is available, even though such evidence is of reduced utility compared with other forms.

Cultural-ecological evidence is essentially the same for the three sets because of the emphasis all sets place on agroforestry trees. There is, however, a division with regard to the evidence that ties individuals to community and land over the long term (such as knowledge of and social attachment to tombs, cemeteries, sacred areas, and village ruins) as opposed to shorter-term forms of cultural-ecological evidence (such as field boundaries and present crops). Subtracting agroforestry trees from the list of cultural-ecological evidence, respondents in Montepuez were more likely than those in other sites to cite evidence that demonstrates shorter-term occupation of an area (Table 8.4). Given that the control villages are the most "intact" communities, it makes sense that social evidence and long-term cultural-ecological evidence were found to be the most prevalent there. For all three samples, the extent of different forms of social and cultural-ecological evidence parallels the degree to which households believe dispute resolution is more "just" and tenure more secure (Tables 8.4, 8.3, and 8.2).

Overall, the ability of smallholders in Montepuez to build a good argument about a land claim is compromised because of the lack of social evidence that can corroborate the existence of other physical or cultural-ecological evidence. This situation most likely arises because most in the Montepuez sample are recent migrants (Table 8.1) and thus do not have the same community-land connection or community cohesion as households within the control or the Monapo village sets. Of the migrants in the Montepuez set, only 3 (out of 94) households indicated some form of social evidence. Thus reductions in the availability of social evidence for populations with significant numbers of migrants appears to result in a shift to favor the forms of evidence that are available—physical evidence and some cultural-ecological evidence—with the relative permanence of older agroforestry trees emerging as one of the most important and durable pieces of evidence available.

Different Approaches to Land Tenure

The interaction of disparate approaches to land tenure in Mozambique influences the legitimacy of forms of evidence in dispute resolution. Whereas the previous section looked at how the availability of evidence shapes preferences for specific forms of evidence, this section considers how the between-group legitimacy of evidence shapes evidence preferences. In postwar Mozambique there are three different general approaches to land tenure: (1) customary, (2) statutory legal, and (3) migrant or "disrupted." The latter approach is characterized by a comparative lack of social connections to the community regarding land and a higher value placed on naturally occurring physical forms of evidence in claims to land. Land disputes involving parties from the different tenure approaches can involve forms of evidence that are regarded as legitimate and therefore respected within a certain approach. If not respected by the opposing party (through enforcement or custom), however, then such forms of evidence have little value. Such cases may force the different parties, particularly the less powerful, to fall back on evidence that is mutually legitimate.

For the customary (control) and largely migrant (Montepuez) groups in the study, there are only two forms of evidence for which both groups express a relatively high preference: soil type and agroforestry trees (Table 8.4), with soil type much less important than trees in both communities. While similar data do not exist for largeholders operating in the formal system, the land law in place at the end of the war acknowledged forms of smallholder evidence that demonstrate "occupation" (soil type does not) and explicitly disallowed social evidence. Although crops and field boundaries are evidence of occupation, they were so severely disrupted during the war that they are problematic for small-holders to use as evidence in a dispute and therefore are less preferred (Table 8.4). Agroforestry trees, on the other hand, especially the older trees, are evidence of occupation in the formal land tenure system and can signify a more direct and permanent connection to land for smallholders. Thus agroforestry trees are the only remaining evidence validated by customs and rules (formal and infor-mal), not only within, but also between, groups subscribing to different tenure approaches. As disputes between smallholders, largeholders, and migrants become common in certain areas, it is likely that agroforestry trees will become increasingly important for dispute resolution.

All else being equal then, the presence of such evidence should influence the outcomes of land disputes. While not comparable in every way, Monapo and Montepuez seem to support this. Both sets show similar measures for value of trees as evidence, conflict number, and perception of land conflict as a prob-lem (Tables 8.5 and 8.1). In the Monapo set, however, with many more cashew trees, a much lower percentage of respondents believe that smallholders lose land (Table 8.1), and higher percentages of the Monapo set indicate that conflict resolution between smallholders as well as between smallholders and large-holders is not a major problem (Table 8.3). That the Monapo sample expresses greater tenure security (Table 8.2) also makes sense. One might speculate that the much larger presence of cashew trees in the Monapo area (Table 8.5), to-gether with a greater presence of social evidence (not allowed in the land law but in many cases connectable to trees), perhaps plays a substantial role in out-comes of land conflict.

Even in the presence of good evidence, conflicts are instigated for a vari-ety of reasons. Many stem from poverty and instability in Mozambique. Mi-grants and largeholders alike seek access to land in better areas with the hope of at least getting a crop from a piece of land before their claim is contested. While the incidence of conflict may not be overly affected by the presence of cashew trees (Monapo has more cashew trees than Montepuez and fewer migrants, but also more conflicts), outcomes of disputes are perhaps resulting in greater tenure security, as well as affecting investment in technology and perceptions on how "just" dispute resolution institutions are.

The Technology's Effect on Property Rights Institutions

Cashew agroforestry has two overall effects on property rights in postwar Mozambique. First, the rules and customs regarding the link between agroforestry trees and land tenure have greatly facilitated (at no cost to the state) the defense and assertion of rights to land in a postwar context. This has helped to organize important aspects of property in a way that might not have occurred had there been no or very few agroforestry trees present in the postwar period. The existence and comparative importance of respected customs and norms regarding the connection between agroforestry trees and land, in an otherwise chaotic postwar tenure environment, therefore holds considerable potential as a starting point for the evolution or re-formation of additional institutions regarding property rights. Over time, forms of social evidence connected to cashew trees could take hold—that is, corroborating testimony regarding lending, renting, and purchase of tree harvests and times of planting and maintenance. This pattern may also occur with other forms of cultural-ecological evidence attesting to short-term occupancy, such as field boundaries and location of crops.

The second effect of agroforestry trees as evidence on property rights concerns the adoption and maintenance of cashew agroforestry. The failure to adopt, or readopt, tree replacement strategies due to the high value placed on older trees as evidence will eventually result in a decrease in this evidence as the older trees die out, with probable negative effects on both cashew production and tenure security. With decreasing numbers of trees, their availability as forms of evidence would eventually reach a point where the customs and norms that uphold trees as evidence would begin to disintegrate.

Very high value will continue to be placed on older trees unless other forms of evidence and their corresponding institutions become available and legitimate among the different groups. By reducing the comparative importance of agroforestry trees as evidence, an expanded array of broadly accepted evidence would enable renewed investment in agroforestry.

For the control sample, even without legal backing for customary social forms of evidence, a wider array of available evidence is regarded as legitimate (Table 8.4). This is also the set where the greatest planting occurs and where cashew trees ranked as a slightly less important form of evidence relative to the other two sets (Table 8.5). These characteristics are due to the wide array of other available evidence as well as the proportionately smaller number of largeholders competing for land in the control area, thus enabling greater consensus on the legitimacy of customary evidence.

In addition to the tenure relationship, significant market disruption may have also affected incentives to replace trees. Damage to market and transport infrastructure during the war reduced the ability of commercial interests to purchase and process cashews and to transport shipments for export and urban consumption. As a result, the economic incentive to smallholders to replace older trees in order to attain economically viable levels of production has no doubt decreased. The relative economic benefit of replacing trees, however, relative to the tenure benefit of nonreplacement is difficult to determine. Presumably, if market and transport infrastructure were optimally in place in the postwar period, there would be some increase in replacement of trees, but the risk of losing land and trees would likely take economic priority over any incentive to increase cashew production. If other evidence becomes available and if legitimate and market infrastructure recovers, however, the role of market incentives will likely increase.

The effect of cashew agroforestry in assisting the organization of land reaccess, and the potential disintegration of this evidence and its associated institutions along with the technology itself, highlight a broader point about the relationship between technology adoption and property rights. In Mozambique the nature of this relationship is not a static, entirely predictable one, but rather is necessarily influenced by a wider sociopolitical context that can influence the trajectory of this relationship.

Factors Important to the Evolution of Nonagroforestry Evidence and Institutions

The successful evolution of property rights and dispute resolution institutions will depend on the widespread recognition of different forms of evidence as legitimate. Customary evidence is largely not legitimate within the formal system, and the statutory system is less than legitimate to many smallholders, especially for dispute resolution. The incorporation of customary forms of evidence into the land law is a fundamental step in making such evidence legitimate within the formal system, and the formal system legitimate to smallholders. This step would act to increase the value of such evidence among smallholders, especially in problematic conflicts with largeholders who operate within the formal tenure system. Furthermore, it tends to be easier to modify national land legislation to accommodate evidence legitimate within the customary system than it is to legislate out of existence customary norms and rules regarding land tenure (Bruce, Migot-Adholla, and Atherton 1994). This is not to suggest that the details of land tenure in all customary systems should be incorporated into formal law (an impossible task), but rather that statutory law should recognize the themes and tenets that embody these and make them operable, such as community membership, testimony, local leadership, history of occupation, present use, and use of in-place dispute resolution institutions for intracommunity disputes. Continued conflicts, however, in which smallholders lose land to largeholders because the formal legal system does not recognize customary evidence are only likely to increase smallholder migration and lead to the loss of important social and cultural-ecological evidence, thereby acting to stagnate the evolution of evidence and their institutions. Adoption of agroforestry could then become more difficult because those dislocated from land will likely, if they continue to farm, be unable to plant trees on rented or borrowed land.

The legitimacy of the formal system from the smallholder point of view also shapes the potential for dispute resolution institutions to evolve. Smallholders residing in critical resource areas, with a much greater exposure to largeholders, believe that land dispute resolution between large and smallholders is more unjust than do those in the control sample (bottom third of Table 8.3). For Montepuez, 64 percent more of the sample believed the formal system was "unjust" when the dispute was between small- and largeholders than when the dispute was between smallholders. For Monapo, this difference was 51 percent, and for the control, 29 percent. Approximately half of the samples from both critical resource areas believed dispute resolution between smallholders using the formal system to be "very just," which is comparable to the control. Thus the government could build upon the smallholders' belief that the formal system has legitimacy by incorporating the much-needed "customs and controls" of communities in enforcing decisions. The problem is that the formal system lacks legitimacy for smallholders when it comes to disputes between small- and largeholders, potentially limiting that opportunity.

The evolution of institutions regarding customary forms of evidence also faces an availability problem. The war disrupted many institutions that support commonly accepted social and cultural-ecological evidence for smallholders, especially for those who are now migrants. In the Mozambique case, customary evidence regarded as legal will clearly be of greater assistance to communities such as the control and Monapo than it will be to areas such as Montepuez, where forms of social evidence are much less available. To the degree that customary forms of evidence are made legal in the national tenure system, however, one could imagine that the time necessary for the evolution or re-evolution of institutions even in areas such as Montepuez would very likely be shortened.

Including customary evidence in statutory legal codes, however, will have little meaning to small-scale agriculturalists if the parameters of the new statutory legal environment are not known at the local level and if smallholders do not have the capacity to engage the new legal environment. Key informant interviews revealed that smallholders and even largeholders and commercial interests are largely unaware of the precise nature of the statutory legal framework regarding use of and access to land resources, including dispute resolution. The government's extremely limited capacity to diffuse this information outside the provincial capitals means that district-level officials are frequently unaware of current and new legal tenets, thereby impeding landholders' ability to take advantage of any legal environment (current or changed) as well as the potential for evolution of effective institutions regarding legal forms of customary evidence. Nevertheless, residents of Montepuez and Monapo, who have significantly more education than residents of the control site (Table 8.1), may be better equipped to gain access to important aspects of the land law, especially given the breakdown of important customary forms of evidence.

Changes to Mozambican Land Law

Responding to the land tenure issues of the postwar period, the Mozambican Interministerial Land Commission, backed up by technical support, took the lead in formulating a revised national land policy and land law for Mozambique. Activities of the Land Commission included research on a number of important topics, local and national debates and discussions, workshops, and three national conferences on land issues, with discussions of land conflict resolution playing a prominent role in these. On July 31, 1997, after two weeks of parliamentary debate, the National Assembly approved a new land law.

The key changes regarding conflict resolution that were adopted as articles in the revised law indicate that:

- the use of nonwritten forms of customary evidence, such as oral testimony, to defend claims to land is permitted;
- rural smallholders are explicitly granted land use rights through "occupation," and such rights are not to be prejudiced by or inferior to rights received through a formal written title;
- local community "participation" is required in the formal titling process; and,
- the registering of land in the name of the local community is permitted.

Efforts are under way in Mozambique to encourage domestic and international nongovernmental organizations (NGOs) to play a role in bringing about local understanding of the revised land law. By communicating important aspects of the revised law to the district levels, NGOs act as advocates to numerous communities. NGOs assist these communities with dispute resolution with largeholders while smallholders continue to learn about the new legal environment. The inclusion of customary evidence in national land law and communication of the revised law to the provincial, district, and local village levels have the potential to encourage the evolution of land dispute resolution institutions by expanding the menu of legitimate evidence.

Direct information on the impact of the revised land law is not yet available. It is expected that smallholders, with an ability to present evidence that is customarily legitimate, yet legal within the formal system, will increasingly be able to retain access to land in dispute resolutions with largeholders. Moreover, largeholders will perhaps be more willing to accommodate communities' use of resources if it is widely known that customary evidence in a land dispute has formal legal standing. Making social forms of evidence legal could eventually result in an expansion of the kinds of available evidence used, particularly in areas like Montepuez and Monapo, where the portfolio of evidence is narrow. Increased smallholder tenure security may take some of the pressure off older agroforestry trees as the sole evidence that is available and respected by different groups. This change could in turn result in employment of the tree replacement strategies important to full adoption and maintenance of cashew agroforestry. Overall, inclusion of customary evidence in formal legal codes is likely to have the effect of increasing communities' control over the resources on which they depend.

Conclusion

The nature of legitimate evidence in land dispute resolution plays a fundamental role in the land tenure security necessary for adoption of natural resource management technologies. In postwar Mozambique the conflict has altered the availability and legitimacy of evidence to put significant evidence value on cashew agroforestry trees. The presence of cashew trees on smallholder land provides evidence of landownership and constitutes legitimate evidence for dispute resolution. As a result, cashew agroforestry as a natural resource management technology has strengthened property rights and heightened tenure security, a uniquely valuable service in the chaotic postwar period. With such value placed on agroforestry trees, further investment in cashew would seem the logical choice. However several forces serve to discourage investment in cashew planting.

- The high evidence value placed on agroforestry trees, together with a comparative lack of other evidence of equal value, means that older, non-producing agroforestry trees are not removed to make space for planting cashew in tree-farm associations or cashew groves.
- With close to half of the national population dislocated during the course of the war, the presence of migrants on land claimed by others is a common occurrence. Migrants are prevented from planting cashew because of the role of tree planting in claiming land and because the duration of their tenure tends to be shorter.
- The war has created significant uncertainty over who owns what in Mozambique, increasing the probability of disputes and decreasing the incentives to invest further in cashew planting.

- The lack of connection between formal and customary land tenure systems has increased the likelihood of land disputes between smallholders and largeholders, particularly in critical resource areas. The resulting uncertainty is aggravated by power distributions that favor commercial and largeholder interests and hence lend greater legitimacy to statutory law regarding administration of land. Smallholders therefore have greater expectations of land loss, resulting in decreased incentives to invest in technologies such as cashew agroforestry.

Such a set of opposing forces regarding the role of cashew agroforestry trees as evidence for land claims reveals important aspects about the adoption of natural resource management technologies. Montepuez had the most migrants and fewest cashew trees, which may explain lower measures of tenure security and perceptions of unjust dispute resolution. Monapo, however, has a greater number of land conflicts than Montepuez, despite a higher average number of cashew trees per person, fewer migrants, and greater tenure security. This finding suggests that numbers of trees and migrants may not affect the incidence of conflict significantly, but they do affect tenure security, investment in technologies, and perceptions of the "justness" of dispute resolution institutions. Thus, incidence of conflicts may not necessarily significantly weaken tenure security, provided that forms of evidence widely perceived to be legitimate (such as cashew agroforestry trees) are available to resolve disputes.

With few alternative forms of evidence available that are as widely legitimate as cashew trees, there exists the risk that continued nonremoval of older trees coupled with little planting of new trees would result in fewer trees in the future. Recent legislative revision by the Mozambican government, however, has resulted in a formal land law that incorporates customary forms of evidence to a significant degree. This change presents the possibility that alternative forms of customary evidence will be recognized as legitimate in land dispute resolution and therefore benefit smallholders. Although it is still too soon to know for sure, the use of new forms of evidence may have the effect of decreasing the near singular importance of cashew trees as evidence and hence remove an important constraint to cashew tree replacement and full adoption of the agroforestry technology.

References

Bruce, J. W., S. E. Migot-Adholla, and J. Atherton. 1994. The findings and their implications: Institutional adaptation or replacement? In *Searching for tenure security in Africa*, ed. J. W. Bruce and S. E. Migot-Adholla. Dubuque, Ia., U.S.A.: Kendall/Hunt.

CCL (Capricorn Consultants Limited). 1994. *National cashew tree population survey, final report*. Nairobi.

FAO (Food and Agriculture Organization of the United Nations). 1987. *The cashew industry in Mozambique.* Rome.

Finnegan, W. 1992. *A complicated war.* Los Angeles: University of California Press.

Fortmann, L., and J. Riddell. 1985. *Trees and tenure: An annotated bibliography for agroforesters and others.* Madison and Nairobi: Land Tenure Center and International Centre for Research in Agroforestry.

Galli, R. 1992. Who will rehabilitate agriculture in the post-war period? Unpublished manuscript.

Lauriciano, G. 1995. Socio-economic. In *Mozambique inview.* Maputo: Mediacoop.

Middleton, J. 1988. Foreword. In *Land and society in contemporary Africa*, ed. R. E. Downs, and S. P. Reyna. Hanover, N.H., U.S.A.: University Press of New England.

MOA/SSTC (Ministry of Agriculture/Sectratariat of the State for Cashew). 1989. Cashew rehabilitation and development project for Gaza and Inhambane. Ministry of Agriculture, Maputo. Project proposal.

Moll, P. 1996. *Call for prompt action on the Mozambique draft bill on land.* World Bank Mozambique land brief position paper. Maputo: World Bank.

Raintree, J. B. 1987. *Land, trees, and tenure.* Madison and Nairobi: Land Tenure Center and International Centre for Research in Agroforestry.

Tanner, C. R. 1996. Personal communication. FAO representative to the Land Commission, Ministry of Agriculture, Maputo.

Tanner, C. R., and J. B. Monnerat. 1995. Bases for a national land program, including the revision of the land law, and the links with other pertinent programs and projects. Project Support to the Land Commission (TCP/MOZ/2335). Ministry of Agriculture and Fishing, Republic of Mozambique, Maputo, and Food and Agriculture Organization of the United Nations, Rome.

Unruh, J. D. 1997. Post-conflict recovery of African agriculture: Critical resource tenure in Mozambique. Ph.D. diss., University of Arizona, Tucson, Ariz., U.S.A.

USAID (U.S. Agency for International Development). 1996. *Mozambique: Country strategic plan FY 1996–FY 2001.* Maputo: USAID Mozambique Mission.

USCR (U.S. Committee for Refugees). 1993. *World refugee survey.* Washington D.C.

Willett, S. 1995. Ostriches, wise old elephants, and economic reconstruction in Mozambique. *International Peacekeeping* 2 (1): 34–55.

9 Between Market Failure, Policy Failure, and "Community Failure": Crop-Livestock Conflicts and Technology Adoption in Sri Lanka

REGINA BIRNER AND HASANTHA GUNAWEERA

In the semi-arid zone of southern Sri Lanka, conflicts over crop damage caused by grazing livestock constitute an important obstacle to the adoption of more sustainable land use practices. They affect the shift from slash-and-burn agriculture to irrigated farming and to agroforestry. At first glance crop damage may appear to be a technical problem, but it has an institutional dimension as well. It reveals an underlying conflict between crop farmers and livestock keepers for property rights over land. This problem is an interesting case for studying the relations between property rights, collective action, and technology adoption for three reasons. First, solving the problem involves collective action at different levels—among the crop farmers and the livestock farmers themselves and between these groups. Second, the case illustrates the decisive role of the political and administrative system in which the groups interact. Third, the problem is not unique to Sri Lanka. It is almost universal during certain phases of agricultural development, especially in areas where both crop and livestock farming are ecologically feasible. The problem typically arises when increasing population pressure induces the expansion of crop farming, and consequently land resources used for pastoral livestock keeping become scarce (Birner 1999).

The chapter is organized as follows: it begins by outlining the study methodology. Next it discusses the emergence and relevance of crop damage by grazing livestock as an obstacle to the adoption of more sustainable land use practices. It goes on to examine the difficulties of reaching a solution in the presence of market failure, government failure, and "community failure." Analyzing the process currently observed in the research region, the chapter then shows how collective action within a given political and administrative arena may lead to a solution.

Description of the Study Site and Methodology

This study is based on empirical data collected in the Hambantota District of Sri Lanka, which is mainly located in the dry zone that receives less than 1,270

186

millimeters of rainfall. Land use in this zone is characterized by the coexistence of two land use systems, which differ considerably in their intensity: (1) irrigated paddy cultivation, mostly in irrigation and settlement projects that have been established in Hambantota District since the 19th century, and (2) slash-and-burn agriculture on nonirrigated land, which traditionally includes fallow periods and in Sri Lanka is referred to as *chena* cultivation. Vegetables and fruits are cultivated to a small extent on plots adjoining houses, referred to as home gardens. Wasteland, fallow land, and the paddy land after harvesting has traditionally been used for keeping of cattle and buffalo in an extensive free-grazing system.

The chapter relies on two empirical data sources: (1) a research project on livestock development conducted from 1994 to 1995 in selected villages of the Hambantota District and (2) a survey carried out from 1995 to 1998 by a committee nominated to develop a proposal for solving the problem of crop damage caused by livestock. The 1994/95 research project applied the methodology of a comparative village case study, which included eight villages in the dry zone section of Hambantota District. Four villages were selected from areas settled in the 19th century and four from areas settled between the 1950s and the 1990s. In each group two villages were situated within major irrigation schemes and the other two in nonirrigated areas. Research methods included a review of the household statistics available at the village level, a survey of all livestock-keeping households in the selected villages (207 households), participant observation over a period of 12 months in one of the selected villages, interviews with crop farmers affected by crop damage caused by livestock, and interviews with representatives of the agencies involved in settling conflicts over crop damage. Information on technology development was also provided by major development agencies in the district and by the Department of Agriculture. Information on political conditions was obtained through informal interviews with local politicians and observation of the election campaigns for the provincial council, parliamentary, and presidential elections in 1994.

The second data source for this chapter, the survey carried out from 1995 to 1998 by the committee mentioned, completely covered one selected Agrarian Services Division of the district, which was particularly affected by the problem of crop damage. The committee reviewed the secondary data maintained by different government institutions and by the livestock farmers' organization of the division. Forty-five key informants involved in settling conflicts concerning crop damage provided primary information. During the process of developing, negotiating, and implementing the proposal for solving the problem of crop damage, the committee collected information on the discussion process taking place within the organized interest groups and on their interaction with administrative and political decisionmakers.

Crop-Livestock Conflicts as an Obstacle to Sustainable Land Use

Land Tenure and Land Use in the Research Region

In the traditional settlement areas of the research region, farmers typically hold paddy lands and home gardens as formal private property. In the irrigation and settlement projects constructed after the enactment of the Land Development Ordinance of 1935, farmers hold individual use rights in paddy lands and home gardens. The only transfer right is the right to bestow, which is limited to handing down the land intact to a single heir. This regulation led to a clear stratification of the rural households among those holding comparatively large parcels of paddy land and those without paddy land (see Tables 9.1 and 9.2). Paddy land is an important status symbol, and access to more than two acres in the research region is commonly considered sufficient to secure the livelihood of a household throughout the year.

Except for home gardens, nonirrigated land resources in the research region are almost exclusively formal state land. They are widely used both for slash-and-burn agriculture (*chena* cultivation) and for livestock rearing. Since the enactment of the Crown Lands Encroachment Ordinance in 1840, *chena* farmers have had to obtain cultivation permits from the local administration. Because of environmental concerns, cultivation permits are now rarely issued in the research region. *Chena* farming is nevertheless widely practiced (see Table 9.3) and tolerated by the authorities because in nonirrigated areas the majority of the rural households depend on *chena* cultivation for their livelihood. In the eight villages surveyed in 1994/95, the average cultivated area was 2.1 acres per household. As a result of low productivity and a considerable risk of crop losses, most of the *chena*-cultivating households must hire out labor or find other additional income sources in order to secure their livelihood. Notwithstanding, these households are referred to herein as *chena* farmers. Most *chena*

TABLE 9.1 Land tenure in the dry zone of Hambantota District

Division	Households owning land	Households owning paddy land	Average size of paddy holdings	Average size of upland owned[a]
	(number)	(percentage)	(acres)	(acres)
Hambantota	8,795	39.6	2.36	1.62
Tissamaharama	8,010	34.4	2.94	1.50

SOURCE: DCS (1984, 25).

NOTE: Data are taken from the 1982 census of agriculture, the last available census data that provide information on tenure of paddy holdings.

[a]Data on *chena* cultivation on state-owned land were not collected in this census.

TABLE 9.2 Distribution of paddy land

Division	Percentage of households owning					
	<1 acre	1–2 acres	2–3 acres	3–4 acres	4–5 acres	>5 acres
Hambantota	12.0	26.1	28.1	23.0	4.8	6.0
Tissamaharama	5.4	16.5	31.5	19.8	9.9	17.0

SOURCE: DCS (1984, 25).

NOTE: Data are taken from the 1982 census of agriculture, the last available census data that provide information on tenure of paddy holdings.

farmers in the surveyed villages fell below the poverty line defined by the government for implementation of poverty alleviation programs.

After the harvest, paddy lands and *chena* lands are traditionally used as grazing resources for cattle and buffalo. Fallow *chena* lands and other land not used for crop cultivation are used for grazing as well. Livestock owners claim that they have customary rights to use these lands for grazing. Interviews with key informants and participant observation revealed that the owners of the larger herds kept outside the village were successful in excluding newcomers and outsiders from using these land resources for rearing cattle and buffalo. They have not, however, developed specific regulations to limit herd sizes and control the stocking rate.

TABLE 9.3 Area cultivated with other crops than paddy

Division	All parcels cultivated with other crops than paddy[a]			Number of home gardens[b]
	Number	Total area	Average size	
		(acres)	(acres)	
Hambantota	5,951	6,093	1.02	4,032
Sooriyawewa	7,415	9,303	1.25	3,617
Tissamaharama	11,639	9,617	0.83	8,913
Lunugamwehera	5,889	5,463	0.93	4,105

SOURCE: DCS (1992/93, 5).

NOTE: This table includes four divisions because both Hambantota and Tissamaharama have been divided since the 1982 census. The census did not distinguish between state-owned and privately owned land. According to information collected from the divisional secretariats in Hambantota and Tissamaharama, however, almost the entire upland cultivation area that is not allocated to home gardens is state owned.

[a]For this survey, a parcel was defined to be a piece of land cultivated singly or jointly, irrespective of legal ownership (DCS 1992/93, 2).

[b]The major definition criterion for the home garden was the dwelling house.

The distribution of cattle and buffalo ownership in the research region is highly skewed. In the villages included in the 1994/95 survey, only 5.6 percent of all households kept cattle, 1.2 percent kept buffalo, and 0.8 percent kept a combination of both. Of the households that kept cattle, buffalo, or both, 6 percent kept fewer than 10 animals and 47 percent kept more than 60 animals. In the division covered by the 1995–98 surveys, approximately 75 percent of the livestock owners keeping more than 10 animals are organized in a cattle farmers' association, which has 150 members. Thirty-five percent of the members keep between 100 and 250 animals, and 18 percent keep more than 250. The average herd size is 158 animals per member.

Herds smaller than 10 animals are typically kept at the homestead of the owners, while the larger cattle and buffalo herds are kept outside the village in a free-grazing system. During the paddy cultivation seasons, these herds are traditionally shifted to more remote areas. Crop damage is mostly caused by these larger herds owned by rather affluent families. All cattle- and buffalo-keeping households included in the 1994/95 survey that owned more than 10 animals also cultivated paddy land. In addition, many engaged in activities such as trade, renting out agricultural machinery, and money lending. For convenience, the term "livestock owners" is used herein to refer to households that keep herds of cattle and buffalo of more than 10 animals outside the villages and are therefore involved in the problem of crop damage.

Crop Damage by Livestock as an Obstacle to Technology Adoption

The problem of crop damage caused by livestock as an obstacle to technology adoption can be placed into the framework of the theory of induced innovation (Boserup 1981; Hayami and Ruttan 1985; see Chapter 1 of this volume). Both the system of slash-and-burn agriculture (*chena* farming) and the system of large-scale cattle and buffalo rearing emerged under conditions of low population density. Accordingly, these systems are non–labor intensive and employ extensive land use. Both systems have come under pressure because of the rapidly increasing population in the dry zone section of Hambantota District. The population density almost doubled from 106 to 204 persons per square kilometer between 1971 and 1994.[1]

Because land in irrigation and settlement projects must not be divided in the course of inheritance, the members of the second generation of settlers who do not inherit paddy land are forced to either apply for land in new irrigation and settlement projects or engage in *chena* cultivation on the nonirrigated land resources. Consequently, reduced fallow periods and increasing soil degradation

---

1. This figure is calculated according to information from the Statistical Branch of the District Secretariat, Hambantota, 1994.

in the nonirrigated areas are common phenomena in the research region, as elsewhere in the dry zone of Sri Lanka. In the early 1980s more than half of the *chena* plots in the research region were cultivated without fallow period (ILO 1984). Contrary to the predictions of induced innovation, however, cultivation practices have not been adapted to the reduced fallow periods, and interviewed farmers frequently reported declining yields.

Since the 1980s public research institutions in Sri Lanka have increasingly been engaged in developing technologies that allow the shift from *chena* cultivation to more sustainable permanent land use systems. The focus has been placed on the development of alley cropping systems (Keerthisena 1995), on the introduction of drought-resistant fruit and timber trees into the upland farming systems of the dry zone (Gunasena 1995), and on moisture conservation techniques such as contour bunds with hillside ditches (Handawela 1995). The interviewed representatives of the agencies promoting alternatives to *chena* cultivation generally reported a low rate of adoption and addressed crop damage caused by the free-grazing cattle and buffalo herds as a major reason. An example of this is a fruit tree project launched in 1993 among women farmer groups. Because of the perennial nature of the trees, households would have to supervise their plots year-round against livestock damage compared with only four months under *chena* cultivation. Although barbed-wire fencing had the potential to substitute for supervision labor, its cash cost was much too high to make it feasible. Another example refers to the Kirindi Oya Irrigation and Settlement Project (KOISP), the major irrigation project in the region. As an alternative to *chena* farming, KOISP promoted the planting of nonpaddy field crops (chilies, groundnuts, onions, green gram, cowpea) within the irrigation tracts during the minor cultivation season, when irrigation water was not sufficient to grow paddy. In 1990, 232 hectares were cultivated with these crops, corresponding to only 12 percent of the targeted extent of 2,000 hectares (HARTI 1995). A study by HARTI identified the danger of crop damage as a major obstacle, next to lack of water and insect attacks. As shown in Table 9.4, for all crops except onions, the farmers reported crop damage by animals as the major constraint to productivity. Almost all farmers reported that they had to take care of the crops day and night throughout the cultivation cycle (HARTI 1995). The impact evaluation study of KOISP assessed the problem of crop damage in paddy and concluded, "The conflict between cattle owners and paddy farmers has become one of the major problems of the project, threatening its sustainability" (IIMI 1995, 54).

The problem of crop damage by grazing livestock is closely related to increasing population density, which has led to competition between crop and livestock farming for land. Following the argumentation of McIntire, Bourzet, and Pingali (1992), one can assume that crop-livestock competition only occurs after the expansion of crop farming has reached the point at which grazing grounds available during the cropping season become scarce. Until this point

TABLE 9.4 Constraints to productivity in crop production

Type of constraint	Chile	Groundnut	Onion	Green gram	Cowpea	Total
		(number of farmers)				
Lack of water	14	3	24	0	0	42
Insect attack	37	0	5	5	2	44
Lack of quality seed	5	0	0	0	0	14
Damage by animals	72	23	14	6	11	121
Unsuitability of soil	12	2	10	0	0	52
Total	140	28	53	11	13	246

SOURCE: HARTI (1995, 26).

is reached, the expansion of crop farming usually increases the potential for livestock farming because crop by-products improve the fodder availability during the dry season.

In the research region, competition probably began occurring during the mid-1980s. Even though cases of crop damage were recorded during the colonial period (Woolf 1983), reports by interviewed persons provide evidence that the incidence of crop damage increased considerably during the 1990s. In the first phase of the KOISP, which was completed in 1986, an area of 8,800 hectares was developed for cultivation. This is more than the total area under all major irrigation schemes that were developed in the area during the entire colonial period (Irrigation Department 1975; IIMI 1995). Moreover, KOISP is situated in an area that traditionally served as a major grazing ground for cattle and buffalo herds during the cropping season. The problem mostly affects the new irrigation scheme, as mentioned, but also the nonirrigated areas to which the livestock owners now shift their animals during the cropping season since having to make way for KOISP. The administrators of villages surrounding KOISP that rely mostly on nonirrigated cultivation reported between 150 and 200 cases of crop damage per season. The damage is usually caused by cattle and buffalo herds owned by people who reside in the traditional paddy cultivation areas. In these areas where livestock owners protect their own crops interviews with village administrators revealed fewer than five cases per season.

Interviews with livestock keepers showed that they consider the expansion of crop cultivation, especially under KOISP, a violation of their traditional property rights to land. Therefore they are reluctant to take measures to prevent crop damage caused by their herds, such as continuously herding their animals throughout the day and paddocking them at night. Rather, they still practice the traditional system that emerged under low population density. There are obvious economic incentives not to change the prevailing system: continuous herding would decrease the return to labor because of increased labor input, and paddocking the herds at night would reduce feed intake, thus affecting milk yields and livestock growth.

Potential Solutions for Crop-Livestock Conflicts

Because crop damage caused by livestock affects individuals beyond the livestock producers themselves, they can be considered an externality of the livestock farming system. The theoretical literature offers three major approaches to solve problems caused by externalities: a neoliberal solution, an interventionist solution, and a communitarian solution. The following sections examine to which extent each theoretical position can be applied to the problem of crop damage in the research region.

The Neoliberal Solution

The neoliberal solution can be expressed by the Coase Theorem, which holds that a clear specification of private property rights is a sufficient solution to the problem of externalities. In the absence of transaction costs, voluntary bargaining between individual agents will lead to an efficient outcome, regardless of how property rights are initially assigned (Coase 1960). Interestingly, Coase used the problem of crop damage caused by livestock to illustrate his argument. Coase assumed that a cattle raiser and a neighboring crop farmer trade for either the crop farmer's right to compensation for crop damage or the cattle farmer's right to damage the crops. Theoretically, whichever way the liability is defined, the trade will lead to an efficient allocation of the land resources according to the comparative advantage of crop and livestock production. The idea that even property rights can be allocated efficiently through the market mechanism and without state intervention fits well into neoliberal economic reasoning and explains to a large extent the popularity of the Coase Theorem in mainstream economics (Medema 1994).

To judge the applicability of the neoliberal solution in the Sri Lankan case, it is useful to consider two major assumptions on which the Coase Theorem is based:

1. the absence of transaction costs, and
2. the irrelevance of equity questions.

ASSUMPTION OF NO TRANSACTION COSTS.   Coase (1960) left no doubt that he considered the assumption of no costs involved in carrying out market transactions to be unrealistic. In the Sri Lankan case considered here, individual bargaining between crop and livestock farmers would certainly involve transaction costs because each crop farmer would have to strike a deal with several livestock farmers in order to protect his or her crops. Otherwise, the crop farmers would have to organize themselves, which also involves transaction costs.

ASSUMPTION OF IRRELEVANCY OF EQUITY QUESTIONS.   Coase
(1960) mentions that his argument does not take questions of equity into account. It is obvious, however, that the assignment of property rights and the
bargaining for them alters the distribution of wealth and income of the parties
concerned. In the Sri Lankan case, the current distribution of wealth and income
between the livestock keepers and the *chena* farmers is already rather unequal,
with livestock owners belonging to the upper stratum of village society and
chena farmers usually living below the poverty line. Even if the right to compensation for crop damage is assigned to the *chena* farmers, the social barriers
created by the difference in status, wealth, caste, and education make it unlikely
that *chena* farmers and livestock keepers could enter any individual bargaining
process as equal partners.

Further implicit assumptions of the Coase Theorem are also unlikely to
apply: the assumption of perfect knowledge of one another's production and
profit or utility functions, and the assumption that agents strike mutually advantageous bargains in the absence of transaction costs (Hoffman and Spitzer
1982).

Because major assumptions of the theorem do not apply, it does matter
how property rights are initially assigned. As long as there are transaction costs
and information costs, as well as social and class barriers between the parties
concerned, private bargaining for property rights may either not take place at
all or lead to an inefficient or undesirable outcome. Therefore, the Coase Theorem's assertion that a market mechanism for the exchange of private property
rights can solve externality problems is not applicable in the Sri Lankan case.
In this sense, one can speak of a "market failure."

The Interventionist Solution

State intervention is the other classical answer to the problem of externalities.
In principle, different types of state intervention are conceivable as measures
to deal with the problem of crop damage, most notably the following:

1. a Pigouvian tax on cattle and buffalo,
2. regulations that make the herding of the animals compulsory and prohibit
   stray animals,
3. regulations that forbid livestock keeping in cropping areas, and
4. regulations that assign the liability for crop damage to the livestock farmers
   and include provisions to enforce this liability by state intervention.

A PIGOUVIAN TAX.   The Pigouvian tax is generally judged to be superior to other instruments of state intervention on efficiency grounds, but this
instrument is difficult to implement in the case under consideration. Besides
the problem of determining the appropriate tax level to internalize the external
costs caused by the crop damage, the implementation of such a tax is affected

by difficulties in recording the exact number of animals kept by the individual livestock owners.

REGULATION OF HERDING. A legal regulation that requires that livestock farmers herd their animals had already been established. According to the Cattle Trespass Acts Number 12 of 1941 and Number 24 of 1949, local administrative authorities such as municipal and town councils have the right to catch unherded animals in their administrative area and demand a fine from the owner. A similar provision was included in the Agrarian Services Act Number 58 of 1979, which applies to irrigation schemes and other cultivated land held as formal private property. So far, these formal legal regulations have rarely been enforced. The interviewed administrative officers mentioned potential conflicts with livestock owners as a major reason.

PROHIBITION OF LIVESTOCK IN CROPPING AREAS. A legal regulation that forbids keeping grazing livestock in cropping areas also existed. According to the Agrarian Services Act, livestock owners are required to move their herds out of the paddy cultivation areas by the date paddy farmers fix at their seasonal meeting for the start of the cultivation. Failure to do so can result in fines by the village administrator. In the traditional paddy-growing areas, this regulation was fairly well enforced because livestock owners often had their own paddy lands situated there. Difficulties enforcing this regulation arose in the more recently established irrigated areas, such as KOISP, to which the livestock owners traditionally used to move their animals during the cropping season.

ASSIGNMENT OF LIABILITY TO LIVESTOCK FARMERS. The assignment of liability for crop damage to livestock farmers was also established in the Sri Lankan case. According to the Agrarian Services Act, each crop cultivator with formal property rights in the land he or she cultivated had the right to seize an animal "trespassing" on his or her land and detain it until compensation for the crop damage was paid. The crop cultivator had to inform the village administrator, who had to assess the crop damage and inform the livestock owner. If the livestock owner failed to pay, the Commissioner of Agrarian Services was entitled to sell the seized animals by public auction and pay the compensation out of the proceeds of the sale. Crop farmers had considerable problems exercising this formal right to compensation, however, because (1) crop farmers were often not able to seize the animals; (2) assessment of the damage was difficult and caused major social conflicts in the villages; and (3) auctioning the animals was not practical because livestock farmers acted in solidarity and did not buy animals at such auctions. Therefore, such auctions were hardly held at all.

The Agrarian Services Act did not apply to *chena* farmers because they did not hold formal property rights to the land on which they grew crops. They could, however, claim compensation for crop damage on the basis of the general legislation that protected their rights to the actual crops. The jurisdiction acknowledged that *chena* farmers were—according to the principle of *fructus industrialis*—the owners of the crops they grew. On this basis, they were granted the right to compensation, but they had to seek the assistance of the police and, if this was not successful, file a case in court. Because several visits to the police were necessary to deal with a single case, this procedure involved considerable transportation costs and resulted in the loss of whole working days, which was difficult to bear during the cultivation season. For the *chena* farmers, there were also social barriers to contacting policemen and advocates. For such reasons, none of the three police stations in the research area recorded more than 10 reports of crop damage in *chena* fields each year, although the number of such cases in a single *chena*-based village easily exceeded 100 per season. Not a single case for compensation for crop damage by livestock had been filed in court by *chena* farmers during recent years.

In conclusion, none of the potential instruments of state intervention that could internalize the external costs of crop damage was effectively enforced at the local level. In this sense, one can speak of a government failure.

The Communitarian Solution

In view of government failures and market failures, the application of institutions and social norms enforced by local communities, herein referred to as the "communitarian solution," offers a third approach to solve externality problems. One can distinguish two types of communitarian solutions: (1) traditional social norms or other institutions that have emerged over time at the local community level, and (2) institutional arrangements that community members have specifically created to solve the crop damage externality problem. This section deals only with the first type of solution. The second type is addressed in the next section.

In the case under consideration, traditional social rules for dealing with the problem of crop damage have been considerably weakened during recent decades. The interviews revealed that livestock owners traditionally used to pay compensation for crop damage to *chena* farmers, even though they were not formally required to do so. The payment of compensation was embedded in a traditional patron-client relationship between livestock owners and *chena* farmers. Livestock farmers usually owned paddy land on which *chena* farmers worked as hired laborers. Livestock owners also interacted as moneylenders and traders with *chena* farmers. The payment of compensation by livestock owners was considered a deed of mercy rather than the fulfillment of a right held by the *chena* farmers. The village community played a role as well, since there was public disapproval if a relatively rich livestock owner refused to pay compensation for the crop damage suffered by a comparatively poor *chena* farmer.

The weakening of the social rule calling for payment of compensation can be related to the dissolution of the traditional patron-client relationship. The mechanization of paddy cultivation since the 1960s reduced the dependence of livestock owners on the labor resources of *chena* farmers. The emergence of semiformal credit organizations in the villages promoted by nongovernmental organizations (NGOs), development projects, and the government reduced the dependence of *chena* farmers on the livestock owners as moneylenders. In addition, many *chena* farmers are descendants of settlers who immigrated during recent decades from other regions of the country to obtain paddy land in irrigation projects. These *chena* farmers have never established personal relations with the livestock owners. Moreover, the livestock owners feel that both the settlers in the irrigation projects and their descendants who engage in *chena* cultivation are invading their traditional grazing rights. Therefore, they perceive no social obligation to pay compensation for crop damage occurring in these areas.

In conclusion, traditional social norms have become defunct with the dissolution of patron-client relationships. New informal rules based on voluntary cooperation are not likely to evolve in a society that is stratified by unequal access to resources and different caste affiliation, no longer perceives benefits from patron-client relationships, and has fragmented because of ongoing immigration. One can draw a parallel to the concept of market and government failure and speak of a "community failure" in this case.

Collective Action and Bargaining as a Solution

The preceding section has shown that the three classical solutions to problems of externalities did not work in the case under consideration because of market failure, government failure, and community failure. This section discusses an alternative solution: collective action and bargaining between organized groups with the participation of state authorities. Such a process is currently occurring in the research region. The politicians and the local administration act as advocates of the *chena* farmers. Under the mediation of an appointed committee, they bargain with the organized livestock farmers for the following "deal": The livestock farmers commit themselves to avoid crop damage in exchange for formal reserved pastureland where they can keep the animals during the cropping season.

This process combines elements of all three classical solutions: the bargaining aspect of the Coase solution; the involvement of the state, which characterizes the interventionist solution; and the engagement of the local communities, which is the essence of the communitarian solution. The following analysis describes the conditions under which a combination of these elements may overcome the failures of the three classical solutions. For this purpose, the process currently occurring in the research region is analyzed as a process of institutional change driven by the interaction of different interest-groups within a given political and administrative arena. This discussion begins by examining the interest groups involved and their organizational capacity. Next it analyzes the political and administrative institutions and actors involved. Finally, it examines the bargaining process taking place in the research region and discusses a model solution that has been developed for one Agrarian Services Division.

The Interest Groups Involved and Their Organization

Three potential interest groups may be distinguished: the paddy farmers, the *chena* farmers, and the livestock owners.

In the research region the livestock keepers organized themselves during the 1980s in three formally registered organizations, which are united under one umbrella organization. The organizational capacity of the livestock farmers can be explained by the fact that they represent a comparatively small and socially homogenous group of relatively wealthy people with easy access to transportation and communication and formal ownership of pastureland where crop farming was not allowed. By organizing themselves, livestock farmers are able to not only reduce their transaction costs, but also solidify their bargaining power. The link between these features and outcomes corresponds to the theoretical frameworks of the new institutional economics (Harriss, Hunter, and Lewis 1997) as well as those explaining organizational capacity put forth by Davis and North (1971), which are noted in Chapter 2 of this volume. Another influential factor was the charismatic leadership provided by one livestock owner who served as the secretary of one of the three livestock farmers' organizations and as the general secretary of the umbrella organization.

The paddy farmers are formally organized in farmers' associations for the purpose of irrigation management. The farmers' organization, in contrast to that of the livestock farmers, is strongly supported by state authorities, especially the Agrarian Services Department. In the irrigation projects, membership is compulsory. Therefore, paddy farmers had in principle the possibility of pursuing their interests with regard to crop damage within these existing organizations. In the new areas of the KOISP project area, however, where crop damage in paddy was important, paddy farmers' organizations were not well functioning, despite state support. Because the settlement project was still new, the settlers' heterogeneity in terms of caste and origin was particularly pronounced. Moreover, widespread disputes among the settlers over the boundaries of the allocated paddy lands, along with some absentee owners, were obstacles to the creation of solidarity.

The *chena* farmers in the research region were hardly organized at all to pursue their common interests with regard to the problem of crop damage. This lack of organization can be attributed to their relatively large number, their sociocultural heterogeneity (different origin and caste affiliation, for example) and their comparatively low income, which implies high risk aversion and a preference for activities that yield short-term benefits. The fact that the *chena*-based villages were poorly connected to the communication and transportation infrastructure also reduced the organizational capacity of *chena* farmers. Moreover, *chena* farmers were not in a position to pursue their interests in already existing organizations, even though many of them were members of various organizations such as semiformal credit societies or village groups created in connection with the implementation of poverty alleviation programs. None of these organizations was directly related to *chena* farming, and the organizations usually included members such as laborers or craftsmen who were not interested in *chena* farming at all. Moreover, these organizations were highly dependent on external "social mobilizers." Experience in the research region has shown that such groups usually stopped functioning when the respective program was terminated and the social mobilizers withdrew.

The Political-Administrative System

To understand the role of the state in the research region, it is useful to conceptualize the state as a system of political and administrative institutions that create an incentive structure for politicians and bureaucrats and influence the bargaining power of the interest groups identified earlier. Sri Lanka's political and administrative system can be characterized as a comparatively stable democracy. Since the 1987 introduction of a decentralization package designed to solve ethnic conflict, political representation in Sri Lanka involves three levels: the Parliament, the directly elected provincial councils, and the Pradeshia Sabhas—town and municipal councils. The members of all these bodies are elected according to a proportional system of representation and a preferential system of voting. This election system creates a particularly strong incentive for the individual candidates to uphold the interests of the voters in their district. Under the present system, District Development Committees involve grassroots organizations in local planning and project implementation and are chaired by elected politicians.

Because the *chena* farmers represent the largest number of voters, politicians of all parties must address their interests if they want to win elections or stay in power. Although the fact that *chena* farmers are not organized limits their ability to articulate their interests, by continuously raising the crop damage problem in meetings with politicians, they were able to make the politicians and the local bureaucracy aware of the urgency of the problem. Moreover, politicians and the local administration have been kept informed about the problems by development projects promoting new crop-farming technologies. Although they tend not to get involved in direct political advocacy, development project and NGO staff can be important in channeling information about issues confronted by *chena* farmers to local administrations, which serve as project-implementing agencies. Interviews with politicians and local administrators showed that they consider the problem of crop damage to be a serious obstacle to agricultural development in the region.

In contrast to *chena* farmers, the political power of livestock farmers rests mainly on their ability to organize themselves effectively and act as a political pressure group. Since their number is comparatively small, their political influence cannot be based on the votes they represent. Because of their high degree of organization, however, they are well prepared for lobbying activities, and their representatives are able to communicate directly with political and administrative decisionmakers. Moreover, because of their comparatively wealthy status, livestock keepers are able to support the election campaigns of political candidates. Politicians thus have an incentive to find solutions that take the interests of livestock farmers into account.

The paddy farmers represent more votes than the livestock farmers do, and as described, they are organized, too. Crop damage, however, is not very prominent in the lobbying activities of paddy farmers' organizations. Other aspects of paddy cultivation, especially the distribution of irrigation water and the farmgate price of paddy, appear to be of greater relevance for paddy farmers as an interest group. This can be related to the fact that only paddy farmers in the new irrigation and settlement projects are severely affected by livestock-related crop damage. As noted, they are less efficiently organized than paddy farmers in traditional areas.

The Process of Negotiating a Solution

Until the early 1990s the strategy of the government, especially the Department of Animal Production and Health, was to convince livestock farmers to switch to a more intensive system of livestock keeping, involving, for example, improved breeds, systematic fodder management, and feeding of concentrates. This approach was seen as an incentive for livestock owners to reduce their herd sizes voluntarily. Both the administration and the politicians considered this strategy an appropriate solution to the problem of crop damage because more restrictive measures were likely to lead to conflicts with livestock owners. The interviews showed that a more intensive system of livestock keeping was considered necessary to "modernize" the prevailing system. Nonetheless, even though the department offered extension services as well as subsidies for breeding animals, concentrates, and establishment of fodder plots, the livestock farmers showed no interest in adopting the proposed innovations. Their reluctance to adopt more labor- and capital-intensive technologies can be attributed to the fact that the present extensive system of keeping large herds offers a competitive return to labor and capital, particularly given that livestock farmers bear relatively low opportunity costs of land (see Table 9.5). In addition, intensive systems of cattle and buffalo farming are generally discouraged in Sri Lanka because of low prices for milk and high costs of concentrates.

In the 1990s it became obvious that the strategy of the Department of Animal Production and Health to convince livestock owners to voluntarily reduce their herd sizes had failed. At the same time, the problem of crop damage gained momentum because of the increasing population density and the expansion of crop cultivation. The three election campaigns of 1994, with their numerous meetings at the village level, provided an excellent forum for the *chena* farmers to launch complaints concerning the crop damage problem. In 1995 the District Development Committee, which is chaired by a member of Parliament

TABLE 9.5 Farm enterprise income from cattle keeping

Item	Small herds	Medium herds	Large herds
Total herd size (number of animals)	5	30	100
Gross output			
From milk (Rs.)	3,470	16,240	89,390
From cull animals and stock increase (Rs.)	3,760	16,210	67,600
Total (Rs.)	7,230	32,450	156,990
Total costs[a] (Rs.) (without imputed labor and capital costs)	2,130	15,010	69,150
Enterprise income I (Rs.) (without imputed labor and capital costs)	5,090	17,440	87,830
Fixed capital (Rs.)	9,460	48,630	224,100
Enterprise income II (Rs.) (with imputed capital costs, without imputed labor costs)	4,050	12,090	63,780
Input of labour (person-days)	216	231	552
Enterprise income I per person-day[b] (Rs.)	24	76	159
Enterprise income II per person-day (Rs.)	19	52	114
Enterprise income I in relation to fixed capital[c] (percentage)	54	36	39

SOURCE: Birner (1999, 212).

[a]Variable and fixed costs including infrastructure depreciation.

[b]The daily labor wage in paddy cultivation during the peak season was Rs. 135.

[c]The interest rate in the formal bank sector ranged beween 20 and 25 percent.

elected for the district, decided to address the problem. The committee organized a large special meeting to which representatives of the livestock farmers' organizations, the paddy farmers' organizations, NGOs, development projects and the local administration were invited. The *chena* farmers did not participate because they had no organizations and therefore no representatives who could speak for them. The interests of the *chena* farmers, however, were expressed by the member of Parliament who chaired the meeting and by members of the administration. Because the number of participants was too large to start a negotiation process, a special committee was nominated to negotiate a solution. It comprised two Sri Lankan counterparts of a foreign-funded agricultural development project and one entrepreneur from the agribusiness sector.

Previously, livestock owners had demanded that the government allocate land to them as exclusive pasture. In 1986 this demand resulted in the government's designating an area of 445 hectares as exclusive pastureland, although these land resources were not officially handed over to the livestock farmers' organizations. Later, the members of the livestock owners' association, who together keep approximately 23,800 heads of cattle and buffalo, demanded an extension of the land area because it was not sufficient to maintain the herds of all members during the cropping season. The available land resources in the region, however, were not sufficient to maintain the total number of animals kept by the association without reducing the land available for *chena* farming.

To reduce this conflict of interest between the livestock owners' association and the *chena* farmers, the committee proposed (1) to declare an area as reserved pastureland where the incidence of *chena* farming was particularly low and (2) to improve the carrying capacity of these land resources by technical measures. The identified pastureland covers 2,000 hectares, including the 445 hectares identified in 1986. The suggested improvement measures include the rehabilitation of land that had been destroyed by gem mining, the restoration of existing tanks (small earthen reservoirs) and the construction of additional tanks, the introduction of water conservation methods, and the establishment of improved pasture and fodder trees. The committee estimated that even if these measures were taken, only half the number of animals currently kept by the members of the livestock owners' association could be maintained in the proposed pastureland throughout the cropping season. Therefore, the problem of crop damage could be solved only if members of the association committed themselves to take measures to prevent crop damage, including a reduction of herd sizes.

One may ask why the livestock owners' association entered into a bargaining process at all under these rather unfavorable conditions. The major incentive probably came from signals from the politicians that they could induce the local administration to enforce the stray cattle legislation if no agreement was reached. This threat was credible because the politicians had publicly prioritized the issue by involving the District Development Committee and therefore had a strong incentive to prove they were able to solve the crop damage problem. Because the local administration participates in the District Development Committee, it also had an incentive not to seem incapable of solving problems of high priority. Moreover, the interviews implied that the attitude of the local administration toward the livestock and the *chena* farmers had gradually changed in favor of the latter group. By implementing poverty alleviation programs, the local administrators had developed a more direct relationship to this group. The local administrators foresaw that many project activities in the crop-farming sector in which they were involved were threatened by the crop damage problem.

The livestock owners knew that, if the administration enforced the stray animals legislation, they would have to reduce their herd sizes and take measures to prevent crop damage without receiving pastureland in return. The committee offered an additional incentive by suggesting that the livestock owners' association itself, and not a state agency, manage the proposed 2,000 hectares of pastureland. The association would receive formal permanent use rights to the area and be in charge of implementing the proposed upgrading activities. The Norwegian-funded Hambantota Integrated Rural Development Project and the U.S. Agency for International Development (USAID) agreed to provide technical and financial support for this purpose.

The livestock owners' association accepted the proposal after a highly controversial discussion, during which the administration promised to enforce the stray cattle legislation if the livestock farmers failed to fulfill their commitment to prevent crop damage. Although this represents the only threat that can prevent the livestock owners from free riding on the proposed solution, the administration has its own incentives to keep its commitment. In addition, the local politicians have—because of the reputation effect—an incentive to induce the administration to keep its commitment. When the study ended in 1998, the livestock owners' organization had already registered a private company with limited liability, as required by the proposal. The local administration was in the process of surveying the respective land resources in preparation for the official transfer of the property rights in the proposed pastureland.

It remains to be seen whether the proposed solution will eventually solve the problem of crop damage. On the one hand, the proposal involves considerable potential. Unlike earlier approaches, it was negotiated with a view to balancing the various interests, and the parties involved gave their explicit consent. Moreover, the process led to the creation of a set of proposed arrangements for managing the pastureland, effectively constituting an induced institutional innovation of the type often highlighted by the new institutional economics theory (North 1995; also see Chapter 2 of this volume). On the other hand, successful implementation depends on a number of critical factors. Enforcement crucially depends on the willingness of the local administration to prosecute livestock owners who do not comply with the provisions of the proposal. The incentive of the politicians to exercise pressure on the administration mainly depends on the political weight that they attach to the loss of reputation from not being able to solve the crop damage problem. It also depends on the extent to which the voting power of *chena* farmers carries weight in comparison with the lobbying efforts and election campaign support provided by the livestock farmers. Moreover, to be sustainable in the long run, the use of the proposed pastureland must be economically viable without subsidies. This remains a major challenge, both from an organizational and a technical point of view.

Conclusions

The study of *chena* farmers and livestock owners in the Hambantota District of Sri Lanka allows one to draw several conclusions on the relation between property rights, collective action, and technology adoption. It demonstrates how induced innovation can be disrupted in a situation characterized by the concentration of traditional informal rights in the hands of the livestock owners and poor enforcement of formal property rights held by crop farmers. Instead, increasing population pressure and competition for land can result in crop damage by livestock and thereby prevent the adoption of more sustainable land use practices. Thus, induced technical change may require institutional change such as a redistribution of property rights and greater incentives to enforce rights. In such situations, institutional change takes precedence over technical change in creating efficient and equitable agricultural development.

The case study also supports the conclusion that institutional innovations like redistribution of property rights, which makes more efficient land use possible, are not simply induced by increased population density. The study rather shows that because of market failures, government failures, and community failures, the classical remedies for externalities may not work. Thus, the case considered here contradicts the efficiency theory of institutional change, which is reflected in Demsetz's (1967, 374) hypothesis that "[p]roperty rights develop to internalize externalities when the gains of internalization become larger than the cost of internalization." The case study is rather an illustration for North's (1990, 16) view that "[i]nstitutions are not necessarily or even usually created to be socially efficient; rather they, or at least the formal rules, are created to serve the interests of those with the bargaining power to devise new rules."

One can conclude from the case study that the bargaining power of the potential interest groups involved in institutional change both depend on their capacity to act collectively in order to pursue their interests and the political and administrative system in which the different interest groups interact. In the case under consideration, the resource users who were most disadvantaged by the prevailing property regime were also those with the lowest organizational capacity: the *chena* farmers. Additionally, the onus was on them to invoke a change in the prevailing property regime in order to make a more efficient, equitable, and sustainable land use possible.

In the Sri Lankan case the political system of a functioning democracy, a decentralized form of government, and a preferential system of voting created an incentive for the politicians and the local administration to act as advocates of the *chena* farmers. Therefore, a platform to start a negotiation process was institutionalized. As well, members of a donor-funded project and a private sector institution were able to play a facilitating role and strengthen the bargaining power of *chena* farmers. Thanks to this combination of factors, a process of institutional change could be induced in spite of the low organizational capacity of the *chena* farmers. Such favorable conditions are not enjoyed in many developing countries.

Nevertheless, this favorable solution was developed without the active participation of the *chena* farmers themselves. Although the traditional patron-client relationships between *chena* farmers and livestock owners had been dissolved, the *chena* farmers had effectively become clients of the politicians and the local administration. One could argue that in the case under consideration, active participation of the *chena* farmers in the bargaining process might not have changed the result. In cases where the political and administrative frame conditions are less favorable, however, active participation of the groups that are disadvantaged under the current distribution of property rights may be essential to induce institutional change that leads to more efficient, equitable, and environmentally sustainable resource use. Current theories of collective action draw heavily on the importance of direct communication, reputation, trust, and reciprocity for explaining how collective action can be achieved and sustained among individuals who have symmetrical interests and access to resources (Ostrom 1998). They are less well equipped to deal with issues of power and how collective action can be induced between groups that have unequal access to resources and are divided by social barriers of status and wealth. Historical evidence shows that collective action has great potential for turning socially and economically disadvantaged groups into agents of institutional change: this potential arises from the group's vision that they are—in spite of their disadvantaged position—able to change the present situation, if they act collectively. Creating this vision has much to do with charismatic leadership and ideology. Regarding both factors, the new institutional economics and theories of collective action still have remarkably little to say.

References

Birner, R. 1999. *The role of livestock in agricultural development: Theoretical approaches and their empirical application in the case of Sri Lanka.* Aldershot, U.K.: Avebury.

Boserup, E. 1981. *Population and technological change: A study of long-term trends.* Chicago: University of Chicago Press.

Coase, R. H. 1960. The problem of social cost. *Journal of Law and Economics* 3 (October): 1–44.

Davis, L. E., and D. C. North. 1971. *Institutional change and American economic growth.* London: Cambridge University Press.

DCS (Department of Census and Statistics). 1984. S*ri Lanka census of agriculture 1982:Hambantota District report (smallholding sector).* Colombo.

———. 1992/93. *Agricultural crops and livestock 1992/93: Hambantota District preliminary report.* Colombo.

Demsetz, H. 1967. Toward a theory of property rights. *American Economic Review* 57 (2): 347–373.

Gunasena, H. P. M., ed. 1995. *Multipurpose tree species in Sri Lanka: Development of agroforestry systems.*Proceedings of the Sixth Regional Workshop on Multipurpose Trees, Kandy, Sri Lanka, August 17–19.

Handawela, J. 1995. Role of agroforestry in stabilisation of upland rainfed farming in the South Eastern Dry Zone of Sri Lanka. In *Multipurpose tree species in Sri Lanka: Development of agroforestry systems,* ed. H. P. M. Gunasena. Proceedings of the Sixth Regional Workshop on Multipurpose Trees, Kandy, Sri Lanka, August 17–19.

Harriss, J., J. Hunter, and C. M. Lewis, eds. *The new institutional economics and third world development.* London: Routledge.

HARTI (Hector Kobbekaduwa Agrarian Research and Training Institute). 1995. *Production and marketing of other field crops in the Kirindi Oya Project area.* Research Study 91. Colombo.

Hayami, Y., and V. W. Ruttan. 1985. *Agricultural development: An international perspective.* 2d ed. Baltimore, Md., U.S.A.: Johns Hopkins University Press.

Hoffman, E., and M. L. Spitzer. 1982. The Coase theorem: Some experimental tests. *Journal of Law and Economics* 25 (April): 73–98.

IIMI (International Irrigation Management Institute). 1995. *Kirindi Oya irrigation and settlement project: Project impact evaluation study.* Vol. 2, *Final Report.* Colombo.

ILO (International Labour Organisation). 1984. *Employment and income generation in agriculture in the District of Hambantota, Sri Lanka.* Colombo.

Irrigation Department. 1975. *Register of irrigation projects in Sri Lanka.* Colombo: Ceylon Printers.

Keerthisena, R. S. K. 1995. Fifteen years of research on alley cropping at Mahailluppallama: Review. In *Multipurpose tree species in Sri Lanka: Development of agroforestry systems,* ed. H. P. M. Gunasena. Proceedings of the Sixth Regional Workshop on Multipurpose Trees, Kandy, Sri Lanka, August 17–19.

McIntire, J., D. Bourzat, and P. Pingali. 1992. *Crop-livestock interaction in Sub-Saharan Africa.* Washington, D.C.: World Bank.

Medema, S. 1994. The myth of the two Coases: What Coase is really saying. *Journal of Economic Issues* 27 (March): 208–226.

North, D. C. 1990. *Institutions, institutional change, and economic performance.* Cambridge: Cambridge University Press.

———. 1995. The new institutional economics and third world development. In *The new institutional economics and third world development,* ed. J. Harriss, J. Hunter, and C. M. Lewis. London: Routledge.

Ostrom, E. 1998. A behavioral approach to the rational choice theory of collective action. *American Political Science Review* 92 (1): 1–22.

Woolf, L. 1983. *Diaries in Ceylon, 1908–1911: Records of a colonial administrator, being the official diaries maintained by Leonard Woolf while Assistant Government Agent of the Hambantota District, Ceylon.* 2d ed. Dehiwala, Sri Lanka: Tisara Prakasakayo.

10 Organizational Development and Natural Resource Management: Evidence from Central Honduras

JOHN PENDER AND SARA J. SCHERR

In recent years a consensus has begun to emerge regarding the importance of local institutional and organizational development in developing countries as a necessary complement to economic, social, and political development. Numerous observers have hailed the increased role for local organizations and other elements of civil society in the wake of structural adjustment policies and declining government budgets in many developing countries (de Janvry and Sadoulet 1993; Farrington and Bebbington 1993; Nugent 1993; Uphoff 1993).

Local (or "grassroots") organizations, defined as those operating at the township or village level or below (Uphoff 1993), have been cited as offering numerous advantages favoring rural development (Farrington and Bebbington 1993). These advantages include increasing economic efficiency where private markets fail; increasing the effectiveness of government and nongovernment programs by involving local people in the design and implementation of such programs; reducing poverty in rural areas by responding to the needs of the rural poor; empowering rural people by increasing their role in decision processes

The authors gratefully acknowledge the financial support of the Swiss Development Cooperation and the Inter-American Development Bank for this research. We are grateful to the study team—Guadalupe Durón, Fernando Mendoza, Carlos Duarte, Juan Manuel Medina, and Roduel Rodriguez—for their tireless efforts to complete the survey; to Oscar Neidecker-Gonzales for research assistance; to Lourdes Hinayon, Nancy Romero, and Nolvia Lagos for administrative support; to Peter Hazell, Gilles Bergeron, Bruno Barbier, and other colleagues at the International Food Policy Research Institute (IFPRI) for advice in the conduct of the research; to Byron Miranda of the Instituto Interamericano para la Cooperación en la Agricultura (IICA), Peter Heffron of CARE and other colleagues outside of IFPRI for advice on the survey design and implementation; to Hector Barreto and Pedro Jimenez of the Centro Internacional de Agricultura Tropical (CIAT) for providing secondary data; to IICA/Honduras for providing logistical support to the research; to numerous government agencies, municipal governments, and local teachers who helped to make arrangements for the survey in the different communities; and to Ruth Meinzen-Dick, Anna Knox, Frank Place, and Stephen Sherwood for detailed and constructive comments on the manuscript. Most of all, we are grateful to the many farmers and representatives of organizations in Honduras who generously agreed to respond to our many questions. Any errors or omissions are solely the responsibility of the authors.

that affect their lives; and improving management of natural resources by helping to foster collective action to manage externalities or common property resources (Uphoff 1986; Rasmussen and Meinzen-Dick 1995; Baland and Platteau 1996). Although substantial work has investigated some of these claims, drawing comparative conclusions about these issues from much of the literature is difficult because of the idiosyncratic nature of many of the case studies that are reported, lack of a representative sampling frame, measurement of different variables in different studies, and lack of use of rigorous statistical procedures to test hypotheses about the impacts of key variables (Rasmussen and Meinzen-Dick 1995).[1]

This study represents a modest effort to address some of these shortcomings through an examination of the development of local organizations and their impacts on natural resource management (NRM) in a representative sample of villages in central Honduras. The issues of local organizational development and natural resource management are critical in Honduras. Local organizational development is relatively limited in most of rural Honduras, and problems of resource degradation—including deforestation, watershed degradation, soil erosion, soil fertility decline, water scarcity, and water contamination—are increasingly critical as population continues to grow rapidly in the fragile hillsides of the country (Pender and Durón 1996). New opportunities have arisen, however, as a result of declining central government presence in rural areas, increased authority of local governments, and greater presence of nongovernmental organizations (NGOs) since the early 1990s (Durón and Bergeron 1995). Now is thus an opportune time to study organizational development in Honduras.

In this study, we do not focus on organizational function or performance, but rather on the determinants and impacts of local organizational presence. We focus on voluntary local organizations, which are the dominant form of local organization in the region. In contrast to some recent literature, we emphasize that local organizational development may affect private NRM decisions as well as affecting collective action to manage resources.

Conceptual Framework

The conceptual model for this study draws upon the theory of induced institutional innovation (Hayami and Ruttan 1985; North 1990; see also Chapter 1 of this volume). This theory posits that institutions are created and evolve in response to changes in relative prices or other changes in the net benefits of innovation. Innovation can also influence farmer decisions and thus have feedback

---

1. The seminal work of Esman and Uphoff (1984) is an exception to this generalization, although the method of selection of their case studies limits the ability to generalize from their findings, as the authors note.

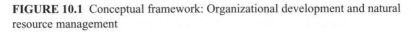

FIGURE 10.1 Conceptual framework: Organizational development and natural resource management

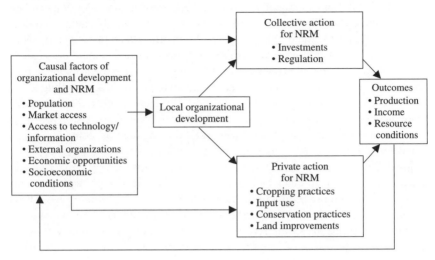

effects on the factors and processes that stimulated the change. In our case, we hypothesize that organizational innovation is a result of changes in the costs and benefits of organizational activity. Although organizations and institutions are not identical, we posit that a similar process of induced change applies to organizational development as to institutional change.[2] As in the case of institutional change, the process of induced organizational development is not likely to be automatic, occurring whenever the aggregate benefits of change exceed the costs, because of the high degree of uncertainty about the benefits and costs, the need for collective action to attain the benefits, and the presence of high fixed costs. In our conceptual framework, changes in factor endowments (that is, labor, capital, and land), market access, economic opportunities, access to technology, interventions by external programs and organizations, local natural resource and socioeconomic conditions, and other factors affecting the benefits and costs of organizational activity are hypothesized to induce local organizational change (Figure 10.1).

Development of local organizations can influence NRM by affecting collective or private actions. Collective action affecting NRM may include

2. Many of the changes discussed by North and Hayami and Ruttan involve organizational as well as institutional change. Uphoff (1986, 8–9) distinguishes organizations, defined as "structures of recognized and accepted roles," from institutions, defined as "complexes of norms and behaviors that persist over time by serving collectively valued purposes." There are many examples of organizations that are not institutions (for example, a particular law firm), institutions that are not organizations ("the law"), and organizations that are institutions (the Supreme Court).

community regulation to address environmental problems, or collective investments to improve common lands, protect watersheds, or otherwise achieve collective benefits. Private actions affecting NRM may include adoption or adaptation of new agricultural technologies; intensification of use of factors of production; investments in land or other resource improvements on private land; adoption of soil and water conservation or organic fertility management practices.[3]

Both collective and private action affecting NRM may be influenced by a large number of factors other than organizational development, including many of the factors that influence organizational development itself. These factors include access to infrastructure, information, local knowledge, risk, factors of production (land, labor, capital), wealth, and the physical or technical factors that determine local comparative advantage (such as rainfall and soil types) (see Chapter 2 in this volume). Changes in NRM as determined by collective and private actions lead to changes in outcomes within the village, including impacts on agricultural production, incomes, and resource conditions. These changes in outcomes may influence the costs and benefits of organizational activity, as well as affect the returns to collective and private action directly, and thus have feedback effects on the process of organizational development and NRM.

Research Method

We investigated the determinants of local organizational development and the impacts of organizational development on collective and private action affecting NRM using data collected from a survey of 48 villages in the central hillsides region of Honduras. The central region was defined to include all *municipios* (analogous to counties) of the department of Francisco Morazan except La Libertad and San Miguelito (which are lowland valley communities) and five adjacent *municipios* in the department of El Paraiso.

Whereas the central region is relatively homogeneous in terms of topography and climate, it includes substantial variation in population density, access to markets, and agricultural practices.[4] More than 90 percent of the region is on hillsides, and the climate is generally subhumid tropical, with annual rainfall ranging from 1,000 to 2,000 millimeters. Rural population density averaged 25 persons per square kilometer in 1988, though it ranged from as low as 9 to as high as 87 in some municipalities. Many villages in the region require up to a half-day by foot or pack animal to reach the nearest road. Although soils are generally of poor quality and thin and natural pastures are limited, agricultural and livestock production are the main sources of rural livelihood.

---

3. Some of these investments may also occur on common or private lands through collective action where collective benefits arise.

4. The region is described in detail in Pender and Durón (1996).

The central region faces serious resource degradation and poverty problems. About half of the region is still covered by pine forest, though nearly one-fifth of the area has been deforested since the 1960s. Soil erosion is a serious problem, with estimated erosion rates ranging from 22 to 46 tons per hectare per year, causing economic losses of as much as 700 lempiras (US$60) per hectare per year (World Bank 1991). Other major resource and environmental concerns include declining forest quality, soil fertility depletion, watershed degradation, water pollution caused by agrochemicals and other factors, and air pollution caused by forest fires and agricultural burning. Poverty is severe; more than 40 percent of children were malnourished, and more than half of households lacked access to potable water or health services in 1991.[5]

Production of basic grains (maize, beans, and sorghum) is the most or second-most important occupation in all but one of the sample communities. Going beyond these common features, however, it is possible to identify six general pathways of development, based on occupations and changes in occupations and land use since the mid-1970s:

1. basic grains expansion (basic grain production is the dominant economic activity and has been expanding during the past 20 years);
2. basic grains stagnation (basic grains production is the dominant economic activity though production has been stagnant or declining);
3. horticultural expansion (vegetable production has increased and has become the first or second important activity);
4. coffee expansion (coffee production has increased and is the first or second most important activity);
5. forestry specialization (forestry activities are the first or second most important activity); and
6. nonfarm employment (nonfarm employment has increased and become the first or second most important source of income).[6]

Study Sample

The villages surveyed were selected by a stratified random sample of 48 of the 325 rural *aldeas* (villages) in this region (excluding Tegucigalpa, the urban center of the region and the capital of Honduras).

The stratification was based on 1974 population density of the *municipio* (municipality) in which each *aldea* was located (more or less than 30 persons per square kilometer) and the distance of the *municipio* county seat to Tegucigalpa

---

5. These figures are based on data from the Fondo Hondureño de Inversión Social for the *municipios* in the central region, excluding Distrito Central, which is dominated by Tegucigalpa.

6. In almost all of the basic grains expansion and stagnation communities, livestock production is the second most important activity. All of these pathways are described and analyzed in detail in Pender, Scherr, and Durón (1999).

(more or less than 60 kilometers). Twelve *aldeas* were selected from each stratum, and all of the *aldeas* selected participated in the study.[7] We oversampled *municipios* with high population density to obtain sufficient variation in population density in the sample.

Sources of Data

The sources of information used for the study included a community-level questionnaire administered with groups of typically 15 to 20 respondents, participatory resource mapping, data from the 1974 and 1988 population censuses, and maps of topography, climate, soils, and other geographical features of Honduras. The questionnaire explored community members' perceptions about the current state of and changes since 1975 in agriculture and NRM (including private and collective action), the factors causing or conditioning these changes (including organizational presence), and some of the consequences of these changes for agricultural production, human welfare, and natural resource conditions.[8]

The questionnaire included a census of all of the organizations that had worked in the *aldea* since 1975 and descriptions of the activities of those that were involved in NRM. Complete information on organizations was obtained for only 40 of the communities, so these are used as the basis for the analysis in this chapter.[9] Participatory mapping was used to identify *aldea* boundaries (needed to compute village area and population density). The census data provided information on population and some indicators of access to social services, literacy, and poverty.

In the respondent groups, we sought to obtain representation of people of different ages and genders and from different neighborhoods in each village. Unfortunately, women were underrepresented in the group of respondents in most communities, probably for cultural reasons. This fact may have reduced the availability and quality of information related to women's organizations (such as housewives' clubs) and activities in which women are more commonly involved. According to the respondents (including the women respondents), however, women are generally less involved than men in most of the agricultural and resource management activities discussed in this chapter, so the bias

---

7. Of the 31 *municipios* in the central region, 12 (representing 153 *aldeas*) were classified as low population density/close to Tegucigalpa, 11 (101 *aldeas*) were classified as low density/far, 4 (31 *aldeas*) as high density/close, and 4 (40 *aldeas*) as high density/far.

8. The questionnaire and details on the implementation of the survey are provided in Pender and Scherr (1997).

9. Information on the extent of participation in local organizations was collected but was not sufficiently complete to be used in the analysis. Nearly all of the organizations mentioned in the organization census still exist in the communities. It is possible that there was under-reporting of organizations that have ceased to exist, though further data collection would be needed to verify that.

in the quantitative results related to underrepresentation of women may not have been large.

Qualitative Findings on Local Organizations' Organizational Presence

Rural organization in the central region has historically been poorly developed. Factors that may have contributed to this include poverty, low population density, poor communications infrastructure, political and economic marginality, a tradition of dependence on government organizations, and the relative lack of ethnic differentiation in the region.[10] In the 1970s most organizations were the local offices of national ministries or programs. Local people organized themselves mainly for marketing coffee, pine resin, and processed forest products.

Externally governed organizations, defined as organizations governed at a level above the *aldea* (village), continue to dominate the landscape. Many national government organizations are directly involved in technical assistance and water and forest management. Other agencies have indirect effects on NRM through infrastructure, social investment, education, and nutrition and health programs.

External NGOs proliferated in the region during the 1980s and early 1990s, with the withdrawal of government social and technical assistance programs, increased availability of international funding, new attention to local environmental concerns, and new philosophies of decentralization and local action for public services, including NRM (Miranda 1997). More than 20 NGOs were operating there in 1997.

The density of locally governed community organizations averages about seven organizations per community (compared with about eight externally governed organizations). Of these, nearly 40 percent are involved to some extent in agricultural or NRM activities, although not usually as their primary or original mandate. All are voluntary organizations.

The *patronato* has official status as the primary local decisionmaking body at the village level and exists in almost all villages. *Patronatos* are involved in NRM activities such as repair and construction of drinking water systems, forest protection, and management or establishment of trees in public areas or near water sources. Water committees are relatively common (found in more than 60 percent of villages) and are responsible for maintaining and protecting drinking water systems. Parent associations are common (in more than three-fourths of villages) and are mainly involved in school improvements, sometimes

---

10. The ethnic composition of the central region is predominantly *ladino* (mixed indigenous/European). Some sociologists hypothesize that rural organizations are more likely to form where there are readily identifiable ethnic or social groups, such as indigenous groups. We are grateful to Stephen Sherwood for this suggestion.

including tree planting. Church groups are common, but they often do not engage in NRM activities, though some have been involved in reforestation, guarding forests, and education about safe use of water. Various cooperatives and work groups are found mainly in the villages with nonfarm activities and coffee production. A few student and school groups undertake reforestation. Some communities have local chapters of indigenous councils or other civic and social groups.

Organizational Activities in NRM

Local organizations in the central region commonly play three roles in natural resource management:

1. service or support to local farmers and residents in managing privately held natural resources (for example, to improve agricultural production and conservation);
2. collective investment in common property resources (community forest management, reforestation, building and repairing water systems, run-off control); and
3. regulation of local natural resource use and management by individuals and groups (watershed and forest protection, water distribution, forest management).

Organizational activities related to common property resources have only recently begun to shift from protection (reducing degradation) to improvement (rehabilitating degraded land or enhancing the quality of existing resources), while organizational activities related to private farm resources are shifting slowly from production to conservation. The greatest concern sparking voluntary collective action has been protection of water resources for local consumption. Local people were also willing to organize to protect forest resources, where these are important economically, or to protect local watersheds. Similar efforts were uncommon for soil conservation. Local people acted mainly through existing organizations, although new temporary coalitions arose in a few cases to address perceived emergencies.

Externally managed organizations have played a pivotal role in introducing and disseminating new agricultural, conservation, livestock, and forestry technologies in the central region, both through direct extension and indirectly through diffusion and local information systems. Municipalities are active in no-burning campaigns. Many external agencies provide inputs and services— for example, technical extension, inputs, bank credit, or forest microenterprise support—through specially organized farmer groups, but these groups typically disband when services are discontinued. Some farmer cooperatives and work groups are supported by outside agencies or supralocal farmer organizations, which provide access to production technology, agricultural inputs, credit, or marketing services for particular commercial products (coffee, resin, sugar, wood products). Most spontaneous diffusion of new NRM practices has occurred through individual, rather than collective, action.

Collective Investment

Collective investment in natural resources is only incipient in the central region. Most activities are organized by *patronatos*, local water committees, the municipality, or special projects partially financed externally; the major local input is labor. Group action was reported mainly for road maintenance or for building and maintaining potable water systems. This finding reflects the local priority for activities with high near-term benefits. There has been little collective investment in irrigation systems; rather, individual farmers have established inexpensive ditch and hose irrigation close to either natural water sources or new drinking water systems.

A quarter of the region's communities have organized to control water drainage or runoff, by planting trees near water sources or building stone walls. Field visits suggested that these walls were constructed principally to protect other infrastructure investments, such as roads or water tanks, or to avoid mass movement of soil. All tree planting was organized by local schools, whereas stone walls were constructed by community members after damage had occurred (Durón 1998). External organizations were involved in only a few of these cases (promoting tree planting near water sources).

Only a tenth of all communities worked collectively on communal land improvements, mainly tree planting and fencing. In one case an external organization had catalyzed the effort by offering food for work to plant trees. All other cases were organized by members of the community through the school or *patronato*.

Local Regulation of Natural Resources

Until recently, rural people have had limited legal control over natural resources other than private cropland. The national Forestry Law of 1974 gave control over forest resources on both public and private lands exclusively to the state. Much of the land was national or municipal land subject to restrictions on its use and sale, although most farmers had relatively secure tenure. In the 1990s the legal and institutional context for local organization for NRM changed considerably. The Law of Modernization and Development of Agriculture (LMDSA) of 1992 led to the withdrawal of many national government services and market controls. Agrarian reform land was given full legal status as privately titled land. The Forest Law of 1993 returned many of the rights of commercial use and access to timber and forests to private landowners, local communities, and municipalities, although usually subject to some rules for resource protection.

Although the area of national or municipal lands had declined in many communities, they were still present in two-thirds of our survey communities in 1996.

Local knowledge and interpretation of the new rules varied greatly. The resulting set of norms actually imposed locally to address externalities in NRM thus varied, sometimes reflecting local priorities as much as legislation. In 1996 fewer than half of the communities in our survey with community, municipal, or national lands restricted the rights of outsiders. A quarter prohibited agricultural cultivation on those public lands; few had grazing restrictions. The top-priority environmental concerns reflected in regulations were water supply and quality. A third of communities with public lands reported having local restrictions on the use of water from those lands. Water restrictions included granting priority for human consumption and prohibiting contamination. Many forest regulations also served to protect water resources. While fewer than half of the communities with public land reported restricting fuelwood collection, most restricted pole and timber extraction (requiring cutting permits or prohibiting clearing around water sources). A few communities regulated or prohibited pine resin collection.

The national forest, water, or other agencies occasionally enforce regulations directly, but in most cases enforcement is the responsibility of the municipality (or its locally based representative) or the local *patronato*.[11] In cases involving problems caused by community members, there are usually attempts to first deal with externality problems informally. If there is no response, then officials or a community group approach the person; the next step is to bring the matter to the attention of the municipal representative. Continued intransigence would lead the community to raise its concerns to higher municipal authorities or a national public agency, or to begin legal proceedings, or both. For externalities caused by people from outside the *aldea*, the initial approach by community members is followed by recourse to the municipality and the public agencies. Formal complaints are uncommon. It is unclear whether this lack of complaints is due to few violations, the effectiveness of informal mechanisms, reluctance to impose sanctions, questions about the legitimacy or effectiveness of the formal mechanisms, or other reasons.

One would expect to find more dependence on nonlocal authorities for regulatory enforcement in situations where local people are affected by few locally important externalities, where external authorities are actively present, or where the problems are caused by outside groups (or powerful individuals) over whom local authorities have no effective jurisdiction. By contrast, one would expect to find more dependence on local authorities where management practices are perceived to generate significant local externalities.

---

11. In some cases, private organizations are contracted to manage protected areas.

These expectations appear consistent with observed differences between the pathways. In the basic grains expansion and nonfarm pathways, participants reported that outside agencies performed all enforcement. In the former, this pattern can be explained by the relatively low level of externalities important to local people, as a result of relatively low population density and resource pressures. In the latter, it may be explained by the greater presence of national agencies and large externalities caused by outsiders. In the horticultural pathway most problems are resolved by the municipality or otherwise by outside agencies; this result may reflect the low level of local organizational development in this pathway. In the coffee and forestry pathways the main actors are local organizations (such as forestry co-ops) and outside agencies. In the relatively densely populated basic grains stagnation pathway, with large local externalities, local and municipal authorities were the principal enforcers of natural resource rules.

Econometric Analysis of Local Organizational Presence

We investigated the determinants of local organizational presence and the impacts of organizational presence using econometric analysis, supported by qualitative information from the survey.

Determinants of Organizational Density

SPECIFICATION AND HYPOTHESES. The dependent variables in the analysis of local organizational development were the number of local organizations existing in the community at the time of the survey and the number involved in NRM activities.[12] These are obviously only rough measures of organizational development and abstract from many important issues such as organizational size, scope, performance, sustainability, and intensity of activity. We were not able to obtain satisfactory measures of such aspects of organizational development given the extensive nature of the survey and the limited time we were able to spend in each village (half a day). More intensive research is needed to study these issues. Nevertheless, we believe that analysis of the data available can yield useful insights about the causes and implications of variation in local organizational density across a fairly large number of communities and can suggest valuable directions for further research.

Least-squares regression was used to investigate the determinants of organizational presence. The explanatory variables included in the regressions were the number of external organizations that have worked in the village, the population of the village in 1974, population density in 1974, population growth

---

12. The survey investigated organizational activities related to NRM, such as promotion of new agricultural technologies, conservation measures, and tree planting.

rate (between 1974 and 1988) and growth rate squared, the distance of the village from Tegucigalpa, the distance to the nearest road, the adult literacy rate in 1974, the percentage of the 1974 population born within the *municipio,* and variables for the different pathways of development identified by the survey, representing different patterns of agricultural and livelihood change (and thus differences in economic opportunities and constraints).[13]

Because they may be endogenous to the process of organizational development, predicted values of the population growth rate, the population growth rate squared, and pathway variables were used in the regressions.[14] We examined the robustness of our findings to use of actual versus predicted values and to exclusion of the pathway variables. The robustness of the findings is discussed later when we review the empirical results.

The presence of external organizations also may be endogenous, since it could have been influenced by local organizational development. There is also the potential for omitted variable bias to cause a spurious correlation, if unobserved factors were responsible for both local and external organizational presence. We were not able to use an instrumental variables approach to correct for these problems, since any variable that influences development of external organizations may also directly affect local organizational development. Thus, a correlation between the presence of local and external organizations could be because local organizations attract external organizations or because of omitted variable bias.

The explanatory variables are expected to affect the benefits or costs of organizational development. A higher population level is expected to positively affect the demand for organizations, but it may also increase the cost of organizing. Controlling for population level, population density represents the scarcity of resources and geographic proximity of village households, both of

---

13. In all regressions, the coefficients and standard errors were corrected for sampling weights, stratification, and the total number of communities in the central region (StataCorp 1997). The results are thus representative of the region as a whole. Standard errors were estimated using the Huber-White estimator and are thus robust to general forms of heteroskedasticity (White 1980).

14. The variables used to predict the population growth rate and growth rate squared include all of the other explanatory variables, plus dummy variables for whether the community had access to a road in 1975, whether road access had been obtained since 1975, and the proportions of households having access to water, sanitation, electricity, or radio in 1974. The development pathway dummy variables were replaced by predicted probabilities from a multinomial logit regression of pathway determinants (this regression is reported in Pender, Scherr, and Durón 1999). The explanatory variables for the pathways include mid-point altitude of the village, average number of rainfall days, 1974 population density, distance to Tegucigalpa, distance to the nearest road, and whether a technical assistance program had worked in the village.

For technical reasons, the standard errors could not be corrected for the fact that predicted values were used in the regressions in this study. We are not aware of formulas to correct the standard errors for the complex two-stage regressions used (for example, including predicted probabilities from a multinomial logit model for an ordered probit model in a second-stage regression). Given the small number of observations per stratum, bootstrapping does not appear justifiable.

which may increase organizational density. Greater scarcity of resources may lead to greater demand for organizations to help allocate and conserve resources (such as water user associations) (Scherr and Hazell 1994), while closer proximity of households is expected to reduce the transaction costs of organizational development (Mumtaz 1995). On the other hand, resource scarcity may increase potential conflict and thus undermine the ability to establish and maintain effective organizations to regulate use of natural resources.[15]

We also include the population growth rate and the square of the population growth rate to reflect the impact of immigration or emigration.[16] Where the population growth rate is unusually low, this is likely due to emigration, whereas an unusually high growth rate is likely due to immigration.

In both cases, lower stability of the community population may reduce the ability to achieve collective action in organizational development (Ostrom 1990; Bardhan 1993; Rasmussen and Meinzen-Dick 1995; Baland and Platteau 1996). Thus we expect an inverted U relationship between population growth and organizational development, with a positive effect of growth rate and negative effect of growth rate squared.

The percentage of the village born within the *municipio* reflects the absence of immigrants and may be related to the social proximity of village members, the presence of relations of trust, and the potential for social sanctions, all of which may determine the ability to achieve collective action in forming and maintaining organizations (Baland and Platteau 1996). On the other hand, the presence of immigrants may increase the demand for organizations to manage potential conflicts or increase awareness of opportunities for organizational development. Thus this variable may have mixed effects.

As with migration, market integration may undermine the ability to attain collective action, since community members may have more "exit" options where markets are more integrated (Baland and Platteau 1996). On the other hand, greater access to markets may increase the demand for some kinds of organizational development related to economic opportunities, unless entry of private firms or state intervention displace the need for such development (Uphoff 1986; Bebbington, Quisbert, and Trujillo 1996). Market access may also influence organizational development by affecting village members' access to information and knowledge of alternative organizational forms, as well as by affecting economic opportunities. Thus the expected impacts of measures of market access, including distance to Tegucigalpa and distance to a road, are ambiguous.

---

15. It may be that resource scarcity induces organizational or institutional development only after a threshold level of resource damage has been realized (Scherr and Hazell 1994; Otsuka and Place 2001). One way to test for this is to include higher-order polynomial terms (for example, population density squared). Unfortunately, the correlation of population density squared with population density in our sample is very high (0.94), limiting our ability to identify such nonlinear effects.

16. The correlation between population growth rate and growth rate squared is 0.81.

Education and literacy may also affect organizational development. Education may increase awareness of opportunities for organizational development and the ability of individuals to organize (Esman and Uphoff 1984; Bebbington, Merrill-Sands, and Farrington 1994; Meinzen-Dick 1997). More educated individuals may have a longer-term perspective owing to greater access to credit or greater ability to save (Pender 1996). Where a high proportion of a community is literate (compared with a moderate percentage as in the less literate communities in the sample), the community may be less heterogeneous in terms of wealth or social status, which many authors argue may favor collective action (Ostrom 1990; Tang 1992; Bardhan 1993), though the negative impact of wealth heterogeneity is disputed by Baland and Platteau (1996). On the other hand, education may increase the awareness of exit options of community members and thus tend to undermine collective action. More educated people may have higher opportunity costs of their time, so they may be less prone to participate in collective action. Thus the net impact of education is theoretically ambiguous.

The presence of external organizations in the village can also have mixed effects. On one hand, such organizations may be catalysts for local organizational development and help to strengthen the capacity of local organizations (Esman and Uphoff 1984; Ostrom 1990; Thomas-Slayter 1992; Farrington and Bebbington 1993). On the other hand, such external influences may compete with or undermine local organizations by reducing the need for local collective action (Thomas-Slayter 1992, 1994).

The different pathways of development may also have different implications for organizational development. We expect greater demand for economic organizations such as producer associations, credit groups, and cooperatives where cash-crop production is occurring, as in the horticultural and coffee expansion pathways, than in the basic grains pathways (Uphoff 1986). But the higher incomes associated with such commercial pathways may undermine organizational development by causing people to have a higher opportunity cost of their time, increased exit options from their communities, or greater social heterogeneity. Thus the net impact of development pathways on organizational development, as with most other factors, cannot be determined a priori but is an important empirical issue.

Cultural, ethnic, or religious heterogeneity in addition to distribution of assets or income are also factors that could affect the costs and perceived benefits of organizing. Lack of variation in ethnic and religious makeup of the study communities prevented inclusion of these variables in the analysis, however. We were not able to obtain information on asset or income distribution so could not include these factors in the analysis.[17]

---

17. In our study design, we intended to use information on land distribution from the agricultural census of Honduras, but we could not obtain this information.

RESULTS. The regression results for organizational density are reported in Table 10.1. Local organizational density is positively associated (at the 10 percent level) with the presence of external organizations, population level, distance from the urban market, and adult literacy; and negatively associated with rapid population growth, the percentage of the community born in the *municipio*, and the basic grains expansion and forestry pathways. The number of local organizations involved in NRM activities is positively associated with the number of external organizations involved in NRM activities, population level, adult literacy, and the coffee expansion and nonfarm employment pathways and negatively associated with population density and the forestry pathway.

We explored the robustness of these findings in additional regressions using actual rather than predicted population growth rate and pathway dummies, and regressions excluding the pathways.[18] Almost all of the coefficients significant at the 5 percent level in Table 10.1 have the same sign and are significant at the 5 percent level in these other regressions.[19] In addition, we find support for the hypothesized inverted U relationship between population growth and organizational development in these additional regressions, with a significant positive coefficient of population growth rate and a significant negative coefficient of growth rate squared.

These results generally support the theory of induced organizational development, particularly as regards the impact of population and population growth. Interestingly, however, land scarcity (as measured by population density) does not appear to induce organizational development and in fact is negatively associated with organizational involvement in NRM. This finding suggests that the greater potential for conflict over resources caused by resource scarcity may undermine organizational development.

The results also suggest that interventions by external programs and organizations have promoted local organizational development in central Honduras, though this conclusion is subject to the possibilities of reverse causality or omitted variable bias mentioned. We know from qualitative evidence that in some cases external agencies have promoted local organizational development (Durón 1998)—for example, efforts by an externally funded forestry project to promote forest management cooperatives.

The greater presence of local organizations in communities further from Tegucigalpa supports the argument that greater market access may undermine local organization by increasing community members' alternatives to participation in such organizations. There may also be greater intensity of government

---

18. Regression results available from the authors.

19. The exceptions are the coefficient of basic grains expansion in the first regression, which is negative and significant at the 10 percent level when actual values are used; and the coefficient of the forestry pathway in both regressions, which is insignificant in the first regression and positive and significant in the second regression.

TABLE 10.1 Determinants of local organizational presence (least-squares regression)

Variable	Total number of local organizations	Number of local organizations involved in NRM[a]
Number of external organizations[a]	0.1976**	0.1443*
	(0.0833)	(0.0807)
1974 population	0.002173***	0.002254***
	(0.000722)	(0.000491)
1974 population density	−0.00675	−0.03850***
	(0.00871)	(0.00822)
Population growth rate, 1974–88[b]	0.380	0.154
(percentage)	(0.230)	(0.331)
Population growth rate squared[b]	−0.0475**	−0.0235
	(0.0190)	(0.0247)
Distance to Tegucigalpa (kilometers)	0.0248**	−0.005
	(0.0108)	(0.0135)
Distance to nearest road (kilometers)	−0.0256	0.213
	(0.0821)	(0.154)
Rate of adult literacy in 1974	0.0459*	0.0818***
(percentage)	(0.0234)	(0.0213)
Percent of 1974 population born in the	−0.0629**	0.0038
municipio	(0.0258)	(0.0289)
Basic grains expansion[b]	−2.775**	−0.115
	(1.059)	(2.037)
Horticultural expansion[b]	0.774	2.368
	(1.633)	(1.840)
Coffee expansion[b]	1.268	2.513***
	(0.866)	(0.876)
Forestry specialization[b]	−4.618***	−3.869***
	(1.390)	(1.339)
Nonfarm employment[b]	1.077	1.667*
	(0.865)	(0.934)
Intercept	5.827	−3.593
	(3.425)	(3.800)
Number of observations	39	38
R^2	0.825	0.742

NOTE: Numbers in parentheses are robust standard errors. Coefficients and standard errors are adjusted for sampling weights, stratification, and finite population.

[a] For the regressions of determinants of the number of local organizations involved in natural resource management (NRM), the number of external organizations involved in NRM is the first explanatory variable.

[b] Predicted values are used for population growth rate, population growth rate squared, and the pathway dummy variables. Standard errors are not adjusted for use of predicted values. The variables used to predict the population growth rate and growth rate squared include all of the other explanatory variables, plus dummy variables for communities that had access to a road in 1975 and for communities that gained road access after 1975, and the proportions of households having access to water, sanitation, electricity, or radio in 1974. Pathway probabilities are from a multinomial logit regression using as explanatory variables midpoint altitude, average number of rainfall days, 1974 population density, distance to Tegucigalpa, distance to the nearest road, and whether a technical assistance program had worked in the village.

*, **, and *** indicate statistical significance at the 10 percent, 5 percent, and 1 percent levels, respectively.

involvement in communities closer to the capital city (even controlling for the number of external organizations involved), which would tend to substitute for local organization. We did not find the same impact of proximity to Tegucigalpa for the presence of local organizations involved in NRM, perhaps because the types of services provided by the government do not substitute well for the NRM functions of these local organizations.

The positive association between literacy and local organizational presence supports the hypothesis that more-educated people may be more aware or more able to take advantage of opportunities for organizational development. More-educated people may also be more receptive to encouragement from external organizations to organize.

The negative association between the percentage of village members born in the *municipio* and local organizational density is interesting. This finding suggests that immigration increases the demand for formal organizations or that immigration helps villages become more aware of opportunities for local organizational development. Immigration, however, appears to have a diminishing impact on organizational development (shown by the negative coefficient of the square of the population growth rate).

The pathways of development had some impact on organizational development, though some of the effects were not robust to the specification. The most robust finding with regard to the pathways is that the presence of local organizations involved in NRM is greater in the coffee than basic grains pathways. The greater presence of organizations involved in NRM in coffee communities may be due to several factors, including the effort by external organizations to promote local organizations in such areas, the greater economic value of resources in coffee communities, and common concerns about pollution problems caused by coffee processing.

Determinants of Collective Action Affecting NRM

SPECIFICATION AND HYPOTHESES.   The community survey asked specifically about whether community members had invested collectively in efforts to control runoff, such as by planting trees and constructing stone walls or ditches, and whether they had invested collectively in improvements to common lands, such as by planting trees or shrubs in community forests or fencing common areas.[20] Because it may have been difficult for respondents to distinguish these questions, for econometric analysis we combined the responses into a single variable representing collective action relating to NRM (a "yes" to either question was treated as a "yes," a "no" to both questions treated as a "no"). Such a yes/no measure provides a rough proxy for NRM activity.

---

20. The questionnaire did not investigate the intensity or frequency of these activities, only whether they had occurred. Future studies would benefit from incorporating these factors in the measurement of collective action.

Measures of how many activities are undertaken or resources devoted to NRM would have allowed more detailed analysis, but getting accurate measures of such indicators was beyond the scope of this study. Information on local rules for managing forests, water, and common lands was already reported, but this information is not suitable for econometric analysis.

A probit model, which regresses the probability of a binary dependent variable on a number of independent variables, was used to investigate the determinants of collective action relating to NRM. Most of the explanatory variables used in the regressions for determinants of local organizational density were included in this regression, since organizational development also involves collective action and thus is affected by many of the same factors. We included the number of government organizations and the number of NGOs as separate variables, to investigate whether these different types of external organizations have different impacts. We also included the predicted number of local organizations from the regressions discussed in the preceding section as an explanatory variable.

It is arguable that all organizations, and not only those involved in NRM activities, may influence collective action related to NRM by affecting the level of "social capital" in the village. Thus in one regression we consider the total numbers of external and local organizations as explanatory variables, and in another we consider the number involved in NRM activities. The models were not estimable when the predicted pathway dummy variables were included, so these pathways were excluded.[21]

We expect that local organizational density will contribute to the possibility of collective investment, whether or not the organizations are directly involved in NRM. The presence of local organizations may increase social interactions and the possibility of enforcing agreements based on the multiplex relationships among community members (White and Runge 1995; Baland and Platteau 1996).

Our expectations about the effects of other variables on collective investment are similar to our expectations about their impact on local organizational development, since local organizational development itself requires collective action, as discussed.

RESULTS.   Interestingly, we find that the presence of local organizations involved in NRM activities is significantly positively related to collective action (significant in one specification), while the number of government organizations is negatively associated with collective action (significant in both) (Table 10.2). In one specification we find that land scarcity is associated with

---

21. When too many regressors were included in the model, the model predicted the outcomes perfectly and not all coefficients could be estimated. This is a common problem in estimating binary probit models with a small data set.

TABLE 10.2 Determinants of collective action to control runoff or improve common land (probit regression)

Variable	Total number of organizations as explanatory variables[a]	Organizations involved in NRM as explanatory variables[a]
Number of local organizations[a,b]	0.343	0.843**
	(0.413)	(0.333)
Number of government organizations[a]	−0.538***	−0.519**
	(0.157)	(0.208)
Number of NGOs[a]	0.809*	0.050
	(0.428)	(0.245)
1974 population	0.00223	−0.00066
	(0.00197)	(0.00117)
1974 population density	−0.0527***	−0.0030
	(0.0137)	(0.0162)
Population growth rate, 1974–88[b] (percentage)	1.210**	0.343
	(0.564)	(0.425)
Population growth rate squared[b]	−0.456**	−0.220*
	(0.192)	(0.119)
Distance to Tegucigalpa (kilometers)	−0.0717**	−0.0122
	(0.0287)	(0.0141)
Distance to nearest road (kilometers)	0.013	−0.210
	(0.356)	(0.146)
Rate of adult literacy in 1974 (percentage)	−0.0342	−0.0660**
	(0.0396)	(0.0316)
Percentage of 1974 population born in the *municipio*	−0.0685	−0.0325
	(0.0526)	(0.0329)
Intercept	10.51	6.83
	(7.65)	(4.70)
Number of observations	39	38

NOTE: Numbers in parentheses are robust standard errors. Coefficients and standard errors are adjusted for sampling weights, stratification, and finite population.

[a]In the first regression, the total number of local organizations, government organizations, and NGOs are the first three explanatory variables. In the second regression, the numbers of these organizations involved in NRM are the explanatory variables.

[b]Predicted values are used for number of local organizations, population growth rate, and population growth rate squared. Standard errors are not adjusted for use of predicted values. Predicted values for number of local organizations are based on the regressions in Table 10.1. Predicted values for population growth rate and growth rate squared are determined as explained in footnote b, Table 10.1.

*, **, and *** indicate statistical significance at the 10 percent, 5 percent, and 1 percent levels, respectively.

less collective action, consistent with the finding of less organizational activity related to NRM. As in the case of organizational development, we find an inverted U relationship between population growth and collective investment (though this is significant in only one specification). Villages more distant from Tegucigalpa are less likely to engage in collective action (significant in one specification), whereas a higher literacy rate is negatively associated with collective action (in the other specification).

We investigated the robustness of these results, using actual rather than predicted levels for the number of local organizations, population growth rate and growth rate squared. All of the coefficients significant at the 5 percent level in Table 10.2 are the same sign and significant in these other regressions, except the coefficient of literacy rate in the second regression (insignificant). In addition, we find statistically significant support for a positive effect of population, an inverted U relationship between population growth and collective action, and a negative effect of distance to roads on collective action in these regressions.

Overall, these results confirm the importance of organizational presence, demographic factors, and market access as factors influencing the potential for collective action. Local organizations appear to promote collective action while external government organizations appear to displace it. It may be that external government organizations displace local collective action, or they may simply choose to work in problem communities where local collective action is not occurring. Even if they do displace local collective action, the net impact of external government organizations on collective action depends on indirect effects (via their positive contribution to development of local organizations) as well as these direct displacement effects. Based on the magnitude of the coefficients in Tables 10.1 and 10.2, the direct effects appear to outweigh the indirect effects, however, so that external organizations tend to reduce collective action on balance.

Qualitative information from the community survey indicates that in most cases, collective action to manage runoff or improve common lands occurred through local initiative, though in some cases external organizations were involved (Durón 1998). Thus external organizations do not always displace local action and in some cases promote it. Furthermore, co-involvement of external organizations and local organizations in constructing and maintaining potable water systems and roads was very common (Durón 1998). Thus the extent to which external organizations displaced local collective action appears to depend greatly on the type of collective action. For drinking water systems and roads, external organizations specialized in providing capital inputs and technical expertise, while expecting local communities to provide labor inputs. The different comparative advantages of external and local organizations in providing these different kinds of complementary inputs explains the motive for the high degree of co-involvement of external and local organizations in such activities. The large benefits of these activities to the recipient communities explains the near universal achievement of collective action in these cases. By contrast, collective action to protect natural resources by, for instance, planting trees likely requires less technical or capital inputs from external agents and provides smaller perceived benefits to the community.

As with local organizational development, population growth appears to promote collective action, although rapid population growth, and thus a less stable population, may undermine it. Population density appears to undermine collective action, also consistent with its impact on local organizational development.

Unlike the case with local organizational development, proximity to the urban market appears to promote collective action in NRM. This result may be because of greater intensity of effort in such areas by external programs seeking to promote collective action in more accessible communities. Since local organizations also favor collective action, the net impact of proximity to the urban market on collective action depends on indirect effects (via its negative impact on local organizational development) as well as positive direct effects. Based on the magnitude of the coefficients in Tables 10.1 and 10.2, the direct effect appears to outweigh the indirect effect, so that communities closer to Tegucigalpa are predicted to have greater collective action.

Determinants of Private Action Affecting NRM

SPECIFICATION AND HYPOTHESES. The variables reflecting private actions affecting NRM include the extent of use of various cropping practices (fallow, burning, irrigation), purchased inputs (chemical fertilizer, insecticides, herbicides, improved seeds), annual conservation or fertility management practices (contour planting, green manure, minimum tillage, mulch, incorporation of crop residues, use of cow manure or chicken manure), and land-improving investments (terraces, live barriers, stone walls, drainage ditches, trees). These variables were measured as an ordinal index from 0 to 6 (0 = no farmers use the practice, 1 = a few [less than 10 percent], 2 = minority, 3 = about half, 4 = majority, 5 = almost all [more than 90 percent], 6 = all). We used ordered probit regressions to estimate the impacts of the explanatory variables on farmers' likelihood of adopting different practices.[22]

The explanatory variables included in these regressions include the predicted number of local organizations, the number of government organizations and number of NGOs involved in NRM activities in the village, population density, the distance of the village from Tegucigalpa, the distance to the nearest road, the literacy rate, and the predicted development pathways.

These variables reflect many of the factors suggested in Chapter 2 of this volume as affecting private technology choice, including access to infrastructure

22. Ordered probit is a simple generalization of a standard binary probit model allowing for multiple ordered categories, estimated by maximum likelihood. See Amemiya (1985) or other advanced econometrics texts for a detailed explanation.

(distance to a road), access to information (presence of external organizations, distance to Tegucigalpa, literacy), credit (proxied by development pathways and literacy rate), labor/land endowment (population density), physical/technical conditioning factors determining comparative advantage (determinants of predicted pathways of development), and collective action (presence of local organizations). Household- and plot-level data and time-series data would be needed to adequately incorporate some of the other factors, such as risk, property rights, prices, and wealth.

There are too many dependent variables reflecting private NRM decisions to discuss hypotheses specific to each one. We focus here on the expected impacts of organizations. Government and NGO technical assistance organizations are expected to increase the adoption of practices they have been promoting, such as various conservation practices, while reducing use of some traditional practices that they have discouraged, such as burning. The presence of local producer associations may favor adoption of more modern commercial practices, such as irrigation and purchased inputs, to the extent that they help farmers obtain access to information about such technologies or access to inputs and credit (Uphoff 1986).

RESULTS.   We investigated the determinants of farmers' general cropping practices, use of inputs, annual soil conservation and soil fertility management practices, and land-improving investments. Because of space limitations and the large number of regressions, we will focus the discussion on the impacts of the organizational variables.

The effects of organizations on cropping practices and use of inputs are mixed. Local organizations are associated with greater use of burning, chemical fertilizer, chicken manure, and mulching but less use of insecticides or plowing in of crop residues (Tables 10.3, 10.4, and 10.5). Government organizations are associated with greater use of insecticides, plowing in of crop residues, and terracing and less use of fallow, burning, and mulching. NGOs are associated with greater use of fallow, minimum till, plowing in of crop residues, and live barriers and less use of chemical fertilizers and chicken manure.

The robustness of these findings was investigated using regressions including actual rather than predicted values of the number of local organizations and the pathway variables, and regressions excluding the pathways. Most of these results were found to be robust.[23]

It is difficult to simply characterize such complex results, but it appears that NGOs and government organizations have a tendency to promote more

---

23. The nonrobust exceptions were the positive association between NGOs and fallow, the negative association between NGOs and chemical fertilizer use, the negative association between government organizations and mulching, and the positive association between government organizations and terracing.

labor-intensive practices and investments such as terracing, live barriers, and plowing in of crop residues, whereas local farmer organizations help to promote more immediately profitable and less labor-intensive methods such as use of chemical fertilizer and chicken manure. The differential association of local and government organizations with burning practices is an example of this pattern; where local organizations are more prevalent, burning is more common, whereas government organizations inhibit the use of burning. The fact that government organizations discourage burning is not surprising, given that it is government policy to prevent agricultural burning. The positive association of burning with local organizations is somewhat surprising. This finding probably does not mean that local organizations promote burning; rather, government organizations may be less actively involved (even if present) in areas where local organizations are well developed, so the discouraging effects of government presence may be lower.

Conclusions and Implications

With regard to the determinants of local organizational development in central Honduras, the main findings of this study are that population growth contributes to organizational development at low levels of growth but has a diminishing and possibly negative effect at high growth rates, that proximity to the urban center reduces local organizational presence, and that the presence of immigrants appears to favor local organizational development. Local organizational development related to NRM is positively associated with larger population levels but negatively with population density (land scarcity) and positively associated with education levels and coffee production.

With regard to the impacts of local organizations on NRM, we find mixed results. Local organizations involved in NRM contribute to collective investment in NRM and assist in regulating use of common property resources and dealing with externalities (the representatives of the municipalities and the *patronatos* are particularly important for these regulations), though these roles vary substantially across the development pathways. Local organizations have mixed impacts on farmers' private decisions to adopt resource conservation measures. In some cases they are associated with less adoption of such measures, such as no-burn practices and plowing in crop residues. This result may be because such conservation measures have a lower priority for many farmers than activities that generate greater income in the near term and that may substitute for conservation practices (such as use of chemical fertilizers rather than organic methods).

In contrast to the impacts of local organizations, we find that external government organizations seem to reduce collective investment in NRM, although they promote other kinds of collective investment such as construction and

TABLE 10.3 Determinants of cropping practices (ordered probit regressions)

Variable	Continuous cropping	Burning	Irrigation	Fertilizer	Insecticide	Herbicide	Improved seeds
Number of local organizations affecting NRM[a]	0.260*	0.749***	0.036	0.432**	−0.498***	0.200	−0.553
	(0.150)	(0.138)	(0.144)	(0.183)	(0.123)	(0.138)	(0.361)
Number of government organizations affecting NRM	0.318**	−0.706***	−0.043	−0.083	0.838***	−0.235	0.723
	(0.153)	(0.160)	(0.157)	(0.183)	(0.164)	(0.180)	(0.457)
Number of NGOs affecting NRM	−0.368***	−0.166	0.156	−0.376***	0.0271	−0.237*	0.386
	(0.127)	(0.133)	(0.113)	(0.108)	(0.1178)	(0.121)	(0.238)
1988 population density (persons/square kilometer)	0.0172**	−0.0122	−0.00142	−0.00171	0.00246	−0.00416	−0.00113
	(0.0077)	(0.0077)	(0.00594)	(0.00495)	(0.00543)	(0.00584)	(0.00876)
Distance to Tegucigalpa (kilometers)	0.0295***	0.0306***	0.0194	−0.0118	0.0302***	0.0174	−0.0014
	(0.0096)	(0.0103)	(0.0117)	(0.0115)	(0.0097)	(0.0142)	(0.0138)
Distance to nearest road (kilometers)	0.0631	0.0558	−0.0857	−0.2353***	−0.0652	0.1639**	−3.594
	(0.0917)	(0.1147)	(0.0903)	(0.0698)	(0.0734)	(0.0721)	(2.996)

1988 adult literacy rate (percentage)	−0.0250	0.0363**	0.0018	−0.0350**	0.0218	−0.0327**	−0.0347*
	(0.0217)	(0.0150)	(0.0161)	(0.0163)	(0.0167)	(0.0135)	(0.0192)
Basic grains expansion[b]	−1.478*	−3.899***	−0.528	4.979***	1.023	−1.712**	−11951***
	(0.855)	(0.960)	(1.010)	(0.776)	(0.970)	(0.789)	(4047)
Horticultural expansion[b]	1.782*	−5.444***	3.726***	3.027***	4.756***	−1.387*	5.891***
	(0.968)	(1.103)	(1.327)	(0.990)	(1.010)	(0.767)	(1.603)
Coffee expansion[b]	−1.985**	−3.550***	−1.291*	2.554***	0.913	−0.761	3.238***
	(0.877)	(0.800)	(0.754)	(0.624)	(0.878)	(0.682)	(1.160)
Forestry specialization[b]	6.497***	−5.996***	−1.308	2.171	−0.308	2.899*	4.934*
	(1.891)	(1.326)	(1.730)	(1.560)	(1.840)	(1.630)	(2.555)
Nonfarm employment[b]	−0.576	−1.259	0.072	−2.095***	2.171**	−1.114	5.046**
	(0.868)	(0.935)	(0.816)	(0.770)	(0.983)	(0.899)	(1.910)
Number of observations	37	36	37	38	37	37	38

NOTE: Numbers in parentheses are robust standard errors. Coefficient and standard errors are corrected for sampling weights, stratification, and finite population.

[a]Predicted number of organizations, based on results of regressions reported in Table 10.1.

[b]Predicted pathway probability, based on the same multinomial logit regression reported in footnote b of Table 10.1.

*, **, and *** indicate statistical significance at the 10 percent, 5 percent, and 1 percent levels, respectively.

TABLE 10.4 Determinants of annual soil conservation/organic fertility management practices (ordered probit regressions)

Variable	Contour planting	Green manure	Minimum till	Mulching	Plowing in crop residues	Cow manure	Chicken manure
Number of local organizations affecting NRM[a]	0.309	0.250	0.051	0.511***	-0.369**	0.077	1.182***
	(0.250)	(0.185)	(0.190)	(0.123)	(0.152)	(0.167)	(0.308)
Number of government organizations affecting NRM	0.106	0.282	0.163	-0.259**	0.602***	0.126	0.149
	(0.155)	(0.181)	(0.167)	(0.123)	(0.199)	(0.158)	(0.192)
Number of NGOs affecting NRM	-0.175	0.314	0.329*	-0.185	0.341**	-0.072	-0.965***
	(0.205)	(0.195)	(0.177)	(0.119)	(0.128)	(0.109)	(0.226)
1988 population density (persons/square kilometer)	-0.00855*	-0.00481	-0.01112	0.00681	-0.00611	0.00158	0.00750
	(0.00447)	(0.00690)	(0.00749)	(0.00414)	(0.00499)	(0.00566)	(0.00610)
Distance to Tegucigalpa (kilometers)	-0.0943***	-0.0363*	-0.0514**	-0.0058	-0.0569***	-0.0315	-0.0378*
	(0.0209)	(0.0212)	(0.0214)	(0.0123)	(0.0149)	(0.0210)	(0.0223)
Distance to nearest road (kilometers)	0.342**	0.117	0.644**	0.1438	0.091	0.263**	-20.22***
	(0.131)	(0.159)	(0.268)	(0.0948)	(0.191)	(0.118)	(2.64)

1988 adult literacy rate (percentage)	−0.0048	−0.0410*	−0.0080	−0.0241**	0.0265	0.0111	−0.0187
	(0.0133)	(0.0220)	(0.0174)	(0.0117)	(0.0169)	(0.0166)	(0.0188)
Basic grains expansion[b]	−1.857*	−1.396	−2.311	−0.929	−23.888***	−2.963***	6.785**
	(0.973)	(1.765)	(2.236)	(1.287)	(8.194)	(0.691)	(3.331)
Horticultural expansion[b]	−3.735***	−7.870*	−2.961	−1.388	−1.302	−2.674**	−2.937
	(1.209)	(3.905)	(1.894)	(1.079)	(0.990)	(1.085)	(2.124)
Coffee expansion[b]	0.441	1.050	1.827	0.462	−1.476*	−0.622	0.245
	(0.765)	(1.152)	(1.245)	(0.483)	(0.768)	(0.793)	(1.013)
Forestry specialization[b]	5.288***	−0.021	−1.138	−3.671	0.080	−0.279	−0.747
	(1.839)	(1.898)	(2.074)	(3.405)	(1.334)	(1.270)	(2.039)
Nonfarm employment[b]	−3.783***	−2.536*	−1.264	−1.657**	−1.705**	−2.179*	−1.232
	(1.242)	(1.370)	(1.526)	(0.724)	(0.726)	(1.109)	(1.314)
Number of observations	37	38	38	38	36	38	38

NOTE: Numbers in parentheses are robust standard errors. Coefficient and standard errors are corrected for sampling weights, stratification, and finite population.

[a]Predicted number of organizations, based on results of regressions reported in Table 10.1.

[b] Predicted pathway probability, based on the same multinomial logit regression reported in footnote b of Table 10.1.

*, **, and *** indicate statistical significance at the 10 percent, 5 percent, and 1 percent levels, respectively.

TABLE 10.5 Determinants of land-improving investments (ordered probit regressions)

Variable	Terraces	Live barriers	Stone walls	Drainage ditches	Trees
Number of local organizations affecting NRM[a]	0.148	−0.168	−0.032	−0.131	0.1442
	(0.169)	(0.145)	(0.215)	(0.192)	(0.0918)
Number of government organizations affecting NRM	0.316**	0.061	−0.024	0.147	0.0610
	(0.144)	(0.111)	(0.189)	(0.159)	(0.0894)
Number of NGOs affecting NRM	−0.043	0.230**	0.237	0.051	0.0744
	(0.152)	(0.111)	(0.145)	(0.125)	(0.1140)
1988 population density (persons/square kilometer)	0.00408	0.01071	0.01579**	0.00259	0.01115**
	(0.00698)	(0.00893)	(0.00669)	(0.00609)	(0.00552)
Distance to Tegucigalpa (kilometers)	−0.0209*	−0.0273***	−0.0121	−0.0345**	0.01162
	(0.0118)	(0.00899)	(0.0119)	(0.0130)	(0.00826)
Distance to nearest road (kilometers)	0.2055**	−0.0416	0.0426	0.0938	−0.1751**
	(0.0919)	(0.0771)	(0.0765)	(0.0999)	(0.0756)

1988 adult literacy rate (percentage)	0.0024	−0.0091	−0.0041	−0.0112	−0.0088
	(0.0140)	(0.0134)	(0.0167)	(0.0150)	(0.0134)
Basic grains expansion[b]	−0.956	1.058	−0.719	1.087	1.795**
	(0.795)	(0.844)	(0.754)	(1.185)	(0.718)
Horticultural expansion[b]	1.972**	−2.605**	−3.286***	−1.143	−0.147
	(0.821)	(1.070)	(1.199)	(1.128)	(0.638)
Coffee expansion[b]	1.553*	1.733	−2.235***	0.771	0.051
	(0.865)	(1.167)	(0.819)	(0.829)	(0.712)
Forestry specialization[b]	2.760*	−0.079	−0.433	3.017	−0.553
	(1.462)	(1.183)	(1.296)	(1.833)	(1.596)
Nonfarm employment[b]	−0.171	−1.044	−1.970**	−0.776	−0.887
	(0.768)	(0.808)	(0.910)	(1.098)	(0.579)
Number of observations	38	38	38	37	38

NOTE: Numbers in parentheses are robust standard errors. Coefficient and standard errors are corrected for sampling weights, stratification, and finite population.

[a]Predicted number of organizations, based on results of regressions reported in Table 10.1.

[b]Predicted pathway probability, based on the same multinomial logit regression reported in footnote b of Table 10.1.

*, **, and *** indicate statistical significance at the 10 percent, 5 percent, and 1 percent levels, respectively.

maintenance of water systems and roads. External organizations have a stronger impact on promoting adoption of some labor-intensive conservation measures (such as no-burn, plowing in crop residues, and terracing) on private cropland. Some government organizations also play an important role in enforcing regulations or managing externalities, particularly in forestry communities (in combination with local organizations) and basic grain expansion communities (where local organizations are not very involved in this effort). NGOs are also important in promoting some conservation practices, such as plowing in crop residues and use of live barriers.

In a broad sense, the findings support the theory of induced organizational development. They also suggest, however, that very rapid population growth may undermine the ability for organizational development to keep pace with population or the ability to achieve collective action for NRM.[24] In many communities (most notably rapidly developing horticultural expansion communities), local organizational development is still very limited, despite (or perhaps because of) very rapid population growth, improvements in road and market access, and increases in demand for credit and other services. Local organizational development may be unable to respond to very rapid change.

The positive association between external and local organizational presence suggests that external organizations are playing a catalytic role in many cases, though the effort still may be insufficient to fulfill the demand where the pace of change is very rapid. On the other hand, the negative impact of external organizations on collective investments in NRM suggests that caution is warranted when such organizations do intervene in local communities, to be sure that they are facilitating and not undermining local initiative. External organizations appear to be essential to promote soil conservation measures on private farmland. Both external organizations and local organizations can play important and complementary roles in fostering more sustainable and productive use of natural resources.

The challenge for policymakers and program managers is to identify and exploit cases where synergies exist between external and local organizational development (such as providing complementary inputs into infrastructure development or in regulating resource use and externalities), to be cautious about intervening in a way that displaces local initiative, and to focus effort on activities that have significant social benefits but are not being addressed adequately by private action (such as many conservation measures). Given the possibilities of unexploited complementarities or unintended competition between the actions of external organizations and local organizations, increased

---

24. Several authors have hypothesized that a rapid population growth rate (as opposed to a high population level) has negative impacts on NRM because of lags in institutional adjustment (see, for example, Templeton and Scherr 1997 and references cited therein).

investment by external actors in understanding the extent and roles of local organizations could yield substantial benefits.

It is important to recognize that the opportunities for and constraints upon efforts to meet this challenge may vary substantially from place to place, depending upon local economic opportunities, population pressure, and other factors. This study focuses on a situation with a relatively low level of economic development and low population density. One might expect to find similar results in similar conditions elsewhere, whereas in more developed or densely populated conditions substantially different relationships between organizational development and natural resource management may exist. As our conceptual discussion emphasized, most determinant factors have theoretically ambiguous impacts, and actual impacts can be determined only through careful empirical research. Such research on organizational development is still relatively limited. We hope that this study will encourage further efforts to disentangle the causes and effects of local organizational development in different circumstances and help policymakers to consider such issues when targeting their efforts to promote more sustainable agricultural development.

References

Amemiya, T. 1985. *Advanced econometrics*. Cambridge: Harvard University Press.

Baland, J.-M., and J.-P. Platteau. 1996. *Halting degradation of natural resources. Is there a role for rural communities?* Oxford: Clarendon Press.

Bardhan, P. 1993. Analytics of the institutions of informal cooperation in rural development. *World Development* 21 (4): 633–639.

Bebbington, A. J., D. Merrill-Sands, and J. Farrington. 1994. *Farmer and community organisations in agricultural research and extension: Functions, impacts and questions*. Overseas Development Institute (ODI) Agricultural Administration (Research and Extension Network) Network Paper 47. London: ODI.

Bebbington, A. J., J. Quisbert, and G. Trujillo. 1996. Technology and rural development strategies in a small farmer organization: Lessons from Bolivia for rural policy and practice. *Public Administration and Development* 16 (3): 195–213.

Boserup, E. 1965. *The conditions of agricultural growth*. New York: Aldine.

de Janvry, A., and E. Sadoulet. 1993. Market, state, and civil organizations in Latin America beyond the debt crisis: The context for rural development. *World Development* 21 (4): 659–674.

Durón, G. 1998. The influence of external organizations in the collective management of resources in Honduras. Master's thesis, School of Development Studies, University of East Anglia, U.K.

Durón, G., and G. Bergeron. 1995. *Las politicas sectoriales agricolas y ambientales y su impact en las laderas de Honduras*. Paper presented at the Seminario Taller las Politicas Sectoriales y Su Efecto en el Manejo de los Recursos Naturales en Areas de Lader en Honduras, September 11–13, Tegucigalpa, Honduras.

Esman, M. J., and N. T. Uphoff. 1984. *Local organizations: Intermediaries in rural development*. Ithaca, N.Y., U.S.A.: Cornell University Press.

Farrington, J., and A. Bebbington. 1993. *Reluctant partners? Non-governmental organizations, the state, and sustainable agricultural development.* London: Routledge.

Hayami, Y., and V. W. Ruttan. 1985. *Agricultural development: An international perspective.* Baltimore, Md., U.S.A.: Johns Hopkins University Press.

Meinzen-Dick, R. 1997. Farmer participation in irrigation: 20 years of experience and lessons for the future. *Irrigation and Drainage Systems* 11 (2): 103–118.

Miranda, B. 1997. Arreglos institucionales para el desarrollo sostenible de las laderas de América Central. In *Desarrollo agricola, sostenibilidad de recursos naturales y reduccion de la pobreza en América Latina: El papel de las regiones de laderas*, ed. O. Neidecker-Gonzales and S. J. Scherr. Feldafing, Germany: Deutsche Stiftung für internationale Entwicklung.

Mumtaz, S. 1995. The demographic determinants of "successful" village cooperatives. *Pakistan Development Review* 34 (4, Part 2): 609–617.

North, D. C. 1990. *Institutions, institutional change and economic performance.* Cambridge: Cambridge University Press.

Nugent, J. B. 1993. Between state, markets, and households: A neoinstitutional analysis of local organizations and institutions. *World Development* 21 (4): 623–632.

Ostrom, E. 1990. *Governing the commons: The evolution of institutions for collective action.* Cambridge: Cambridge University Press.

Otsuka, K., and F. Place, eds. 2001. *Land tenure and natural resource management: A comparative study of agrarian communities in Asia and Africa.* Baltimore, Md., U.S.A.: Johns Hopkins University Press.

Pender, J. 1996. Discount rates and credit markets: Theory and evidence from rural India. *Journal of Development Economics* 50 (2): 257–296.

Pender, J., and G. Durón. 1996. Pathways of development in the central hillsides of Honduras: 1970s–1990s. International Food Policy Research Institute, Environment and Production Technology Division, Washington, D.C. Photocopy.

Pender, J., and S. J. Scherr. 1997. Community survey of hillside development patterns in the central region of Honduras. International Food Policy Research Institute, Environment and Production Technology Division, Washington, D.C. Photocopy.

Pender, J., S. J. Scherr, and G. Durón. 1999. *Pathways of development in the hillsides of Honduras: Causes and implications for agricultural production, poverty, and sustainable resource use.* Environment and Production Technology Division Discussion Paper 45. Washington, D.C.: International Food Policy Research Institute.

Rasmussen, L. N., and R. Meinzen-Dick. 1995. *Local organizations for natural resource management: Lessons from theoretical and empirical literature.* Environment and Production Technology Division Discussion Paper 11. Washington, D.C.: International Food Policy Research Institute.

Scherr, S. J., and P. B. R. Hazell. 1994. *Sustainable agricultural development strategies in fragile lands.* Environment and Production Technology Division Discussion Paper 1. Washington, D.C.: International Food Policy Research Institute.

StataCorp. 1997. *Stata statistical software: Release 5.0.* College Station, Texas, U.S.A.

Tang, S. Y. 1992. *Institutions and collective action: Self-governance in irrigation systems.* San Francisco: ICS Press.

Templeton, S., and S. J. Scherr. 1997. *Population pressure and the microeconomy of land management in hills and mountains of developing countries.* Environment and

Production Technology Division Discussion Paper 26. Washington, D.C.: International Food Policy Research Institute.

Thomas-Slayter, B. P. 1992. Implementing effective local management of natural resources: New roles for NGOs in Africa. *Human Organization* 51 (2): 136–143.

———. 1994. Structural change, power politics, and community organizations in Africa: Challenging the patterns, puzzles and paradoxes. *World Development* 22 (10): 1479–1490.

Uphoff, N. 1986. *Local institutional development: An analytical sourcebook with cases.* West Hartford, Conn., U.S.A.: Kumarian Press.

———. 1993. Grassroots organizations and NGOs in rural development: Opportunities with diminishing states and expanding markets. *World Development* 21 (4): 607–622.

White, A. T., and C. F. Runge. 1995. The emergence and evolution of collective action: Lessons from watershed management in Haiti. *World Development* 23 (10): 1683–1698.

White, H. 1980. A heteroskedasticity-consistent covariance matrix estimator and a direct test for heteroskedasticity. *Econometrica* 48 (May): 817–838.

World Bank. 1991. Honduras: Environmental agenda. Washington, D.C. Photocopy.

11 Collective Action in Space: Assessing How Cooperation and Collective Action Vary across an African Landscape

BRENT SWALLOW, JUSTINE WANGILA,
WOUDYALEW MULATU, ONYANGO OKELLO,
AND NANCY McCARTHY

Economists are beginning to show more interest in the spatial aspects of economic relationships. Spatial patterns of prices and land use have perhaps received most attention to date. Jayne (1994) and Omamo (1995) have analyzed spatial patterns of crop choice in Zimbabwe and Kenya. Bockstael (1996) studied spatial patterns of land use and land prices in the Patuxent watershed in the state of Maryland. Chomitz and Gray (1996) analyzed the spatial patterns of land use conversion resulting from road construction in Belize.

Collective action for natural resource management also has important spatial aspects. The location of individuals relative to each other and the collective good determine both the benefits and costs of collective action. Consider, for example, a collective good available at a single fixed location—for example, a water well managed by a collective. On the one hand, households located near the well incur relatively low transaction costs from participating in maintaining the pump and from collecting water from the well. On the other hand, households located near the well, or near roads leading to the well, may also incur relatively high costs from the disturbance caused by neighbors walking past. Aggregate benefits and costs also depend upon the spatial distribution of individuals and resources. The more densely populated the area served by the well, the lower the monitoring costs per individual, the greater the total transaction costs associated with queuing, and the greater the incentive to free-ride on others' cooperative behavior.

The focus in this chapter is on individual adoption of a technology that produces a mixed public-private good. The technology is a formulation of insecticide that is applied to cattle as a "pouron." The mixed public-private good is control of external parasites and animal disease vectors. Household demand for pourons is hypothesized to depend upon three spatial factors: (1) the distance from the household to the place where the cattle treatments are sold; (2) the density of cattle owners in the neighborhood around each household; and (3) the ability of the local administrative unit to foster collective action. The distance to the treatment center determines the transaction costs incurred in obtaining treatments. The density of cattle owners in the neighborhood affects both

240

the opportunities for collective action and the incentives to free-ride on neighbors' use of the cattle treatments. The ability of the local administrative unit to foster collective action determines the incentives to free-ride or cooperate in provision of the public good.

Those hypotheses are tested through an analysis of individual use of cattle treatments in a study site in the Ghibe Valley in southwest Ethiopia. The behavior of individual households regarding the use of cattle treatments is related to the characteristics of the households themselves and the characteristics of their neighbors. Neighbor variables are created using geographic information systems (GIS) software and brought into a logistical regression model. The outcome of successful collective action is captured by an index of cooperation that varies from negative and statistically significant for areas where free-riding is evident to positive and statistically significant for areas where cooperation is evident. Follow-up analysis confirmed that areas with negative indexes of cooperation appeared to have little collective action for pouron use and areas with positive indexes appeared to have significant collective action for pouron use.

The next section provides some background on the technical and economic aspects of the problem and the particular case study. The following section presents a model of household demand for pouron treatments. That model provides a mathematical definition of the three spatial dimensions of demand for the mixed public-private good. The chapter goes on to discuss the methods used to collect, process, and analyze household-level census data and present the econometric results. The econometric results led to a subsequent qualitative study of local communities' ability to cooperate in the use of the pourons. Both the methods and results of that phase of the research are described.

Individual and Collective Action for Tsetse Control by Use of Pourons

Background

African animal trypanosomosis is a disease that constrains livestock productivity and agricultural development across much of Sub-Saharan Africa. Trypanosomosis is caused by parasitic protozoa and transmitted by several species of tsetse fly (*Glossina* spp.). Trypanosomosis is particularly important in Ethiopia, where about 7 million cattle are at risk of contracting the disease. Cattle are the main source of traction for crop cultivation.

Since January 1991 the International Livestock Research Institute (ILRI) has been conducting a tsetse control trial using a cypermethrin high-*cis* pouron (Ectopor, Ciba-Geigy, Switzerland) in the Ghibe Valley (Gullele area) of southwest Ethiopia (Leak et al. 1995; Swallow, Mulatu, and Leak 1995). A solution of the insecticide is applied directly to farmers' cattle as a pouron. Tsetse flies and other external parasites that attempt to feed on the treated animals contact the insecticide and die. Individual cattle owners pay 3 Ethiopian birr (about

US$0.50) for each of their animals that is treated (Swallow, Mulatu, and Leak 1995). Any farmer who wishes to have animals treated can present their animals at one of the nine treatment centers where ILRI makes the pourons available one day each month. Figure 11.1 is a map of the study site that indicates the locations of the nine treatment centers and the names and locations of the 23 local administrative units (*kabeles*).

The Private and Local Public Benefits of Pouron Use

Previous studies in the Ghibe Valley show that farmers perceive three main benefits from use of the pouron: (1) less trypanosomosis in cattle; (2) fewer problems with biting flies; and (3) fewer problems with ticks (Leak et al. 1995; Swallow, Mulatu, and Leak 1995). Farmers who treat their cattle with pourons obtain private benefits. Animals that receive treatments carry fewer ticks and may receive fewer bites from tsetse and other biting flies. Private treatment of animals with the pourons also generates local public benefits—namely, suppression of the numbers of tsetse and other biting and nuisance flies in the local area. Given the dispersal patterns of the species of tsetse flies found in the study site, most of the benefits of tsetse suppression in one location likely accrue to people keeping cattle within a one-kilometer radius of that location (Leak 1997).

Pourons are thus described in economic terms as mixed public-private goods or impure public goods (Cornes and Sandler 1986). Individual farmers will purchase pouron treatments on the basis of their expectations of the marginal costs, marginal private benefits, and marginal benefit from the public good. The marginal costs will include the cash cost of the treatment and transaction costs associated with procuring the treatments. The marginal private benefit will depend upon the productivity effects of biting flies and ticks and the efficacy of the pourons in alleviating those effects. The public-good benefit will depend upon the presence or absence of collective action for pouron use. A priori, we assumed that there would be differences in collective action between *kabeles*. *Kabeles* are the lowest level of government administration in rural Ethiopia (200–250 households) and are responsible for a wide range of public services and local organization. Although *kabele* governments were not formally involved in the pouron trial, we had some anecdotal evidence that there were differences in collective action between *kabeles*. While there are other social-spatial units that affect collection action in the area, none are observed across the study area, none are mutually exclusive, and none have fixed and observable boundaries.

A Model of Household Demand for Pouron Treatments

This section presents a model of household demand for pourons that considers the private and local public benefits that they generate. Equation (1) defines the profits from cattle keeping for individual *i* as the difference between expected

FIGURE 11.1 Study site in the Ghibe Valley of Ethiopia

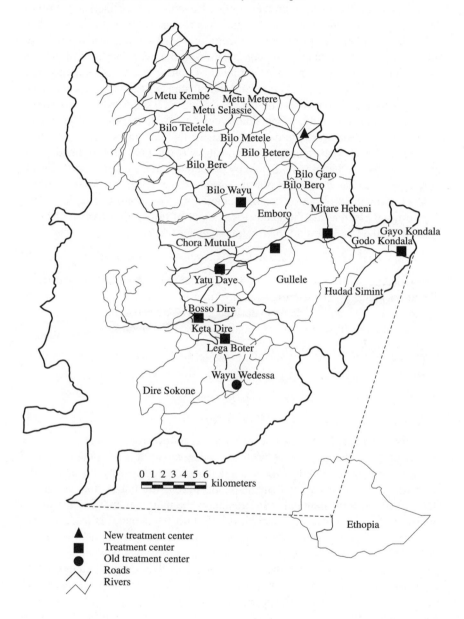

revenues and costs. We assume that livestock producers will choose the level of pouron use (*Poi*) that maximizes profits. Revenues are defined as the product of an aggregate product price (*P*) and the productive capacity of individual *i*'s cattle herd (*Hi*). The productive capacity of a herd is a function of the number of cattle in the herd (*Li*), the composition of the herd, the level of pouron use by individual *i* (*Qi*), the expected level of pouron use by others who raise livestock in the area ($QJ = \sum_{n} Qj\backslash i$), and the attributes of the herd owner. Two variables were used to measure herd composition: *LOi* is the proportion of oxen in the herd, and *LCi* is the proportion of cows in the herd. Age and gender of the household head were the two attributes of the herd owner that were considered. Herd size (*Li*) and herd composition (*LOi, LCi*) are assumed to be quasi-fixed assets that are unaffected by pouron use in the short term. Thus the only costs associated with the pouron use are the costs of the pourons themselves (*c*) and the transaction costs associated with the pouron treatments (*ti*). A priori, we assume that the main determinant of transaction costs is the distance from the homestead to the treatment center (*ti(di)*).

$$\pi i = E\,[P * Hi(Qi, QJ; Li, LOi, LCi, Agei, Sexi)] - (c + ti(di)) * Qi \quad (1)$$

Differentiation of equation (1) with respect to *Qi* produces the first-order condition given by equation (2) and the implicit demand function given by equation (3). The explicit demand derived is given by equation (4). We assume that the function *H* is concave and continuously differentiable.

$$\partial \pi i / \partial Qi = E[P(\partial H/\partial Qi + (\partial H/\partial QJ) * (\partial QJ/\partial Qi)] - c - ti = 0 \quad (2)$$

$$\partial \pi i / \partial Qi = P\,\partial H/\partial Qi + P\,\partial H/\partial QJ\,E(\partial QJ/\partial Qi) - c - ti = 0 \quad (3)$$

$$Qi^D = f(P, c, ti, \partial H/\partial QJ * E(\partial QJ/\partial Qi);$$
$$Li, LOi, LCi, Agei, Sexi) \quad (4)$$

The expected signs of five of the variables follow from the standard model of variable input demand: (1) $\partial Qi^D/\partial P > 0$—demand is increasing in the price of the aggregate output; (2) $\partial Qi^D/\partial c < 0$—demand is decreasing in the cost of the pouron; (3) $\partial Qi^D/\partial ti < 0$—demand is decreasing in transaction costs; (4) $\partial Qi^D/(\partial H/\partial Qi) > 0$—demand is increasing in the marginal contribution of the pouron to herd productivity; and (5) $\partial Qi^D/\partial Li > 0$—demand is increasing in herd size. The expected signs on both of the herd structure variables, $\partial Qi^D/\partial LOi$ and $\partial Qi^D/\partial LCi,$ are positive because oxen and cows are the most preferred age-sex cohorts in the cattle herds. This hypothesis is supported by the earlier analysis by Swallow, Mulatu, and Leak (1995). $\partial Qi^D/\partial Agei$ is expected to be positive since the pouron is a risk-reducing input and households whose heads are older are expected to be more risk averse. $\partial Qi^D/\partial Sexi$ (*Sexi* = 1 if the household head is male and 2 if the household head is female) is also expected to be positive since female-headed households are expected to be more risk averse. This hypothesis is supported by the findings of Echessah et al.

(1997) that female-headed households in the Busia area of Kenya were willing to contribute a significantly higher proportion of their income to tsetse control than male-headed households.

The component of equation (4) that relates to collective action and cooperation is $(\partial H/\partial QJ * E (\partial QJ/\partial Qi)$. We assume that $\partial H/\partial QJ$ is always positive: the marginal benefits derived from additional units of the pouron are positive for all relevant levels of pouron use. $E (\partial QJ/\partial Qi)$ may be positive or negative. Without effective collective action between neighbors, $E (\partial QJ/\partial Qi)$ would be negative. That is, individual i would expect his or her neighbors to free-ride on their use of the pouron by reducing their own level of use to the Cournot-Nash outcome. The more pouron used by i, the less pouron used by i's neighbors. With effective collective action between neighbors, $E (\partial QJ/\partial Qi)$ would be positive. That is, individual i would expect his or her neighbors to reciprocate his or her use of the pouron by using more themselves, thereby moving away from Nash equilibrium. We therefore define $E(\partial QJ/\partial Qi)$ as λi, the index of expected cooperation held by individual i. Following the discussion earlier, we hypothesize that λi will vary between *kabeles*. Differences in the index of expected cooperation between one *kabele* and another thus produces differences in cooperative outcomes. Follow-up research reported later in this chapter shows that differences in cooperative outcomes were clearly related to differences in collective action between *kabeles*. Differences in collective action and cooperative outcomes between *kabeles* appear to be related to the transaction costs of collective action.

Data Collection, Generation, and Analysis

Georeferenced Household Census

A georeferenced census of all households in the "marketshed" of the nine supply points for the pouron was undertaken between March and July 1996. Administration of the census questionnaire began with the villages immediately adjacent to the supply points and moved from village to village in all directions away from the distribution points until the enumerators came to villages that reported no use of the pourons during the previous year. A village was judged to be within the marketshed if more than two households in the village reported having cattle treated with pourons during the previous year. A village was judged to be outside of the marketshed if fewer than two households reported having cattle treated during the previous year.

The census questionnaire was prepared in English, translated into Amharic, pretested with 20 households, modified, and administered by enumerators during personal interviews with household heads. The census questionnaire was brief and took an average of 10 minutes to administer to each household. Data were collected on livestock ownership, use of pouron treatments, crop production, and migration. Almost all of the questions were precoded closed-ended questions. Enumerators carried portable global positioning system (GPS) units and recorded the longitude and latitude coordinates for each household.

Generation of Neighbor and Neighborhood Variables Using GIS

After translation into English, all data were entered using Visual dBase (Borland International 1995) and verified in SPSS 6.1 (Norusis 1994). Data were then moved into PCARC/INFO (ESRI 1996), a GIS software, for creation of the spatial variables. The PCARC/INFO POINTDIST command was used to create a point attribute table (PAT) file on neighbors in the one-kilometer-radius neighborhood. Microsoft FoxPro Version 3.0b (Kennamer 1995) was used to sort the PAT data file created by the POINTDIST command and to generate attribute data on neighbors within a radius of one kilometer of each household. The NEAR command was used to calculate the nearest treatment center for each household. ArcView (ESRI 1995) was used to map the locations of households and treatment centers. The augmented data set was then brought into SPSS for econometric analysis.

In this analysis we relate the behavior of households to the characteristics of neighbors within a one-kilometer radius. The one-kilometer radius was chosen for two reasons. First, group interviews show that farmers appreciate the fact that most of the benefits of tsetse suppression in a particular location will accrue within three to four square kilometers of that location (Leak 1997). Second, people are able to easily monitor the tsetse control actions of households located within one kilometer of their homesteads.

A Logistical Model of Pouron Demand

Equation (4) specifies a general version of the pouron demand function. In the empirical analysis we have focused on the probability that a household treated some of their animals with pouron during the previous wet season. While there were direct measures for most of the household-level variables that would affect that probability, an instrumental variable was constructed to represent expected cooperation. As a measure of the effects of others' pouron use on the productive capacity of the individual household ($\partial H/\partial QJ$), we use the number of cattle-owning households within a one-kilometer radius. The higher the number of cattle-owning households in that area, the greater the potential gains from cooperation in pouron use and also the greater the incentive to free-ride on others' behavior.

As noted, we hypothesized that the degree of cooperation or noncooperation ($E(\partial QJ/\partial Qi)$) would depend upon the *kabele* in which the household is located. That is, the demand of households living in *kabeles* with low cooperation would be negatively influenced by the density of cattle-owning households, while the demand of households living in *kabeles* with high cooperation would be positively influenced by the density of cattle-owning households.

Binary variables were created to represent the 23 *kabeles* in which the households were located. The household density and *kabele* variables were multiplied together to create a set of 23 new variables, $CGNL = CGNL1$, $CGNL2, \ldots, CGNL23$, measuring the gains from cooperation or loss from non-cooperation. $CGNL$ stands for cooperation gain or noncooperation loss. For each household 22 of the 23 variables were equal to zero, and one was equal to the number of households within the one-kilometer radius around the household. A negative sign on a $CGNL$ variable indicates that households in that *kabele* did not overcome the incentives for free-riding. A positive sign on the $CGNL$ variable indicates households in that *kabele* were able to cooperate.

Thus the logit analysis computes the probability of i as a function of household attributes (age and sex of the household head); herd attributes (herd size, proportion of oxen, proportion of cows, distance to the treatment center, and the square of distance to allow for diminishing marginal costs associated with distance); composite variables of number of animals in the one-kilometer radius; and *kabele* binary variables ($CGNL1, CGNL2, \ldots, CGNL23$).

Statistical Results

About 5,000 households were enumerated during the census, two-thirds of which owned cattle (3,267). The average cattle-owning household held 4.7 cattle at the time of the survey, 51 percent of which were oxen and 17 percent of which were cows. Ten percent of cattle-owning households were headed by women, and 90 percent by men. Seventy percent of cattle owners treated some cattle during the previous wet season (June–August 1995), 46 percent treated some cattle during the dry season, 44 percent treated some cattle during both the dry and wet season, and 1.6 percent treated some cattle during the dry season only.

The average cattle-owning household in the area was located 2.5 kilometers from the nearest treatment center and had 53 cattle-owning neighbors within a one-kilometer radius. Neighbors of the average cattle-owning household treated 59 cattle during the previous dry season and 102 cattle during the previous wet season. The average household owned 3.8 percent of all cattle within the one-kilometer radius of their household. There was large variation in these spatial variables between households. One household had 143 cattle-owning neighbors within a one-kilometer radius; others had no cattle-owning neighbors within a one-kilometer radius (Table 11.1).

Households in the marketshed of the nine treatment centers resided in 23 *kabeles*. The average *kabele* had 142 cattle-owning households and 216 total households. *Kabeles* ranged in size from 27 to 317 households.

Several findings stand out from the results of the logistical regression model of wet-season demand presented in Table 11.2. First, neither the age nor sex of the household head were significant in any of the models. Second, the

TABLE 11.1 Descriptive statistics on household population included in household census

Variable name deviation	Mean	Standard deviation	Minimum	Maximum
Use of pourons				
Percentage of households using pourons in dry season	46			
Percentage of households using pourons in wet season	70			
Cattle treated in dry season	1.38	1.95	0	25
Cattle treated in wet season	2.16	2.36	0	30
Household characteristics				
Age (years)	41.50	14.60	16	111
Sex (1 = m, 2 = f)	1.10	0.30	1	2
Herd characteristics				
Number of cattle	4.70	4.60	1	56
Percentage of oxen	51	0.36	0	1
Percentage of cows	17	0.20	0	1
Distance to treatment center (kilometers)	2.50	3.10	0	19.8
Neighbor traits (number of cattle owners within 1 km)	52.67	33.23	0	143

NOTE: Data are for 3,267 cattle-owning households.

coefficients on the herd size and herd structure variables were significant in all versions of the model ($p < .001$). The relative size of the estimated coefficients indicate that large holdings of oxen are more likely to prompt farmers to treat some animals than equally large holdings of cows. Third, the results from Version 2 of the model indicate a significant nonlinear relationship between distance to the treatment center and the probability that a household treated any animals. The findings that the probability of treatment actually increases for some distance, then decreases, might indicate that the relationship is nonlinear but poorly represented by the quadratic. It might also indicate that proximity to the treatment center provides people with a stronger incentive to free-ride; this incentive might outweigh the difference in transaction costs.

Results from Version 3 of the model indicate large differences between *kabeles* in their ability to cooperate. The estimated coefficients on the *CGNL* variables were negative for about half of the *kabeles*, indicating overall free-riding behavior, and positive for the other half, indicating overall cooperative behavior. Seven of the negative coefficients are statistically significant at $p < .001$, three of the positive coefficients are statistically significant at $p < .001$.

Figure 11.2 illustrates these results on a map of the *kabeles* in the study area. The *kabeles* indicated by vertical hatched lines have positive coefficients on the ability-to-cooperate variable. The three *kabeles* with the narrowly spaced vertical lines have significant positive coefficients, while the nine *kabeles* with the widely spaced vertical lines have insignificant positive coefficents. On the other hand, *kabeles* indicated by horizontal lines have negative coefficients on the ability-to-cooperate variable. The four *kabeles* indicated with widely spaced horizontal lines have insignificant negative coefficients, and the seven *kabeles* indicated with narrowly spaced horizontal lines have significant negative coefficients.

The spatial distribution of the four types of *kabeles* indicates that the ability of the *kabele* to cooperate is correlated with distance to the treatment centers. *Kabeles* with low cooperative abilities tend to be on the periphery of the study area, while *kabeles* with high cooperative abilities tend to be in the center of the area. Differences in index of cooperation between *kabeles* with similar distance to the treatment centers suggest that factors other than distance to treatment center also affected cooperation. For example, in the southwest of the study area, there are four neighboring *kabeles* with different levels of cooperative ability that are all located near to treatment centers.

What Caused Differences in Cooperation?

The quantitative results indicate significant differences between *kabeles* in their abilities to foster cooperation in pouron use among neighbors. These results raise additional questions. First, do the results capture real differences in cooperation or some other phenomenon that is only statistically related? Second, are *kabeles* important in their own right, as assumed a priori, or are they spatially correlated with some more important social groupings? Third, why is it easier to undertake collective action in *kabeles* close to the treatment centers than in *kabeles* further from the treatment centers?

Follow-up research was conducted to address those questions. Results from the econometric analysis were used to select three pairs of *kabeles*, including one *kabele* with a high index of cooperation and a nearby *kabele* with a low index of cooperation. In the southwest part of the study area, Wayu Wedessa was selected as an area of low cooperation and Bosso Dire was selected as an area of high cooperation. Group interviews were held in each of the six *kabeles* during February 1998, with between 5 and 30 livestock owners participating in each interview. About 10–12 open-ended questions were asked during interviews lasting one to two hours. The level of participation in the group interviews was the first indication that the statistical results were accurate. No more than 10 livestock owners attended the group interviews in the low-cooperation villages. Twenty to 30 livestock owners attended the group interviews in the high-cooperation villages.

The information collected through the interviews provides answers to the three questions posed. Regarding the actual significance of the statistical find-

TABLE 11.2 Results for versions 1, 2, and 3 of the model of pouron demand

Variable	Version 1		Version 2		Version 3	
	Coefficient	P-value	Coefficient	P-value	Coefficient	P-value
Constant	−.8919	.0000	−.2936	.0000	−1.3841	.0000
Household traits						
Age of hh head	.0006	.8336	.0013	.6520	.0013	.6644
Sex of hh head	−.1135	.3881	.0247	.8538	−.0319	.8253
Herd traits						
Number of cattle	.1889	.0000	.1820	.0000	.1858	.0000
Proportion of oxen	1.8617	.0000	1.7873	.0000	1.8571	.0000
Proportion of cows	.7935	.0006	.8185	.0004	1.1066	.0000
Distance to treatment center						
Meters			.0003	.0000	$7.6E-5$	.0750
Meters squared			-2.0×10^{-8}	.0000	-3×10^{-9}	.4829
Kabele1*cattle-owning hhs in 1 km					.0188	.0002
Kabele2*cattle-owning hhs in 1 km					−.0002	.9641
Kabele3*cattle-owning hhs in 1 km					.0152	.0042
Kabele4*cattle-owning hhs in 1 km					.0070	.0358
Kabele5*cattle-owning hhs in 1 km					−.2441	.0000

Kabele6*cattle-owning hhs in 1 km			−.0077	.1657
Kabele7*cattle-owning hhs in 1 km			−.0050	.4738
Kabele8*cattle-owning hhs in 1 km			−.0994	.0008
Kabele9*cattle-owning hhs in 1 km			.0156	.0182
Kabele10*cattle-owning hhs in 1 km			−.0268	.0000
Kabele11*cattle-owning hhs in 1 km			−.0046	.2353
Kabele12*cattle-owning hhs in 1 km			.0071	.0171
Kabele13*cattle-owning hhs in 1 km			−.0170	.0000
Kabele14*cattle-owning hhs in 1 km			−.0072	.0000
Kabele15*cattle-owning hhs in 1 km			−.0135	.0435
Kabele16*cattle-owning hhs in 1 km			.0072	.0072
Kabele17*cattle-owning hhs in 1 km			.0177	.0012
Kabele18*cattle-owning hhs in 1 km			.0165	.0001
Kabele19*cattle-owning hhs in 1 km			.0459	.0000
Kabele20*cattle-owning hhs in 1 km			.0030	.7334
Kabele21*cattle-owning hhs in 1 km			.0053	.4043
Kabele22*cattle-owning hhs in 1 km			−.0145	.0000
Kabele23*cattle-owning hhs in 1 km			−.0130	.0000
Chi squared	367.8	410.6	804.1	
% correct predictions	75.8	75.4	77.6	

NOTE: Data are estimated for 3,221 cattle-owning households in the Ghibe Valley of Ethiopia.

FIGURE 11.2 Index of cooperation for 23 *kabeles* in the ectopor area, Ghibe Valley, Ethiopia

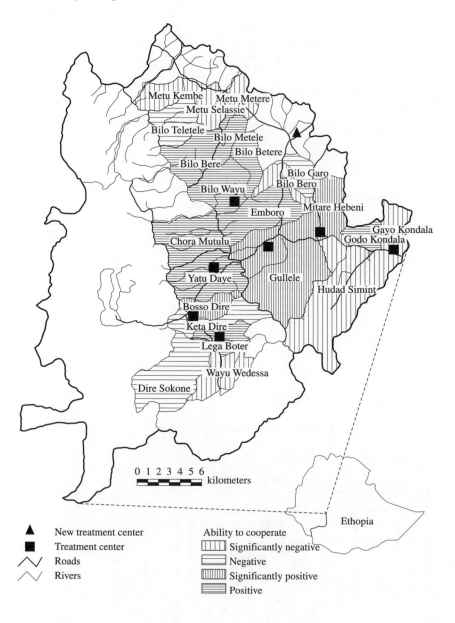

Metu Kembe   Metu Metere
Metu Selassie
Bilo Teletele
Bilo Metele
Bilo Betere
Bilo Bere
Bilo Garo
Bilo Bero
Bilo Wayu
Emboro   Mitare Hebeni
Chora Mutulu   Gayo Kondala
Godo Kondala
Yatu Daye   Gullele
Hudad Simint
Bosso Dire
Keta Dire
Lega Boter
Wayu Wedessa
Dire Sokone

0 1 2 3 4 5 6
kilometers

Ethopia

▲ New treatment center
■ Treatment center
Roads
Rivers

Ability to cooperate
Significantly negative
Negative
Significantly positive
Positive

ings of cooperation and noncooperation, all three *kabeles* that were identified through the econometric analysis as having low cooperation did indeed report low levels of pouron use and little or no active collective action to support pouron use. On the other hand, the three *kabeles* that were identified as having high cooperation reported much higher levels of pouron use and a great deal of collective action for pouron use. For example, the livestock owners and *kabele* officials that we interviewed in Bilo Metele reported several forms of active collective action, most of which were led by the *kabele* officials:

1. Information about the dates when pouron treatments are available was disseminated through individuals who were appointed to share information about upcoming meetings and important events with particular groups of households.
2. People took each other's animals to the treatment center despite the difficulties of handling others' animals in strange places.
3. The chairman of the *kabele* had met with nearby *kabeles* to organize joint work to clear the road along which they walk their animals to the crush where treatments are available.
4. A village of recent immigrants who live farther away from the crush were allowed to graze their animals around the village en route to getting treatments.

In contrast, in Wayu Wedessa, farmers participating in the group interview admitted that they had deliberately discouraged their neighbors from receiving pouron treatments. Their logic was this: if they told their neighbor that pouron treatments would be available on a certain day, that neighbor would ask them to take their animals when they went. The strange animals would be difficult to handle and may cause crop damage along the way.

An answer to the question about the importance of the *kabele* as a focus of collective action is provided by both the econometric analysis and the group interviews. A fourth version of the model, not reported here, included eight binary variables for the nine treatment centers. None of the coefficients on the treatment center binary variables were significant, implying that the *kabele* was more important than the treatment center as a focus of collective action. In addition, the groups of farmers interviewed in the three *kabeles* with high levels of cooperation mentioned examples of collective action at the *kabele* level but did not mention examples of collective action for pouron use around any other social group.

The group interviews also provided a possible answer to the third question about why it appears to be more difficult to sustain collective action in *kabeles* farther from the treatment center. The types of collective action that the farmer groups mentioned involve transaction costs. Gathering and disseminating information about the dates when pouron treatments will be available is costly. Taking neighbors' animals to and from the treatment centers is costly. Maintaining a clear walking path through intensively used farmland is also costly. All of these transaction costs are positively related to distance to the treatment centers. The greater the distance, the higher the transaction costs associated with cooperation, and thus the less likely was cooperation.

Transaction costs are also positively related to ethnic heterogeneity. We propose two hypotheses that are consistent with this result. First, the greater the ethnic heterogeneity within a *kabele*, the greater the transaction costs associated with collective action. This hypothesis is consistent with both theory and other case study evidence (see Baland and Platteau 1994). Second, the greater the ethnic difference between the *kabele* that hosts a treatment center and another outlying *kabele*, the greater the transaction costs associated with the collective action in the outlying *kabele*. Two of the noncooperative *kabeles* were populated by mixtures of Oromo-speaking and Amhara-speaking people, whereas the third was mostly populated by Oromo speakers. The pattern of settlement in the study area is such that all of the crushes are located in areas where Amharic-speaking persons predominate. Because they do not interact as freely with Amhara speakers, the Oromo speakers had to bear greater costs to obtain information about the treatment dates. In addition, Oromo speakers do not feel welcome to walk their animals through the Amhara areas en route to the crushes or to wait around the crushes to have their animals treated. Crop damage cases would be more costly and difficult to resolve.

Discussion and Conclusions

The Case Study

The results from the case study indicate significant differences between *kabeles* in their abilities to foster cooperation in pouron use among neighbors. The subsequent group interviews confirmed these findings and provided three important insights. First, *kabeles* are an important locus of cooperation even though they are not formally involved in the control program. Second, cooperation is costly, in terms of both acquiring and exchanging information and moving animals to the treatment centers. Third, anything that increases the costs or risks of cooperation will reduce the likelihood of successful cooperation. Differences in ethnicity and distance to the treatment center increase those costs.

The pilot tsetse control trial was changed in two ways because of the insights obtained from this study. First, new treatment centers were opened in two low-cooperation areas that are mostly populated by Oromo-speaking people. This change should make the treatments more easily accessible to Oromo-speaking people in the area and increase cooperation. Second, the dates when pouron treatments will be given are now announced at least a month in advance. This should make information more easily and cheaply available.

Implications for Analysis of the Economics of Space

Several features of this study distinguish it from most other studies of economic behavior and economic activity in developing countries. First, the large number of observations allowed more accurate estimation of parameters than is usual. The costs per household of data collection and data processing were very low because there were no costs associated with sampling (for example, compilation of an accurate sampling frame and location of selected households) and because the questionnaire was very focused.

Second, the large number of observations allowed the accurate estimation of the parameters and thus more complete testing of hypotheses. Version 2 of the model included 31 variables, over half of which were statistically significant at $p < 0.001$. Two additional versions of the model, not shown here, were run with several more variables.

Third, the georeferenced census yielded information about all of the neighbors of every household. Manipulation of the census data with the GIS tools allowed the creation of the neighbor variables and the tests of hypotheses about ability to cooperate. This approach could be extended to the many other types of economic behavior and economic outcomes that are related to space. This approach was possible because of close contact and collaboration between economists and geographers and the availability of computer software and hardware for GIS and econometric analysis.

Fourth, the georeferencing of the census data allowed us to create several new spatial data layers that can be used for other purposes. For example, we now know the location of all households in our study area, the year that they established their homestead in its present location, and where they originated. Those data are being used to estimate the temporal and spatial patterns of in-migration into the study area and the effects of tsetse and trypanosomosis on those patterns.

References

Baland, J.-M., and J.-P. Platteau. 1994. *Halting gradation of natural resources: Is there a role for rural communities?* Rome: Food and Agriculture Organization of the United Nations (FAO).

Bockstael, N. 1996. Modeling economics and ecology: The importance of a spatial perspective. *American Journal of Agricultural Economics* 78 (5): 1168–1180.

Borland International. 1995. Visual dBase. Scotts Valley, Calif., U.S.A.: Borland International.

Chomitz, K. M., and D. A. Gray. 1996. Roads, land use, and deforestation: A spatial model applied to Belize. *World Bank Economic Review* 10 (3): 487–512.

Cornes, R., and T. Sandler. 1986. *The theory of externalities, public goods and club goods.* Cambridge: Cambridge University Press.

Echessah, P. N., B. M. Swallow, D. W. Kamara, and J. J. Curry. 1997. Willingness to contribute labor and money to tsetse control: Application of contingent valuation in Busia District, Kenya. *World Development* 25 (2): 239–253.

ESRI (Environmental Systems Research Institute). 1995. PC Arc/Info version 3.5. Redlands, Calif, U.S.A.

———. 1996. PC ArcView version 2.16. Redlands, Calif., U.S.A.

Kemmamer, W. 1995. Microsoft FoxPro version 3.0b. Seattle, Wash., U.S.A.: Microsoft Corporation.

Jayne, T. 1994. Do high food marketing costs constrain cash crop production? Evidence from Zimbabwe. *Economic Development and Cultural Change* 42 (2): 387–402.

Leak, S. G. A. 1997. Personal communication. September.

Leak, S. G. A., W. Mulatu, G. J. Rowlands, and G. D. M. D'Ieteran. 1995. A trial of a "cypermethrin pouron" insecticide to control, and *G. morsititans submorsitans (diptera: glossinaidae)* in southwest Ethiopia. *Bulletin of Entomological Research* 85: 241–251.

Norusis, M. J. 1994. SPSS advanced statistics 6.1. Chicago: SPSS.

Omamo, S. W. 1995. Smallholder agriculture under market reform: The case of Southern Siaya District, Kenya. Ph.D. diss., Stanford University, Stanford, Calif., U.S.A.

Swallow, B. M., W. Mulatu, and S. G. A. Leak. 1995. Potential demand for a mixed public-private animal health input: Evaluation of a pouron insecticide for controlling tsetse-transmitted trypanosomosis in Ethiopia. *Preventive Veterinary Medicine* 24 (4): 265–275.

12 Collective Action in Ant Control

HELLE MUNK RAVNBORG,
ANA MILENA DE LA CRUZ REBOLLEDO,
MARÍA DEL PILAR GUERRERO,
AND OLAF WESTERMANN

Leaf-cutting ants are a serious problem for farmers in many parts of Latin America. In La Laguna, a community in the Andean hillsides of southwestern Colombia, small-scale farmers ranked the damage caused by leaf-cutting ants *(Atta. cephalotes)* as one of their most serious agricultural problems.[1] Accounts both from La Laguna and from elsewhere in Latin America of leaf-cutting ants eating an entire plot of cassava or destroying one or more fruit trees overnight are not uncommon (Cherrett 1986). In general La Laguna farmers estimate that they lose between 20 and 50 percent of their cassava to attacks from leaf-cutting ants. The most common control practice is the use of the chemical chlorpyrifos (an organophosphorus), known in the area by the commercial name Lorsban. The manufacturer recommends that Lorsban be pumped into the ant nest, but because many farmers lack the cash to purchase both the pump and sufficient quantities of Lorsban, the most common practice is to place Lorsban around the entrances and exits of the anthill directly from the bag. Farmers complain about the ineffectiveness of this method as well as the human and environmental health problems associated with it.

In many ways crop damage caused by leaf-cutting ants is a problem related to collective action. Ants do not respect farm boundaries. Farmers who control anthills on their own fields might still face damage to their crops caused by ants coming from neighboring fields where no control measures are taken.

We are indebted to Marleny Aranda Morales, who acted as our local field assistant and played a tremendously important role in helping and stimulating farmers in their efforts to undertake collective ant control. We also wish to thank farmers in Los Zanjones for wishing to work with us and making our many Saturdays at Los Zanjones truly pleasant memories. We are grateful to Ruth Meinzen-Dick, Anna Knox, and Brent Swallow for their valuable comments on an earlier draft of this chapter. Last but not least, we wish to thank the International Development Research Centre (IDRC) and Danish International Development Assistance (DANIDA) for financing this research.

1. In a group diagnosis of agricultural and natural resource management problems, the problem of ant control ranked second to the cassava pest (*Cyclocephala* sp.) among the problems identified, while in a questionnaire survey concerning crop pest and disease problems in the area, the ant control problems came out as the most frequently mentioned problem.

Thus crop damage caused by leaf-cutting ants constitutes a transboundary natural resource management problem.

The transboundary nature of many agricultural and natural resource management problems has not only technical implications for experiment design and resource monitoring approaches (Ravnborg 1997) but also organizational implications for farmer coordination of management practices. It means that the search for alternative solutions or management practices cannot be seen as a purely technical endeavor, taking into consideration only the technical effectiveness and the economic and financial aspects of potential solutions. Alternative solutions must also include mechanisms that stimulate and facilitate coordinated or collective management efforts at various levels. This chapter illustrates the importance of organization in the case of ant control.

The chapter gives an account of site selection and methods used and describes an attempt to assess the need for collective ant control in La Laguna. It briefly summarizes the ant control practices employed in the area before the search for alternative ant control methods. In response to farmers' identification of ant control as one of their most important and widespread problems, the research team from the Centro Internacional de Agricultura Tropical (CIAT) committed itself to assisting farmers in searching for alternative solutions, technical as well as organizational, and the chapter goes on to describe an experiment to test some of the potential technical solutions identified through this joint search and its results. One of the potential solutions tested in this experiment was evaluated favorably by farmers, and we thus describe some of the organizational problems—and challenges—encountered when seeking to implement this solution at a landscape level and draw some tentative conclusions from this work in progress.

Methods

In early 1996 CIAT's hillsides project began undertaking "participatory landscape-level experimentation" on a pilot basis to explore the methodological implications of addressing natural resource management problems at a landscape level rather than solely at a plot level. CIAT has a long history of undertaking both researcher-led and farmer-led on-farm experimentation, particularly in the municipality of Caldono in the Department of Cauca, an area characteristic of much of the medium altitude and culturally diverse hillsides of Latin America where small-scale farming dominates. Participatory landscape-level experimentation was initiated in a contiguous area big enough to include different types of land uses and users and small enough to make it possible for landscape users to meet face to face. Because many natural resource management problems relate to movements of water and soil within a landscape (though not all—including the ant control problem treated in this chapter), site identification was done on a watershed basis, identifying all watersheds in the area of a size between 25 and 150 hectares. Previous research done in the area (Ravnborg and Guerrero 1996) yielded a set of selected watersheds with great diversity in terms of land uses and land users, including Los Zanjones, located in La Laguna. Los Zanjones comprises 44 hectares, subdivided among 14 individual owners. In addition to owner cultivation, various other forms of access to land are common in the area, such as renting in land, sharecropping, or employment as caretakers. Including these forms of tenure in addition to owner cultivation, Los Zanjones has a total of 17 land users.

CIAT invited all land users to a series of meetings to explore their interest in working collectively to solve agricultural and natural resource management problems that farmers could not solve on an individual basis. In the meetings land users identified, ranked, and analyzed problems. The meetings also served as fora within which land users planned and monitored experiments. In parallel with the meetings, researchers undertook open-ended, semistructured interviews with individual land users selected through contrast sampling (Ravnborg and Guerrero 1999) to examine their perceptions of natural resource management problems, interests, and conflicts more closely. A structured questionnaire survey provided more detailed information about pest and disease problems and current management practices in the area (de la Cruz and Cardona 1996). In addition to ant control, the group identified and worked on other high-priority problems such as decreasing soil quality and protection of riverbeds and springs. Throughout the period of experimentation, regular meetings were held and occasionally conversational interviews were undertaken to obtain a more detailed understanding of farmers' perceptions of progress and problems.

Ant Control: A Transboundary Natural Resource Management Problem

Following farmers' identification of ant control as a major problem, one of the objectives of the CIAT research team was to find ways to analyze, and to some extent quantify, the transboundary nature of the ant control problem and thus raise awareness of the need for a coordinated effort. Researchers had land users in Los Zanjones conduct an inventory of major anthills. Thirty-nine major anthills or nests were identified and located on a detailed map. Figure 12.1 shows the boundaries of the 19 plots, overlaid by the location of the 39 major nests. Farmers followed the ant tracks from the anthills in the area and found that the ants move an average distance of 80 meters from the nest to forage.[2] A circle with a radius corresponding to 80 meters has therefore been drawn around each nest in Figure 12.1 to indicate their respective area of influence. Thus the map shows that each plot is potentially affected by an average of 5.5 anthills

---

2. The 80-meter action radius is, however, a conservative estimate since leaf-cutting ants are known to cut leaves at distances up to 200 meters from the nest (Cherrett 1986, 179).

FIGURE 12.1 Location of anthills, their radius of action, and farm boundaries, Los Zanjones, La Laguna, Colombia

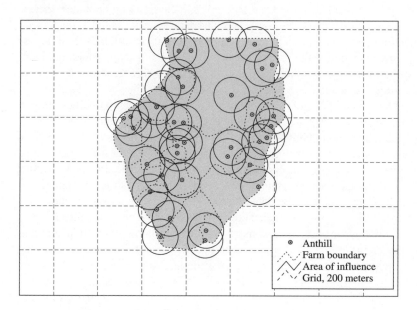

(ranging from 1 to 13), of which 3.4 anthills (ranging from 0 to 9) are located on plots belonging to other farmers—on average belonging to 2.5 other farmers (ranging from 0 to 6). In addition to the damage caused by ants whose nest lies within the farm boundaries, farmers can expect crop damage to be caused by ants coming from more than three nests located outside their own farm, belonging to two to three other farmers. Controlling the ants on one's own plot thus provides limited security against crop damage by leaf-cutting ants unless one's neighbors also control ants originating from their plots.

Current Ant Control Practice

The current ant control method employed in the area is the use of a powdered insecticide with the commercial name Lorsban, in which chlorpyrifos is the active ingredient. In Los Zanjones 88 percent of households use Lorsban for ant control. It is recommended that Lorsban be pumped into the ant nest to be effective, but the most common method of application, used by 41 percent of the farmers, is to pour Lorsban directly from the bag around the entrance and exit holes of the anthill (see Figure 12.2). As soon as the ants detect the poison, they leave the old entrances and start opening new ones. Farmers say they use

FIGURE 12.2 Ant control methods used, Los Zanjones, La Laguna, Colombia (percentage of farmers)

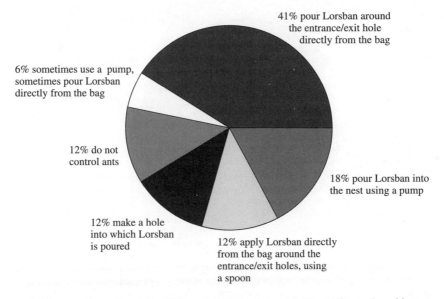

NOTE: The percentages do not total 100 because of rounding errors. $N = 17$; the number of farmers does not correspond to the number of landowners because of the existence of tenure arrangements other than owner cultivation, such as sharecropping and caretaker cultivation.

this suboptimal method because they lack a pump for pumping Lorsban into the nest and because pumping Lorsban into the ant nest requires the use of larger quantities of Lorsban (and is therefore more costly).

Figure12.3 shows the amounts of Lorsban used during the period May 1996 to May 1997 as recalled by farmers in May 1997. The most frequently used quantity was between 1 and 3 kilos, used by 41 percent of the farmers. For comparison, controlling an anthill by pumping Lorsban into it requires on average three applications of 0.5 kilos each, or a total of 1.5 kilos of Lorsban. Figures reflect the total amount of Lorsban used per farm, and it may be used to control one or more anthills or to spray crops.

Less than 10 percent of farmers in Los Zanjones use protective gloves or masks when applying Lorsban. This situation is unfortunate because chlorpyrifos, classified by the World Health Organization as having class II toxicity, easily penetrates the skin.

The failure to control ants in Los Zanjones with the use of Lorsban is assumed to be due to a combination of the suboptimal method of application and the lack of coordination among farmers. Moreover, farmers complained

FIGURE 12.3 Amount of Lorsban used in Los Zanjones from May 1996 to May 1997, La Laguna, Colombia (percentage of farmers)

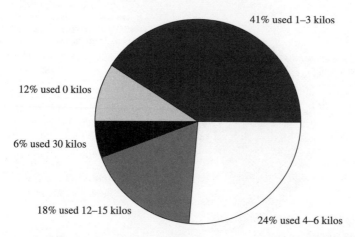

41% used 1–3 kilos

12% used 0 kilos

6% used 30 kilos

18% used 12–15 kilos

24% used 4–6 kilos

NOTE: N = 17 farmers. Thirteen farmers (76 percent) indicated use of Lorsban only for ant control while 2 farmers (12 percent) used Lorsban both for ant control and to spray crops. This partly explains the large quantities used by some farmers.

One kilogram of Lorsban costs US$2 (for comparison, an agricultural laborer is paid US$4.5 per day).

about the cost of Lorsban and expressed their general environmental concerns about the use of insecticides. These deficiencies and concerns motivated the search for alternative ant control methods.

Alternative Ant Control Methods: The Experiment

Four alternative treatment methods and a control (no treatment) were selected for farmer experimentation in La Laguna for control of existing anthills.[3] These methods were

1. agricultural lime, pumped into the anthill;
2. lime mixed with Lorsban, pumped into the anthill;

---

3. In addition, CIAT researchers proposed a fifth treatment method to prevent young queens from establishing new anthills by awarding prizes to young children who collected the queens. A total of 4,616 queens were collected in 1997 during the brief period when queens leave their old nests to establish new ones. Because only 0.5–1 percent of all young queens manage to establish new nests, this number translated to the prevention of between 23 and 46 new nests. By 1999 an association of extension workers formed a subcommittee that undertook a queen-catching competition in the broader Rio Cabuyal watershed. Twenty-three villages participated, resulting in the capture of more than 100,000 queens.

3. gasoline, poured into the anthill and set afire in order to produce an explosion; and
4. washing powder, poured into and around the entrances and exits of the anthill.

Agricultural lime does not work directly to kill the ants. Rather, it increases the pH of the interior of the anthill and thereby creates conditions under which the fungus that the ants cultivate and feed on cannot survive.[4] Thus, lime causes the gradual starvation of the ants. In response to initial experiences with the application of lime, farmers proposed mixing lime with Lorsban for combined application in a proportion of 3:1 and gradually decreasing to zero the amount of Lorsban added to the lime. Since Lorsban works by directly killing the ants, this method offers farmers immediate ant control while the effects of the lime build up. In the experiment the average ratio of lime to Lorsban was 6.33:1, calculated over all the applications.

Gasoline works by exploding and thus physically eradicating the anthill. Young male farmers, especially, proposed this method.

Female farmers proposed a fourth method involving the use of washing powder, poured into and around the anthill. Presumably, alkaline washing powder has an effect similar to that of lime—that is, it increases the pH of the anthill, thus inhibiting the growth of the fungus on which the leaf-cutting ants live.

Farmers were asked to volunteer to participate in the experiment, each with one anthill. Fifteen anthills were included in the experiment,[5] and a lottery was used to assign a treatment to each anthill, resulting in three replications per treatment.

After testing several methods of evaluating anthill activity,[6] the group chose a relatively simple method: all holes (entrances and exits to the nest) were closed following the treatment.

After about two weeks farmers counted the number of holes that had been opened or reopened. Although it was recommended that farmers visit the anthill

---

4. Leaf-cutting ants do not directly feed on the leaves they cut but rather on a fungus cultivated in the nest on the basis of the leaves.

5. Because of the inclusion of controls (no treatment), two farmers insisted on participating with two anthills in the experiment. Thus a total of 13 farmers participated in the experiment.

6. In addition to the method of counting holes, two other methods were tried. The first method, proposed by Fowler (1993), consisted of cutting drinking straws of different colors into pieces of 2.5–3.0 millimeters and impregnating these pieces in mashed banana. These pieces were placed on plates around the entrances and exits of the anthill, and the number taken into the anthill was used as an indicator of activity. For the ants to leave any little pieces of impregnated straw, however, the number of pieces placed around the nest had to exceed 1,000, making this method time-consuming, and thus impractical for farmer evaluation. The second method involved excavating the nest and counting the number of healthy and destroyed "garden cells," that is cells or chambers containing the fungus. This method was employed occasionally, but it cannot be recommended as a regular evaluation method because the ant nests can be very deep—up to five meters.

every fortnight to apply treatment, to monitor ants, or both, in practice the interval between individual applications and monitoring varied from a week to a month. The periods of application of the various techniques were uniform (with the exception of the applications around Christmas), except of course for cases in which the anthill had been effectively controlled before the last application or monitoring date. The last application or monitoring date was the same for all treatments.

Results from the Experiment

Table 12.1 shows the results of the experiment using the four treatments mentioned, measured as the initial number of entrance and exit holes to the ant nest and the number of holes opened or reopened after each application or monitoring visit over the five-month period covered by the experiment. It should be noted that anthill activity varies over the season as well as with the age of the anthill. Thus even without any treatment, the number of holes can be expected to change. The table shows that lime mixed with Lorsban and gasoline were the two most effective treatments, reducing the number of holes by 95–100 percent.

Table 12.2 summarizes the costs of the treatments and shows that washing powder was not only the least effective, but also the most costly treatment, averaging US$11.76 per anthill. On the other hand, the use of lime mixed with Lorsban was one of the two cheapest alternatives, with a total average cost per anthill of between US$5.36 and US$5.60, depending on the type of lime used.[7]

This cost is the same as that calculated for pumping Lorsban into the anthill (US$5.56). For cash-constrained farmers, however, the composition of the cost is important. While both the use of washing powder and gasoline have high input (cash) costs (US$6.86 and US$8.05, respectively), lime mixed with Lorsban and particularly lime (Cal Viva) alone, have relatively low input (cash) costs (ranging from US$0.56 for Cal Viva alone to US$1.15 for Supercal mixed with Lorsban). Lime alone has higher labor costs because of the need for more applications. The input cost calculated for the use of Lorsban pumped into the anthill of US$2.89 is somewhat above the input costs for lime and lime mixed with Lorsban.

In an open-ended evaluation, farmers included both cost and effectiveness in controlling ant activity in their assessments of the different methods. They discarded the use of washing powder because of its low effectiveness and its high costs. In addition, farmers included a third, environmental, aspect in their

---

7. Two types of fine-powdered lime with a 100 percent calcium content are available in the area: one called Supercal, which is available in 10-kilo bags at a cost of US$2.22 (or US$0.22 per kilo) and another called Cal Viva, which is available in 50-kilo bags at a cost of US$5.55 (or US$0.11 per kilo). Although it is more expensive per kilo, farmers prefer Supercal to Cal Viva for its ease of transport, local availability, less risk of storage losses, and lower cost per bag.

TABLE 12.1 Results of ant control treatment, La Laguna, Colombia

Anthill number	Treatment	Number of holes at first application/ monitoring visit	Number of holes at last application/ monitoring visit	Total number of applications	Percentage reduction in number of holes
1	Washing powder	44	7	7	84
2	Washing powder	135	20	9	85
3	Washing powder	25	43	9	-72
4	Lime	109	1	10	99
5	Lime	257	18	9	93
6	Lime	22	26	9	-18
7	Lime + Lorsban	70	3	7	96
8	Lime + Lorsban	25	0	3	100
9	Lime + Lorsban	13	0	4	100
10	Gasoline	8	0	2	100
11	Gasoline	35	0	2	100
12	Gasoline	102	0	3	100
13	Control	30	6	n.a.	80
14	Control	8	6	n.a.	25
15	Control	17	9	n.a.	47

NOTE: n.a. indicates not applicable.

TABLE 12.2 Average total costs per anthill of different ant control treatments (US$, 1998 prices)

Treatment	Input costs[a]	Labor costs[b]	Total costs
Washing powder	6.86	4.90	11.76
Lime (Cal Viva)	0.56	8.89	9.44
Lime (Supercal)	1.11	8.89	10.00
Lime (Cal Viva) + Lorsban	0.97	4.44	5.36
Lime (Supercal) + Lorsban	1.15	4.49	5.60
Gasoline	8.05	2.06	10.11
Lorsban pumped into nest *(calculated; treatment not included in experiment)*	2.89	2.67	5.56
Queen-catching competition	1.20–2.41	n.a.	1.20–2.41

NOTE: n.a. indicates not applicable.

[a]Calculated on the basis of retail prices at the local markets.

[b]Calculated on the basis of the local payment for an agricultural day-laborer, corresponding to US$0.6 per hour.

assessment. They evaluated the use of lime and particularly lime mixed with Lorsban positively because, apart from cost-effectively controlling ants, they perceived that these products improved the soil, which is rather acid in that area (pH around 5).

After being treated with lime, a large anthill that had been completely bare for many years began producing vegetation. Farmers attributed this effect to the lime. Also, compared with the current practice of applying Lorsban alone, farmers preferred the use of lime mixed with Lorsban, primarily on environmental grounds, since it used less insecticide. On the other hand, although the young male farmers found the use of gasoline effective and liked the excitement involved in its application, they discarded it as a feasible control method because of the high cost of restoring the soil's nutrients, life, and structure where the explosion had occurred.

Consequently, the use of lime mixed with gradually decreasing amounts of Lorsban was the treatment farmers evaluated most favorably, and they considered how to initiate ant control on a collective rather than an individual basis.

Toward Collective Ant Control

Testing alternative technical methods of ant control constitutes only part of the solution to the ant control problem and the participatory landscape-level experiment initiated in Los Zanjones. Equally important is identifying mechanisms to facilitate the adoption of promising ant control methods in a coordinated fashion. Undertaking ant control in a coordinated fashion does not imply that the actual treatment—that is, the pumping of lime and Lorsban into the ant nest—should be done collectively. Rather, collective action is necessary to ensure that all anthills are treated simultaneously. Not surprisingly, this part of the ant control problem has proven to be the most difficult to solve, and the solution still has not been perfected. This section describes some of measures taken and experiences gained in the joint efforts between farmers and researchers to stimulate collectively coordinated ant control.

In a meeting on the technical evaluation of the various ant control methods, farmers decided to use part of a fund established by CIAT for purchasing a pump to be shared between the 17 farmers in the area for application of lime mixed with Lorsban. They decided that the pump should rotate between farmers, each of whom could use it for one day every two weeks. Although the pump has been rotating, farmers encountered two problems. First, some farmers were persuaded by agricultural supplies dealers to buy a type of powdered lime that was too coarse. This lime apparently damaged the pump and discouraged farmers from continuing lime-Lorsban ant control. The pump was repaired, however, and in mid-1998, a survey was conducted at adjacent local markets to establish the commercial names of the feasible kinds of fine-powdered lime (and the ones to be avoided) as a guide to farmers when they make their purchases. No further pump breakdowns have occurred.

The second problem, still only partly resolved, concerns the difficulty of transporting the pump from one place to another in the rather hilly watershed. The farmers initially proposed a system whereby the pump would always be returned to the pump caretaker. The advantages of this system are that the pump caretaker assumes responsibility for the pump and everyone knows where to find the pump. The drawback, however, is that it is always the same group of farmers, namely those living at some distance from the pump caretaker, who have difficulty getting access because they must walk long distances over hills to get the pump. The farmers therefore decided to purchase a second pump with the fund, and this solution has somewhat eased the problem of transportation. Moreover, the system of returning the pump to the pump caretaker after every use has gradually been relaxed and evolved into a more rotational system. This change has made it difficult for farmers to locate the pump, and a local field worker employed by CIAT has, to a large extent, stepped in to help farmers locate the pump. Finally, a number of farmers decided to purchase their own pump, which has increased the availability of pumps in the area to all farmers. The cost of the type of mechanical pump used in the area is approximately US$55.

The second decision made by farmers relates to the organization of work. Pumping lime into an anthill is hard work, and lime can get damp if stored for long during the rainy season. It is only commercially available in bags of 10 kilos or more, whereas each application consumes only about half a kilo. For these reasons, farmers suggested subdividing themselves into working groups of two to four neighboring households, who would collaborate in applying treatment as well as purchasing lime. Six groups were established, each of which decided upon different arrangements for sharing input purchase and work. Only one group, however, consisting of two Guambiano farmers (a man and a woman) and one female mestizo farmer, has succeeded in dividing the purchase of inputs between them and jointly treating the anthills on a fortnightly basis. The remaining groups have managed in varying degrees to buy inputs and work together, but because of problems of cooperation, lack of time, and the unwillingness of some to undertake ant control, many farmers have ended up doing the ant control on an individual basis. Thus some farmers still complain that undertaking the applications *alone* is hard work.[8]

Encouraged by CIAT researchers, farmers decided to monitor the number of opened and reopened holes after each application as well as locate all anthills in Los Zanjones, whether receiving treatment or not, on a series of maps. The maps depict approximately 90 anthills in Los Zanjones, including smaller anthills. These two measures combined have allowed for more global monitoring of the success of ant control for the whole microwatershed. Farmers complained, however, that the monitoring sheet was difficult to complete and that including all anthills and not just the major ones made monitoring cumbersome. The monitoring sheet has been simplified, but ways to overcome farmers' uneasiness about writing and the great number of anthills to be monitored must still be found. Since monitoring change is so central to the understanding of many transboundary natural resource management problems, including the problem of ant control, developing monitoring systems that farmers can manage and analyze themselves remains an important challenge to participatory landscape-level research.

Finally, farmers who had participated in the experiment, the meetings, or both concerning ant control encouraged farmers who hitherto had not participated to undertake ant control. They took this step because of the perceived importance of controlling all anthills simultaneously to effectively protect against crop damage by leaf-cutting ants. Before the 1997 mapping exercise, efforts by farmers to elicit the participation of their neighbors were largely discouraged. Some farmers did not feel economically affected by the ants because their land was lying fallow or was planted with a crop, like beans, that is not attacked by the ants. Other farmers were sharecropping or taking care of someone else's farm and would not undertake any ant control unless the owner gave his acceptance or paid for the inputs. On the other hand, some farmers whose crops were damaged by ants coming from neighboring fields responded by trespassing into the neighboring field to undertake ant control themselves.

---

8. Each application requires an average of half an hour just for pumping, in addition to time for carrying the pump and the lime to the ant nest.

In 1998 farmers decided to try another way of encouraging more global ant control throughout Los Zanjones: they launched a competition. Over a period of three months (the time it takes on average to effectively control an anthill using lime mixed with Lorsban), they would record the control of anthills in the area and reward the person who had controlled the most anthills on his or her own fields as well as on fields belonging to neighbors. The reward would be a *minga*, a labor party on the winner's land, in which the workers would be farmers who had participated in the competition. Lunch would be paid for by the fund established by CIAT. To identify a winner, farmers developed a scoring system, as follows:

For every anthill controlled on own farm	5 points
For every anthill controlled on neighbor's farm (with the permission of the neighbor)	10 points
For every anthill a farmer could convince a neighbor to control (based on consent between the "convincer" and the "convinced" that this was what happened)	20 points
For every anthill controlled in groups, every member of the group receives	20 points

Only about half (nine) of the farmers participated in the competition. Through the competition, however, an additional four farmers were convinced to undertake ant control, and all participants in the competition got permission from their neighbors to control anthills on their land. Despite favoring ant control in groups, the scoring system did not succeed in encouraging farmers to do so. Only three of the participants undertook ant control in groups. Participants in the competition collected between 5 and 180 points, and the winner managed to control 14 anthills on her own farm and 7 at a neighbor's farm, in addition to convincing one of her neighbors to control some anthills on his farm. The fact that all competitors participated in the *minga* at the winner's farm provides an indication of their commitment and their recognition of the efforts of the winner. In total the competition controlled 56 anthills, or approximately two-thirds of the estimated total number of anthills in the area.

Thus the competition itself and the fact that farmers developed a stronger sense of the transboundary nature of the ant control problem turned out to be an effective means of stimulating a coordinated ant control effort. As a somewhat ironic indication of success, farmers in Los Zanjones today do not wish to continue their work in ant control because they no longer perceive it as a major problem (although they do recognize the importance of controlling remaining anthills). Instead, they wish to embark upon solving other problems, such as land use around riverbanks and springs and erosion control, which also require coordinated efforts.

Conclusion

Technical designs are rarely sufficient to solve transboundary natural resource management problems. The case of crop damage caused by leaf-cutting ants described in this chapter illustrates that, although technically feasible ant control methods were developed, it was not until a mechanism was identified to encourage a significant proportion of the farmers of Los Zanjones to control their ant nests simultaneously that progress was made in effectively limiting ant activity. Thus the case of participatory experimentation to solve the ant control problem was successful in curtailing the crop damage caused by leaf-cutting ants in Los Zanjones as well as in demonstrating the importance of collective action in addressing the transboundary ant control problem.

Yet coordination is cumbersome, particularly in groups that are as heterogeneous in terms of livelihood strategies (day-laboring farmers, small-scale farmers, sharecroppers, and caretakers and absentee landlords), ethnicity, and resource endowments as the land users of Los Zanjones. Heterogeneity can contribute to lack of trust and mutual understanding within the group and lack of experience working together. The multifaceted relationships between neighbors can also create fears that encouraging someone to undertake practices such as ant control might be taken as a reproach and thus endanger future relationships and perhaps block future favors. The solution to many natural resource management problems depends upon the coordinated efforts of diverse, rather than homogeneous, land users and their ability to negotiate conflicts between short-term and long-term interests, as well as between individual and collective interests.

In the case of Los Zanjones, CIAT has been instrumental in overcoming many of the organizational difficulties involved in coordinated ant control, such as organizing meetings, facilitating the rotation of the pump, undertaking a market survey to establish the types of lime compatible with pumping, and promoting and partly conducting the monitoring of ant control. The participatory experimentation initiated and supported by CIAT shows that with third-party organizational support, it is possible to achieve coordination among individual farmers even in heterogeneous groups and thus reach results that critically depend upon such coordination. Inspired not only by the project's technical results (the use of lime mixed with Lorsban), but also by its organizational lessons, an association of extension workers employed by a range of governmental and nongovernmental organizations has decided to undertake a joint effort in ant control in the 7,000-hectares Río Cabuyal watershed, of which Los Zanjones is part. Still, it is important to explore more effective means to support coordination and stimulate farmers to assume responsibility for organizing their collective efforts, not only in ant control but also more widely in natural resource management. This task should be a major goal of future research on collective action in agricultural development and natural resource management.

References

Cherrett, J. M. 1986. The economic importance and control of leaf-cutting ants. In *Economic impact and control of social insects*, ed. S. B.Vinson. New York: Praeger.

de la Cruz, A. M., and M. C. Cardona. 1996. Caracterización fitosanitaria de la microcuenca de La Laguna, Municipio de Caldono, Cauca. Cali: Centro Internacional de Agricultura Tropical (CIAT). Photocopy.

Fowler, H. G. 1993. A simple method for determining location of foraging ant nests using leaf-cutting ants as a model. *Journal of Applied Entomology* 116 (4): 420–422.

Ravnborg, H. M. 1997. Beyond the farm and within the community: Issues of collective action in participatory natural resource management research. In *New frontiers in participatory research and gender analysis*. Proceedings of the international seminar on participatory research and gender analysis for technology development, September 9–14, 1996. Cali: Centro Internacional de Agricultura Tropical (CIAT).

Ravnborg, H. M., and M. del Pilar Guerrero. 1996. Poverty profiles for designing and evaluating rural research and development activities: A methodology. In *CIAT hillsides program annual report 1994–1995*. Cali: Centro Internacional de Agricultura Tropical (CIAT).

―――. 1999. Collective action in watershed management: Experiences from the Andean hillsides. *Agriculture and Human Values* 16 (3): 257–266.

13 Institutions and the Intensification of Cattle-Feeding Techniques: A Village Case Study in Kenya's Coast Province

KIMBERLY A. SWALLOW

Throughout Sub-Saharan Africa, policy makers have seen intensification of dairy production as a possible solution to three problems: (1) dairy market supply deficits, especially in urban areas; (2) increasing land scarcity; and (3) insufficient income-earning opportunities for smallholders. It was anticipated that these problems would translate into opportunities and constraints for smallholders that would lead them to seek more intensive cattle-feeding techniques. To aid this process, technical assistance programs were designed to add intensive cattle feeding to the options available to smallholder cattle keepers. The technique most widely recommended across Sub-Saharan Africa was stall feeding based on specialized feeds grown on-farm, such as Napier grass (*Pennisetum purpureum*) and *Leucaena l.*, and purchased agroindustrial by-products. Smallholders have chosen stall feeding in the highlands of Kenya and Tanzania, but a slower-than-anticipated pace of intensification has been the norm throughout the remainder of the region (McIntire, Bourzat, and Pingali 1992; Gass and Sumberg 1993).

The research reported here was originally carried out to provide a detailed view of the issues involved in intensifying cattle-feeding techniques, and thereby offer input into the process of reevaluating this technical support. It is hoped that such insight can provide policymakers, development workers, and extensionists with a more realistic understanding of the process of technical change and thereby engender respect for the time required and, if necessary, inspire the creation of a broader range of options.

This chapter opens with a description of the case study situation, including descriptions of the case study village, its institutions, and its cattle enterprises and cattle-feeding techniques. The research objectives and methods are

The author thanks the editors for helpful comments on an earlier draft. The research reported here was assisted by a grant from the Joint Committee on African Studies of the Social Science Research Council and the American Council of Learned Societies with funds provided by the Rockefeller Foundation. The support given by the center director and staff of the Kenya Agricultural Research Institute's Regional Research Centre, Mtwapa, and the International Livestock Research Institute is acknowledged with thanks.

then explained. The eight case study homesteads' heads are described in general while focusing on the personal wealth and networks of the three operators of commercial dairy enterprises. The research findings are then reported in two sections: one on the transactions used to obtain cattle feed and one on institutional transactions. Transactions used to obtain cattle feed are described with respect to the village's collective support for transactions in general. This discussion is followed by a description of the transaction institutions and bargaining transactions used by operators of cattle enterprises for their herder- and tethered-grazing and then stall-feeding techniques. The section reporting findings on institutional transactions discusses the ways in which villagers supported, bargained over, and adapted institutions governing transactions over cattle feed, especially during times of change. Finally, conclusions are discussed.

Case Study Background

Intensification of dairy production was expected in the area of the study because of high market demand for milk in Mombasa, as well as the area's relatively high population density and declining income-earning potential from the traditional cash crop of copra, derived from coconuts. In 1992 the annual shortfall of milk production in Coast Province was 113 million liters (Mullins 1992). Between 1980 and 1995 the National Dairy Development Project extended a technical package of improved breeds of dairy herds and stall feeding in Coast Province. The project recommended complete confinement and use of the stall-feeding technique. Feed recommendations were based on forages planted on homestead plots—mostly Napier grass (*Pennisetum purpureum*)—or purchased agroindustrial by-products such as copra cake (Maarse, Tesha, and Wainaina 1990). A major obstacle for potential adopters was the high cost of production stemming from a variety of factors including (1) lack of formal credit, (2) increasing scarcity of land, (3) variable availability of feeds, (4) high labor requirements, (5) lack of adequate veterinary services, and (6) lack of marketing infrastructure such as a milk collection service. Although as many as 350 coastal dairy operators at one time fully implemented the National Dairy Development Project package, field visits in 1994 revealed that very few still adhered to the prescribed package (Mullins et al. 1994).

The case study village was connected to Mombasa by 5 kilometers of dirt road followed by 45 kilometers of paved road with good public transportation. Livelihoods in the village were primarily based on subsistence production and remittances from income earned in Mombasa. Income from on-farm production was low and unreliable. Bimodal rains averaging 1,100 millimeters annually supported an intercrop of maize, cowpea, and cassava with coconut palms planted throughout the area (Jaetzold and Schmidt 1983). There was little to no use of chemical or organic fertilizers or improved seed stock. In general, the farming system was a low-input, low-output system.

The village's human population density of 591.7 persons per square kilometer (Swallow 1996) and the low productivity of its soils meant that it was at a threshold of increasing population density and land scarcity. During the cropping season of 1992, only 44 (17.5 percent) of the 252 plots used by case study villagers contained some fallow (Swallow 1996). Nevertheless, there was little use of manure or other fertilizers. Consequently, the village land area was not sufficient to produce enough to feed the villagers year-round, and basic food items were purchased during the long dry season (Waaijenberg 1994).

The Village and Its Institutions

The village was established in the 1800s and at the time of the study consisted of 132 extended-family homesteads. Although ethnically the village's membership was almost exclusively Giriama, it was religiously diverse, with 58.3 percent followers of the customary religion, 25.8 percent Christians, and 15.9 percent Muslims (Swallow 1996). There was little in- or out-migration, although many homestead heads and young people were nonresidents working in Mombasa, who remitted income to their village homesteads.

In keeping with Giriama culture, the village was organizationally decentralized. Customary institutions were derived from councils of elders and secret societies and consisted of diffuse monitoring and enforcement. Overlapping personal networks among villagers were based principally on relationships among family members, neighbors, friends, and those who shared the same religious affiliation.

There was to some extent a duality of local and national control of land in the village. Officially, land was managed under a system of individualized ownership and use. Indeed, the village's entire 3.5 square kilometers were held under individual title. Villagers had registered their titles in the early 1970s during a compulsory governmental land registration program. There were no spatial niches, such as a forest, pasture area, or roadside, lacking individual claims other than the roadways themselves, footpaths, and water holes. However, coexisting in the same spatial niche with this de jure individualized system administered by the national government was a multiple-use system that had customary roots and was managed by villagers through an evolving set of rules and conventions.

Historically, the latter set of institutions stipulated that cattle keepers could graze their cattle on any piece of land in the village that was either in fallow or had been harvested, with no need to seek permission. Use rights were acquired by virtue of group membership. At the time of the case study, the vast majority of cattle keepers in the village depended on forage obtained from land that was registered to another homestead. Few cattle keepers held title deeds to enough land to herd their cattle year-round. Given the importance of obtaining cattle feed from diverse agroecological niches, even those cattle keepers with a favorable ratio of land to cattle could benefit from using other villagers' land periodically.

Recently, however, some villagers were viewing the institutions that supported secondary access to others' land in a new light. One cattle-keeping homestead head built the first two fences in the village to protect the forage that he planted for his commercial dairy operation. Some non-cattle-keeping homestead heads had started grumbling about upholding the stipulations of good neighborliness when their cattle-keeping neighbors appeared to be doing better than they were. Several such homestead heads refused to allow use of their land by their cattle-keeping neighbors.

Cattle Production

Of the village's 132 homesteads, 37 (28.0 percent) kept cattle.[1] The average herd size was 10.5 animals; the range was 1 to 35 animals. Traditional subsistence-oriented, multiple-output enterprises were operated by 35 homesteads, while 3 homesteads operated the new commercial dairy enterprises. The herds of the multiple-output enterprises consisted of mainly zebu (*Bos indicus*) cattle, while those of the commercial dairy enterprises consisted of either pure dairy cattle or at least second-generation crosses. The herds of the latter enterprises were small, containing only 2 to 3 animals.

Multiple-output enterprise operators sought a variety of ends: (1) milk for home consumption, (2) plowing, (3) milk sales, (4) savings and investment, and (5) social benefits (that is, funeral sacrifices, bride wealth payment, and status). In fact, of the 35 multiple-output enterprises, only 6 (17.1 percent) sometimes sold milk. By contrast, operators of commercial dairy enterprises exclusively sought profit. Of the three operators of commercial dairy enterprises, 2 sold milk locally and 1 sold milk to a small café in Mombasa. The latter transported the milk by bicycle and public bus. No milk collection, refrigeration, or transportation services were offered in the village.

Each cattle keeper in the village used one or more of three types of cattle-feeding techniques: herder grazing, tethered grazing, and supplemental stall feeding. For the most part, cattle keepers maintained the same combination of cattle-feeding techniques throughout the year. They responded to seasonal variations in feed supply mainly by changing the way that the techniques were used. The area usually used for cattle grazing—whether herder or tethered grazing—was typically less than a 30-minute walk from the homestead and within the borders of the case study village.

The vast majority of the 37 cattle-keeping homesteads in the village used herder grazing, and it was the only cattle-feeding technique used by 19 (51.4 percent) of those homesteads. While herder grazed, the cattle were never left un-

---

1. Although there were only 37 cattle-keeping homesteads in the village, there were 38 cattle enterprises because one homestead operated two separate cattle enterprises—one each of the two cattle-enterprise types under operation in the village.

supervised. They were guided through irregularly shaped fallow fields scattered among cropped fields during the cropping season, and both fallow and harvested fields during the noncropping season. Tethered grazing was used by 18 (48.6 percent) of the 37 cattle-keeping homesteads in the village. It was done on the same types of fields as herder grazing; the difference was that with tethered grazing the cattle were tethered and left unsupervised while grazing.

Four homesteads in the village used stall feeding as a supplement to grazing. No cattle enterprise depended solely on stall feeding. Three of the four homesteads that used the technique were the village's three operators of commercial dairy enterprises, and one was an operator of a multiple-output enterprise. Cattle were stall fed during the morning or evening milking sessions or both. A great variety of feeds were stall fed: (1) species of natural vegetation, (2) crop and tree by-products and residues (such as maize bran),[2] (3) specialized planted cattle feeds (such as Napier grass [*Pennisetum p.*] and *Leucaena l.*), and (4) specialized purchased cattle feeds (such as copra cake). Cattle keepers used larger quantities of the relatively cheap bulk feeds such as natural vegetation, or if possible Napier grass, and smaller quantities of the more expensive, higher-quality feeds such as maize bran, or if possible *Leucaena l.* or copra cake.

The majority of cattle enterprise operators did not think that land scarcity was acute enough to necessitate the cultivation of specialized cattle feeds. Only two homestead heads—both operators of commercial dairy enterprises—engaged in the practice. Cattle enterprise operators chose other methods of responding to increasing land scarcity: (1) reducing the size of their herds, (2) limiting their use of the herder-grazing cattle-feeding technique, and (3) increasing their use of the more land-use-intensive cattle-feeding techniques of tethered grazing and supplemental stall feeding.

Objectives and Methodology

The objective of the research was to identify the factors that affected the transaction costs of obtaining feed for different cattle enterprises and cattle-feeding techniques in an environment of technical and institutional change. The study also sheds light on how institutions governing cattle feeding were adapted in response to change.

Collection of Data

A detailed case study was undertaken between November 1991 and February 1995. A village located within the milkshed of Kenya's second largest city,

---

2. The maize bran that was used in the case study village was a by-product of maize being pounded into flour that was used to produce *ugali*, the main staple for human consumption.

Mombasa, was chosen because this area had both demand-pull and cost-push factors to encourage commercial dairying, it provided an opportunity to study the early stages of land use intensification, and a dairy intensification extension program had been in place for 12 years prior to the study. Although the case study villagers knew about the latter program's technical package, most had chosen not to adopt it.

Data were collected using both qualitative and quantitative methods, including village census, semi-structured interviews, direct observation, survey questionnaires, and longitudinal monitoring. Primary data were collected from all 132 extended-family homesteads in the village. The purpose of the village case study phase was to identify the characteristics of the village as a collective that conditioned the transaction costs of institutional transactions. During this phase a village census, semistructured key-informant interviews, and single-visit questionnaire interviews were conducted.

In the next phase a detailed study was carried out for 105 weeks between 1992 and 1994 to document on a weekly basis the cattle feed transactions of eight operators of cattle enterprises that were differentiated by commercial orientation and level of intensification of cattle-feeding technique. Longitudinal monitoring was used to collect data on a variety of variables: (1) the cattle-feeding technique used, (2) feed use, (3) the source of feed item, (4) the means by which feeds were obtained, and (5) the relationship between transaction partners. Three commercial dairy enterprise operators who used stall feeding year-round were studied in the most depth. Finally, information on institutions used to reduce the information gathering, contracting, and monitoring and enforcement costs of transactions was assessed through qualitative methods and secondary sources.

Case Study Homesteads

The original case study homesteads were eight of the nine[3] homesteads in the case study village that reported using something akin to the stall-feeding technique at some point during the year before the start of the longitudinal-monitoring exercise. During that exercise, however, only four of these homesteads used the technique—one a multiple-output enterprise and three operators of commercial dairy enterprises in the village. The latter homesteads used the technique during almost every week that they were interviewed.

The three commercial dairy operators shared common socioeconomic characteristics that set them apart from the average villager, but they maintained greatly different local personal networks. Like 93 (70.5 percent) of the 132 homestead heads in the village, each of these 3 homestead heads had worked off-farm. All three were Muslims—a minority religion in the village—with greater than average sources of personal wealth. The greater atomism of Islamic

---

3. One homestead did not wish to participate in the exercise.

TABLE 13.1 Use of others' feed sources for all three cattle-feeding techniques

Feeding technique	Some use	No use	No data	Total
Herder grazing (weeks)	361	217	26	604
	(59.8)	(35.9)	(4.3)	(100)
Tethered grazing (weeks)	301	361	24	686
	(43.9)	(52.6)	(3.5)	(100)
Stall feeding (use-instances)				
Individuals	332			
	(28.8)			
Private businesses	247			
	(21.5)			
Subtotal	579	552	20	1,151
	(50.3)	(48.0)	(1.7)	(100)

SOURCE: Longitudinal-Monitoring Exercise, July 1992–1994 (Swallow 1996).

NOTE: Figures in parentheses refer to percentage of weeks that a technique was used (for herder or tethered grazing) or percentage of use-instances (for stall feeding).

beliefs had historically been used among the Giriama to resist the claims of kin for assistance and to justify individual gain from production (Parkin 1972).

With respect to reliance on other individuals' feed sources, cattle enterprise operators who used the stall-feeding technique relied on other individuals' feed sources in only 28.8 percent of their use-instances, while operators who used the herder- and tethered-grazing techniques relied on these sources for 59.8 percent and 43.9 percent of the weeks that they used the techniques respectively (Table 13.1).[4] The three operators of commercial dairy enterprises did, however, vary in their reliance on the different sources of cattle feed, as is described next.

One of the operators of a commercial-dairy enterprise was considered by other villagers to be an outsider. This person was one of the few non-Giriama members of the village. He was also a relative newcomer, and neither he nor any other adult male homestead member actually resided in the village. This homestead head lived in Mombasa, where he had been engaged in salaried employment for the 10 years prior to the study. Although a Muslim, he used his English name, suggesting a Westernized image. He had in fact attained one of the highest levels of formal education of the village's members. All of these factors limited his personal network within the village. For the remainder of this report, this cattle-enterprise operator is referred to as the "self-reliant outsider."

---

4. The commercial dairy operator who also operated a multiple-output cattle enterprise used other individuals' feed sources far more for the latter—over 90 percent of weeks—than the former enterprise, which suggests that this practice is not individual-specific, but rather enterprise- and technique-specific.

TABLE 13.2 Source of stall-fed feed items by homestead (use-instances)

Homestead	Private businesses	Other individuals	Own	No data	Total
Multiple-output enterprise operator	0	110 (78.0)	31 (22.0)	0	141 (100)
Self-reliant outsider	67 (22.4)	12 (4.0)	215 (71.9)	5 (1.7)	299 (100)
Model cattle keeper	145 (29.2)	131 (26.4)	209 (42.1)	12 (2.4)	497 (100)
Moderate innovator	35 (16.4)	79 (36.9)	97 (45.3)	3 (1.4)	214 (100)
Total	247 (21.5)	332 (28.8)	552 (48.0)	20 (1.7)	1151 (100)

SOURCE: Longitudinal-Monitoring Exercise, July 1992–1994 (Swallow 1996).
NOTE: Figures in parentheses refer to percentage of use-instances.

As can be seen in Table 13.2, he only used cattle feeds obtained from other individuals in 4.0 percent of his use-instances. He relied on feed produced on his own land, including Napier grass, for 71.9 percent of his use-instances and he relied on feed purchased from private businesses, including a small quantity of specialized feeds, for 22.4 percent of his use-instances.

The second operator of a commercial-dairy enterprise, although an insider to the village, placed himself too far above others to be accepted within the village. He did this by creating an image of himself as a model cattle keeper. He was frequently visited by extension agents and had successfully attempted many of the innovations presented to him, including the raising of a pure dairy cow and the cultivation of specialized cattle feeds—Napier grass and *leucaena l.* He also used some specialized purchased feeds. The infrastructure for his cattle enterprise was the most extensive of any homestead in the village. His was the only homestead in the village that owned a donkey—useful in transporting the substantial quantities of water required by pure dairy cattle. The head of this homestead also showed his dairy cow at the provincial agricultural show. The extent of this homestead head's personal network within the village was limited not only by this reputation, but also by the fact that a good portion of his land—the portion used for cultivating specialized cattle feeds—was fenced such that other cattle keepers could not use it. The jealousy of his neighbors caused them to spread rumors that he was crazy to take land out of food for humans and put it into feed for cattle. His neighbors also thought that his use of a formal-sector loan to purchase his pure dairy cow was too risky. This homestead head is henceforth called the "model cattle keeper." As shown in Table 13.2, he relied on his own sources of feed for 42.1 percent of his use-instances and on private businesses for 29.2 percent of his use-instances, leaving 26.4 percent of use-instances in which feed was obtained from other individuals.

The third operator of a commercial dairy enterprise started his enterprise after first successfully establishing his multiple-output enterprise. This latter enterprise was, in fact, based on one of the largest herds of cattle in the village. This homestead head had an extensive personal network within the village because he maintained an image of being one of the villagers, and he had more moderate investment in and success with his dairy enterprise. Although he was a Muslim, he used his Giriama name. He had no formal education and had worked off-farm for only six years. The very fact that he kept zebu cattle contributed to his image of being like the others in the village. He used no infrastructure for the commercial dairy enterprise, planted no forage, and used only a negligible amount of specialized purchased feeds. This homestead head will be called the "moderate innovator." As shown in Table 13.2, this cattle-enterprise operator's reliance on his own feed sources—45.3 percent of his use-instances— was about the same as that of the model cattle keeper, but he obtained feeds from private businesses in only 16.4 percent of his use-instances and from other individuals in 36.9 percent of his use-instances.

Transactions over Cattle Feed

Collective Support for Transactions

Collective support among villagers for transactions over cattle feed came in the form of a set of shared expectations about ownership rights, incentives for cooperation, the extent of personalization of the transaction, and the degree to which the transaction was reciprocal or quid pro quo in nature. Rights of ownership of feed sources were based on the principle that individuals owned the product of their labor and should reap the benefits. This principle was balanced against beliefs about good neighborliness, an ethos of sharing, and expectations of the rights and duties of personal relationships. Desirable behavior was encouraged through reciprocity and helping others in need. Undesirable behavior was discouraged through inflicting guilt and shunning errant individuals.

This collective support for cattle feed transactions enabled cattle-enterprise operators to reduce their transaction costs. In general, information-gathering costs were reduced through multiple spheres of interaction among villagers. Contracting costs were reduced through the maintenance of expected contracting procedures such as the use of witnesses. Enforcement costs were reduced through the use of fines, the sanctioning of some types of right-holder enforcement (such as certain uses of physical force), and stipulations against theft and physical violence. In extreme cases, support for enforcement could be found through ad hoc councils of village elders or the national government via the subchief.

How transactions over cattle feed were carried out—whether on a private paid basis, on a reciprocal no-payment basis, or based on established community norms—depended to a large extent on the physical-technical attributes of the techniques, particularly the rivalry of consumption or competition over resources and the cost of excluding others from using the resource (Table 13.3).

Herder- and Tethered-Grazing Techniques

TRANSACTION INSTITUTIONS. Intensification of land use had gradually increased to the point that competition over use of fallow growth for crop production and cattle enterprises was beginning to be evident. With only two of the plots in the village fenced, the costs to landowners of physically excluding others' use were prohibitive. As a result, cattle keepers gained access to other villagers' land most often without seeking permission. At other times they used others' land with permission but without payment. This situation suggests that cattle keepers preferred the use of impersonal relationships[5] for herder and tethered grazing, because retaliation for unfavorable behavior is less likely than in personal relationships. The exception to this finding occurred in the case of tethered-grazing transactions undertaken by operators of commercial dairy enterprises. These operators were twice as likely as operators of multiple-output enterprises to seek permission for the use of tethered-grazing spots. In fact, the only cattle keeper who paid for tethered-grazing spots was the model cattle keeper.

BARGAINING TRANSACTIONS. For the most part, cattle keepers' interests were to rely on the customary norms governing their rights to graze fallow land, and landowners' interests were to draw on the evolving expectations of reciprocity or payment. Bargaining between these differing institutions was more reactive than proactive: a cattle keeper would for the most part assume his right to graze and wait for a response, if any, from the landowner. Given the existing institutional structure, the burden of changing the situation rested on the landowner.

Nevertheless, cattle keepers who used the tethered-grazing technique as well as those who operated commercial dairy enterprises did enjoy benefits from the newer arrangements. For users of tethered grazing, if a request had been made for use of the land, the cattle were more likely to be observed while being tethered by members of the landowner's homestead. This fact reduced the likelihood that they would get loose and damage crops, which would result in conflict and fines. There was also a greater assurance that the cattle would not be harmed, inadvertently or intentionally, while they were grazing. In addition, if use was based on permission, a contract for exclusive access could be established. The moderate

---

5. Personal relationships were relationships defined by respondents as those of relative, friend, or neighbor.

TABLE 13.3 Characteristics of commodity transactions

Characteristic	Private transactions	Gray area	Reciprocal transactions	Gray area	Community transactions
Rivalry of consumption	High	Intermediate	Moderate	Intermediate	Low
Costs of exclusion	Low	Intermediate	Moderate	Intermediate	High
Holder of ownership rights	Individual (collective member)	Individual (collective member)	Individual (collective member)	Contested	Collective
Structure of transaction					
Incentives for cooperation	Utility	Contested	Normative-voluntary	Normative-voluntary	Normative-voluntary
Personal/impersonal	Impersonal	Contested	Personal	Contested	Impersonal
Means of access	Pay	Contested	Ask-but-don't-pay	Contested	Don't-ask

innovator negotiated one such contract. For commercial dairy operators, the profitability of their operations meant there was greater value attached to a reliable supply of tethering points, and a greater cost of harm done to cattle.

Cattle keepers used several methods to capture as much bargaining power as possible. First, cattle keepers guarded the historical precedent stipulating that others' fallowed and harvested fields were open for grazing by all. Second, much effort was invested in establishing reputations as assertive cattle keepers. The moderate innovator reported that he had to keep landowners accustomed to the idea that he would use their land unless they made it clear that they would stop him. He did this by routinely returning to the fields of homestead heads who asked him to leave. He continued to do this unless these landowners asked him to leave more than three times or threatened to use force. Third, cattle keepers developed tit-for-tat relationships such that if a cattle keeper asked another cattle keeper's herder to leave his land, the offended cattle keeper would reciprocate. The moderate innovator had several tit-for-tat relationships with other cattle keepers.

Although non-cattle-keeping homesteads would gain if access to their land were transacted using reciprocal or paid arrangements, the low level of land use intensity and the potentially high costs of restructuring existing norms prevented them from trying to change the existing practice. On top of the actual costs of monitoring and enforcement that would be required to exclude unwanted use, there would be the social cost of going against the traditional norm of good neighborliness and access to others' land. In addition, almost all villagers aspired to own cattle one day and would want these customary norms to apply to themselves. A final cost was the possibility that beneficial relations with trespassing homesteads would be curtailed and would damage reciprocal practices in other spheres of interaction. These norms tended to prevail over national ideologies of private land ownership, particularly in transactions between villagers who were not engaged in a commercial enterprise.

Even given these costs, if a landowner chose to defend his interests he could do so by complaining to the local government representative—the subchief—or consistently or fiercely demanding herders to leave his land. In one case the moderate innovator's herd was chased away by a machete-wielding landowner. In the case of tethered grazing, landowners' had several unique factors in their favor. Since exclusion was less costly, the overall cost of contracting was less than that for herder grazing. With tethered grazing, incidences of trespassing were less costly to detect, and information about the owner of the cattle was easier to obtain. Enforcement was easier in that cattle could potentially be removed or harmed by the landowner if they were left unsupervised.

Stall-Feeding Technique

TRANSACTION INSTITUTIONS. Given their variety of physical-technical attributes, stall-fed items were transacted in a variety of ways. Copra cake and maize bran were obtained exclusively by quid pro quo payment; in fact, copra cake was exclusively purchased from private businesses. Although maize bran was a by-product of human food preparation within the homestead and therefore had near zero physical-technical costs of exclusion, it did have an opportunity cost as a feed in the subsistence poultry enterprises that were operated by the majority of homesteads in the village. The preference for the use of impersonal relationships in maize bran transactions (Table 13.4) is striking given the prevalence of personal relationships within the village. Maize bran was also the only feed frequently purchased from non–case study villagers.

Only planted feeds and miscellaneous crop and tree residues and by-products were obtained exclusively by asking-but-not-paying, and, even then, only 10 use-instances were recorded.[6] More often, they were obtained from cattle keepers' own sources. These items are characterized by moderate rivalry of consumption and lack of opportunity cost. The physical-technical costs of excluding others' use of mango and cassava leaves were theoretically high as these plants were often far from homestead buildings. Once the plants were harvested, the costs of excluding others' use of maize husks, cassava peels, and potato peels was near zero as these items were by-products of crop processing that took place within the homestead. The self-reliant outsider, however, did report a problem of theft of parts of maize and cassava plants. Planted feeds' high rivalry of consumption indicated that they would most likely be transacted as private goods, even though they were characterized by relatively high costs of exclusion. The fact that they were exchanged on a reciprocal basis among matrilineal kin is probably due to the strength of these relationships, which may have carried more weight than physical-technical characteristics. A summary of the different types of transactions over feed sources used in all three cattle-feeding techniques can be seen in Table 13.5.

BARGAINING TRANSACTIONS.   Banana pseudo-stems, natural vegetation, and maize stalks were transacted in institutional gray areas such that transaction partners often bargained between the different norms and institutions in order to gain access to these items. In general, enterprise operators were more proactive in bargaining for stall feeding than in transactions for the herder- and tethered-grazing techniques. Bargaining transactions over stall-fed items were differentiated by several factors: (1) the physical-technical characteristics of the feed item, (2) seasonal scarcity of feeds, (3) the enterprise type, (4) the degree of commercialization of the cattle enterprise, and (5) the enterprise operator's personal networks.

---

6. One use-instance is one instance of use of a feed item by one homestead at least once during one week. Since no long-term storage of feeds was practiced in the case study village—with the exception of feeds purchased in bulk from private businesses—an instance of use of another individual's feed item corresponded roughly to an instance of transaction over that feed item.

TABLE 13.4 Means of access to other individuals' stall-fed items by feed-type category and relationship to the feed owner (use-instances)

Feed type	Relationship to feed owner[a]	Pay	Ask-no-pay	No-ask	Subtotal	No data	Total
Maize bran	Impersonal	55 (78.6)	0	0	55 (78.6)	7 (10.00)	70 (100)
	Personal	8 (11.4)	0	0	8 (11.4)		
Banana pseudo-stems	Impersonal	7 (24.1)	2 (6.9)	0	9 (31.0)	1 (3.4)	29 (100)
	Personal	0	19 (65.5)	0	19 (65.5)		
Planted feeds	Impersonal	0	0	0	0	0	4 (100)
	Personal	0	4 (100)	0	4 (100)		
Miscellaneous crop and tree residues and by-products[b]	Impersonal	0	2 (33.3)	0	2 (33.3)	0	6 (100)
	Personal	0	4 (66.7)	0	4 (66.7)	0	
Natural vegetation and maize stalks	Impersonal	0	19 (8.5)	26 (11.7)	45 (20.2)	9 (4.0)	223 (100)
	Personal	0	102 (45.7)	67 (30.0)	169 (75.8)		
Total		70 (21.1)	152 (45.8)	93 (28.0)	315 (94.9)	17 (5.1)	332 (100)

SOURCE: Longitudinal-Monitoring Exercise, July 1992–1994 (Swallow 1996).

NOTES: Figures in parentheses refer to percentage of use-instances.

[a]Personal relationships were relationships with relatives, friends, or neighbors.

[b]Miscellaneous crop and tree residues and by-products include cassava leaves and peels, mango leaves, maize husks, and potato peels.

TABLE 13.5 Means of access to others' feed sources for all three cattle-feeding techniques

Feeding technique	Private transactions (pay)	Gray area	Reciprocal transactions (ask-no-pay)	Gray area	Community transactions (no-ask)
Herder grazing					X
Tethered grazing		X[a]		X	
Stall feeding					
Copra cake and maize bran	X				
Banana pseudo-stems		X			
Planted feeds			X		
Miscellaneous crop and tree residues and by-products[b]			X		
Natural vegetation and maize stalks				X	

SOURCE: Longitudinal-Monitoring Exercise, July 1992–1994 (Swallow 1996).

[a]This gray area was used by only one commercial dairy enterprise.

[b]Miscellaneous crop and tree residues and by-products include cassava leaves and peels, mango leaves, maize husks, and potato peels.

The high degree of rivalry of consumption and low costs of exclusion of banana pseudo-stems favored the use of private transactions. However, their zero opportunity cost meant that they were transacted reciprocally or made available to the wider community, except during the dry season when banana pseudo-stems were one of the only feed items available. This was the season when they were purchased by the self-reliant outsider who did not have many personal relationships in the village. As shown in Table 13.4, banana pseudo-stems were obtained by asking-but-not-paying in 72.4 percent of the instances in which cattle keepers used others' sources. In 65.5 percent of these instances, transactions were based on personal relationships, and in only 6.9 percent, transactions were based on impersonal relationships.

Natural vegetation and maize stalks accounted for the vast majority of use-instances[7] in which stall-fed items were obtained from other individuals, and they were the only stall-fed item obtained without permission (Table 13.4). Their access mode is consistent with their rising opportunity cost in terms of lost benefits to the farming system and high costs of exclusion.

---

7. The commercial dairy operator who also operated a multiple-output cattle enterprise used other individuals' feed sources far more for the latter—more than 90 percent of weeks—than the former enterprise, which suggests that this practice is not individual-specific, but rather enterprise- and technique-specific.

Cattle keepers who used the stall-feeding technique were less likely than those who used the two other techniques to obtain natural vegetation and maize stalks without permission. Cattle keepers who used the stall-feeding technique obtained these feed items without permission in 41.7 percent of the instances in which others' sources were used, while those who used the other two techniques did so an average of 82.5 percent of the time. In addition, cattle-keepers who used the stall-feeding technique were more likely to use personal relationships in transactions over natural vegetation and maize stalks than those who used herder and tethered grazing (see Tables 13.4 and 13.6). This greater reliance on personal relationships to obtain natural vegetation and maize stalks for stall feeding suggests that such access may have been contingent on having a more extensive personal network.

When the degree of commercialization of a cattle enterprise was analyzed, it was found to influence the cost of transactions for stall-fed items. The operator of the single multiple-output enterprise who used stall feeding obtained feed through distinctly different means than the two operators of commercial-dairy enterprises who made consistent use of others' feed sources for stall feeding—the model cattle keeper and the moderate innovator. As shown in Table 13.7, the operator of the multiple-output enterprise used feed items without seeking permission in 50.0 percent of the instances in which he used others' feed sources, and he never paid to use a feed item. The two operators of commercial dairy enterprises, in contrast, used feed items without seeking permission in only an average of 18.1 percent of their use-instances, and they paid to use feed items in an average of 31.9 percent of those instances. The tradition of allowing the village's cattle keepers access to natural vegetation and maize stalks without permission was called into question when these feeds were used in a nontraditional technique, especially if that technique was used exclusively to make a profit, as was the case in the commercial dairy operations.

The personal network of the cattle enterprise operator was another factor related to means of access to the stall feed items. Given his limited local personal network, coupled with his relatively sufficient personal wealth, the self-reliant outsider used only three other villagers' feed sources, and he used them only during the severe dry season. This enterprise operator paid for feed in 66.7 percent of his use-instances (Table 13.7). The model cattle keeper, although an insider in the village, also had a limited local personal network and therefore less bargaining power with his neighbors. He also had less land than the self-reliant outsider. As a result he was the only cattle enterprise operator who paid for tethered-grazing spots. This commercial dairy operator relied on private businesses for 29.2 percent of his use-instances (Swallow 1996). He only relied on feed obtained through transactions with other individuals for 26.4 percent of his use-instances (Table 13.2), and he paid for feeds in 35.9 percent of those use-instances (Table 13.7).

The moderate innovator had personal networks and thus more opportunities to use multiple relationships to gain access to feed. He was also highly motivated to use his personal networks since he had less personal wealth than

TABLE 13.6 Means of access to others' feed sources by relationship with the feed owner for all three cattle-feeding techniques

Feeding techniques	Relationship to feed owner[a]	Pay	Ask-no-pay	No-ask	No data	Total
Herder grazing (weeks)	Impersonal		22	164	0	186
			(41.5)	(53.2)		(51.5)
			(11.8)	(88.2)		(100)
	Personal		31	144	0	175
			(58.5)	(46.8)		(48.5)
			(17.7)	(82.3)		(100)
	Subtotal		53	308	0	361
			(100)	(100)		(100)
			(14.7)	(85.3)		(100)
Tethered grazing (weeks)	Impersonal	0	23	85	0	108
			(47.9)	(35.4)		(35.9)
			(21.3)	(78.7)		(100)
	Personal	13	25	155	0	193
		(100)	(52.1)	(64.6)		(64.1)
		(6.7)	(13.0)	(80.3)		(100)

Stall feeding[b] (use-instances)

Subtotal	13 (100) (4.3)	48 (100) (15.9)	240 (100) (79.7)	0	301 (100) (100)
Impersonal	52 (67.5) (54.2)	21 (13.7) (21.9)	23 (24.7) (24.0)	0	96 (28.9) (100)
Personal	18 (23.4) (8.2)	131 (85.6) (59.5)	70 (75.3) (31.8)	1 (11.1) (0.5)	220 (66.3) (100)
No data	7 (9.1) (43.8)	1 (0.7) (6.3)	0	8 (88.9) (50.0)	16 (4.8) (100)
Subtotal	77 (100) (23.2)	153 (100) (46.1)	93 (100) (28.0)	9 (100) (2.7)	332 (100) (100)

SOURCE: Longitudinal-Monitoring Exercise, July 1992–1994 (Swallow 1996).

NOTES: Figures in parentheses refer to percentage of weeks that a technique was used or percentage of use-instances, with column percentage above row percentage.

[a]Personal relationships were relationships with relatives, friends, or neighbors.

[b] These figures include only cases in which other individuals' feeds were used. They do not include cases in which private businesses' feeds were used.

TABLE 13.7 Means of access to other individuals' stall-fed items by homestead
(use-instances)

Homestead	Pay	Ask-no-pay	No-ask	No data	Total
Multiple-output	0	55	55	0	110
enterprise operator		(50.0)	(50.0)		(100)
Self-reliant outsider	8	3	0	1	12
	(66.7)	(25.0)		(8.3)	(100)
Model cattle keeper	47	62	20	2	131
	(35.9)	(47.3)	(15.3)	(1.5)	(100)
Moderate innovator	22	33	18	6	79
	(27.8)	(41.8)	(22.8)	(7.6)	(100)
Total	77	153	93	9	332
	(23.2)	(46.1)	(28.0)	(2.7)	(100)

SOURCE: Longitudinal-Monitoring Exercise, July 1992–1994 (Swallow 1996).
NOTES: Figures in parentheses refer to percentage of use-instances.

the other commercial dairy enterprise operators. He was able to gain more access to other villagers' feed sources through nonpayment arrangements than were the two other operators of commercial dairy enterprises. While this homestead head relied on his own feed sources about as often as the model cattle keeper, he relied on other individuals' feed sources in 36.9 percent of his use-instances and private businesses in only 16.4 percent of his use-instances (Table 13.2). In addition, he only paid for stall-fed feed items in 27.8 percent of the instances in which he used other individuals' feeds (Table 13.7).

Institutional Transactions

In the previous section, it was shown that at the time of the study many of the transactions over cattle feed in the case study village were conducted through bargaining in institutional gray areas rather than being determined by an explicit and consistent set of rules for all transaction partners as was the customary case. This was true for transactions over feed sources for herder and tethered grazing, and it was true for 75.9[8] percent of the instances of use of other individuals' stall-fed items (Table 13.4). Extensive gray area bargaining can be attributed to the situation of techno-institutional change in the village whereby expectations about the rules that should govern transactions over some feed items had become dis-

---

8. As is shown in Table 13.4, the feed categories that were obtained through more than one means of access were banana pseudo-stems, natural vegetation, and maize stalks. The number of instances of use of these feeds was 252, which is 75.9 percent of 332, the total number of instances of use of other individuals' stall-fed items.

located. It is likely that bargaining transactions in these gray areas would, through repetition, create new collective expectations about the transaction institutions governing specific feed items and techniques.

A high transaction cost of organization prevented villagers from engaging in collective action to establish more definitive transaction institutions. These high costs emanated from village members' heterogeneous values and beliefs about legitimate principles of leadership and processes for making collective choices. The main source of this heterogeneity lay in the religious diversity of the village. Different beliefs contributed to conflicting views on local leadership, social organization, and land ownership.

The high cost of institutional transactions also resulted from the way that the village nested organizationally with the national government. Although the government involved itself in some local issues, it did not involve itself in others, and as a result its role was not clear to villagers. Because the national government provided an alternative, competing forum for dispute settlement and decision enforcement with respect to land ownership, individuals could theoretically choose their forum and change forums if their first choice resulted in an unfavorable outcome (Spear 1978). Government officials were involved in keeping order by enforcing national laws and implementing public policy, but they neither effectively involved themselves in the day-to-day management of local resources nor delegated authority to the local level (Waaijenberg 1994). The national government lacked the resources and legitimacy to be effective in securing local expectations and in monitoring and enforcing laws and policies. Lack of delegation of authority to the local level meant that there was confusion about which collectives' domain encompassed local resource management. Poorly defined and overlapping roles between local authority and the national government, as well as changes in land scarcity and commercialization, contributed to a generalized state of instability of expectations about access to land-based resources in the village.

Finally, differences in production interests as well as personal sources of power—in terms of personal wealth and personal networks—made it difficult to create institutions to govern transactions over cattle feeds in particular. Though few in number, those homestead heads with commercial dairy operations yielded sufficient power to prevent the subsistence landholder majority from shaping new institutions that reflected their interests. Furthermore, personal sources of power were becoming more heterogeneous through religious conversion and unequal access to education, off-farm employment, and the national governmental system.

Conclusions

Findings from a detailed case study undertaken in a village located within the milkshed of Mombasa, Kenya, suggest several possible factors that influenced the adoption of cattle-feeding techniques: (1) the cost of excluding others from the feed and therefore the capacity to capture private benefits at a low cost, (2) the relative bargaining power of the different stakeholders—in this case cattle-keeping households and non-cattle-keeping landowners, (3) the wealth of cattle keepers, and (4) the extent and strength of personal networks and the degree to which a person is considered a community insider and worthy of community support.

Although the in-depth case study approach limits the ability to extrapolate findings, the study shows that neither optimistic project expectations for rapid change nor pessimistic predictions of resistance to change are necessarily accurate. Cattle keepers in the case study village were in fact intensifying their use of cattle-feeding techniques; however, they took different routes than anticipated. It was foreseen that cattle keepers would respond to the need to intensify land use with complete confinement of cattle, planted forage, self-reliance in cattle feed, and use of the private sector for transactions. Among the villagers' varying responses to the need to intensify land use, however, the common thread was the choice of a middle road of marginal, step-wise change rather than the radical change that was anticipated.

At the village's low but rising level of intensification of land use, alternatives to complete self-reliance in feed were available: feed could be obtained from other villagers through secondary means. Use of these feed sources had the disadvantages of providing less nutrition and requiring higher transaction costs, but these sources also required lower inputs in terms of land, labor, and cash than the recommended feeds. Cattle-enterprise operators blended their use of the traditional, less-intensive cattle-feeding technique of herder grazing with the more-intensive techniques and different types of feeds, which resulted in different levels of transaction costs. This choice of a marginal, step-wise style of technical change enabled learning on both the technical and institutional fronts.

Although the common thread was the choice of the middle road, the three cattle keepers who had come the farthest along the road of intensification at the time of the study did so by making use of their varying sources of personal wealth and networks. The two cattle keepers with the greatest sources of wealth but the most limited personal networks within the village were the least successful in their bargaining transactions with other villagers, but they could afford to rely on their own resources. The cattle keeper with the least sources of personal wealth but largest personal network relied the most on secondary access to other villagers' feed sources, and he was able to use his personal network to bargain for favorable access to that feed. Contrary to the usual view that transaction institutions are applied uniformly to all transaction partners based on collective choice rules, this study suggests that rules are applied differentially and may depend to a large extent on personal relationships and perceptions. The cumulative effect over time may be change in the institutions governing cattle feeding.

References

Gass, G. M., and J. E. Sumberg. 1993. Intensification of livestock production in Africa: Experience and issues. University of East Anglia, Norwich, U.K. Draft.

Jaetzold, R., and H. Schmidt. 1983. *Kilifi District farm management handbook of Kenya.* Vol. 2C, *East Kenya.* Nairobi: Ministry of Agriculture and German Agency for Technical Cooperation.

Maarse, L. M., F. T. Tesha, and G. M. Wainaina. 1990. *Lessons from 10 years' NDDP experience at the Kenya Coast.* Mtwapa, Kenya: Kenya Agricultural Research Institute and International Livestock Centre for Africa.

McIntire, J., D. Bourzat, and P. Pingali. 1992. *Crop-livestock interactions in Sub-Saharan Africa.* Washington, D.C.: World Bank.

Mullins, G. R. 1992. Dairy production, marketing and consumption in coastal Kenya. In Proceedings of the All Africa Conference on Animal Agriculture, November 23–27, Nairobi, Kenya.

Mullins, G., P. Tsangari, L. Wahome, and L. Maarse. 1994. Benefits or burdens?: The impacts of intensive dairy production on smallholder farm women in coastal Kenya. In Proceedings of a workshop on women in livestock development, sponsored by Heifer Project International, held in Mombasa, Kenya, May 16–20.

Parkin, D. J. 1972. *Palms, wine, and witnesses: Public spirit and private gain in an African farming community.* San Francisco: Chandler.

Spear, T. T. 1978. *The Kaya complex: A history of the Mijikenda peoples of the Kenya coast to 1900.* Nairobi: Kenya Literature Bureau.

Swallow, K. A. 1996. Economic development, institutions, and technique change: Intensification of cattle-feeding techniques by the Giriama of Kenya's Coast Province. Ph.D. diss., University of Wisconsin, Madison, Wisc., U.S.A.

Waaijenberg, H. 1994. *Mijikenda agriculture in Coast Province of Kenya.* The Hague, the Netherlands: Royal Tropical Institute.

14 Conclusions and Policy Implications

ANNA KNOX, RUTH MEINZEN-DICK,
BRENT SWALLOW, AND FRANK PLACE

Researchers and policymakers often attribute low levels of technology adoption in developing countries to problems of insecure property rights and ineffective collective action. Customary property regimes are often equated with insecure property rights, which are in turn associated with inefficient resource use and underinvestment in land improvements. Constraints on communities' ability to undertake collective action are similarly seen as obstacles to the adoption of large capital investments. But despite the growing body of theoretical and empirical studies of how property rights and collective action institutions can constrain or facilitate the adoption of agricultural and natural resource management technologies, the effects of these institutions have often been misinterpreted, either because the studies have looked only at the direct effects or because their outcomes have been confounded with the effects of other factors.

This volume weaves together conceptual frameworks, guidelines for empirical research, and original empirical evidence on the relationships between property rights, collective action, and technology adoption. Overall, the volume shows the importance of considering the interrelations between property rights and collective action institutions, the feedback effects of new technologies on property rights, the importance of social capital on collective action, and the direct and indirect effects of property rights, collective action, and the many other determinants of technology adoption.

In Chapter 2, Knox, Meinzen-Dick, and Hazell present two new conceptual models. One illustrates how the spatial and temporal dimensions of technologies shape concerns about the effects of property rights and collective action on technology adoption. This conceptual model provides a helpful basis for predicting how property rights and collective action institutions are likely to affect the adoption of new agricultural and resource management technologies. Another conceptual model presented by Knox, Meinzen-Dick, and Hazell illustrates that property rights and collective action not only have direct effects on technology adoption but also filter the effects of other important factors. In doing so, this model seeks to provide a new approach for framing empirical research that specifies and tests these indirect effects.

294

Property Rights and Technology Adoption

The initial chapters in this volume focus primarily on the relationships between property rights and technology adoption. The underlying message that emerges is that there is no clear relationship between security of land and resource tenure and adoption of technologies. Whereas Place and Otsuka suggest that stronger rights to agricultural land may catalyze tree planting and lead to higher tree densities on those lands (Chapter 4), Gavian and Ehui's study show input intensities to be higher on lands held under tenures with shorter durations and a narrower range of rights (Chapter 5). The marginal correspondence between weaker tenure status and lower levels of productivity emerges because land that is rented, borrowed, and shared tends to be inherently less productive and used by farmers with less experience. Smucker, White, and Bannister (Chapter 6) go even further in highlighting this ambiguity by drawing on a variety of studies on the relationship between land tenure and adoption of natural resource management technologies in rural Haiti. While there is some indication that tenure status may be correlated with the types of technologies farmers employ, it has little or no bearing on their overall levels of investment.

The three case studies support several of the contentions Knox, Meinzen-Dick, and Hazell make in Chapter 2. In particular, Place and Otsuka confirm the importance of secure property rights for long-term investments, such as trees, while the finding by Gavian and Ehui suggests that agricultural productivity in the Ethiopian case is more dependent upon short-term input use than upon long-term capital investment. All three case studies demonstrate that a host of other factors besides tenure security determine adoption outcomes. Place and Otsuka point in particular to the importance of markets and infrastructure in shaping the incentives to cut and cultivate trees. Gavian and Ehui stress the impact of soil fertility and farmers' levels of human and physical capital. Smucker, White, and Bannister argue that economic and political security take precedence in the priorities of rural peasants. Rather than tenure security per se, they conclude that it is the strength of the relationships among people in rural communities that affects the adoption of sustainable resource management practices. This finding marks the first indication from the case studies that collective action is important for upholding local institutions to sustain natural resources and enable livelihood security.

Smucker, White, and Bannister also address the issue of titling as a reliable indicator of tenure security. Their literature review reveals that in environments characterized by high transaction costs of maintaining a formal cadastre and titling system, by distrust and incapacity of the judiciary, and by poor access by rural peasants to the formal system, local institutions are apt to more effectively address the livelihood security needs of rural peasants and foster better natural resource management practices. In such instances the issuance of land titles may reduce, rather than increase, overall land tenure security. Land titling may thus have a role in tenure policy in some, but certainly not all, situations found in the developing world. Like other dimensions of land policy, land titling schemes must be designed in light of the specific circumstances that prevail in a particular circumstance.

The study by Gavian and Ehui also shows that the results from empirical studies should be judged with considerable caution. First, it was only because of a careful and thorough study design that the authors were able to identify the underlying causes of the differences in productivity across the three tenure types. Second, at the time of this study, all forms of land tenure in Ethiopia were somewhat insecure. The formal policy of the Ethiopian government was that all agricultural land belongs to the state and that agricultural land should occasionally be redistributed to ensure that all qualified rural households have access to land. The overall effects of this insecurity cannot be assessed through a cross-sectional survey. It perhaps is worth noting that virtually all of the trees planted in this area of Ethiopia are planted not in agricultural fields but in homesteads that are not reallocated.

Uncertain Property Rights, Local Institutions, and Technology Adoption

Evidence of the capacity and resilience of local institutions for governing tenure and natural resource management is further exemplified in Chapter 7 by Rae et al. Built on the accumulated local knowledge of ecological and socioeconomic realities in the arid Syrian rangelands, pastoral institutions generally embody the necessary flexibility and dynamism to respond to environmental conservation and livelihood needs. Yet the state's interest in diffusing the power of pastoral tribes led it to support plantation and shrub technologies in an effort to sedentarize the tribes. Although the government and other external actors have failed to appreciate the importance of herder mobility, livestock feed preferences, and the delicate relationships and territorial claims of the different tribes, local institutions have endured. A more promising strategy for increasing livestock production, improving rangeland management, and enhancing pastoral welfare lies in state recognition of local institutions and building on their strengths.

Similar conclusions can be drawn from Smucker, White, and Bannister's study of Haiti (Chapter 6) and Unruh's study from Mozambique (Chapter 8). Common to both studies is a climate of political and economic uncertainty that exacerbates the incapacity of and distrust for the formal judicial system. But although local tenure institutions appear to be sufficient for sustaining the adoption of natural resource technologies in Haiti, the situation is more complex for agroforestry in Mozambique. Here, the fact that cashew trees have emerged as one of the few enduring forms of legitimate evidence of land claims following the war has led farmers to avoid replacing older, less-productive trees. This situation is a clear example of how technology can affect institutions, not just the reverse, and is an interaction that is still largely underresearched.

Because cashew tree production has environmental benefits and significant potential for contributing to smallholder incomes, stimulating tree replacement and wider-scale adoption will necessitate strengthening the legitimacy of alternative forms of evidence of tenure security. In the process of rebuilding the country, the Mozambican government has a unique opportunity to recognize and revive alternative forms of customary evidence in addition to cashew trees and to support the legitimacy of local conflict resolution institutions. Such a strategy is more likely to succeed in strengthening the claims of smallholders and cultivating popular trust in the government than imposing new rules from above.

Collective Action and Technology Adoption

Whereas a number of previous studies have provided evidence on the effect of property rights on the technology adoption process, there has been less empirical research on the effect of collective action on application of natural resource management technologies. A number of studies in this volume contribute important insights for understanding this relationship.

Pender and Scherr's quantitative analysis of factors contributing to investment in natural resource management technologies (Chapter 10) shows that much depends on the type of investment. Differences in adoption arise depending on whether investments are undertaken privately or involve collective action and whether organizations involved in the community are local or external. This finding underlines the importance of the interrelationships between property rights and collective action discussed by Knox, Meinzen-Dick, and Hazell in Chapter 2. This finding also shows that policies and programs designed to promote adoption of conservation measures need to carefully examine the potential impacts of involving government organizations or nongovernmental organizations and supporting measures for strengthening local cooperation.

Three of the chapters in this volume explore processes of induced technical and institutional change, mainly drawing attention to the limitations of theories predicting efficient outcomes and highlighting implications for collective action. Pender and Scherr's study of Honduras demonstrates that in areas of rapid population growth, the pace of change may overwhelm the potential for robust local organizational development. Examining the tension between livestock owners' traditional property rights and the formal rights held by *chena* (swidden) cultivators in Sri Lanka, Birner and Gunaweera (Chapter 9) demonstrate how inequitable distribution of power can thwart the predicted efficiency outcomes of induced technical and institutional innovation. K. Swallow's in-depth case study of cattle-feeding techniques in Kenya (Chapter 13) suggests that bargaining power is achieved not only through wealth, but also through social networks and personal relations with one's neighbors. The source of bargaining power can in turn influence the pathways of innovation. Although Birner and Gunaweera affirm that collective action can be the key to redressing power imbalances, they assert that it does not always constitute a necessary condition. In the Sri Lankan case a well-functioning democratic political system allowed the rights of *chena* farmers to be upheld despite their lack of organizational capacity. In the absence of such democratic political institutions, development agencies and nongovernmental organizations may be able to play key roles in strengthening the collective political voice of groups suffering from insecure property rights.

The model of spatial and temporal scale presented by Knox, Meinzen-Dick, and Hazell in Chapter 2 illustrates several landscape-level technologies that require collective action for their efficient use. While irrigation systems and watershed management technologies require both secure property rights and collective action, the large spatial scale but limited temporal scale of integrated pest management (IPM) techniques requires collective action. Although IPM technologies often have significant environmental advantages over chemical pesticide sprays, the collective benefits of lower pest populations are usually possible only if there is a high degree of participation in exercising pest control techniques. Such collective action is costly. B. Swallow et al. (Chapter 11) and Ravnborg et al. (Chapter 12) point to heterogeneity as a factor that increases the costs of collective action because of lack of trust and mutual understanding. Spatial factors such as information dissemination and coordinating actions across large distances also add to costs. Both studies suggest that the intervention of external actors can help mitigate collective action costs. In the case of pouron treatments for cattle to contain disease caused by tsetse flies in Ethiopia, the results of B. Swallow et al. led authorities to relocate treatments centers to lessen the costs associated with livestock transport, information exchange, and interethnic tensions. The results achieved by the Centro Internacional de Agricultura Tropical (CIAT) in providing organizational support and facilitating conflict negotiation among farmers in the Rio Cabuyal watershed has spawned similar efforts by governmental and nongovernmental organizations in Colombia.

Methods and Implications for Researchers

Empirically testing the relationships between property rights, collective action, and technology adoption presents serious methodological challenges given both the number of factors involved and the complexities of their interactions. Place and Swallow (Chapter 3) suggest that particular attention must be given to definition and clarification of terms, the simultaneous and complex relationships between technology adoption and property rights variables, the challenges involved in data collection and measurement issues, and the difficulties associated with analysis and interpretation of findings. They recommend that researchers consider the following factors in all stages of their studies (design, data collection, analysis, and interpretation):

1. the intended use and audience for the results—study design affects how the results will be interpreted;
2. the nature of the cause-effect relationships that are being addressed;
3. the dimensions of property rights that are thought to affect adoption;
4. whether or how to differentiate different quantities and qualities of technologies;
5. how to distinguish a farmer who has adopted a technology from one who is still testing it;
6. the multiple and subtle ways that different groups of farmers may have received different access to a technology, especially farmers who interact with research institutions in the development of new technologies;
7. the step-wise time path along which farmers often adopt the components of technology packages;
8. the other factors that influence adoption and confound the direct effects of property rights;
9. the units of analysis and sociospatial scale at which the relationships have effect; and
10. the timing of a study of adoption relative to the time profile of research and dissemination efforts.

The chapters presented in this volume illustrate many examples of the best practice described by Place and Swallow. For example, it was only by considering the broader components of productivity that Gavian and Ehui were able to capture factors beyond technology applications that can explain the correlation between institutions and productivity. Likewise, spatial and mapping techniques, such as those employed by B. Swallow et al., may offer new insights on factors underlying the adoption of technologies whose implementation and impact are relevant at higher scales.

Although empirical methods are important for deepening our understanding of relationships between technologies and institutions, they alone are not sufficient. Studies in this book relied on case study methods and the application of political economy, new institutional economics, and legal pluralism perspectives to grapple with the complexities of property rights and collective action and to capture such elusive and difficult-to-quantify determinants as power and social relations. Such approaches are also useful for illustrating the path dependency of certain processes and for showing how a myriad of contextual factors can influence technical and institutional change. Detailed, interdisciplinary analyses of the interrelationships between technological and institutional change are needed to understand the dynamic processes if sustainable resource management technologies are to be adopted and lead to improved productivity, equity, and environmental outcomes.

At the same time it is important for researchers to appreciate that institutions do not always need to adapt to technology. The existing base of knowledge of property rights and collective action provides adequate guidance for developing technologies that fit the institutional, as well as the physical environment. Researchers can assess the degree of tenure security and collective action in a location as a starting point for developing techniques with an appropriate scale and time horizon, as indicated in the framework introduced in Chapter 2.

Implications for Policymakers and Development Practitioners

Strengthening local institutions of property rights and collective action increases the probability that people will use many of the new technologies for resource management. No single instrument, however, provides the key to understanding and influencing people's use of different technologies. This volume has illustrated some of the complexities in the linkages between property rights, collective action, and technology choices. Because of the many interrelationships and the number of site-specific factors involved, it is not straightforward to prescribe a certain type of property regime as "most appropriate" for a particular technology or resource management practice. Even if it were, identifying policy tools and approaches to develop such property rights is far from straightforward. Simply passing laws specifying the rights and responsibilities of individuals, groups, or government agencies is not enough. Laws alone do not create property rights unless there are institutions to monitor and enforce those rights. When one recognizes the importance of legal pluralism, it becomes clear that local law derived from a number of sources may have equal or greater influence on actual behavior. The evolution of property rights must be understood as a process of institutional change, in which resource users themselves play an active role. Although this understanding certainly limits the ability of outside "experts" or policymakers to shape property rights, it also recognizes that local users themselves have greater knowledge of their specific physical, socioeconomic, and institutional context.

Similarly, collective action cannot be externally dictated (unless there is considerable coercion). Certain policies and practices, however, have been shown to be effective in fostering local organizations for voluntary resource management activities. Employing a cadre of institutional organizers can help strengthen organizational capacity and has shown high returns in terms of uptake and sustainability of resource management practices when outsiders are well trained and sensitive to the priorities of local stakeholders. The use of organizers can be thought of as subsidizing initial leadership development and as an investment in the institutional infrastructure required for sustainable resource management.

Finally, property rights can provide an important policy tool for strengthening collective action for natural resource management. Just as individuals are unlikely to invest in soil fertility, terracing, or tree planting unless they have secure tenure, communities cannot be expected to collectively invest in resource management practices if they have no long-term rights to the resource. Yet many governments have been unwilling to transfer rights to water, irrigation infrastructure, rangelands, or forests when they devolve management responsibility to user groups. The issues of community rights and ways of creating new common property regimes (in place of state ownership) are emerging as critical issues in devolution programs (Meinzen-Dick, Knox, and Di Gregorio 2001).

Reference

Meinzen-Dick, R. S., A. Knox, and M. Di Gregorio, eds. 2001. *Collective action, property rights, and devolution of natural resource management: Exchange of knowledge and implications for policy.* Feldafing, Germany: Zentralstelle für Ernährung und Landwirtschaft.

Contributors

George Arab is a researcher at the International Centre for Agricultural Research in the Dry Areas, Aleppo, Syria.

Michael Bannister is assistant director of the Center for Subtropical Agroforestry, School of Forest Resources and Conservation, University of Florida, Gainesville, Florida.

Regina Birner is assistant professor at the Institute of Rural Development, University of Göttingen, Germany.

Ana Milena de la Cruz Rebolledo, engineer in agronomy, worked at the Centro Internacional de Agricultura Tropical (CIAT), Cali, Colombia, from 1987 to 1997 on the entomology of beans and hillside agriculture.

Simeon Ehui is coordinator of the Livestock Policy Analysis Program of the International Livestock Research Institute (ILRI), Nairobi, Kenya.

Sarah Gavian is a senior associate at Abt Associates, Bethesda, Maryland, U.S.A.

Gustave Gintzburger is a range ecologist at Montpellier University, Montpellier, France.

María del Pilar Guerrero is a consultant to the Centro Internacional de Agricultura Tropical (CIAT), Cali, Colombia. She is a rural sociologist.

Hasantha Gunaweera, formerly a project officer at the Smallholder Integrated Livestock Extension Project in Hambantota, Sri Lanka, is now with CARE International in Anuradhapura, Sri Lanka.

Peter Hazell is director of the Environment and Production Technology Division of the International Food Policy Research Institute (IFPRI), Washington, D.C.

Khalil Jani is a senior officer at the Steppe Directorate, Syrian Ministry for Agriculture and Agrarian Reform, Palmyra.

Anna Knox is assistant coordinator of the Participatory Research and Gender Analysis Program of the Centro Internacional de Agricultura Tropical (CIAT), Cali, Colombia.

Nancy McCarthy is a research fellow in the Environment and Production Technology Division of the International Food Policy Research Institute (IFPRI), Washington, D.C.

Ruth Meinzen-Dick is a senior research fellow in the Environment and Production Technology Division of the International Food Policy Research Institute (IFPRI), Washington, D.C., and coordinator of the System-wide Program on Collective Action and Property Rights of the Consultative Group on International Agricultural Research (CGIAR).

Woudyalew Mulatu is project supervisor of impact assessment at the International Livestock Research Institute (ILRI), Addis Ababa, Ethiopia.

Thomas Nordblom is a senior research fellow at the Cooperative Research Centre for Weed Management Systems, Charles Sturt University, Wagga Wagga, Australia.

Onyango Okello is a research technologist at the International Livestock Research Institute, Nairobi, Kenya.

Keijiro Otsuka is a professorial fellow at the Foundation for Advanced Studies on International Development, Tokyo.

John Pender is a senior research fellow in the Environment and Production Technology Division of the International Food Policy Research Institute (IFPRI), Washington, D.C.

Frank Place is an economist in the National Resource Problems, Priorities, and Policies Unit at the International Centre for Research in Agroforestry, Nairobi, Kenya.

Jonathan Rae is a lecturer in geography in the School of the Environment at Brighton University, United Kingdom.

Helle Munk Ravnborg is a senior research fellow at the Centre for Development Research, Copenhagen, Denmark. Until 1998 she was a research fellow in the hillsides project at the Centro Internacional de Agricultura Tropical (CIAT), Cali, Colombia.

Sara J. Scherr is a senior policy analyst at Forest Trends, Washington, D.C.

Glenn R. Smucker is senior researcher and policy analyst at Smucker Consulting, Milwaukee, Wisconsin. He is a cultural anthropologist with extensive experience in agriculture and natural resource management.

Brent Swallow is principal economist and program leader for Natural Resource Problems, Priorities, and Policies at the International Centre for Research in Agroforestry (ICRAF), Nairobi, Kenya.

Kimberly A. Swallow is a consultant in the field of socioeconomic development in Nairobi, Kenya.

Jon D. Unruh is associate director of the Center for the Study of Institutions, Population, and Environmental Change and associate professor in the Department of Geography, University of Indiana, Bloomington, Indiana.

Justine Wangila is an agricultural economist in the Natural Resource Problems, Priorities, and Policies Unit at the International Centre for Research on Agroforestry (ICRAF), Nairobi, Kenya.

Olaf Westermann is a rural sociologist with the hillsides project of the Centro Internacional de Agricultura Tropical (CIAT), Cali, Colombia.

T. Anderson White is director of policy and market analysis at Forest Trends, Washington, D.C.

Index

Page numbers for entries occurring in figures are followed by an *f;* those for entries occurring in notes, by an *n;* and those for entries occurring in tables, by a *t.*

African animal trypanosomosis, 241

Africa, North. *See* West Asia and North Africa

Africa, Sub-Saharan: agricultural productivity, 28; dairy production, 272; household plots, 3; kinship and marriage practices, 27–28; land markets, 53; livestock diseases, 241; poverty, 102; private property, 75, 76–77, 100; property rights systems, 19, 101–2. *See also specific countries*

Agricultural land: fallowing, 48, 172; fragmentation, 62, 125; plot scattering, 23

Agricultural productivity. *See* Productivity, agricultural

Agricultural technology: alley farming, 19, 191; effects of organizations, 228–29, 230–31t; Green Revolution, 16, 30; in livestock raising, 200; mechanization, 196; sustainable land use, 191. *See also* Agroforestry; Irrigation; Soil conservation practices; Technology adoption

Agriculture: credit for, 25–26; labor, 26–27; slash-and-burn, 187, 188–89, 190–91. *See also* Grains

Agroforestry: collective action in, 18; factors in, 96; in Haiti, 139; relationship to property rights, 18, 132–37. *See also* Cashew agroforestry in Mozambique; Trees

Agropastoral economies. *See* Herders

Aleppo steppe, 149, 158–60

Algeria: shrub species, 153

Alley farming, 19, 191

Animals. *See* Cattle; Crop damage in Sri Lanka; Grazing rights; Herders; Sheep

Ant control: alternative methods, 258, 262–66; collective action in, 257–58, 259, 266–69; costs, 264, 266t; evaluations of effectiveness, 263, 264–66, 265t; failures, 261; queen collection, 262n; transboundary issues, 259–60. *See also* Colombia ant control study; Lorsban

Ants, leaf-cutting: anthill locations, 259–60, 260f, 268; damage caused, 257

Arab Center for the Studies of Arid Zones and Dry Lands, 149

Arid zones. *See* Rangeland management; Steppes, West Asian

Asia: agricultural productivity, 28; taboos on women's labor, 27. *See also* West Asia and North Africa; *and specific countries*

Atriplex shrubs, 151–52, 163

Ba'ath Party, 156

Bambara people, 27

Bangladesh: groundwater rights, 24–25

Banking, 25–26

Burkina Faso: property rights of women, 27

Cadastral surveys, 119, 128, 141

Camel herders, 158–60. *See also* Herders

Cameroon: alley farming, 19

Caribbean. *See* Haiti

Cashew agroforestry in Mozambique, 168–69; ages of trees, 168, 172, 173–76, 179, 183; effects of land disputes, 181; effects of war, 168, 173–77, 179–80, 183; effects on property rights, 179–80; exports, 168, 180; factors discouraging investment in, 183–84;